Electronic Highways
for World Trade

The Atwater Series on
the World Information Economy

International Transactions in Services: The Politics of Transborder Data Flows, Karl P. Sauvant

Electronic Highways for World Trade: Issues in Telecommunication and Data Services, edited by Peter Robinson, Karl P. Sauvant, and Vishwas P. Govitrikar

The Atwater Institute:
The World Information Economy Centre

The Atwater Institute is an independent, international, nonprofit organization devoted to public policy issues in the field of information and communication. The Institute organizes conferences, commissions and disseminates research, and develops educational materials on the information economy. Currently, its principal project is to facilitate the creation of an enlightened international policy framework for information and communication services.

The Atwater Institute ˙
3940 Côte des Neiges, Suite D-3
Montreal, Québec, Canada H3H 1W2
tel. (514) 931-2319

Electronic Highways for World Trade

Issues in Telecommunication and Data Services

EDITED BY

Peter Robinson, Karl P. Sauvant, and Vishwas P. Govitrikar

The Atwater Series on the World Information Economy

Westview Press
BOULDER, SAN FRANCISCO, & LONDON

The Atwater Series on the World Information Economy

Acknowledgment is made for permission to reprint: Appendix B, from G. Russell Pipe and Chris Brown, eds., *International Information Economy Handbook*, Springfield, VA: Transnational Data Reporting Service, Inc., 1985; Figure I, p. 31, from Raymond Krommenacker, "Uruguay Round Services Negotiations," in *Transnational Data and Communications Report*, Springfield, VA: Transnational Data Reporting Service, Inc., 1987; and Table II, p. 326, from Robert Stern and Bernard M. Hoekman, "Issues and Data Needs for GATT Negotiations on Services," *World Economy*, March, 1987, copyright © 1987 by Basil Blackwell Ltd.

This Westview softcover edition is printed on acid-free paper and bound in softcovers that carry the highest rating of the National Association of State Textbook Administrators, in consultation with the Association of American Publishers and the Book Manufacturers' Institute.

Published in 1989 in the United States of America by Westview Press, Inc., 5500 Central Avenue, Boulder, Colorado 80301, and in the United Kingdom by Westview Press, Inc., 13 Brunswick Centre, London WC1N 1AF, England

Library of Congress Cataloging-in-Publication Data
Electronic highways for world trade : issues in telecommunication and
    data services / edited by Peter Robinson, Karl P. Sauvant, and
    Vishwas P. Govitrikar.
      p.   cm.—(The Atwater series on the world information economy:
no. 2)
    Bibliography: p.
    Includes index.
    ISBN 0-8133-7764-1
    1. Service industries—Communication systems.   2. Service
industries—Data processing.   3. International trade.
4. Telecommunication—International cooperation.   I. Robinson,
Peter, 1925–   . II. Sauvant, Karl P. III. Govitrikar, Vishwas P.
IV. Series.
HD9980.5.E44   1989
384'.041—dc20   89-32797
                                                                      CIP

Printed and bound in the United States of America

 The paper used in this publication meets the requirements of the American National
    Standard for Permanence of Paper for Printed Library Materials Z39.48-1984.

10   9   8   7   6   5   4   3   2   1

CONTENTS

Foreword, *Frank B. Common and Knut O.H.A. Hammarskjöld*   ix

Acknowledgements   xi

Editors' Note   xiii

INTRODUCTION

Services and Data Services: Introduction, *Karl P. Sauvant*   3

OVERVIEWS

Trade in Telecommunication and Data Services: A "Constitutional"
Analysis, *R. Brian Woodrow*   15

Services: National Objectives, *Sidney Dell*   43

Participation of Developing Countries in a Telecommunication
and Data Services Agreement: Some Elements for Consideration,
Bruno Lanvin   71

Global Trade in Services: A Corporate Perspective on
Telecommunication and Data Services, *James C. Grant*   101

International Views on the Tradeability of Telecommunications,
G. Russell Pipe   121

CONCEPTS & PRINCIPLES

International Trade in Services: The Issue of Market Presence
and Right of Establishment, *V.N. Balasubramanyam*   131

"Appropriate Regulation" for Communication and Information
Services, *Ester Stevers and Christopher Wilkinson*   155

viii

Most-Favored-Nation Principle and Negotiating Strategies,
Henning Klodt   181

Institutional Aspects, *Francis Gurry*   197

TELECOMMUNICATION & DATA SERVICES

Telecommunications, *Toshio Kosuge*   223

Market Access and Telecommunication Services,
Jonathan D. Aronson   239

International Network Competition in Telecommunications,
Geza Feketekuty   257

Legal Rights of Access to Transnational Data,
Anne W. Branscomb   287

About the Editors and Contributors   305

Appendix A   309

Appendix B   311

Appendix C   315

Appendix D   325

Bibliography   331

Index   361

FOREWORD

This is the second volume in The Atwater Series on the World Information Economy. The first -- *International Transactions in Services: The Politics of Transborder Data Flows* by Karl P. Sauvant -- was a comprehensive review of the international policy discussion on services and data services up to 1985. Since then, there have been a number of developments which form the background against which the present volume must be seen.

In September 1986, ministers from 92 countries met in Punta del Este, Uruguay, and agreed to inaugurate a new round of multilateral trade negotiations: the Uruguay Round. For the first time, they also agreed that, in addition to the customary negotiations on trade in goods, there should be 'parallel-track' negotiations on *trade in services*. This volume addresses some of the most fundamental issues raised by the discussion on an international framework for trade in services and, in particular, these issues in the context of a core sector in international service transactions: telecommunication and data services.

The recent merging of the technologies of computing and telecommunication has had several major consequences, one of which is the increase in tradeability of 'information-intensive' services -- examples are banking, insurance, advertising, tourism and consultancy services of various sorts. This increase in tradeability and the consequent increase in the share of services in world trade, coupled with the rapidly rising proportion of services in the GNP of most countries, has made trade in services in general and trade in telecommunication and data services in particular high-priority items on the international agenda. Also high on the international agenda is the need for and nature of the rules, regulations or disciplines necessary to cover international telecommunication and data services in an era of unprecedented technological change. While questions relating to trade are being discussed mainly under the auspices of the Uruguay Round, questions relating to regulatory change are being discussed mainly under the auspices of the International Telecommunication Union.

There is clearly a need for greater understanding of the issues involved, for conceptual clarification, and for bridge building among the divergent interests and positions. This volume is a partial response to these needs. The approach taken is to explain each issue or concept, to examine its role in trade in services generally, and to analyze its implications for trade in telecommunication and data services specifically. Each issue is addressed by a recognized international expert, and the concerns of both developed and developing countries are taken into account.

The aim of the Atwater Series is to stimulate serious, informed and constructive discussion on public policy in the information and communication area. The only criterion by which contributions to it should be judged is whether they succeed in facilitating such discussion. We hope that you feel as we do that the present volume passes this test.

Frank B. Common, Jr., Q.C.
Chairman and Founder

Knut O.H.A. Hammarskjöld
Director General

ACKNOWLEDGEMENTS

The Atwater Institute's work on trade-related issues in telecommunication and data services, leading to the publication of the present volume, was made possible by a major grant from The Donner Canadian Foundation, one of the largest Canadian foundations with a long-standing interest in international affairs. The Institute gratefully acknowledges this support on the occasion of the publication of the result of this work.

The Institute's work was also supported by others, prominent among whom were: the Department of Communications, Government of Canada; the Canadian International Development Agency (CIDA); the Atwater Development Foundation, U.S.A.; and Teleglobe Canada, A Memotec Company. The Institute is grateful to all sponsors of its work.

Peter Robinson
Karl P. Sauvant
Vishwas P. Govitrikar

EDITORS' NOTE

The views expressed in the papers herein collected are solely the authors'. They do not necessarily reflect the views of the Atwater Institute or the views of the organizations with which the authors are associated.

P.R.
K.P.S.
V.P.G.

INTRODUCTION

SERVICES AND DATA SERVICES

INTRODUCTION

Karl P. Sauvant

When the Uruguay Round of Multilateral Trade Negotiations was launched in Punta del Este in September 1986, it was decided that, as part of this undertaking, an appropriate framework for trade in services should be established. Specifically, the ministers decided that:

> Negotiations in this area shall aim to establish a multilateral framework of principles and rules for trade in services, including elaboration of possible disciplines for individual sectors, with a view to expansion of such trade under conditions of transparency and progressive liberalization and as a means of promoting economic growth of all trading partners and the development of developing countries. Such framework shall respect the policy objectives of national laws and regulations applying to services and shall take into account the work of relevant international organizations.[1]

This decision represents formal international recognition of the importance of services for growth and development:. The services sector is now the single largest sector in most economies and services trade accounts for one-fifth of total trade.

But the share of services in world trade has not expanded as rapidly as its share in the domestic economy. For many policy- makers and trade negotiators in developed countries, the principal reason for this failure to transmit the sector's domestic dynamism to international trade has been the absence of a stable, predictable and transparent framework for trade in services and especially the preponderance of trade-restricting national regulations. Accordingly, they advocate the establishment of a framework which would lead to the progressive liberalization of regulations restricting trade in services and thereby unleash the dynamism of the services sector in the international arena. This is expected to give a major new impetus to the world economy, accelerate economic growth, create new jobs and facilitate structural adjustment. A liberal trading system and expanding trade in services is seen to benefit all and therefore to contribute to the development of the developing countries as well.

Policy-makers and trade negotiators in developing countries recognize the importance of the services sector for economic growth. But, unlike those from developed countries, not all of them believe that the distribution of benefits associated with an international framework leading to progressive liberalization and expanded trade would necessarily be equitable. In particular, although it is recognized that developing countries can benefit from cheaper and more efficient service imports, a number of policy-makers from these countries fear that, in the absence of appropriate protection, their infant service industries would be overwhelmed by foreign competition. This fear is intensified by any proposal that the traditional trade framework be broadened to include all or some forms of foreign direct investment. And their perception of unequal benefit is strengthened by the difficulties of including service-related labour movements in a liberalizing international framework. In brief, a number of policy-makers and trade negotiators from developing countries do not see how the framework desired by developing countries would, on balance, benefit the development of the developing countries.

In spite of these differences, agreement does exist that an international framework for trade in services should be established which stimulates the economic growth of all trading partners and promotes the development of the developing countries.

The importance of this task is further increased by the advent of telecommunication and data services - henceforth 'data services' for short (Sauvant, 1986). These services are the result of the convergency of computer and telecommunication technology. Operating on the basis of digital signals, they comprise data processing, information storage and retrieval (data bases), software and telecommunication services. Together with data goods (computers, peripheral equipment, etc.), they constitute the nexus around which economies are being restructured in the process of becoming information economies.

In the context of this volume, data services are particularly important because these services increasingly enter international trade and perhaps even more importantly, because they increase the tradeability of other services.

The characteristic of most services is that they are intangible and non-storable and must therefore be produced when and where they are consumed. Hence, most services are difficult to transport and consequently difficult to trade. This is reflected in the fact that only some 10 percent of the world's production of services (mainly transport and tourism) enters international trade, compared to some 45 percent of manufacturing products. To give an example: banking required in the past that customers go to a bank to transact their business, e.g., to inquire about a cheque-book balance or to obtain funds; the services were produced when the customers were in the bank.

The advent of data services changes this situation fundamentally because data services permit instantaneous, long-distance interactive interactions *via* transnational computer-communication systems. More specifically, by collapsing time and space (at decreasing costs), data services permit certain services to be produced in one place and consumed in another place. In other words, the unity of time and space is no longer required to produce and consume certain services, especially information-intensive services. The result is an increase in the transportability and, consequently, tradeability of certain services -- they can be delivered *via* the telecommunication network. To return to the example of banking: a number of banking services can now be obtained *via* automated teller machines (ATMs) or computer-communication systems, i.e., (banking) services are being produced in one place and consumed in another.

The extent to which this is already taking place can be observed in the corporate networks of transnational corporations. These corporations are using data services to undertake a considerable range of corporate functions transnationally and they expect to expand the use of data services even further. Thus, in many transnational corporations transborder data flows are important or crucial for such functions as financial management, marketing, distribution, inventory control, accounting, and research and development. In each case, the product being transported is information in the form of digital data and such data can be sent *via* transnational computer-communication systems. For transnational corporations, these systems have acquired a central importance, not only for sending information faster and more efficiently but, above all, for managing their worldwide operations more efficiently and for undertaking activities which are closely related to, or already a part of, the production process.

There is no reason why the services currently being provided via transnational computer-communication systems *within* transnational corporations cannot be made available *outside* those systems as well. It is only a question of time until the processes of differentiation, specialization and standardization of knowledge lead to the emergence of economies of scale which make it feasible and sensible to take the provision of these services out of their corporate framework and to place it instead in the international market-place. The emergence of closed user-group networks which link independent firms -- such as SWIFT for the banking industry and SITA for the airline industry -- is a step in this direction.

Thus, it is quite conceivable, if not predictable, that the increased application of data services will make a whole range of normally untradeable services tradeable and thereby create trade options for firms which in the

6

past served foreign markets primarily through foreign affiliates. This option may become particularly important in such industries as banking, insurance, other financial services, data services, accounting, research and development, design and engineering, advertising, management consulting, legal services, and education. The potential for growth in trade in these and other information-intensive service industries is substantial.

In sum, data services play a key role in increasing the tradeability of certain services. As mentioned earlier, they are also of crucial importance for the operations of transnational corporations. And, one may add, they are becoming an important part of the infrastructure for trade in goods -- for instance, through their use in inventory control or the handling of trade documentation. Altogether, these features of data services make them a *core service,* a service central to the growth of international economic transactions and economic development.

But the potential of data services can only be fully realized in an international environment which is relatively free from restrictions on the flow of data services. In any framework for trade in services which is oriented towards growth and development, data services therefore deserve special attention.

This raises again the question of who benefits from such a framework -- in this case, from a framework for trade in data services. Generally, all those stand to benefit who can utilize the underlying technology, be it to increase the import or export of services, to manage transnational affiliate networks better or to promote trade in goods. This means, first of all, firms from developed countries because they are the most advanced in the application of data services. But developing countries should be able to benefit as well, because data services provide them with a wider range of options to obtain services important for their development, be it in terms of mode of delivery (trade vs. foreign direct investment), range of suppliers or, more generally, information about international markets. Developing countries also have certain opportunities to develop exports of services which are information-intensive and in whose production they either have or can develop a comparative advantage, e.g., software, information storage and retrieval, engineering services, accounting -- in principle, all services whose tradeability has been increased through the application of data services. For some services, increased tradeability may even help to sidestep, at least to a certain extent, the thorny question of labor movement: instead of software specialists moving to another country to produce their services there, for instance, they can provide them via computer-communication systems from home. The point is that a whole range of new opportunities is being opened up and that all countries are potential beneficiaries.

There are a few conditions, however, which appear to circumscribe the extent to which these opportunities can be exploited and which define, therefore, the benefits countries can derive from an international framework.

One is the extent to which the international environment guarantees access to data resources located elsewhere. Particularly under conditions of a highly uneven global distribution of data goods and data services, it is of obvious importance that countries which rely on data resources located elsewhere can rest reasonably assured that their access to these resources is not disrupted.

Secondly, countries -- and particularly developing countries -- which can realize some of the new opportunities offered by the increased tradeability of certain services ought to be assured that they have access to the markets in which the services they can provide are in demand and they ought to be protected in a reasonable way from the use of restrictive business practices by dominant data-service providers.

A third condition relates to the ability of countries to obtain data goods and data services, to acquire the skills to use them, to obtain the technology to produce and reproduce them, and to build the telecommunication infrastructure to utilize and apply them. This is particularly important for developing countries, most of which, in all these areas, lag far behind the developed countries. For some developing countries, the question may arise whether they ought to encourage the indigenous growth of at least some data industries. Given the importance of data resources for development in general and international economic transactions in particular, it would be surprising if a number of countries did not want to pursue this possibility and, for that purpose, to preserve certain policy options related to infant industries, whether individually or in concert with other developing countries. Apart from such infant-industry strategies, virtually all developing countries may have to embark on a major training effort, may require liberal access to technology and, perhaps above all, may need a massive infusion of technical assistance to strengthen their telecommunication infrastructure. Without such a broad-based effort, many developing countries may simply be unable to take advantage of the new opportunities created by data services and the increased tradeability of other services -- in fact, they may fall further behind in their development.

The establishment of a framework for trade in services and data services is a difficult undertaking because the effort addresses unchartered territory characterized by a dearth of data and broad intellectual neglect of the services sector. It is not accidental that trade theory is based on the exchange of cloth for wine and not, for instance, of banking for shipping. It is also not accidental that, when it comes to economic policy, most countries strive to 'industrialize' or 're-industrialize'. And, finally, it is not accidental that institutional development in many countries has led to the creation of ministries of industry, but not of services, and that the international community has established a framework for trade in goods, but not for trade in services. These are all examples of a mind-set in which services do not matter. The services sector has long been the stepchild of economic theory, policy and institution-building. And data services, begot by the marriage of computers and telecommunications and barely in their teens, have so far escaped theoretical attention almost entirely.

Progress in understanding the subject is not made easier by the dispersion of responsibilities relating to international transactions in services. The Uruguay Round, serviced by the GATT Secretariat, is responsible for trade in services; the UNCTAD for trade and development in services (UNCTAD, 1988); the UNCTC for foreign direct investment in services (UNCTC, 1988); the UN Statistical Office and IMF for statistics on services; and the ITU for the technical infrastructure of data services. In addition, a number of specialized institutions (e.g., ICAO, the World Tourism Organization) are responsible for *specific* service industries. While this dispersion may encourage a competition of ideas, it does not facilitate a concentrated effort to illuminate the subject and to provide policy-makers with empirically based insights.

At the moment, the trade aspects of international transactions in services are in the forefront of international attention, crystallized in the Uruguay Round. (Data services have received separate attention as well, but only in the context of the OECD and especially in the form of a Declaration on Transborder Data Flows, adopted by the OECD Council of Ministers in April 1985 - see Appendix B.) But technical aspects related to the data-services infrastructure of trade in services are also being considered and quite intensively by the ITU, especially in preparation for the World Administrative Telegraph and Telephone Conference in November and December 1988 (WATTC 1988). The two efforts are discrete. It is perhaps ironic that while the technical experts of WATTC will meet in Melbourne, Australia, beginning 28 November 1988, the trade experts of the Uruguay Round will meet for a mid-term review in Montreal, Canada, beginning 5 December 1988. The former will define the rules according to which the (data-services-trade) roads are constructed; the latter will determine what traffic should be permitted under what conditions on these roads. One can only hope that some invisible hand co-ordinates these efforts in the interest of economic growth and development.

There is obviously a need for greater understanding, for conceptual clarification and for bridge-building. This volume is meant as a modest contribution towards these objectives.

A number of issues and concepts central to the current discussion on trade in services and data services have been chosen for examination and clarification. These are issues and concepts which have emerged primarily in two contexts: (1) the negotiations on an international framework for trade in services, undertaken in the Group of Negotiations on Services of the Uruguay Round and (2) the international discussions on transborder data flows and telecommunication regulation in a number of international fora. An effort has been made to explain these issues and concepts, followed by an examination of their significance for trade in services in general and trade in data services in particular. The focus of most of the contributions is on data services -- and, in fact, a few deal only with data services -- precisely because of their *core-service* nature.

The first set of contributions discusses in some detail the scope of what constitutes trade in services and data services and reviews the different objectives negotiators bring to the bargaining table of the Group of Negotiations on Services, paying special attention to the developing countries. When defining the scope of the negotiations, the key task, undertaken by *Brian Woodrow*, is to draw the boundary lines between trade, foreign direct investment and labor movement. Given that many services are not tradeable -- and hence require foreign direct investment or labor movement to be delivered to foreign markets -- a certain temptation exists to expand the traditional concept of trade to include these transactions or parts of them. This issue is closely interrelated with the national objectives of the countries participating in the Uruguay Round negotiations. As *Sidney Dell* points out, the primary aim of the developed countries is to achieve progressive liberalization of a wide range of services in as many countries as possible, preferring a definition of trade which includes foreign direct investment or at least certain forms of such investment. The national objectives of developing countries, on the other hand, are primarily concerned with the effects of a liberalization of trade in services on development, especially when the governing liberalizing regime includes foreign direct investment but not labor movement. Given the structurally disadvantaged situation of the developing countries, *Bruno Lanvin* looks at the safeguards that these countries would look for in any agreement, focusing especially on balance-of-payments and infant-industry concerns, preferential treatment, control of restrictive business practices, and the need for technical assistance.

The second section deals with some of the key concepts and principles that have dominated the negotiations. Particularly important among them are the most-favoured-nation (MFN) principle and the rights of presence and establishment. The applicability of the MFN principle is examined by *Henning Klodt.*. This principle is central to the international trading system as embodied in the GATT. It provides that all parties to an agreement have to grant to each other treatment as favorable as that given to any other country in the application and administration of import and export duties and charges. The principle is meant to protect weaker countries from the bilateral pressures of stronger ones. At the same time, the unconditional granting of MFN treatment may decrease the incentive to live up to any liberalization provisions of an agreement. Not surprisingly, therefore, the negotiating positions on this issue in the Uruguay Round reflect largely the relative strength and aspirations of individual countries. "Right of establishment", on the other hand, which refers to the conditions under which foreign investors can establish commercial facilities in another country, is traditionally a concept central to the debates on the creation of an international framework for foreign direct investment, together with such concepts as national treatment, fair and equitable treatment and transparency. (UNCTC) [2] *V.N. Balasubramanyam* dissects this right, together with the novel right of presence. Both rights have been introduced into the debate on the establishment of an international framework for trade in services by the developed countries, precisely because these countries wish this framework to cover at least part of foreign-direct-investment transactions. Somewhat short of a right of establishment is the right of presence which does not necessarily involve equity ownership by foreign corporations but involves rather a bundle of rights that are meant to guarantee access to a given market (and especially its telecommunication network) by foreign service providers. In many instances, this involves the relaxation or abolition of national regulations impeding such access. Such a liberalization of regulations need not proceed at equal pace or go equally far in all service industries and in all aspects of a particular industry. Rather, this process is a gradual one which has to take into account a number of factors, among them especially the policy objectives of national laws and regulations applying to services. Regulations, in other words, have to be "appropriate" -- the subject of the contribution by *Ester Stevers* and *Christopher Wilkinson*. To find the proper balance between the disciplines imposed by an international framework and the legitimate regulatory objectives of individual countries is one of the greatest challenges of the negotiations on both services and data services. Most probably, this will require an ongoing process, undertaken in the framework of an international machinery. But the purpose of such a machinery would most likely be broader and concern itself also with the monitoring and enforcement of any agreement ultimately concluded. This, in turn, raises the need for dispute settlement procedures, the topic of *Francis Gurry's* paper. Dispute settlement has a dual function: it maintains the order and credibility of the established system and it contributes to the evolution of the system through the definition of the range of acceptable norms and practices. And since, typically, an effective procedure for dispute settlement requires concessions of sovereignty, agreement on such procedures is frequently the ultimate litmus test for the seriousness with which the negotiating parties view an agreement.

The third section, then, focuses on data services. Central to a realization of the increased tradeability of certain services are telecommunication services -- which is why they receive special attention throughout this volume. *Toshio Kosuge* concentrates on the implications of technological innovation for the creation of a modern telecommunication infrastructure as a network of highways for services trade and, in particular, emphasizes the need for an open international system as a pre-condition for the full unfolding of the potential of the latest technological developments in this area. Regulatory rather than technological innovation is the starting point of *Geza Feketekuty's* analysis of international network competition in telecommunication. The key innovation here is the introduction of competition in the provision of international telecommunication services. Pioneered by the United States, the United Kingdom and Japan, this change, together with the changes in the underlying technology, has created pressures on other countries to follow suit. And it has raised a host of issues which, given the nature of telecommunications, require international attention. Trade-based rules defining the terms of network competition and reciprocal access, especially between countries that do permit competition and those that do not, may be the most appropriate route to take. Part of this rule-making is about access -- access to networks, facilities and markets. *Jonathan D. Aronson* looks at this matter in his contribution. In so doing, he also re-examines some of the questions related to the rights of establishment and presence in the specific context of trade in data services. Another aspect of access, that related to access to data, is taken up separately by *Anne W. Branscomb*. Since data have become a resource central to the functioning of economic processes, the legal rights of governments, corporations and individuals to have access to data located in other countries are moving to be forefront of international discussions. Any international agreement will most probably have to pay attention to this issue.

Ultimately, any international understanding on trade in services and data services is meant for users, those who actually engage in trade transactions. In practice, this means mostly corporations and especially transnational corporations. The "practical" contribution in this volume is therefore written by a user, *James C. Grant*. Based on his experience, he describes how data services have affected trade in services, using international financial services as an example and outlining issues and challenges confronting this industry. More than any other paper in this volume, Grant underlines the centrality of data services: they are not just another service but rather the principal facilitator of trade in most services as well as in goods.

The contributions in this volume have been written by experts who bring their own specific expertise and approach to bear on the issues and concepts selected for analysis. Their contributions are meant to be expository in nature. The aim is to illuminate an issue rather than to argue a position. This approach has been chosen because the Atwater Institute -- which commissioned these papers -- understands itself as a bridge between various positions, interests and disciplines and, in that capacity, seeks to encourage informal discussions and consensus building. This approach has also been chosen in order to maximize the usefulness of this volume as a reference tool for the intended readers: those involved in the development and implementation of international policy with regard to services generally and data services especially and those, of course, who in universities and research institutions seek to broaden our understanding of the issues involved.

The world economy is evolving into a service economy in which data services occupy a central position. It is a transformation of historic proportions, driven by technological innovation and transcending North-South divisions. Like any transformation on this scale, it tests the managerial capabilities of decision makers at the national and international levels. If this volume helps to bring about a better understanding of the international dimension of this transformation, if it helps to stimulate constructive debate and to build bridges of understanding between the various interests and communities involved, it will have served its purpose.

Endnotes

1 See Appendix A to the present volume. For the events leading up to the adoption of this text, see Karl P. Sauvant, *International Transactions in Services: The Politics of Transborder Data Flows* (Boulder: Westview Press, 1986).

2 See UNCTC, *The United Nations Code of Conduct on Transnational Corporations, UNCTC Current Studies*, Series A, No.4, United Nations Sales No. E.86.II.A.15.

OVERVIEWS

TRADE IN TELECOMMUNICATION AND DATA SERVICES

A "CONSTITUTIONAL" ANALYSIS

R. Brian Woodrow

Introduction

It is no exaggeration to assert that telecommunication and data services constitute the essential core of today's service economy, at least within and among developed nations. They also give every promise of being perhaps the most important spur to economic growth and development globally in the years to come. The long-heralded convergence of computers and communications is now a practical reality as varied and often hybrid technologies and new and improved services are becoming widely and readily available. Broadband data networks, cellular mobile radio, interchanging use of satellites and cables, facsimile transmission of documents and access to online data bases are but a few examples of this new reality. Nationally, the provision and use of telecommunication and data services is changing markedly in many countries as domestic policy and regulation - - traditionally monopolistic and restrictive at least in the area of telecommunications -- have come under review and as user needs and industry boundaries are evolving. This process of change is most obvious and most advanced in the United States, but it is also occurring in the United Kingdom, Japan and Canada, while even the staunchest West European PTT nations and some developing nations show signs of moving in a similar direction. Internationally, the cooperative technical and administrative arrangements among the world's nations and their still largely monopolistic telecommunication administrations - as evidenced most specifically through the International Telecommunication Union - are likewise being challenged by essentially the same forces of service diversification and increased competition in the domestic arena. At the same time, through trade and foreign investment, a growing internationalization in the provision and use of telecommunication and data services is taking place as certain countries and business and user interests press strenuously for more open access to foreign networks and markets.

It is in this form that the issue of trade in telecommunication and data services currently presents itself. The roots of the issue, however, trace back to two main sources. First of all, dating from the early 1970's and as articulated most clearly in the OECD's 1985 Declaration, there has been a persistent interest in the phenomenon of transborder data flows and its implications, initially in terms of privacy concerns relating to individuals but later in terms of promoting and ensuring widespread and relatively unrestricted information flows worldwide while acknowledging the legitimate policy and sovereignty concerns of individual nations (Robinson, 1985 and 1987). Secondly and more recently, there has of course been mounting pressure since the 1980's to bring services under multilateral and bilateral trade agreements - one prominent component of which would presumably be trade in telecommunication and data services - and, of course, a separate negotiation on the whole range of services is now proceeding as part of the Uruguay Round of trade negotiations (Bhagwati, 1987b). Simply put, what is at stake is whether and how the extensive and diverse range of data flows endemic to information economies worldwide and the telecommunication networks on which they ride internationally as well as nationally should *ab initio* be treated within a trade context.

The underlying dynamics of the trade-in-services issue is also quite straightforward: the United States in particular has taken the lead in pressing other industrialized countries and the developing nations to create and institutionalize a more liberalized regime for dealing with a wide range of services trade issues, supportive of and complementary to that already in place for goods trade through GATT and other multilateral and bilateral arrangements. With regard to telecommunication and data services as on other issues, the often quite divergent interests and approaches of different national governments and affected groups, operating both domestically and internationally, come obviously and immediately to the forefront. However, at least some of the difficulty with regard to telecommunication services as a trade-in-services issue is also definitional and conceptual and stems very much from the considerable differences between a trade-policy perspective and a telecommunication-policy perspective on this issue.

In this sense, the task facing nation-states, the world community and those interested in the issue is essentially a "constitutional" one. Speaking to the somewhat analogous issue of reconciling the right of free speech to First Amendment guarantees of separation of church and state, the noted American educator Robert Maynard Hutchins described the exercise of creating rules of conduct where different but equally important principles are involved as one of "building a fence around a vacant lot". The image is most instructive and transferable to the case before us. A fence represents on the one hand the establishment of boundaries for those activities which take place within its confines while, on the other hand, it also implies rights of ownership and/or usage -- for common as well as for individual purposes

- which must be acknowledged by all who wish to trespass upon that territory. The lot itself may appear to be vacant but that does not mean that it is currently unused even in its nominal state nor does it mean that the land is somehow lacking in value. Rather, quite the opposite is the case in that those who own, rent, use or otherwise appropriate the land can do so potentially for a variety of different purposes -- and often for more than one at the same time -- and these multiple possible uses can, singly or in aggregate, have significant and quite differing value. Drawing the analogy back to the trade in telecommunication and data services issue, what a constitutional solution attempts to accomplish is to build that fence -- a set of "disciplines and arrangements" in the jargon of the traders -- around the increasing range and diversity of telecommunication and data services which now and in the future might take place upon this lot. It is exactly this kind of "constitutional" [1] exercise -- focused to be sure on the global rather than the national level -- which the Atwater Institute is promoting through this project.

This paper and the others commissioned for this project can then be viewed as contributions to the ongoing process of establishing the constitutional underpinning for one crucial feature of the services economy of the twenty-first century. The task I have been given is to examine the essential character of the activities which currently do and in the future might take place on this vacant lot -- the inherent tradeability of telecommunication and data services -- and whether and how a fence might be built to encompass these activities. The first section of the paper focuses specifically on a sampling of the kinds of telecommunication and data services activities which do or might take place and how these activities can be analysed. The second highlights the different perspectives of trade-policy and telecommunication-policy officials who must play a major role in arriving at any major agreement. The paper then reviews the literature on how telecommunication and data services can be conceptualized in terms of services trade. The fourth section tackles the matter of what constitutes "trade" in the telecommunication and data services realm. And, finally, the paper analyzes in a general way the boundary-line issues involving on trade in telecommunication and data services and other concepts such as foreign investment, transborder data flows, domestic and international regulation and the process of development.

Some Current Examples of Trade in Telecommunication and Data Services

Consider for a moment the following examples of how the provision and/or consumption of telecommunication and data services -- might be seen as constituting trade in services:

CASE #1: An elderly lady in Montreal places a *normal long-distance call* to her nephew in San Francisco. Instantaneously, Bell Canada transfers that call westward along the Telecom Canada network via microwave or satellite to the West Coast where BC Tel interconnects with AT & T Longlines which uses its fibre-optic facilities to pass the call on to Pacific Telesis ROC where her nephew picks up his phone. The call is billed by Bell Canada at published Canada/US rates, with Telecom Canada settling revenues among its member companies and AT & T between itself and Pacific Telesis. The international transaction between Telecom Canada and AT & T Longlines would be handled between the companies on a net basis depending upon the number, distance and duration of all Canada/US calls and in accord with recognized ITU accounting procedures.

Does this transaction across international borders -- based upon cooperative technical and administrative arrangements and mutually agreed-upon settlement procedures -- constitute an internationally traded service? If Telecom Canada were able to choose - as it presently can - to interconnect under similar cross-border arrangements with alternative providers like MCI or Sprint rather than A T & T, would this degree of competition somehow enhance the trade-in-services component of the transaction? If A T & T were allowed to extend its network physically into Canada or, through foreign investment, to take over an existing Canadian carrier, what implications would either of these actions have for the status of the transaction as trade in services? Finally, would it make any difference if this elderly lady -- thoroughly modern nonetheless -- linked her computer to her nephew's and communicated data rather than voice information? Under prevailing conceptions of trade in services and irrespective of the variations suggested in the questions above, this normal cross-border telephone call would indeed be considered an internationally traded service, although telecommunications policy officials would have considerable difficulty seeing it in those terms.

CASE #2: Telecommunication services are provided internationally in most countries -- the exceptions presently being the United States, Japan and the United Kingdom -- on a monopoly basis typically using INTELSAT as well as regional satellite and cable facilities. Data services which make use of international telecommunication circuits, however, are offered in many countries on a competitive and unregulated basis. Telecommunication and data services offered internationally have normally used the established monopoly transmission arrangements but alternative distribution possibilities are opening up. For example, domestic satellite providers in one country may attempt to *sell transborder capacity or even specialized services* into contiguous countries. Designated international telecommunication providers may begin to compete more aggressively with one another for *transit business*. Providers of data services providers may attempt to use or create *alternative distribution possibilities* such as global private networks or customized satellite or cable facilities and thus to bypass the prevailing international telecommunication arrangements.

Does a normal overseas telephone call from Paris to Melbourne -- handled as it would be by the French PTT and Telecom Australia internationally and domestically within each country -- both of which operate as monopolies domestically and according to cooperative technical and administrative arrangements internationally -- constitute an internationally traded service? Would it make any difference to the tradeability of the service if the telephone call was between Tokyo and Washington where all the international linkages could now be provided competitively? If domestic satellite providers were to attempt to market their services into contiguous countries or international telecommunication providers to compete aggressively with each other for transit business, what implications would this have for international telecommunication policy and regulation? Also, what would be the implications for international telecommunication policy and regulation if international data-service providers were able to bypass the present monopoly arrangements and were systematically to pursue alternative distribution possibilities? Just as normal cross-border telecommunication traffic can be treated as an internationally traded service, so too can overseas telecommunication services as well as other activities such as the sale of satellite capacity or competition for transit business. In the latter instances, however, competitive trade-in-services activities -- as distinct from those activities governed by international cooperative arrangements -- could be viewed as representing a purer form of trade where notions of comparative advantage are more clearly applicable.

CASE #3: A large multinational corporation wishes to use *private leased lines* in several countries to link headquarters with its subsidiaries throughout the world, each of which must also be linked to several plants and an extensive dealer network. Alternatively, major financial institutions or the world's airlines, as is the case in SWIFT and SITA respectively, agree to participate in a *closed-user leased-line arrangement* for continuous, large-scale data transmission. Even more elaborately, Cable and Wireless in the U.K. wishes to patch together a *global private network* using private transoceanic cable facilities and terrestrial leased lines to link Western Europe to North America and Japan and provide service to large business customers in competition with the international public-switched network providers. In each of these instances, there are specific difficulties to be overcome. While it may be easy to obtain volume-insensitive leased-line capacity within the United States or Canada, this may be considerably more difficult in West Germany or France where monopoly PTTs have been anxious to safeguard the public-switched network or in some developing nations where telecommunication facilities are rudimentary in nature and strained to capacity. In the case of specialized closed-user networks, ITU sanction is required for the establishment of these arrangements and the series D recommendations of the ITU regulations seriously limit other types of international leased-line arrangements. And finally the patching together of global private networks offering services internationally to large customers may often require interconnection with the public-switched network in the various countries where those services might be initiated or received.

Irrespective of how the public-switched network is treated in trade-in-services terms, do not these uses of leased-line capacity purchased in foreign countries -- whether for intracorporate, closed-user or alternative-network purposes -- constitute examples of internationally-traded services? Should actions taken by monopoly PTTs to restrict the availability of leased lines or even ITU provisions governing certain leased-line arrangements be construed either as deliberate or implicit barriers to trade? What about policy and regulatory actions taken by countries to introduce volume-sensitive pricing for leased lines or to impose taxes on transborder data traffic which may have a similar inhibiting effect? And could not the introduction of ISDN -- as it is now being planned and put into place by governments and the world's telephone companies -- be interpreted as a bold attempt to upgrade the capability of the public-switched telephone network and so to obviate the need for private leased lines and other alternative arrangements? Indeed, private leased lines configured to operate across national boundaries would be considered internationally traded services and restrictions on access and use of leased lines and on resale and sharing could be construed as trade barriers.

CASE #4: A national regulatory agency in country X, operating separately but under some degree of policy direction from the responsible political officials, faces the task of determining whether specific telecommunication and data services should be regulated or left to open competitive provision. Over the years, most developed countries have evolved regulatory and ownership policies based upon distinctions among types of services and the kinds of facilities appropriate for their provision. In this particular case, an aspiring telecommunication service provider applies to offer *network-based services* such as call-forwarding and account recording along with some electronic mail capability and this is denied by the regulator on grounds that the service is primarily a basic rather than an enhanced service to be provided by a Type I rather than a Type II carrier and thus not open to competitive provision. Alternatively, a *data services provider* in the same country offers an information retrieval service available not only domestically but also internationally which makes roughly similar use of the network but which is treated as a Type II enhanced service and open to competitive provision. To complicate the matter even further, if each of these services were to be subsumed under a trade-in-services regime based upon national treatment and the distinction between basic and enhanced services was applied differently or not recognized as applicable at all, then the difficulties of taking domestic regulatory decisions and relating them to international trade considerations become readily apparent.

In terms of domestic policy and regulatory practice as well as international trade considerations, should network-based telecommunication services be treated differently from data or other services which make essentially similar use of the network? As a general rule, should domestic policy and regulatory distinctions - which vary widely around the world and are constantly subject to change - be absorbed directly or implicitly into any international trade-in-services regime? Unless regulatory systems are already broadly similar or some degree of policy harmonization is mandated, can national treatment obligations realistically form the basis for any trade-in-services regime? And finally, if either telecommunication services or data services could be rendered by means of software rather than transfered across communication networks, then would not what is a trade-in-services transaction in one form be treated as a trade-in-goods transaction in another form? Distinctions between basic and enhanced services are domestic policy and regulatory devices which are used in a largely similar fashion in countries like United States and Canada but have not been adopted by other countries like the United Kingdom or Japan which favour a Type I/Type II facilities-based approach or by most PTT nations which recognize no such distinctions at all. While sometimes useful in terms of domestic policy and regulation, these distinctions must generally be viewed as too transitory, insubstantial and varied to provide a basis for either a trade-in-services regime or an international telecommunication regulatory regime.

CASE #5: A researcher in Country A wishes to *use an online database* available from a company in Country B. Normally, all that would be required is a long-distance telephone call linking the researcher's computer with the database service provider abroad and the payment of whatever access, transmission and usage fees are prescribed. Several quite different problems relating to transborder data flows could inhibit this seemingly innocuous commercial transaction. Network access at reasonable costs and conditions could be effectively restricted either in country A or Country B as a consequence of normal governmental policy and regulations such as restrictions on bypass or cross-subsidization. Country B could restrict database access on the part of foreign researchers for reasons of national security or copyright. Alternatively, country A might restrict market access on the part of the foreign database supplier in order to protect domestic database suppliers. Additional considerations, however, could also come to bear. If both country A and country B happened to be adherents to the 1985 OECD Declaration on Transborder Data Flows, then each would be under an obligation not to engage in any of the above practices. If the transborder data flow were to be intracorporate rather than commercial, it is unlikely that the governments of each country would even know about the transaction let alone restrict it in one way or another. And finally, if the database were to be rendered on disc or tape and transported across borders in this fashion, the character of the transborder data flow would have changed dramatically.

Does this kind of information transfer provided across borders constitute an internationally traded service? Where does transborder data flow end and trade in telecommunication and data services begin? Can and should the data component of the service be effectively separated from the telecommunication component of the service and, if not, what does this mean for the scope of any trade agreement on telecommunication and data services? What kinds of access - - market access, network access, database access -- are relevant to any trade-in-services negotiation? To be sure, it will be no easy task to separate data services from the telecommunication networks upon which they are normally provided and consideration of the two elements together along with other modes of provision such as software is virtually a necessity.

CASE #6: A developing nation with aspirations to build a future in the area of information technology decides to expand and upgrade its domestic telecommunication network. The international subsidiary of a major telecommunication company in a developed nation wins the contract to. *plan, install and advise upon the operation of* that new telecommunication system. For providing services to the project, the subsidiary naturally draws upon the experience and expertise built up over the years by its parent company and also its preferences with regard to the supply of network and transmission equipment. Financing for the project may well be guaranteed by the foreign aid or export development agency of a service-exporting country or by an international organization. The subsidiary earns payment for its services internationally which, as an accounting matter, turns up as a receipt in its country's balance of payments under the heading of professional and consulting services. The service-exporting country acts as an intermediary in facilitating the service transaction which takes place in a third country. And the developing country in question modernizes its telecommunication system as the result of this rather complicated international service transaction.

Does the supply of such professional and consulting services for projects abroad constitute a telecommunication service *per se*? Just as it is recognized that telecommunication and data services can be embodied in goods such as sophisticated digital switches or in software on disc, is it not possible for them also to be embodied in the experience and expertise of people? Should the transaction outlined here be treated as trade in telecommunication services, professional and consulting services or even as a financial service transaction? Also, what does this imply about labor mobility as a constraint on internationally traded services in addition to the more normal constraints usually seen in foreign investment controls or unfair regulatory practices? Clearly, any proper conceptualization and definition of internationally traded services will have to be expansive so as to take into account the different ways in which services can be delivered and the various forms which service transactions can take.

This catalogue of examples of how trade in telecommunication and data services might occur is meant to provoke thought and underline the complexity of the phenomenon rather than to provide definitive answers. It should be clear that the conceptualization of services, the distinction between services and goods, the nature of *trade* in this area, and the applicability of trade concepts to telecommunication and data services all require analysis. Before proceeding to these tasks, however, it is important first to confront the basic differences between the trade-policy perspective and the telecommunication-policy perspective which lie very much at the root of the problem.

Trade-Policy Perspective *vs.* Telecommunication-Policy Perspective

The fundamental difficulty with telecommunication and data services as a trade-in-services issue is that it is both a telecommunication-policy issue *and* a trade-policy issue *simultaneously and interactively*. As a trade-policy issue, telecommunication and data services present themselves as one single sector or possibly two separate sectors among the several trade-in-services sectors, including financial services, computer services, travel and tourism services and many others in which liberalized trade rules could usefully be negotiated at the international level. From a telecommunication-policy perspective, however, trade in telecommunication and data services arises primarily as a new policy dimension -- and a very controversial one -- among such matters as regulatory practices, facilities planning, ownership and control, social and national objectives which together compose an overall telecommunication policy responsive to user needs and provider capabilities. This clash of different perspectives will be crucial to the evolution of telecommunication and data services as a trade-in-services issue, especially because each community seems to be pursuing its own separate agenda according to its own timetable (Pipe, 1987).

In terms of *trade policy*, trade-in-services issues have become increasingly significant during the 1970s and 1980s as the world's industrialized nations have become predominantly "service economies" domestically and are moving more and more in that direction globally.[2] As the country with the largest and probably the most dynamic service component and under consistent pressure from its own domestic service sectors, the United States has taken the lead in pressing for inclusion of services within multilateral and bilateral trade agreements (Dizard, 1984; Aho and Aronson, 1985). International trade agreements after World War II, and specifically the successive rounds of GATT, moved progressively to lower tariffs and remove some non-tariff barriers to trade in goods but certain other key areas such as investment, agricultural trade and, of course, services were *not* covered except indirectly. Other international organizations including the OECD, the World Bank and the various UN agencies also paid little attention specifically to services until the 1980s (Krommenacker, 1984; Sauvant, 1986). Following the conclusion of the Tokyo Round negotiations in 1979 where services received virtually no attention, however, U.S. service industries particularly in the data processing and financial services area made common cause with the newly-elected Reagan administration to press the issue in the GATT, the OECD, the UNCTAD and elsewhere (Spero, 1982; Brock, 1982; Feketekuty and Aronson, 1984a,b).

Over the past five years, *slow but steady progress* has been made -- at least on the process level - in advancing the trade-in-services issue as it relates to telecommunication and data services. In 1984, GATT empowered its secretariat to provide support for preliminary meetings on trade-in-services and encouraged interested member states to submit national studies pending an explicit decision on whether or not to proceed with formal negotiations (GATT Preliminary Negotiations on Services, 1984-86). In 1985, the United States concluded a bilateral free-trade agreement with Israel, one component of which dealt with trade in services including telecommunications, but this agreement was largely declaratory and is only now being turned into one with contractually binding rights and obligations. In 1985, the OECD -- through its Committee on Information, Computers and Communications Policy -- developed and adopted a precedent-setting Declaration on Transborder Data Flows which committed members not to take measures in the future to hinder information flows. In 1986, the OECD's Trade Committee prepared an initial "conceptual framework for trade-in-services" which was subjected to "sectoral testing" within the organization and subsequently approved for public distribution as a contribution to the evolving debate (OECD Trade Committee, 1987). As is well known, the GATT Council of Ministers agreed in 1986 to launch the Uruguay Round of trade negotiations including the establishment of a Group of Negotiations on Services (GNS) to run on a parallel track with the mainstream goods negotiations (GATT, 1986). More recently, in 1987, Canada and the United States have signed a bilateral free-trade agreement which includes a major section on trade in services including a detailed "sectoral annex" on "telecommunications network-based enhanced services and computer services". And finally, the GNS has, since early 1987, been discussing a range of trade-in-services issues and is now exploring the possibility of achieving a multilateral framework agreement for the GATT mid-term meeting to be held in Montreal in December 1988. Thus, slow but steady progress has been made over the past five years towards liberalization of trade in services and more substantive action is clearly at hand.

It is important at this stage to understand what *a trade-policy perspective on telecommunication services* entails. As set out clearly by one of the key U.S. trade officials in this area, Geza Feketekuty, a trade-policy perspective has *an inherent bias towards trade liberalization*:

> The principal objectives of international trade negotiations are to establish fair and mutually beneficial rules for trade among commerical enterprises operating in a market environment, the reciprocal reduction of barriers to mutually beneficial trade, and the establishment of principles and procedures that will minimize the extent to which domestic regulations distort trade.

> The GATT rules for multilateral trade are based on the underlying assumption that trade based on market competition is generally both fair and mutually advantageous, and that government intervention in commercial transactions based on market criteria should be kept within agreed limits. The GATT system of rules gives competing enterprises from different countries considerable flexibility and freedom to carry out commercial transactions within the limits established in trade agreements.

> In summary, the strength of a trade policy approach is in its emphasis on mutual commercial advantage, competition on a market-oriented basis and the reciprocal removal of obstacles to mutually beneficial trade. Trade officials have a dual role in the government - to act as guardians of the country's general commercial interest, and simultaneously as guardians of a system of trade rules that permit market-based competition among enterprises from different countries (Feketekuty, 1988b:18).

From the trade policy perspective, then, telecommunication and data services constitute only *one among many service sectors*, although admittedly a particularly crucial one which governs the infrastructure over which many other services are traded. The negotiation of common international rules and procedures is viewed as contributing greatly to the satisfaction of domestic and international business concerns and as breaking down unwarranted barriers to trade in an increasingly important area of the world economy.

The telecommunication-policy perspective on trade in services is a sharply different one. National policy-makers and regulators in the telecommunication field are primarily concerned with the *efficient and effective operation of telecommunication networks* and with the broader *economic, social and national objectives* which those networks have traditionally been expected to serve. Depending upon a country's particular history and tradition as well as its continuing political preferences, the telecommunication system may be monopolistic or competitive, owned and controlled either publicly or privately, and subject to widely varying degrees of regulation (Bruce et al., 1985). Also, at the international level, telecommunication policy-makers and service providers must work with their counterparts in other countries, both bilaterally and through international organizations like the International Telecommunication Union, to develop and maintain the complex technical and administrative arrangements necessary to allow for the conduct of modern international telecommunications (Codding, 1982). Bilateral and multilateral coordination combined with domestic regulation has become the prime instrument whereby nations have agreed to organize and manage international telecommuications. However, telecommunication policy-makers today find their world in considerable turmoil and disarray as the result of rapid technological advance which brings about persistent pressures for greater competition and new services and which is challenging long-established institutional structures and practices in the telecommunication field.

From *the telecommunication-policy perspective*, international telecommunication has simply not been viewed in terms of trade between nations but rather as a cooperative technical and administrative arrangement (Herzstein, 1985). Moreover, the new services constantly coming on stream often seem to have more to do with computing and the content which telecommunication systems carry than with the carriage function and the telecommunication network itself. Nevertheless, telecommunication policy-makers in various countries have moved somewhat reluctantly in recent years to recognize -- if not yet to respond to -- increasing interest in the trade in telecommunication and data services issue. In 1982, at its last Plenipotentiary Conference, the ITU scheduled a World Administrative

Telegraph and Telephone Conference for the late 1980s to deal with new telecommunication services and this conference is now to be held in Melbourne late in 1988 (ITU, 1987a). A WATTC-88 Preparatory Committee was established in 1984 to begin drafting the International Telecommunication Regulations which would deal with the new telecommunication services environment and, after four sets of meetings, a highly contentious set of draft regulations was produced in 1987 (ITU, 1987b). At the same time, planning is proceeding apace both on the national and international level for the introduction of the Integrated Services Digital Network(s) which will allow the world's telecommunication networks to handle new telecommunication services more efficiently and effectively [Rutkowski, 1986]. Within OECD as well, work is proceeding on assessing the policy implications of telecommunication-network-based services and also on the application of conceptual frameworks for trade in services to the telecommunication and informatics field (OECD Committee on ICCP, 1987; OECD Working Party on Transborder Data Flows, 1987). And finally, the ITU as an organization and, of course, the national policy-makers and telecommunication administrations which participate within it are currently holding a "watching brief" on the Uruguay Round services negotiations, contributing to that process when requested but clearly concerned about the possible implications for the technical and administrative aspects of international telecommunication regulation. Thus, the stance taken towards the trade-in-services issue by the telecommunication policy-community -- governments, regulators and providers -- is considerably more cautious and incremental than that taken by trade-policy officials.

The *telecommunication policy perspective*, as evident specifically on the international level, is well captured by Secretary-General Richard Butler in a recent treatment of the problems facing the International Telecommunications Union:

> The primary purpose of the ITU is to produce broad agreements among affected countries in the field of telecommunications, through those countries negotiating between themselves the rights and obligations which the parties to the agreements, i.e. governments, will have vis-a-vis one another. These agreements are reflected in treaty principles and regulations, CCITT and CCIR recommendations, procedural obligations and provisions to be followed by all those concerned. Each country reserves the right to regulate its telecommunications in accordance with its own national law. However, the application of the latter is tempered by the built-in, compelling need for agreements with the other parties concerned...

We in the ITU will be following closely the issue of 'services negotiations' between the GATT contracting parties, in order to avoid duplication or conflict of potentially related international treaty legislation, for the preservation of worldwide interconnectivity is fundamental. At the international level there is close liaison between the GATT and ITU secretariats. Future developments in this area will depend, however, upon coordination at national level within the individual countries. At that level a clear understanding of the issues is needed between the telecommunications authorities and the GATT contracting parties (Butler, 1988:16-17).

The proliferation of new telecommunications and data services and the trade-in-services issue -- as opposed to essentially technical matters with which it normally deals -- then poses the kind of challenge to the telecommunication-policy community which it is perhaps least equipped and able to deal with.

Mention should also be made of data-services providers and users -- that services component which is perhaps most integrally related to telecommunication services -- and how they view the trade-in-services issue. At first glance, data services providers and users would seem more likely to view the issue from the trade policy rather than the telecommunication-policy perspective. Clearly they want unrestricted access to networks and services all around the world in order to market and use their services and their interests have been an important driving force behind the transborder-data-flow issue and now behind the trade-in-services issue. At the same time, however, there is some recognition that the telecommunication-policy perspective, as reflected in concern about the integrity and efficiency of telecommunication networks, remains crucial and that trade-policy considerations cannot be allowed simply to override telecommunication policy concerns (Sauvant, 1987).

Conceptualizing Trade In Services and Distinguishing It From Trade in Goods

There is a vibrant ongoing debate on how to distinguish trade in services from trade in goods and on the conceptualization of services themselves which has considerable importance for the treatment of internationally traded telecommunication services. The longstanding tradition in the economic literature is to treat services primarily as an "intermediate" stage in the production/consumption process and even, following Adam Smith, to dismiss services altogether as "unproductive" or, at best, a "tertiary" sector of modern economies (Hill, 1977; Bhagwati, 1984 and 1987). Services have supposedly differed from goods in that they must be used in close proximity to where they were produced, they had relatively low intrinsic value vis-a-vis the final product in which they were embodied, and they were not easily measurable and tradeable across jurisdictional boundaries. This limited and static view of services simply does not conform to the realities of modern services economies in industrialized nations, where services contribute a larger share than goods to gross domestic product, employment and wages although goods still predominate in trade. In recent years, economists and others have been scurrying to rethink and revise their conceptualization of services in the modern economy.

Harald Malmgren (1985:15) presents a concise summary of the *reasons why services have become so significant* within the world economy and at the same time are so difficult to measure:

First, in their monitoring of international transactions in services, governments have not been able to keep pace with developments in the sector, particularly because technological advances in telecommunications are revolutionising the means of delivering services.

Second, many services are provided by multinational enterprises with a number of offices in different geographical locations working simultaneously and collectively. The value added is diffused geographically, but the final fee may be booked at a particular location for tax or regulatory reasons.

Third, manufacturing enterprises are increasingly providing services in conjunction with trade in goods and foreign investment.

Fourth, the configuration of service industries is being transformed by mergers, acquisitions and other forms of agglomeration which transcend the traditional boundaries that separate particular types of services.

Fifth, many new kinds of services are being made available, as in the provision of software for the management and delivery of engineering services, medical and health-maintenance services, remote retailing and so on.

Sixth, many services are transacted in a non-market or 'black' market environment.

Not only is our understanding of the significance of services in the modern economy changing but so too is its prevailing conceptualization and the work of T.J. Hill is often cited as a major contribution to this process of redefinition. Hill interprets the traditional characteristics of services in more dynamic terms: first of all, he argues that "a service may be defined as a change in the condition of a person, or a good belonging to some economic unit, which is brought about as a result of the activity of some other unit"; second, services may not be storable but they can be "embodied" either in people or in goods, they are transactional and tradeable between economic units and even across borders, and the "change of condition" which takes place can be expressed in terms of value added (Hill, 1977:315-18).

Building upon this more dynamic notion of services, other economists (Bhagwati, 1984:136-38; Sampson and Snape, 1984:172-75) have proceeded to construct *typologies of different categories of services* according to the proximity of producers and consumers of services and the extent to which services can be "disembodied" from the supplier and provided without a physical presence being necessary. Several conceptual categories have been identified:

- "separated" or "long-distance" services, where physical proximity is unimportant and the service may at some point be "disembodied" into goods or people. Examples would include financial, insurance, or information services and, in the latter instance, discs full of data might be construed more as a service than a good;

- mobile-provider, immobile-user services, such as is the case with consulting projects, guest worker programs and many other service activities where the provider moves to the user;

- mobile-user, immobile-provider services, such as is the case with regard to tourism services where the user moves to the provider;

- services where proximity is important either in the form of immobile providers serving immobile users, as is the case with many local services in the domestic economy or in the form of mobile providers serving equally mobile users who make contact "on the go".[3]

Whereas the above categorization emphasizes the proximity criterion, other writers have focused more on the "embodiment" criterion and some would go so far as to argue that services can be conceptualized as having no independent status of their own but that all services can be treated as being "embodied" either in goods or in people (Grubel, 1987).

The late Jacques Nussbaumer sought to develop a functional categorization of services (including services embodied in goods) according to their function within national and international economies and their tradeability. Primary services such as unskilled labor are little more than a normal factor of production common to many economic activities without reference to the scope or purpose of the activity performed and are tradeable only in a nominal sense. Intermediate services which perform a linkage or communication function, e.g. telecommunications, transport, insurance, maintenance, etc., serve essentially as a complement to the production or consumption of other goods and services and the tradeability of these intermediate services is more problematic. Final services are most easily identified in that they represent basic additions to consumer welfare, e.g. all types of content services including information services, health services, education services, etc., and many of these are internationally tradeable (Nussbaumer, 1987a:12ff). In his most recent work, Nussbaumer carried his analysis further by relating his categorization more closely to the value-added information content of intermediate and final services (Nussbaumer, 1987b: Chapter 4).

Rather than a categorization of services themselves, Raymond Krommenacker has recently proposed *one particularly promising typology of service transactions in terms of the character of the trade taking place* (Krommenacker, 1987). Four main categories are identified according to the mobility of consumers and of factors of production as set out in Figure I:

Figure I: Conceptual Framework for Categorizing Services Trade			
		FACTORS OF PRODUCTION	
		Dont't Move	Move
CONSUMERS OF SERVICE	Don't Move	Across-the-border trade	Foreign-earnings trade
	Move	Domestic-establishment trade	Third-country trade

Krommenacker's conceptualization of services trade - as opposed to the character of the services themselves - is a promising contribution to the trade-in-services debate which deserves further exploration and elaboration.

At least four points about telecommunication and data services and their relation to trade-in-services concepts grow out of this discussion. First of all, telecommunications and data services are very seldom treated explicitly or distinctly within these categorizations and typologies cited above but, rather, different examples of such services often fit into different categories. Second, a major weakness of these categorizations and typologies -- to which this absence of attention to telecommunication and data services *per se* is testimony -- is the failure to take into account the "transportability" of services, i.e. the infrastructure provided by the public-switched network or, alternatively, the postal system, the frequency spectrum or various transportation modes - -as a distinct and explicit set of intermediary services, at least conceptually separate from the "content" services usually treated. Third, whether telecommunication and data services should be treated together or separately as "transport" plus "content" services needs to be examined further. Finally, it needs to be recognized that categorization and typologies of services or services trade are analytical devices which contribute relatively little in the final analysis to a resolution of conflicting interests among nations but may be considerably more important in reconciling differences of approach among trade-policy and telecommunication-policy officials.

What Constitutes "Trade" in Trade in Telecommunication and Data Services?

The concept of "trade" underlying *trade in telecommunication and data services* is also a matter of some controversy. As was noted in the examples given earlier, the forms which trade in telecommunication and data services might take are quite varied and there is much resistance within the telecommunication policy community to treating normal international telecommunication activity in trade terms. It is also not clear whether conventional trade theory can adequately be applied to services transactions and how the concept of trade relates to other concepts like foreign investment and features of industry structure such as monopoly, competition or regulation. The divergence of views and confusion on these matters is readily apparent both in the literature on trade in telecommunication and data services and in ongoing discussions and negotiations at the international level. And once again, the trade-policy perspective differs considerably from the telecommunication-policy perspective on what actually constitutes "trade" in the area of telecommunication and data services.

Conventional trade theory explains trade between nations in terms of the *theory of comparative advantage*. Basically, trade occurs because countries are differently emdowed with resources -- raw materials, skills and size of labour force, capital -- and therefore produce goods and services at different costs. The exchange of goods and services thus makes possible a more efficient allocation of resources and benefits consumers in all countries. The nineteenth-century British economist David Ricardo demonstrated by his law of comparative costs that trade in specific goods and services can be beneficial to both trading partners, A and B, even if A produces all goods and services more cheaply than B. The reason for this is that it is rational for A to import a product from B, which it could produce more cheaply at home, *if* the resources needed to do so can be more efficiently allocated to another product which can be *exported* to B at a significant advantage. Note that this also means that it is possible for a country (B) to be an exporter even if none of its producers is more efficient than competitors in its trading partner (A). (For further discussion, see Feketekuty, 1988A, Ch. 6.) In the view of most economists and trade-policy officials, the theory of comparative advantage provides a very firm foundation for international trade and it is only in very special circumstances and for a limited period that governments can justify domestic protection from international competition on such grounds as infant-industry considerations. (Corden, 1974).

But does the theory of comparative advantage hold with equal rigour and relevance for services as for goods? Does the export and import of services pose special problems which compromise the applicability of that theory? Again, most economists conclude that the theory of comparative advantage *does indeed apply to trade in services* (Jussawalla, 1982; Hindley and Smith, 1984; Grossman and Shapiro, 1984; Bhagwati, 1987a). However, some also recognize that trade in services has some peculiar characteristics. First of all, almost everyone recognizes that services trade cannot be monitored and measured when it crosses national boundaries in the same way that goods trade can and therefore it is much more difficult to determine if "trade" is actually taking place (Stern and Hochman, 1987). Second, foreign direct investment in service industries, where this is allowed, is often either a substitute for or a complement to trade in services between countries and the intrafirm transfer of technology and transborder data flows which also occur so extensively represent little more than a hidden form of "trade" (Grossman and Shapiro, 1985). Third, it is recognized by many that developing nations face particularly severe "terms of trade" in dealing with developed nations in the services area because their own service sectors are usually so poorly developed that they must be large net importers of services at the same time that such services are increasingly essential for them for modernization and growth (Jussawalla, 1982; Bhagwati, 1984). And finally, despite the inherent mobility of factors in many service sectors, at least some would argue that comparative advantage can be artificially engineered in certain sectors such as financial services in ways that are not possible with regard to many goods.

Even the task of coming up with an *adequate definition of trade in services* has been difficult and epitomizes the problems of conceptualization in this area. The recent OECD draft on "a conceptual framework for trade in services" suggested three possible definitions, only slightly different from one another but carrying quite different implications. One simple and straight-forward definition -- "services exported from a supplier country and imported into another country" -- may be too simple and straight-forward and would not capture the variety of ways certain services like tourism or telecommunications can be exchanged. Another definition - "services produced by residents of one country and used/received/paid for by residents of another country" - captures the basic element of exchange but hinges too much on the idea of residency and location. A third definition - "services essentially produced in one country and used/received/paid for by residents of another country" - subtly introduces the notion of "value added" as part of the exchange process and perhaps comes closer to the mark (OECD Trade Committee, 1987:4). As of now, however, neither the OECD nor those involved in the Uruguay Round negotiations have come up with what can be regarded as an adequate definition of the phenomenon.

With regard to telecommunication services specifically, there is more pointed debate over *whether "trade" is the appropriate concept to apply to the provision of international telecommunication services*. Prior to the emergence of the trade-in-services issue in the late 1970s and early 1980s, no one in the telecommunication-policy field viewed international telecommunication activity as in any real sense a trade issue. Since that time, however, trade-policy proponents have been successful in establishing the notion of trade in telecommunication and data services as being broadly applicable to virtually all international telecommunication activity. In one recent study prepared for the OECD and generally available though never officially released, Reid (1985) challenges that trade policy view in terms of its specific applicability to international public-switched network and leased-line activities while at the same time demonstrating why trade in services does in fact occur -- and will occur increasingly in the future -- with respect to other types of telecommunication services. The crux of her argument hinges on the elaborate set of international arrangements, developed and implemented primarily through the ITU, whereby *"worldwide service is provided on a cooperative basis by national administrations"*. She demonstrates how these arrangements set out the basic categories of telecommunication services which can be provided (e.g. public-switched network service, leased lines but not when used by third parties, and no data-processing services), how tarification principles have been agreed to so as to cover costs and to deter "harmful competition", and the various ways in which revenues are settled between national administrations according to agreed procedures. These arrangements, she concludes, do not constitute "trade":

> If the purpose of trade can be said to be allowing a country to exchange products and services in which it has a comparative advantage for those in which it has a comparative disadvantage, it is difficult to see how the telecommunications structure described above fulfills this purpose. Far from encouraging countries to exchange different services, it instead has ensured that all countries produce the same services. The capability of producing these services has then been shared among countries, not traded. An international flow of funds results, but it does not so much represent the purchase

by one country of a service from another as the balancing of accounts between different sections of the same organization (Reid, 1985:18).

Reid, however, does not dispute the fact that *genuine trade can and indeed currently does take place* with regard to some telecommunication services. Technological innovation, the availability of alternative facilities and product differentiation among service providers are altering the boundary lines between what constitutes basic services, provided primarily using cooperative arrangements, and other value-added services provided competitively and suited more explicitly to trade.[4]

From a telecommunication-policy perspective, such a skeptical view of what constitutes internationally traded telecommunication service would probably find considerable sympathy because it accords with widely-held views within that community. At the same time, however, viewed from a trade-policy perspective, her eventual conclusion would also be welcomed but not necessarily her exemption of cooperative international telecommunication activity from the range of trade in services. Even within the OECD Secretariat and among several member governments, although often for different reasons, her view is regarded as "not sufficiently nuanced, in that it ignores that some scope for limited competition exists" (OECD ICCP Committee, 1986:5). They point out, in rebuttal to Reid, that limited competition does already exist within the existing international arrangements in terms of "diverging telecommunications charges among countries", "limited inter-service competition" or "competition between telecommunication administrations for traffic to a third country" and also that "the possibility exists for firms to lease lines or transmit traffic from one country to another and then use the public-switched network of the second country for distribution of the traffic to final destinations" (OECD ICCP Committee, 1986:5). Thus, in their view, trade in telecommunication services is possible and can and does take place even within existing or modified international arrangements. The trade-policy community -- supported by many data service providers and users -- would of course press for *more extensive and unrestricted forms of competiton and trade* in the telecommunications field.

By way of summary, we can make at least three points about what constitutes "trade" in internationally traded telecommunication services. First, telecommunication services -- more so than other services sectors -- fit rather uncomfortably into conventional trade theory and it is likely that a proper conceptualization of "trade" in this area will have to take into account the specific features of how international telecommunications presently operate. Second, the argument that most international telecommunication activities presently take place within cooperative arrangements which do not really constitute trade according to normal notions of "comparative advantage" must be confronted squarely. One obvious way of doing so would be to define the category of internationally traded telecommunication and data services broadly to include all activities using telecommunication transport infrastructure and then to differentiate between transactions accomplished through cooperative arrangements and competitive trade in telecommunication and data services. Third, the international telecommunication scene is changing rapidly as many industrialized nations modify their domestic regulatory practices and major industrialized countries and transnational business interests press for market access in all countries. It is virtually a certainty that the competitive mode will in the future become more prominent than the cooperative mode and, in fact, one might go further and raise the issue of whether some minimum degree of domestic and international competition is necessary for effective trade in services.

On Domestic and International Telecommunication and Data Services and Their Implications for Trade-In-Services Negotiations

From their inception, international telecommunication services have been provided according to what is *essentially a monopoly model* in accord with similar practices then followed domestically in countries all over the world. Monopoly provision of local and long distance as well as telegraph service was the norm in terms of domestic telecommunication systems and, only with the advent in recent years of new services and alternative facilities for their provision, has even a modicum of competition been allowed. In addition, foreign investment in domestic telecommunication systems was usually restricted or prohibited and, where public ownership through PTTs or their equivalent was not adopted, regulation of private monopoly providers has been predominant. This pattern of public policy for domestic telecommunications is now breaking down in a number of industrialized countries as *competition in services and, to a lesser extent, in facilities* is supplanting long-standing monopoly practices. The United States has, of course, led the way in deliberate deregulation, divestiture and the introduction of greater competition within its domestic telecommunication system, while other countries are moving in the same general direction although in their own way and at their own pace. Privatization of publicly-owned telecommunication providers and liberalization or re-regulation of telecommunications services are also allied in countries like the United Kingdom, Japan and Canada to this move towards increased competition (Bruce, 1987; Ergas, 1987). In terms of international telecommunication activity, with special attention directed at West European PTT nations and key developing nations, U.S. government and business interests in particular are pressing for the curbing of restrictive practices and the acceptance of increased competition in other countries and on the international level (Eward, 1985; Aronson and Cowley, 1988). Meanwhile, the provision and use of international data services remain, to a large extent, restricted by prevailing domestic and international telecommunication policy and regulation.

Trade in telecommunication and data services, specifically as it follows the competitive mode, is serving as a wedge to open up and gain access for foreign service providers to domestic telecommunication systems, previously protected by restrictions on direct foreign investment and often hidden domestic regulatory barriers. *Ownership and control restrictions and regulatory practices* have been the traditional instruments of telecommunication policy in all countries, including the United States, to maintain the integrity of domestic networks and keep out unwanted foreign competition. It's a fact of life that all countries require that foreign ownership and control of telecommunication network providers of basic services be completely excluded or limited to a low percentage. Similar restrictions may also apply to other telecommunication service providers using the basic network, although the United States has claimed since the early 1980's to maintain no overt foreign ownership and control restrictions on enhanced service providers. Foreign direct investment in services -- as distinct from cross-border trade in services -- is increasingly important in many service sectors, and especially in data services though not yet in telecommunication services. Until now, foreign direct investment has been treated quite separately and differently from trade, with the emphasis squarely on the sovereign right of states to admit or refuse investment and, if admitted, to regulate it. Increasingly, the issue is being raised as to whether foreign direct investment and the various concepts which relate to it -- right of establishment, right of non-establishment, temporary presence -- need to be absorbed more directly within an overall trade-in-services regime (Sauvant and Zimny, 1987).[5]

The other major policy instruments have been various domestic and international regulatory practices -- in addition to normal price and rate of return regulation -- which have effectively drawn the lines between monopoly and competitive provision of services. In these cases, there is considerably more variation among countries in drawing the line between monopoly and competitive provision of services. The United States, in the wake of the FCC's "Computer Inquiry I" and, especially "Computer Inquiry II", continues to pursue the distinction between "basic services", where the message is merely being transported without being processed or changed, and "enhanced services" where some value is added to the basic services, although now, after "Computer Inquiry III", with greater ambiguity and the recent addition of market-dominance criteria. In Japan, the demarcation is made on the basis of facilities rather than services, with a distinction being made between Type I carriers, offering services on their own facilities and subject to regulation, and Type II carriers, offering unregulated services on Type I carrier facilities. In the United Kingdom, both facilities and services are used to draw the line, with facilities providers (two at the moment) providing basic conveyance on a regulated basis, while value-added services can be provided only on resold telecommunication capacity but competitively by any willing entrant (Bruce, 1987). The recent Canadian government policy statement establishes Type I carriers which own interprovincial and international transmission facilities and provide basic services to the public and Type II carriers which rent capacity from Type I carriers and provide enhanced services in a competitive environment (Woodrow, 1988: Chapter 3). Likewise, the ITU, through explicit regulations accepted by member states as well as more informal recommendations to national telecommunication administrations, maintains a panoply of regulatory practices relating to the conduct of international telecommunications. Those domestic and international regulatory practices which unduly restrict or distort trade in telecommunication and data services will undoubtedly be a central component of any multilateral agreement (Richardson, 1987).[6]

One other prominent feature of the trade-in-services issue should also be mentioned. The relationship between *levels of development and trade in services* has been crucial from the very beginning. Many developing nations were concerned about any extension of GATT principles and practices from goods to services because of what they view as the inadequate way in which the interests of developing nations have been treated in the past and the possibility of inappropriate trade-offs between goods and services. As articulated initially by countries like Brazil and India and more recently by other countries like Argentina and Mexico, they have argued that, if multilateral agreements on trade in services are to be negotiated, the concept of economic development must be treated as a major objective and development concerns -- from preservation of national sovereignty to questions of labor mobility -- must be effectively handled (Riddle, 1987; Gibbs, 1985). It is clear that any broad and substantive agreement on a trade in services regime must take account of the special concerns of developing nations that services trade not be allowed merely to make the rich richer and the poor poorer.[7]

Mention should finally be made of the relationship between trade and transborder data flow. One recent contribution typifies the problem involved. Herbert Grubel has argued that telecommunication services in general are "splintered services" and that electronic signals should not be treated as in any sense a "special case". In his view, the essential service involved in the transmission of information is embodied in "material substances", i.e., the signals themselves, which have the same characteristics as goods. Thus, he concludes that "all international trade involving electronics results in the crossing of borders by material signals that in principle are recordable and measurable, much like books, letters and floppy discs" and further that "in principle, registering of the trade should not give rise to special difficulties, for it can be monitored whenever the substances cross borders" (Grubel, 1987:326). To anyone who is familiar with transborder data flow issues as they have developed over the past decade and also with the laws and regulations which prescribe how domestic and international telecommunications take place -- let alone the difficulties encountered in measurement -- this assertion arising out of a trade-policy perspective can only be amusing (Robinson, 1985 and 1987).

The negotiation and implementation of multilateral and bilateral agreements covering trade in telecommunication and data services thus offers a unique opportunity to confront some of these barriers to services trade and to establish a new and more liberal trade regime for the future. Successful agreement(s) can alter or affect existing domestic and/or international practices and could allow foreign service providers greater access to domestic markets. This constitutional exercise -- for that is what is effectively being undertaken -- spawns conflict among different nations and interests and necessitates wise and careful choices as to how to proceed. Who should take the lead in negotiating a trade-in-telecommunication-and-data-services regime? For all intents and purposes, that question has already been answered. The Uruguay Round Group of Negotiations on Services has clearly taken the lead in this regard. Telecommunication and data services are one of the two or three priority sectors which most nations regard as crucial to any successful outcome. In this regard, there is some disposition to involve the ITU more directly in the negotiations but also a concern on the part of trade-policy officials that sectoral discussions in this area not be allowed to turn into a "regulator's negotiation".

What format might such a regime take? Most likely, a multilateral or bilateral trade in services agreement would establish a mutually agreeable set of principles which together would create a *framework* for how all services sectors should be treated. Further provision might then be made - through *sectoral annexes or annotations* - for specific treatment of individual sectors requiring additional detail or exemption from the application of certain principles. This is the general format presently being considered in the Uruguay Round negotiations on services. There is some feeling, however, that, while a services agreement may be negotiated broadly within the GATT forum, the subsequent agreement need not necessarily be lodged within that body on a permanent basis but rather in a separate but related institution.[8]

Establishing the scope and limits of trade in services negotiations is as important for successful trade policy as drawing lines and setting boundaries for services and markets is for successful telecommunications policy. There are several possible options in this regard for negotiating trade in telecommunication and data services, each with its own strengths and weaknesses, as we move beyond a framework agreement towards subsequent sectoral negotiations. A *narrow-gauge sectoral approach* might focus on telecommunication networks alone, the essential transport infrastructure for the growth and internationalization of other trade-in-services sectors like computer services or financial services. This approach would attempt to separate carriage from content and would parallel most closely the ongoing work of the ITU as well as what has been done in the proposed Canada-U.S. free trade pact. One major benefit of this approach is that it focuses due attention specifically on the telecommunications transport function (ITU, 1987; Canada-U.S. Free Trade Agreement, 1987:Chapter 14). A *broad-gauge sectoral approach* would focus on telematics and combine telecommunications with the various computer-based uses to which the network can be put, i.e., telecommunication network-based services. This approach would mix both carriage and content functions and respond to the concerns of many observers that computer communications should be confronted head on, while also recognizing the fact that clear dividing lines between the two functions cannot easily be drawn. This seems to be the approach followed for many years within the OECD and its Committee on Information, Computer and Communications Policy (Robinson, 1985; OECD Committee on Information, Computer and Communications Policy, 1987). While both of the above approaches treat their respective subject matter as essentially sectors within a multi-sectored trade-in-services negotiation, yet another approach might be to aim for a *separate information technology agreement* which would treat not only services but also high-technology goods together. This approach would recognize the growing variety of forms which trade in services takes in this area and could establish the essential transformative role which information technology is coming to play in modern economies (Grey, 1986; Rada, 1987). Each of these different approaches to negotiation clearly has different implications for how trade in telecommunication and data services would be handled within negotiations. Nevertheless, it is clear that, whatever approach is taken and whatever set of principles is eventually adopted, the concept of internationally traded telecommunication and data services has -- with only minor reservations and qualifications -- come to be generally accepted.

Concluding Comments

This paper has attempted a preliminary 'constitutional' analysis of trade in telecommunication and data services. In using the term 'constitutional', I have presented the exercise in terms of "building a fence around a vacant lot". In particular, this paper has explored the different perspectives of telecommunication-policy and trade-policy officials, the conceptualization of services and the special dynamics of trade in this area. I must admit that I have spent more time talking about what is taking place on the lot than precisely how the fence can best be built. That is perhaps not so bad, however, since many of the papers prepared for this volume take up the task of fence-building in greater detail.

Endnotes

1 The use of the term "constitutional" is unusual in this instance but by no means unprecedented. Professor John Jackson has in the past used such a formulation to highlight the need for a "rule-oriented" rather than "power-oriented" approach to multilateral and bilateral trade negotiations (Jackson, 1982 and 1987). It is also the same basic concept which Ambassador Jaramillo, the Chairman of the Uruguay Round Group of Negotiations on Services, has used in describing the work of the GNS (Jaramillo, 1987).

2 The growth of "service economies" domestically and internationally is beyond the scope of our discussion. However, a brief overview of the major evidence is presented in Appendix D.

3 See also the paper by Henning Klodt in this volume.

4 More specifically, see the papers by Aronson and Feketekuty in this volume.

5 Professor Balasubramanyam's paper in this volume deals with this issue.

6 On treatment of regulation within a trade-in-services regime, see the paper by Stevers and Wilkinson in this volume.

7 Bruno Lanvin takes up the issue of developing nations' participation in trade-in-services negotiations later in this volume.

8 On institutional aspects of a trade-in-services regime, see the paper by Francis Gurry.

SERVICES: NATIONAL OBJECTIVES

Sidney Dell

Introduction

It has been said (Aho and Aronson, 1985) that the push for rules to govern trade in services is consistent with the long-term restructuring going on within national economies and in the world economy as a whole. The input of services into the production of goods is increasing and there is a growing recognition of the fact that tradeable producer services - particularly in the information and telecommunication sectors - are playing a rapidly increasing role in the production of and trade in goods.

At the same time there is concern among the major industrial countries that trade in services is, as they see it, being hampered by government measures that restrict or discriminate against imported services by various means, including the erection of barriers to the entry and establishment of foreign enterprise. Such measures, it is felt, are against the best interests of the countries imposing them as well as of the international community as a whole. What is needed is a more open and competitive international environment for the expansion of world trade in services, which, it is believed, would bring benefits to all countries - to importers of services as well as to exporters and to developing countries as well as to industrial countries.

Many of these ideas are the subject of intense controversy not only between industrial and developing countries but within both groups of countries themselves, as will be seen subsequently. The whole question of the liberalization of trade in services is still in its infancy, and the available information, both quantitative and qualitative, leaves much to be desired in analyzing the various points of view advanced from the one side or the other and above all in assessing the potential costs and benefits of alternative policy options. Developing countries feel particularly vulnerable on this score and many of them are not persuaded that the potential short-term gains in resource allocation that might result from liberalization would justify the loss of opportunities for achieving long-run gains in comparative advantage through the protection of infant industries, even in some of the high-tech sectors.

According to the GATT Secretariat, the issue of services first came to the forefront of GATT concerns in 1982 as a result of a request by the U.S. Government that services be included in the Work Programme established by the Ministerial Declaration of 1982 (GATT, 1987, 1). While the proposal received the support of a number of industrialized countries, a number of developing countries opposed the idea on several grounds, including the contention that GATT had no legal authority to address itself to services.

There followed a period of study and discussion that did not lead to any agreement and the eventual decision to proceed with multilateral negotiations on trade in services was adopted only as a political compromise at the Special Session of Contracting Parties in Punta del Este in 1986. Part II of the Ministerial Declaration at Punta del Este set the aim of the negotiations as being to establish "a multilateral framework of principles and rules for trade in services, including elaboration of possible disciplines for individual sectors, with a view to expansion of such trade under conditions of transparency and progressive liberalization..." Two fundamental criteria were to be applied in establishing the framework:

- it was to be a means of promoting economic growth of all trading partners and the development of developing countries;

- it was to respect the policy objectives of national laws and regulations applying to services.

The underlying objective of the industrial countries is to apply in the area of services the same basic policy of liberalization that is believed to have made a major contribution to the expansion of trade and growth of national output that resulted from the seven previous rounds of multilateral trade negotiations since the end of World War II. Services account for a major and increasing share of national output and employment. Productivity growth in both industrial and developing countries will, it is believed, depend increasingly on the harnessing of new technologies in the service sector, particularly those concerned with the processing and transmission of information. Trade in services is, however, being held down by government regulation and lack of competition is believed to be a particularly serious shortcoming in some service sectors, including telecommunications. Industrial countries do not question the right of governments in both developed and developing countries to regulate services and to allow certain services to be provided by state or private monopolies. Where, however, national regulations or restraints on competition tend to prevent the expansion of trade, the issue arises whether it might be possible to negotiate changes in regulatory or competitive regimes that would reduce the obstacles to trade in services without damage to the growth or development prospects of the countries concerned. Among the regulations to be considered in this context are those that limit or constrain transnational corporations in establishing affiliates abroad to supply certain services to the local market and, in some cases, to other markets.

The underlying objective of developing countries is to promote development, though in common with many of the industrial countries their concerns go beyond economic considerations and include questions of culture, privacy and national security, especially as regards transborder data flows. They are well aware that the maintenance and improvement of their competitive position as suppliers of both primary products and manufactures may depend on their keeping abreast of rapidly developing technologies in several of the service sectors and especially telecommunication and data services. But it has not been established to their satisfaction that liberalization of their regulatory systems, including systems for controlling direct foreign investment, will necessarily work in their favour. On the contrary, since these systems are mainly intended to protect the growth of their infant industries, the effect of weakening them might be to downgrade their development prospects. For example, liberalization might in certain circumstances make it easier for foreign companies to establish and exploit dominant positions in domestic markets to the detriment of domestic enterprise. It might also strengthen the resistance of foreign enterprise to the transfer of technology which is indispensable in promoting autonomous development in the host countries.

Developing countries nevertheless accept the point in principle that it may be possible to adjust their regulations so as to expand trade without losing development potential and are prepared to explore such possibilities in the negotiations. They point out, however, that much preliminary work will be required, notably in assembling the statistical and other information that they will need to permit them to reach judgments on the costs and benefits of particular proposals for the amendment of regulations.

Objectives of the United States

The main objective of the United States is to bring about liberalization of trade in services and, to that end, to secure international acceptance of the principle that trade is services, like trade in goods, should be liberalized. The Advisory Trade Panel of the Atlantic Council of the United States has suggested the following "illustrative list" of the specific areas or sectors that might be included in a new international agreement on trade in services:

- merchant shipping, civil aviation and other forms of transportation;

- travel and tourism services;

- communications, including computer and data services;

- construction, engineering and related architectural and consultancy services;

- banking, insurance and other financial services;

- professional services: advertising, accounting, management, consulting, law and education;

- medical and hospital services; and

- artistic and cultural services (Atlantic Council, 1987, 67)

The panel notes, however, that the above list is more comprehensive than governments might wish to adopt. For example, some may prefer to deal with such services as education and health on a bilateral or otherwise more restrictive basis. Some, like the United States for consitutional reasons, may wish to qualify their acceptance of certain categories. Diebold and Stalson (1983) note certain U.S. restrictions such as American ownership of radio and telegraph services, limitation of coastal shipping to U.S. vessels and possible restrictions in the construction industry.

The considerations prompting the U.S. initiative on services appear to have included the following:

- The contributions of services to total output is substantial and has been increasing steadily in most if not all countries.

- Trade in services is also very substantial and growing rapidly. The Advisory Trade Panel of the Atlantic Council estimates international trade in services as being of the order of $400 billion a year, equivalent to about a quarter of world trade in merchandise.

- It is suggested that liberalization of trade in services could be expected to bring major benefits to all countries, just as the liberalization of trade in goods has done.

- The United States, it is believed, has a comparative advantage in trade in services and could expect, in the event of liberalization, to be able to increase its share in such trade, thereby compensating in whole or in part for losses of market share in the world trade in goods.

- An expansion of services provided by U.S. firms under engineering and construction contracts may lead to larger U.S. exports of goods.

- A major impetus has come from industry itself, especially large international firms in the fields of finance and insurance, as well as accounting, law, telecommunications and data processing. In many cases, these firms anticipate considerable demand from foreign affiliates of major domestic clients. Consequently, as Professor Rachel McCulloch has pointed out, the global expansion of competition in services is in part a reflection of the earlier globalization of U.S. manufacturing industries (McCulloch 1987, 14).

The success of U.S. efforts to obtain inclusion of services as well as of intellectual property and trade-related investment rules in the Uruguay Round is seen as the first step in opening the way to a mutually advantageous exchange of concessions with developing countries in the Uruguay Round. In return for concessions in the above three areas, the United States would be prepared to consider standstills and rollbacks on merchandise trade restrictions of interest to the developing countries. As U.S. trade representatives have stated repeatedly, negotiations on goods in the Uruguay Round cannot be concluded successfully without an agreement on services. This means, as Professor Bhagwati (1987, 565) has pointed out, that "the United States...cannot be expected to trade access to its markets any longer without significant elements of reciprocity from the development countries, even if the balance-of-trade deficits are somehow eliminated."

There is no dispute about the fact that any framework of rules and principles would have to allow for exceptions. The existing General Agreement allows contracting parties:

- to introduce temporary import restrictions in cases of difficulty resulting from a rapid increase in imports;

- to impose temporary restrictions on imports to deal with serious balance-of-payments deficits;

- to restrict imports endangering public health, safety, morals, the environment or the general public welfare; and

- to restrict imports for reasons of national security.

Similar provisions would have to be made in the field of services. Moreover if agreement were sought not merely on services *per se* but also in related areas such as investment, information flows or immigration, it would probably be necessary to allow for a considerably more extensive list of exceptions.

In October 1987 the U.S. delegation to GATT circulated a paper to the contracting parties setting out "a number of considerations and concepts" that should, in its view, be reflected in a multilateral framework of principles and rules for trade in services.

Six general considerations should, in the U.S. view, be "given great weight" in elaborating the framework:

- The framework should be designed to achieve a progressive liberalization of a wide range of service sectors in as many countries as possible.

- The framework should recognize the sovereign right of every country to regulate its service industries and must "ensure against" measures restrictive or distortive of trade.

- Countries should avoid adopting new restrictive measures on foreign service providers and should apply the framework to the greatest extent possible to existing measures.

- The framework should benefit every country regardless of its stage of economic development, and, through progressive liberalization, should provide a more competitive environment enabling local consumers to utilize services embodying the most advanced technology at the lowest possible prices.

- The framework should apply both to cross-border movement of services and to the establishment of foreign affiliates to deliver services within the host country.

- The coverage of the framework should be broad but flexible. The negotiation of individual sector agreements in the light of the framework should allow for greater precision and flexibility in attempting appropriate degrees of liberalization, depending on the sector in question.

The paper goes on to elaborate a number of specific concepts as follows:

Transparency

Government measures affecting service industries should operate in a clear and predictable manner and information on such measures should be readily accessible and made known to all interested parties on an equal basis. Obligations should be twofold:

- The obligation to publish proposed and final rules and regulations affecting services, and with certain exceptions, to provide interested parties with an opportunity to comment on them.

- The obligation to notify other countries of government measures affecting services. Measures so notified would be subject to consultations.

Non-Discrimination

In general, signatories to the framework agreement should extend the benefits of agreement unconditionally to all signatories. These benefits need not be extended to non-signatories, but there could be flexibility for signatories to make exceptions, within limits, to the coverage of the agreement.

National Treatment

Foreign service providers should receive treatment no less favourable in like circumstances than that accorded to domestic service providers with respect to government measures affecting the service sector in question. The concept of national treatment should include, but should not be limited to:

- Assess to local distribution networks.
- Access to local firms and personnel.
- Access to customers.
- Access to licenses.
- Right to use brand names.

Where the entry of new firms has been severely limited, provision should be made for a degree of foreign participation.

Discipline on State-Sanctioned Monopolies

The framework agreement should provide disciplines governing the behaviour of state sanctioned monopolies, whether public or private, without interfering with a government's sovereign right to provide a service by way of a monopoly.

Subsidies

The framework agreement should contain rules governing the use of government subsidies to service providers, whether they be domestic or export subsidies. A mechanism should be created for the resolution of disputes over the interpretation of the subsidy provisions. Authority to take offsetting measures equivalent to the impact of the injurious subsidy should be allowed.

Non-Discriminatory Accreditation Procedures

Licensing measures unrelated to competence and ability to perform should be discouraged and measures whose purpose or effect is to discriminate against foreign providers of licensed services should be prohibited.

Consultation/Dispute Settlement

The services framework should contain appropriate consultation and dispute-settlement provisions, which might be similar in concept to Articles XXII and XXIII of GATT or similar provisions of the various Non-tariff Measure Agreements.

Conclusion

The framework agreement should be negotiated at an early stage of the Uruguay Round so as to provide a point of departure for the negotiation of sectoral agreements during the later stages of the Round.

Objectives of Other Industrial Countries

Although most if not all industrial countries supported the idea of including negotiations on services in the Uruguay Round, many of them were at first concerned about the dangers of undue haste in dealing with the issues involved. They, as well as many developing countries, saw difficulties in the lack of agreement on the definition of the service sector, the inadequacy of statistical and other information on the sector, and uncertainly as to the nature and extent of barriers to trade in services. Consequently serious problems confronted most countries in determining precisely what they stood to gain or lose from the liberalization of services in general as well as of individual service sectors in particular.

More recently the interest of European Community countries in the negotiations on services has been strengthened as a result of the appearance of new data indicating considerable potential for gains in this field. It has, however, been difficult for these countries to agree on a common position because of differences regarding the specific sectors having the greatest potential for gain, depending on the particular service specialization developed by each country.

European Community Objectives

According to the representative of the European Commission to the Uruguay Round negotiations:

> In our view, the aim of the services agreement which we are now negotiating in the GNS (Group on Negotiations on Services) must be to provide the framework within which the dynamism which is so evident in our service sectors domestically can be unleashed internationally, leading to a major new impulse to the world economy and an acceleration of its growth (Richardson, 1988, 2).

Although trade in services is "inextricably linked" to trade in goods and should therefore be handled within the same institutional system, a tailor-made framework of rules will, in the view of the Commission, be required. In particular, an agreement on services should from the very beginning take account of the needs of development instead of providing for derogations from its rules for developing countries as required under the arrangements for "special and differential treatment" for developing countries, including the principle of non-reciprocity, contained in Part IV of the GATT.

Despite this and other differences, many of the principles of GATT should apply to any agreement on services, notably "some form of most-favoured-nation principle," progressive liberalization of market access, the negotiation of periodic packages of liberalization measures to ensure a balanced exchange of benefits, rules on transparency and dispute settlement procedures.

Three major characteristics distinguish trade in services from trade in goods:

- movements of consumers or of production factors are an integral part of trade in services and will need to be provided for;

- national regulation of the service sector is legitimate "so long as it has no protectionist intent";

- while tariffs on goods can be eliminated in the long run, some of the obstacles to trade in services represent "appropriate, desirable regulation."

The judgement that a liberal trading system allowing countries to trade on the basis of market prices will "bring benefits to all participants" stands on its own feet and does not require the support of the theory of comparative advantage.

The criteria for a successful agreement on services are that

it must reflect the realities of services trade, not preconceived ideas based on an earlier era of trade policy;

- it must be of mutual benefit to a very broad range of countries;

- it must have the broadest possible coverage in terms of sectors;

- its rules must be clear and unambiguous;

- it must lead to early results.

A number of "core concepts" underlie the basic structure of an agreement on services. The central motivation is to promote the growth of all trading partners and the development of developing countries through trade expansion. Trade expansion is not being pursued for its own sake: thus trade expansion under non-competitive market conditions or hindering development would not be desirable.

In order to allow market forces to stimulate the expansion of trade in services, a high degree of *transparency* will be needed as well as the *progressive liberalization* of market access.

Principles of behavior by producers will be needed to prevent the abuse of dominant positions or collusion between suppliers. There will also be a need for countries to be able to obtain redress if their interests are injured by non-competitive practices.

The agreement should *respect the policy objectives* behind national regulations, implying the development of a concept of *appropriate regulation* and the establishment of a permanent Regulations Committee.

Trade expansion should be compatible with development. Priority might, for example, be given to the liberalization of service sectors in which developing countries have an actual or potential comparative advantage. With respect to developing-country imports, the idea would be to encourage those that aid development rather than those that hinder it. Trade through establishment under national regulatory control offers opportunities in this direction.

Developing countries could be given access to international networks such as those for telecommunications, accountancy etc.

The Regulations Committee would accumulate a list of regulations regarded as inappropriate as well as case law on the types of regulation that should be regarded as appropriate or inappropriate. In this regard the principles of *non-discrimination* and *national treatment* would play an essential role. In some areas, however, such as telecommunications and cultural services, regulations discriminating against foreign producers have been adopted for valid reasons other than protection and here it should be agreed that such regulations are appropriate.

The definition of trade in services will have to be negotiated in a way that balances divergent national interests resulting from differences in the relative abundance of various types of production factor.

It may be noted that several industrial as well as developing countries question the use of the words "appropriate" and "inappropriate" in relation to government regulations as well as the proposal that a Regulations Committee should accumulate a list of "inappropriate" regulations. It is pointed out that the legitimacy of government regulations is not open to question, especially in view of the explicit instruction in the Ministerial Declaration that the multilateral framework "shall respect" the policy objectives of national laws and regulations applying to services. As noted earlier, the issue could be regarded rather as whether certain regulations might be amended in such a way as to avoid interfering with trade expansion without exerting any adverse impact on development, which the Ministerial Declaration emphasizes as being an objective of the multilateral framework for services.

Objectives of Switzerland

Switzerland interprets the Punta del Este Declaration as follows:

- The multilateral framework must not seek to impose general liberalization or oblige countries to adopt a uniform behaviour. The objective should be rather to offer countries the possibility of progressively liberalizing their trade in services by establishing the multilateral consequences of the agreements they will have negotiated for this purpose.

- The regimes for trade and services should be consistent, at least in substance, notably as regards freedom of trade and equal treatment of contracting parties.

- There will be a need for innovation both as regards the opening of markets for services, which should concern factors of production and/or the provision of services; and as regards equal treatment of the parties.

Switzerland proposes an optional most-favoured nation clause (OMFN) whereby any third country could adhere to an agreement concluded between two or more other countries by making an offer formally identical to that furnished by the original parties to the agreement. It is admitted that OMFN cannot be combined with the general GATT principle of non-discrimination. On the other hand it would be wise, according to Switzerland, to provide explicitly that no country should be deliberately injured by agreements in which it does not participate. Nor should such agreements discriminate between countries not participating in them.

Canada and the United States: the Free Trade Agreement

The recent negotiations between Canada and the United States on a Free Trade Agreement illustrate the types of inter-country differences that are apt to arise in dealing with the service sector. One controversy between the two countries that was the subject of prolonged discussion in the Canadian Standing Senate Committee on Foreign Affairs concerned the compulsory licensing of pharmaceuticals by Canada. During the Free Trade negotiations the United States pressed Canada hard to eliminate such compulsory licensing. The Canadian reply was that this demand was non-negotiable. Independently of the bilateral negotiations, the Canadian government has proposed legislation that would provide a new and more liberal regime for the system of compulsory licensing, but abolition of the system itself was stated to be "absolutely out of the question." This particular disagreement generated severe tension between the two delegations (Senate of Canada, 1987 (a) 8:48).

In regard to the film and video distribution legislation contemplated by Canada, President Reagan intervened personally with the Canadian Prime Minister to stress U.S. concerns, but the Canadian government stood firm on its intention to separate the Canadian and American markets in this field.

In other areas, on the other hand, Canada and the United States were in broad agreement in raising the level of intellectual property rights, each country undertaking to adhere to some intellectual property conventions to which the other was already a party (Ibid. 8:60). As pointed out by one of the Canadian negotiators it could be argued that in doing this the two parties, so far from promoting greater market flexibility, were seeking actually to restrict market flexibility by extending the monopoly rights of patent-holders and copyright-holders.

On performance requirements for foreign corporations, the Canadian position is in some ways closer to that of the developing countries than to that of the United States. It is true that in the Free Trade Agreement, under the heading of Investment, there is a provision that there be "no new performance requirements." But, as explained by the Canadian negotiator, this provision relates only to performance requirements exacted as a condition for the approval of acquisitions. Performance requirements are imposed by Canada in a great many other circumstances, and remain unaffected by the Free Trade Agreement (Ibid. 8:62).

The Free Trade Agreement provides a useful indication of the positions of the two countries with regard to temporary access of personnel, a position that is probably typical of the industrial countries as a whole.

One of the issues that was raised by Canada during the negotiations on this subject was the difficulty in servicing the U.S. market either directly with professional services or with equipment involving after-sales servicing because of the administrative typing that has recently occurred in the U.S. immigration system.

To solve this problem, Canadians will be given a special category under the U.S. regime to permit substantially free access to the U.S. market for business purposes for recognized professions and for sales and after-sales personnel. These provisions apply on both sides - they do not greatly affect present Canadian procedures but they will require significant changes in the United States regime. It is therefore possible that the United States might be prepared to negotiate a similar regime with other countries, though it cannot be taken for granted that the United States would always be willing to make the same concessions to other countries that it extends to its immediate neighbors.

More important, however, is the fact that the provisions for free access do not apply even as between Canada and the United States to blue-collar workers. The reason for this, as explained to the Canadian Senate by the Canadian Deputy Chief Negotiator, Ambassador Gordon Ritchie, is that "organized labour on both sides of the border would have neither truck nor trade with the free movement of other people" (Ibid. pp.8:27 and 28).

In the case of maritime transport, as a result of strong pressure from U.S. shipping interests, the U.S. proposal was that this sector should, in effect, be excluded not only from the provisions of the services chapter of the Free Trade Agreement but from those of the investment chapter as well. Canada, under pressure from its own shipping sector, replied that it could not accept an agreement on the transport sector that would exclude maritime transport. The result was that transport services - maritime, air and land - were excluded completely from all provisions of the agreement (Senate of Canada, 1987 (b) pp.11:6-8).

National Objectives of Developing Countries

As in the case of the developed countries, a variety of views, interests and objectives is to be found among developing countries.

The G-10 is a group of ten developing countries (Argentina, Brazil, Cuba, Egypt, India, Nicaragua, Nigeria, Peru, Tanzania and Yugoslavia) which in June 1986 tabled a draft declaration proposing a new Round of multilateral trade negotiations in certain goods sectors. Most of them are strongly opposed to any expansion of GATT responsibilities to cover trade in services. Although they accepted the agreement to negotiate on services contained in the Punta del Este declaration, they attach great importance to the fact that the declaration separated the negotiations on services from those on goods, thus leaving open the question of the future institutional auspices of any agreement on services. Their concerns include questions of national sovereignty, the possible demands of reciprocity, the infant-industry case for protection of service sectors and the role of transnational corporations in services.

On these latter points, their views coincide with those of most other developing countries. Of key importance, as they see it, is the fact that exports of services by the industrial countries are, on the whole, only a small percentage of the sales of services abroad by foreign affiliates of transnational corporations (TNCs) headquartered within those countries. It has been estimated that U.S. exports of private non-factor services in 1982 amounted to about $33 billion, compared to approximately $178 billion of sales by foreign affiliates of U.S. TNCs. Similarly U.S. imports of services in 1982 amounted to about $33 billion, compared to approximately $125 billion of sales by foreign affiliates of non-U.S. TNCs in the United States. (Sauvant, 1986). Estimates for Canada, Japan and the United Kingdom suggest that the volume of sales of foreign affiliates of TNCs headquartered in these countries is about twice as high as the volume of their service exports: in the Federal Republic of Germany the sales of service affiliates exceeded exports from the home country, though by a small margin. Thus for several of the industrial countries, and particularly for the United States, conventional trade in services is far less important than the overseas sales of services by affiliates of home-based TNCs.

Thus any process of bargaining about the service sectors, whether in GATT or anywhere else, cannot fail to arise a whole host of issues connected with the overseas operations of TNCs. These are questions that have occupied various agencies of the United Nations for many years, and relatively few of these issues can be said to have been settled. If the same issues are taken up in GATT, the same disputes will arise, and the same ground and bargaining process will have to be retracted.

It is, of course, true that certain kinds of leverage may be available in GATT that were not available in the UN agencies dealing with these matters. But the leverage, as developing countries see it, operates to the advantage of the industrial countries, not to that of the developing countries. Developing countries believe that many of the restrictions imposed by the industrial countries on their imports from developing countries violate GATT rules and they consider it unreasonable that they should be required to make concessions on services in order, as they see it, to obtain better treatment for their exports of goods.

It may be noted here that such a transaction may well represent a negative sum game. On the one hand, since developing countries are currently operating under extreme foreign exchange constraints, which are likely to continue for an indefinite period into the future, any additional expenditure on imports of services would have to be at the expense of imports of goods just as the servicing of debt is at the expense of such imports at the present time. Consequently, the service sectors in the industrial countries that make gains as a result of the liberalization of trade in services by developing countries will do so at the expense of the industries exporting manufactures. From the standpoint of a substantial number of developing countries, on the other hand, any sacrifice of protection by their own service industries may well be damaging to the overall development of the countries concerned.

This raises the question of the role of services in the development of developing countries and the extent to which these countries should invoke the right of infant-industry protection. Joan Spero (1985) of the American

Express Company has argued that it would be in the interest of the developing countries themselves to open their markets to the high-tech service industries of the industrial countries since otherwise, in her view, these countries will fall further and further behind in the rapid advance of technology taking place in these industries.

The instances of technological advances in banking cited by Spero may be impressive in and of themselves but one could hardly say that without them the development programmes of low-income countries would be jeopardized. It is by no means obvious that the electronic sophistication of global trading in commodities, currencies, stocks and futures has added significantly even to the gross output of the countries where this trading takes place, let alone to world output and income. A case could, in fact, be made that the new technologies have been a major factor in promoting instability in financial markets, thereby adding considerably to the risks of investment in the production of goods, and possibly also of certain services.

There are, however, other areas in which the new technologies of telecommunications, informatics and telematics may make important contributions to the economies of developing countries. Here the pros and cons of liberalization and infant-industry protection require more careful evaluation and there may well be considerable variation in appropriate strategies from country to country depending on such factors as stages of development and size of market.

It cannot be taken for granted that because the industrial countries have a long head start in these technologies, they also have a long-run comparative advantage in them. It is true that in many cases a technological lead may well be self-perpetuating in a free market, especially if the technological leaders are protected by patent rights and/or restrictive business practices. But it is precisely in such circumstances that the case for infant-industry protection may be particularly strong. There are also important considerations regarding the distribution of benefits. As Rachel McCulloch has pointed out:

> Moreover, while scale economies increase the potential benefits from liberalization, they also complicate the issue of how these benefits are shared. In particular, the possibility that a given nation may lose by expanding trade even though global efficiency is improved is more difficult to rule out when scale economies are important.

> Mutual gains are assured only if each country is able, on average, to expand production in industries with scale economies.

> Information-based and knowledge-based services are the areas in which U.S. firms and U.S. policymakers seem most confident of

expanding global sales. These services are likely to exhibit strong economies of scale. The theoretical analysis of comparative advantage and gains from trade suggests both that the apparent U.S. advantage in these industries (as measured by domestic prices) may be overstated under current conditions and that the cautious approach of other nations toward the liberalization of trade in services may have a firm economic basis (McCulloch, 1987).

Deepak Nayyar (1987, 15) has pointed out that while some services, such as telecommunications and informatics, are infants in terms of their age, others, such as banking, shipping and insurance, though not infants in terms of age, are infants in terms of technological level. "It is plausible to argue," he says, "that developing countries possess a potential comparative advantage in many of these sectors, which cannot be realized if there is an immediate liberalization of trade in services that does not allow them to time to learn and become competitive in world markets" (Ibid.).

It is true that many cases can be cited and documented in which developing countries jeopardized their own development through excessive protection that was unduly prolonged. But errors in the implementation of an infant-industry strategy do not destroy the case for such a strategy prudently applied. Strategies of this kind were employed by all of the currently industrialized countries at certain stages of their development as well as by most of the more successful newly industrializing countries of recent years. The proposition cited earlier from the representative of the European Commission that a liberal trading system would necessarily benefit *all* participants simply flies in the face of the evidence, which clearly shows that in the absence of protection infant industries are frequently destroyed by foreign competition. The collapse of industry in southern Italy following the unification of the country is a well-known example.

There are, however, other considerations. In the case of insurance, for developing countries it is a simple question of retaining domestic savings for use at home, although there are certain areas of reinsurance in which costs and risks may be sufficiently high to justify recourse to transnational corporations (TNCs) in one or more of the industrial centres. In banking, the integrity of national macro-economic management is involved but in addition countries are bound to be concerned as to how far domestic savings may be drawn off or may be diverted away from domestic priorities. This is a case where the desire of TNCs for "national treatment" within the host country encounters particular difficulty. If TNCs had access to local banking resources not less favourable than that available to domestic companies, there might well be a serious diversion of domestic resources to the TNCs, if only because of the greater confidence of banks in the credit-worthiness of the foreign companies. Moreover, countries under severe balance-of-payments pressure would have considerable grounds for concern that the TNCs might have an incentive to borrow in the local market while transferring the profits earned abroad. Similar considerations apply to transnational banks: national treatment would imply giving them the same degree of access to local savings that domestic banks have, which could distort the pattern of intermediation and interfere with domestic development priorities.

While the benefits of free trade in high-technology services are being recommended to the developing countries for the Uruguay Round, it has proved impossible thus far to reach agreement on the prohibition of restrictive licensing practices in the proposed code of conduct on transfer of technology that is being negotiated in UNCTAD. The developed countries have insisted on a commercial "rule of reason" to justify many licensing restrictions. The developing countries, on the other hand, reject this approach and wish to leave it to national authorities to make exception. Alternatively, these countries seek a standard for judgment under which the development interests of the recipient country would weigh far more heavily than the commercial interests of the licensing enterprises.

In addition, the developing countries have for many years insisted on an absolute ban on export restrictions while the developed market economies have urged that export restrictions are justified in a variety of situations, such as where they are designed to protect the exclusivity of rights being granted or utilized in other countries (Davidow, 1985).

The above illustrates rather neatly the point made by Harald Malmgren to the effect that information has value only if it is not freely available, and that the more restricted the access to information, the more valuable it is likely to be. (Malmgren, 1985.) It is hardly surprising that the developing countries are reluctant to forego the creation of their own capabilities in high-technology service industries if they cannot rely on gaining access to such technology through the free market.

Even the industrial countries have had difficulties over this kind of issue, as evidenced by the concern expressed by Lord Kearton, former chairman of the British National Oil Company, that foreign companies operating in the North Sea were not transferring their technology to the United Kingdom, so that in the event that they gave up their holdings, the United Kingdom would have the difficulty in taking over from them. Recently concluded legal proceedings by the European Community over an extended period of years intended to compel disclosure by IBM of certain technologies embodied in its products. Although the ultimate agreement between the parties required certain steps by IBM along the lines desired by the Community, expert opinion was generally to the effect that IBM had succeeded in avoiding a commitment to disclosures of major significance. If this was the result in a case where a powerful group of developed countries found it impossible, despite years of litigation, to secure their objectives, the difficulties that face developing countries in similar circumstances will be apparent. In India, where the market is, of course, of much less interest to a computer manufacturer than the European Community is, IBM discontinued its activities rather than comply with a new Indian law requiring majority domestic ownership of TNC affiliates unless the latter were engaged in substantial transfer of technology. In the view of the Indian government, IBM was not transferring technology to the extent that would have been needed to qualify as an exception to the rule.

Thus in many countries, developed as well as developing, there is concern about the potential costs and benefits of a liberalization of international services, particularly since much depends on the policies pursued by the respective TNCs and the extent to which such TNCs would seek to exploit the advantages flowing from liberalization. Many countries see the need for some kind of regulatory framework and, since there is for the time being little chance of the establishment of such a framework at the international level, they feel that it is all the more necessary to maintain their national rules and restrictions. That does not mean that negotiations could not take place on an easing of restrictions on both sides, but the types of negotiation that would have to take place on transfer of technology, transborder data flows and other complex matters would not necessarily lead to the best results if conducted in the environment of GATT preoccupations rather than in the institutions that have been seized of these questions for many years. It should not be beyond the bounds of human ingenuity to devise an arrangement whereby the GATT negotiations could rely, to the extent necessary, on other institutions in dealing with some of the questions arising under Part II of the Punta del Este Ministerial Declaration.

Difficult questions also arise with regard to services of which developing countries could expect to be substantial exporters in a truly free-trade world. Deepak Nayyar (1987, 8) points out that proposals by industrial countries for liberalization of services are confined, by and large, to capital-related services, the production of which is finance-capital intensive, human-capital intensive or technology-intensive. These are sectors in which the industrial countries clearly have the lead (though not necessarily a comparative advantage in dynamic terms). If, however, there is to be a right of establishment, considerations of symmetry and equity require, in Nayyar's view, that such a right should be available also for labor services. Industrial countries have argued that this would impinge on immigration policies, and reference was made earlier to the statement of a Canadian official that organized labor both in his country and in the United States "would have neither truck nor trade with the free movement of other people." Deepak

Nayyar is undoubtedly speaking for many developing countries when he says that "it is essential to redress this imbalance" by including sectors in which developing countries have a revealed comparative advantage, notably labor services. A temporary movement of labor, he points out, does not mean permanent migration, and there has been considerable experience of the temporary migration of workers from South and East Asia to the Middle East. Such temporary movements of labor would generally be from low-wage to high-wage countries, thereby offsetting to some extent the movement of capital-related services predominantly in the opposite direction. Consequently a working consensus on the coverage of the proposed multilateral framework is needed before any significant progress can be made in the negotiations on services. "The element of symmetry and equity is essential in deciding upon the coverage, for that will determine who gains how much from a liberalization of trade in services" (Op. cit. 8-9).

In view of the controversy between some of the industrial countries and the G-10 countries over the international division of labor in high-technology services, it is of interest to examine the objectives of one of the G-10 countries - namely Brazil - which has set out its views on this matter in detail in a paper circulated to the contracting parties as well as in a study entitled "Transborder Data Flows and Brazil" published by the United Nations Centre on Transnational Corporations (1983).

Brazil pointed out that while developed countries had introduced extensive regulations in all service sectors, both traditional and high-tech, regulations in developing countries cover almost exclusively the traditional service sectors. It would be unacceptable, in the Brazilian view, for the negotiations on services to institutionalize this asymmetrical situation, for example through a standstill on regulations. Governments had the sovereign right to regulate the service sectors in the pursuance of vital national policy objectives. Such actions were by definition legitimate and could not be submitted to international scrutiny. What followed from the Punta del Este declaration was the political willingness of developing countries to consider the incidental positive or negative effects that such regulations might have on the expansion of trade without in any way putting into question the aim, common to the national regulations and the negotiations on services, of furthering the economic growth and development of the developing countries.

The idea that the negotiations should provide for the movement of capital and labour across national frontiers was inconsistent, in the view of Brazil, with a key assumption of the classical theory of free trade that had been invoked for the service sector - namely the assumption of the international immobility of factors of production.

In any case the idea that "establishment" should be a "right" to be ensured in foreign markets to providers of services was in conflict with the right of States - recognized by the United Nations and the OECD - to regulate the entry of foreign investment and the conditions of establishment of foreign enterprise.

Brazil was ready to consider the possibility of applying certain GATT principles, such as unconditional MFN treatment, to trade in services. It would, however, be difficult to accept the notion of cross-linkages between concessions in the areas of goods and services.

As far as the treatment of developing countries was concerned, negotiations on services would start from a totally different standpoint from the negotiations on goods. While the latter negotiations involved derogations from the general trade rules for the benefit of developing countries, the ministerial agreement of negotiations on services required that development should be an integral part of any set of rules that might be devised.

The Brazilian study on transborder data flows (TDF) emphasizes the importance of ensuring that countries desiring to benefit from the technology underlying transborder data flows are given the opportunity to do so since otherwise a new set of imbalances between developed and developing countries could emerge (Op. cit. para. 6). This does not imply any change in Brazil's traditionally liberal policy toward foreign direct investment - which includes various incentives as well as tariff protection for local production (para. 55). Of the 200 largest corporations in Brazil in 1980, 39 were foreign affiliates (Table I-6).

Brazil has adopted and implemented a set of policies on TDF and the underlying fields of telecommunications, informatics and telematics. The objectives of this policy are the following:

- to maximize the amount of information resources - such as computers, software, data bases, technical and managerial skills - located in its territory;

- to acquire and maintain national control over the decisions and technologies relating to Brazilian industries;

- to enable the Brazilian society to have universal access to information;

- and to enhance generally Brazil's internal and external political structure as well as its cultural milieu through the appropriate use of information resources (para. 7).

The study points out that TDF links are not only used to move data internationally but also to shift such information resources as managerial and engineering skills, computer power, technological capacities, data-base management systems, specialized software and intelligence in general. Thus TDF, if left unregulated, tends to concentrate information resources and skills in developed countries while relegating developing countries to the less sophisticated periphery of corporate structures. In the long run, it is argued, this could lead to the intellectual impoverishment of developing countries (para. 39).

The Brazilian government considers, however, that the above trend can be arrested through a national strategy that emphasizes autonomous decision-making by foreign affiliates. Such a strategy is no threat to transnational corporations because it does not necessarily imply a change of affiliate ownership (para. 40).

Brazil's policy is believed to have "generally neutralized a number of those impacts of (TDF) links that would otherwise have been negative" (para. 520). In the field of telecommunications, Brazilian policy has met successfully an increasing demand for better domestic and international telecommunication and postal services. It has also stimulated industrial development and encouraged a viable Brazilian-owned telecommunication industry which has begun to generate its own technology and to manufacture a number of locally developed products (para. 497).

In the informatics sector national control has increased and access to information has improved while local production, technology and skills have been augmented. The Government has proceeded cautiously "with the basic consensus of all interest groups involved" (para. 505). Finally, the infant telematics industry has benefited from market protection under a policy that seeks to create a competitive environment for domestic services, to maintain national control over data services, to encourage data structuring in Brazil and to assure privacy protection of personal data (para. 507).

The Brazilian government's study concludes by expressing recognition of the possibility that its experience "may contain elements of a special case" and may be too recent to permit general conclusions to be drawn that would be applicable elsewhere. The study therefore suggests that it would be useful for other countries to make their own studies in cooperation with the Centre on Transnational Corporations (ll the elements to be addressed.) In other words, as John Richardson had pointed out, trade expansion was not being pursued for its own sake. Ambassador Hill sought to refine the chairman's point by indicating that a contribution to development would have to imply more than mere increments in output. "Unless each developing country benefits by increasing productivity and capital formation and the creation of interlinkages among the different sectors of the economy, its development could be retarded even though output as conventionally measured increased" (p. 6). Dissenting from Richardson, Hill saw merit in the application to services of Part IV of GATT and the concept of "special and differential treatment" for developing countries.

Ambassador Hill also noted that between 1979 and 1982 developed and developing countries alike were ranged on both sides of the question whether GATT was an appropriate forum for negotiations on services: he did not, in his paper, address the question of how far the major groups of countries were still divided on the outstanding issues confronting them. Another consideration was that emphasis on the "new" services, particularly those produced by high technology, if accompanied by insufficient attention to the traditional service products and sectors, would lead a number of developing countries to the conclusion that their interests were being ignored (14).

Hill states further that in a world where rich countries still maintain controls over the movement of some factor services (i.e. capital and technology) and where TNCs engage in transfer pricing and are the dominant providers and users of traded services, it is not surprising that developing countries should wish to proceed with the utmost caution. "It would," he says, "be an unbalanced, inequitable and unworkable multilateral agreement if it covered only *access* issues for providers and did not include *exit* issues for users, especially in those new services sector including telecommunications and others revolutionizing the production process."

National Objectives for Telecommunication and Data Services

Within the broad objectives set out above for services as a whole, particular importance attaches to objectives for telecommunication and data services which form one of the most dynamic of the service sectors. The following discussion will do no more than outline some of the issues arising in this sector, which is the subject of much more detailed examination in the other papers to this volume.

After more than a decade of international discussion, crucial problems of definition remain unsolved for this sector. Experts given the task by the International Telecommunication Union (ITU) of defining telecommunication services found little common agreement on how to distinguish between categories of existing and emerging telecommunication services and there are no agreed multilateral definitions for "value-added network services", "information services" or "enhanced services". As a result the Preparatory Committee for the World Administrative Telegraph and Telephone Conference in 1988 was compelled to make reference only to the very general concept of telecommunication. Indeed, the ITU definition even of telecommunication services as a whole is very broad and imprecise.

It therefore appears that a service-by-service approach may not be feasible in the trade negotiations. And it has been suggested in the OECD that the main issue for trade in telecommunication-network-based services concerns the basic conditions for market access, how the conditions are maintained, and how to implement guarantees to ensure that markets are open and not distorted by unfair practices and/or abuse of a dominant position.

A second point of controversy among governments involves the scope of regulations affecting telecommunication services. Some consider that only basic services should be subject to regulation while others believe that all telecommunication services should be covered by regulations, regardless of who the service providers are. Many OECD countries follow the non-binding recommendations of the ITU's International Telegraph and Telephone Consultative Committee (CCITT). Many of these recommendations are designed to constrain competition, while others constrain the choice of network facilities made by users. Some OECD countries, on the other hand, would like to open up the international provision of value-added network services, thus bypassing certain of the CCITT recommendations.

Much of the inter-country controversy on definitions, scope of regulations, and policies is related to differences of opinion on the role of monopoly in the provision of services. Thus attainment of the objective of competitive trade in network-based services will depend on the development of a consensus as to which services should be provided on a competitive basis and on the terms and conditions of market entry. In his paper for this volume Geza Feketekuty concludes that for the foreseeable future the market structure in global communications is likely to be a patchwork of market segments, some with very considerable competition, some with limited competition and others with no competition. Each country will make its own choices with respect to the level of domestic competition it is willing to allow in each segment of the market and with respect to the extent to which it is prepared to allow foreign firms to participate in markets opened up to domestic competition. In the field of data resources, the principal objectives of leading developed countries as well as of a few of the developing countries that are advanced in this field, are to create an international environment in which the maximum possible exchanges of information among countries can take place. In telecommunications their objective, as indicated by Feketekuty, is to establish ground rules for the interconnection of national telecommunication networks, regardless of the regulatory philosophy of the countries involved.

In June 1987, the Commission of the European Communities published a Green Paper on the Development of the Common Market for Telecommunication Services and Equipment (Commission of the European Communities, 1987). The Green Paper stated that

The strengthening of European telecommunications has become one of the major conditions for *promoting a harmonious development of economic activities and a competitive market throughout the Community* and for achieving the completion of the Community-wide market for goods and services by 1992. (Op. cit. Summary Report page 2)

The Commission stated further that "national frontiers should not be allowed to hamper the development of a consistent communications system within the European Community" (Op. cit. page 1). Moreover, competition should be "substantially expanded": all services should be provided on a competitive basis except basic services explicitly reserved for the Telecommunication Administrations. (Op. cit. Figure 3). The Commission emphasized that "*any service monopoly which is maintained implies constraints* on the activities of those connected to this network or using network facilities. The justification of continued exclusive provision where it still exists must therefore be weighted carefully against the restrictions which this may impose on those connected to the network." (Commission of the European Communities, 1988, 9)

These are strong views and much care and thought have undoubtedly been devoted to their elaboration. At the same time it has to be recognized that there are sharply increasing returns to scale in this sector and that, as Feketekuty points out, certain markets will only support a limited number of competitive firms. Even in a market as large as that of the United States, views differ as to whether, as it has turned out, the break-up of AT&T was in the public interest. The question has even arisen whether the entire world market is large enough at the present time to support more than one INTELSAT operating at maximum efficiency.

In the course of her Per Jacobsson Lecture on 27 September 1987, Sylvia Ostry, Canadian Ambassador for Multilateral Trade Negotiations, had the following comments on the significance for developing countries of the "information revolution":

The trend to increasing international integration which is inherent in the information revolution is likely, at least for a time, to enhance the role of the multinational enterprise as a carrier of leading-edge technology. Access to this new generic technology and the flows of capital by which it will in considerable part be transferred will become a prime determinant of growth and development around the world. For this reason an "infant industry" approach to strategic service industries will prove increasingly costly and inappropriate. This *point is especially important for developing countries since the new technology is labour-energy-and materials-saving. Developing countries, which in previous Rounds have not played a major role, have suffered to some extent as a consequence. Hence it is vital that they participate actively in the present negotiation. Otherwise they are likely to suffer again.*

The difficulties facing developing countries along these lines were confirmed in a statement by the Indian Finance and Commerce Minister N.D. Tiwari on 7 November 1987:

Technological developments have made it possible to expand the service sector much before the industrial phase is fully developed. In fact rapid technological advancement faces national planners in developing countries with a difficult range of choices in regard to the pace of absorption of these technological services. The application of new technologically advanced services like informatics could reduce labour costs per unit of output and thus undermine the competitive position of developing countries in the production of labour intensive goods and services. Data have been collected to show that this effect is already evident in the production of textiles and clothing. Given that this competitive advantage is likely to be further reduced as a result of the adoption of new technologies in the developed countries, we have to examine our trade policy and development strategy. For doing so it is necessary to understand and appreciate the role envisaged for the service sector in national development. (Indian Institute of Foreign Trade, 1987)

Developing countries do not, however, accept the proposition that because they are losing some of their advantage in textiles and clothing, it would be advisable for them to abandon the infant-industry approach to strategic service industries. If anything, as they see it, the loss of competitiveness in labour-intensive industries makes it more urgent, not less, to speed the development of industries that can supply alternatives to traditional manufactured exports. Indian exports of information technology/computer services were expected to exceed $200 million by 1990, the terminal year of the Seventh Plan, and exports of software, having reached a level of $38 million in 1986, were expected to grow at an average rate of 80 percent per annum between 1987 and 1989. (Indian Institute of Foreign Trade, 1987) It is possible that India as well as certain other developing countries are competitive in computer software without any government stimulus or support, but even if they are not, there would probably be a *prima facie* case for infant-industry support, especially having regard to the expected growth of world market demand for software to $125 billion by 1990.

Whether they would also benefit from protecting the production of certain types of hardware is another matter, and here the danger of technological lags in a segregated market has to be carefully evaluated. But it cannot be taken for granted that the outcome of such an evaluation would be negative, especially since several developing countries have already acquired capabilities in the exports of microcomputers. If the possession of a technological lead in an industry had been a decisive argument against the development of that industry elsewhere under protection, Britain would still be the principal supplier of textiles to the world market, as it was in the immediate aftermath of the Industrial Revolution.

Developing countries are also greatly concerned about the rapidly increasing outflow of data that is taking place which may give the recipients of the data in other countries, including the headquarters of transnational corporations, a major advantage even as compared with domestic enterprise within the countries from which the data originate. These countries are seeking to regulate or control such outflows, or, to the extent that such outflows take place, to obtain access to the processed information based upon them as well as to the raw data.

Conclusion

The foregoing review of the various national objectives suggests some of the major issues on which discussions and negotiations will need to concentrate. These have been identified by the GNS as follows (GATT, 1987):

1. Definitional and statistical issues.
Considerable work will be required to achieve a commonly accepted set of definitions, together with quantitative data for measurement, comparison and the assessment of various alternative outcomes of the negotiations. In addition, it will be necessary to reconcile the views of those who consider that trade in services should be treated as relating strictly to transfers across national frontiers with the views of others to the effect that a large number of international service transactions take place without the service itself actually crossing the frontier (e.g. tourism) and with the means of producing the service moving (permanently or temporarily) to the country of purchase.

2. Broad concepts on which principles and rules for trade in services, including possible disciplines for individual sectors, might be based.
Ambassador Hill has identified some of the broad concepts as follows (Hill, 1987):

• specialization based on comparative advantage;

- efficiency of the allocation of national and global resources;

- equity;

- competition and restraint of monopolistic or oligopolistic practices which may inhibit the functioning of markets; and

- economies of scale.

Among broad non-economic concepts are the following:

- standards (health, safety, moral and cultural values, etc);

- national security;

- employment creation; and

- distributional objectives.

Among the principles proposed are the following:

- most-favoured-nation treatment (implying non-discrimination among participants and non-discrimination as between services produced and traded domestically and those traded internationally);

- right of establishment; right of commercial presence;

- national treatment;

- reciprocity (and "relative" reciprocity in the case of less developed service sectors or less developed participants); and

- transparency.

3. Coverage of the multilateral framework for trade in services.

In the nature of the case, countries differ as to the service sectors that they wish to liberalize and those that they wish to protect. The question has been raised as to how far the concepts which have been presented (non-discrimination, national treatment and transparency) would apply not only to services involving essentially the movement of capital but also what may be described as labor-intensive activities and labor itself. This could of course touch on the broader question of the possibility of devising a framework and disciplines both globally and for individual sectors which would provide an adequate trade-off between the interests of different countries.

4. Existing international disciplines and arrangements.

It will be necessary to assess the extent to which existing disciplines and arrangements conform to the growth and development objectives of the negotiations and whether they cover both traditional and "new" services adequately. There are, for example, inter-governmental sectoral arrangements to maintain and develop the technical, legal and economic environment for international civil aviation (International Civil Aviation Organisation) and telecommunications (International Telecommunication Union). Account should also be taken of the negotiations of a United Nations Code of Conduct on Transnational Corporations.

5. Measures and practices contributing to or limiting the expansion of trade in services, including specifically any barriers perceived by individual participants to which the conditions of transparency and progressive liberalization might be applicable.

As suggested in John Richardson's paper, certain types of regulation that may constitute barriers to trade in services are not necessarily protectionist in intent. A line will therefore have to be drawn between appropriate and inappropriate regulations.

PARTICIPATION OF DEVELOPING COUNTRIES IN A TELECOMMUNICATION AND DATA SERVICES AGREEMENT

SOME ELEMENTS FOR CONSIDERATION

Bruno Lanvin

Introduction

Development, Trade, Services and Information: An Intricate and Evolving Relationship

Since the end of the Second World War, the once widely held belief that international trade would be mutually beneficial for all those involved has progressively eroded. For many developing countries, integration in world trade seemed to have brought more disappointments than it had fulfilled promises. The failure of the international community in its attempt to agree on the Havana Charter, and the resilience of colonial-type economic relationships between developed and developing countries contributed to the emergence of sometimes conflicting ideologies (as embodied in Prebishian thinking). The continuous erosion of the terms of trade of commodity exporters led to open North-South economic conflicts in the seventies. The failure of GATT to halt protectionist tendencies (especially in the area of non-tariff measures) strengthened even further the already strong doubts developing countries had about the 'fairness' of the international trading system.

The United States proposal to include services in a New Round of Multilateral Trade Negotiations (November 1982) came at a time when a substantial literature was emphasizing the merits of a 'de-linking' of developing economies from international trade. Although simplistic at times, such literature used the example of India and of other developing countries to argue that the few developing countries that had maintained acceptable growth rates in the seventies and eighties were precisely those that had relied less than others on international trade.

If one adds to this already less-than-fertile background the fact that services were seen by developing countries as an area where most of them were running a structural deficit (especially in information-intensive services), one can hardly be surprised by the rather lukewarm greeting given so far by developing countries to proposals to liberalize international trade in services. One could even predict that developing countries should be even less responsive to a proposal to negotiate the more advanced services, i.e., data and telecommunication services. The vision suggested in the present paper is that *this need not be the case* and that, once the objectives and concerns of developing countries have been properly understood and acknowledged by all the parties involved, the basis for a mutually beneficial international agreement on international trade in services, and in particular on information services, could be identified.

Specificity of the Uruguay Round of Multilateral Trade Negotiations

The so-called 'New Round' of Multilateral Trade Negotiations (Uruguay Round) is definitely different from previous Rounds. The scope of discussions is different, and the relative weights of the actors are different. Wandering into new grounds, the discussions that have been taking place under GATT auspices after the Punta del Este Meeting of 1986 look more and more like a dual exercise, where 'pure' trade discussions are but a part of a much more ambitious endeavor.

Soon after the Uruguay Round was officially launched, some analysts expressed their fears that the ambiguities of the Punta del Este Declaration would be difficult to manage when real negotiations start. One such ambiguity relates to data services, which have not yet been identified as an "animal of a different kind". The point was also made that, unless these ambiguities were soon clarified, negotiators might find themselves involved in rather artificial sectoral and sub-sectoral discussions.

From the point of view of developing countries, this state of affairs constitutes an additional reason not to rush to the negotiating table. Some of them have even expressed suspicions that the United States' proposal to liberalize trade in services was neither about trade nor about services, but rather about international investment and information flows. At this intermediate stage, and only a few weeks before the Montreal "mid-term review", two important conclusions can already be drawn from the experience of the last two years:

- As far as services are concerned, the working out of the 'framework' necessary to a successful Uruguay Round will require a clear understanding of the specifics and of the role of information services.[1]

- In this context, however, the participation of developing countries (which all involved in the negotiations have come to recognize as key to their success) hinges on the *ex ante* clarification of a number of issues, including balance-of-payment concerns, preferential treatment, restrictive business practices and technical assistance.

The Relevance Of Safeguards, and Their Applicability In a Data Services Agreement

After years of negotiations, the Ministers in Punta del Este agreed upon the following carefully balanced text:

> Negotiations in this area shall aim to establish a multilateral framework of principles and rules for trade in services, including elaboration of possible disciplines for individual sectors, with a view to expansion of such trade under conditions of transparency and progressive liberalization and as a means of promoting economic growth of all trading partners and the development of developing countries. Such framework shall respect the policy objectives of national laws and regulations applying to services and shall take into account the work of relevant international organizations. (Appendix A to the present volume)

Thus, a clear hierarchy is established between the final goal of the negotiations (i.e., world economic growth and the development of developing countries), the means to achieve this goal (i.e., trade expansion), and some of the modalities that such means may benefit from (i.e., progressive liberalization and transparency). The text also stipulates that 'establishing a multilateral framework of principles and rules for trade in services' would be a natural prerequisite to 'the elaboration of possible disciplines for individual sectors'. As a consequence, one may expect that the participation of developing countries in a telecommunication-and-data-services agreement would necessitate the *ex ante* fulfilling of at least two prerequisites, namely that (1) the contents of such a sectoral agreement not prejudge the rules and disciplines to be included in the general framework and that (2) trade liberalization not be given a higher status in such an agreement than in the Ministerial Declaration (i.e., not more than one of the possible modalities of trade expansion, such expansion being only a means of achieving growth and the development of developing countries).

These basic elements being recalled, some realities should also be kept in mind when trying to outline the elements of a telecommunication-and-data-services agreement of interest to developing countries. One of these inescapable realities is the following: if one took the position of advocating the application of the General Agreement on Tariffs and Trade (GATT) to services, one would be implicitly advocating that all the provisions of GATT should apply to services (including balance-of-payments provisions under Articles XII and XVIII, as well as Preferential Treatment under Part IV). At this point in the discussions, however, no country seems to be in favour of a straightforward application of GATT to services; therefore, the question of possible safeguards to be included in an agreement on trade in services becomes worth posing, and all the more so in the context of data services.

Whereas developed countries are not suggesting the full and straightforward application of GATT to trade in services, they have also come to acknowledge the fact that the accession of developing countries to an agreement on services will need more exceptions (and probably more time) than an agreement on goods. At the same time, it is becoming obvious to negotiators and observers that the interests of developing countries may vary substantially from one country to another and, for the same country, from one sector to another. While these elements undoubtedly complicate the landscape of negotiations on services, they also clearly show that there is room for mutually beneficial negotiations in this area.

One of the important issues that remain to be examined and possibly negotiated is the nature and extent of safeguards that developing countries would benefit from in a possible agreement. It is therefore useful to look first into existing safeguards (i.e., elements contained in the GATT) in order to assess their possible applicability to new agreements, especially in the context of data services. Of particular interest are balance-of-payments-related and infant-industry-related arguments (which are examined in Part 1 of the present chapter), as well as the overall issue of preferential treatment (Part 2). These discussions will then lead us to examine two connected issues, namely Restrictive Business Practices (Part 3) and Technical Assistance (Part 4).

PART ONE : THE BALANCE - OF - PAYMENTS DIMENSION

Overall Context: Trade Integration and the Balance-of-Payments Concerns Of Developing Countries

General economic considerations

The elements mentioned earlier about the 'simple arithmetic of de-linking' (i.e., the temptation to consider that developing countries might be better off if less 'integrated' in international trade) found fertile ground in the international climate of the 1980s: faced with enormous debt-service problems, many developing countries have found creditor countries rather unreceptive to their adjustment efforts. At the same time, the attempt made by debtor countries to reduce their balance-of-payments deficits has often taken the form of massive reallocation of domestic resources towards the external sector (e.g., substituting cash crops for food crops). Faced with deteriorating terms of trade and with spreading protectionism (mostly of a non-tariff kind), these countries found little relief in 'integration'.

For many developing countries, the basic principles of the GATT [2] have been applied neither coherently nor consistently to the realities of international trade. The increasing amount of international trade 'managed' outside GATT rules (the Multi-Fiber Agreement for instance) as well as the relative lack of efficiency of 'special and differential treatment' (part of it resting with the inability of many developing countries to take full advantage of Preferences schemes) have increased the overall lack of confidence of developing countries *vis-á-vis* GATT.

As balance-of-payments constraints were growing heavier for developing countries, the temptation was increasing for them to rely on 'parallel measures' (such as voluntary currency depreciation) and 'parallel trade' (such as barter arrangements). The prospect of an extension of GATT disciplines to services could not thus be expected to receive enthusiastic support from developing countries.

Existing GATT provisions

GATT has two provisions relating to safeguards for balance-of-payments reasons, included in Article XII and Article XVIII of the Agreement; both provisions allow Contracting Parties, among other things, to restrict imports for balance-of-payments reasons (Appendix C).

- The balance-of-payments provisions under Article XII, which have been part of the Agreement since its inception, allow contracting parties to temporarily restrict imports in order to offset balance-of-payments deficits which, in the early years of GATT, were considered 'by definition' to be temporary.

- It was after developing countries expressed their discontent with this underlying assumption of Article XII -- that balance-of-payments deficits were necessarily a temporary affair --that Article XVIII of the General Agreement (dealing with Government Assistance to Economic Development) was amended to incorporate some special provisions for developing countries. Such provisions recognize the structural character of the balance-of-payments deficits of developing countries and allow these countries to make autonomous decisions on the imports of different classes of products, i.e., to identify products that are key to their development process (capital goods, for instance). Article XVIII also provides for surveillance and review of the balance-of-payments restrictions through consultations with the other members of GATT within the Balance-of-Payments Committee of GATT.[3]

Balance-of-Payments Effects of Trading Services: the View from Developing Countries

Economic effects of trading services

Seen from the balance-of-payments angle, [4] international trade in services has several original characteristics, which can be read more or less directly from available data. Such characteristics include in particular the following:

- international trade in services is taking place mainly between industrialized countries;[5]

- it is characterized by a large proportion of intra-industry trade; [6] and

- overall, international trade in services has yielded a steady surplus for developed countries, and a steady deficit for developing countries; [7]

As emphasized earlier, balance-of-payments figures and considerations give a highly distorted vision of international service transactions. As the information-intensity of the services considered grows, the proportion of intra-firm exchanges of services is also likely to grow. Moreover, a large proportion of services internationally transacted are not recorded as such by customs administrations (the main source of IMF balance-of-payments data) because they are imbedded in some other item. It is often stressed in some circles that negotiators have yet to agree on a definition of 'trade' in services. [8] Going beyond mere balance-of-payments arithmetic thus appears more necessary than ever. However, from a negotiating point of view, one question of key importance to developing countries *vis-a-vis* ongoing services discussions is whether or not existing GATT provisions should apply to an agreement on services.

Transferability of Articles XII and XVIII into a services context

It has been argued that Articles XII and XVIII of the General Agreement were among the very few elements of the GATT that could be fully transferred to a services-trade agreement. Indeed, it is rather easy to imagine that a developing country might identify 'infant service industries' deserving government assistance (and protection) before they are exposed to international competition: the wording of Sections A, C and D of Article XVIII would then be fully relevant.

However, the peculiarities of many service industries are such that the opposite point of view can also be substantiated. Some analysts have suggested that a balance-of-payments clause might be less appropriate in the case of services than in the case of goods (largely because of the different relationship that exists between international trade and foreign direct investment in many service sectors).[9] It is also unlikely that developed countries will accept any 'permanent' kind of safeguard to be introduced in a Multilateral Trade Agreement, i.e., accept the introduction of a provision intended to compensate for 'structural' balance-of-payments deficits.

Thus, the question of whether or not an international agreement of trade in services should include a balance-of-payments provision to the benefit of developing countries remains open. Since developing countries would consider as necessary that such a provision refer explicitly to the structural nature of their balance-of-payments deficits, it is to be expected that the issue will be difficult to discuss in the context of the General Framework and might be considered more efficiently in subsequent discussions on sectors and schedules.

Balance-of-Payments Objectives of Developing Countries in a Data Services Agreement

Macro-economic considerations: direct and indirect balance-of-payments effects of trading data services

As mentioned above, international service transactions are the source of an important deficit for developing countries. As far as telecommunication and data services are concerned, this deficit has many of the characteristics of a structural deficit. However, one should distinguish between direct balance-of-payment effects (i.e., data services credits minus data services debits, according to the IMF terminology) and indirect effects (taking into account the import-content of exports, as well as the impact of imported data services on the competitiveness of national firms). In such a context, developing countries will have to carefully consider the line they should adopt *vis-a-vis* foreign companies wishing to provide data services locally.

Traditionally, developing countries have been seen as endowed with two production factors, raw materials and labor, whereas the other factors (capital and knowledge in particular) had to be imported from developed countries. The balance-of-payments situation of developing countries generally reflects this perception. Considering that data services do constitute the most advanced part of world output, one is thus tempted to jump to the conclusion that the emergence of a liberal information-intensive world economy will have a negative impact on the balance of payments of developing countries. When examining this issue, it is important to distinguish direct balance-of-payments effects from indirect ones.

- As far as *direct effects* are concerned (i.e., the credits and debits corresponding to provision or use of data services), it is clear that most developing countries do not have the technological base necessary to be net exporters of most data services. It should be noted, however, that the successes of some countries in this respect (India for software and Singapore for financial data services, among others) show that possibilities exist, even for developing countries, to derive positive direct balance-of-payments effects from integrating in the information economy. However, imports and exports of information services remain largely impossible to quantify, since such services are generally imbedded in goods, people or capital. Analysts have good reasons to think that the proportion of information services is rather high in certain items of the balance of payments such as 'Other private services' and 'Property income', but the heterogeneity of such items forbids the making of any final judgement regarding the direct balance-of-payments effects of international information flows. [10]

- International information flows can have many important *indirect effects* on the balance of payments of developing countries. If one takes the point of view of an importer of data services (which happens to be the situation typical of most developing countries), one can consider two main types of indirect balance-of-payments effects of such imports, namely competitiveness effects and capital-balance effects.

Competitiveness effects should be considered both on domestic markets (where national productions may have to compete with attractive information-intensive imports) and on international markets (where exports of developing countries may become more competitive as their import content increases, if this import content is information-intensive). The point made earlier about services in general (presence of an important proportion of intra-industry trade) is even more valid in information services: the example of airline services shows that competition between national companies is being restructured by computerized reservation systems (Bressand 1988).

Capital-balance effects, although indirect, can be quite substantive when a country decides to integrate into the information economy. By creating local information infrastructures, a country will undoubtedly facilitate the establishment and operations of foreign investors. If such a choice is made (i.e., if the country considers that it has the necessary guarantees that foreign investors will not pursue their interest in ways that conflict with the interests and objectives of the host country), one of its indirect effects would be to attract foreign capital to the country.

Foreign Direct Investment and Factor Movements

This latter point immediately raises the issue of the strategies to be adopted by developing countries *vis-a-vis* foreign direct investment (FDI) flows. From a strict balance-of-payments point of view, FDI seems to be preferable to trade since the consuming country receives capital instead of making payments. The situation is not so simple however. First, as far as services are concerned, investment is generally *not* an alternative to trade, since some services have to be traded (like franchising) whereas others demand a local presence of the provider (like retailing).

In the specific case of data services, however, physical transportability is the rule. A distinction therefore may need to be made between foreign TNCs providing data services (for which establishing locally will generally not be necessary) and foreign TNCs using data services (generally imported from their home country) in order to deliver their services locally. The host country, after pondering the consequences of the presence of the TNC on its soil, may very well find itself in a situation where it will be denying certain companies (of the second type) the right to establish, while requesting that others (of the first type) establish locally. It is therefore crucial that any international agreement on international flows of data services recognize this *'right to selectivity'* of host countries *vis-a-vis* foreign investors and providers of data services. [11]

Eventually, another point should be mentioned in the context of the international transactions of information services *vis-a-vis* the balance-of-payments constraints of developing countries: it concerns the evolving relationship between information services on the one hand and the overall tradeability of services on the other. A few years ago, several authors including J. Bhagwati developed the argument that the international delivery of a service generally required either its producer or its consumer to move across a national border. In the formulation given by Sampson and Snape of the same idea (Sampson and Snape, 1985), modes of delivery are being affected by technological advances in the area of information services: as more services become internationally tradeable, the movement of people across borders becomes less necessary to international trade in services (Lanvin, 1987).

From the point of view of developing countries, this also has important consequences since it means that access to and mastery of information networks and technologies will open more doors to would-be exporters of services. From a strict balance-of-payments point of view, this element alone might justify two types of attitudes from developing countries: (1) a more open stand vis-a-vis the import of intermediate information services, considered as 'capital goods' or, more appropriately 'capital services' and/or (2) growing concern about existing and emerging barriers to entry to the networks and markets involved. This consideration gives special importance to the notions of 'special treatment' and 'restrictive business practices', which will be developed below.

Balance-of-Payments Provisions in a Telecommunication-and-Data-Services Agreement

It clearly emerges from the elements mentioned earlier that developing countries have important reasons to consider a number of information-intensive services to be crucial to their development prospects. In that sense, the phrase 'capital services' (on the analogy of 'capital goods') carries a certain weight and suggests that 'infant industry' types of arguments could validly be raised in the context of a data-services agreement. At the same time, the fact that most such services are produced and exported almost exclusively by a handful of advanced countries suggests that the deficit that developing countries are experiencing in many data-services industries will indeed not shrink rapidly in the absence of a number of safeguards to a free-trade agreement in this sector. Consequently, the question of whether or not a balance-of-payments clause should be a part of such an agreement is worth raising.

From the strict point of view of development, the considerations enumerated in Article XVIII of GATT are fully relevant (and, probably, particularly relevant) in the case of data services, which are both crucial to the development and integration of developing economies and almost exclusively produced outside these countries. However, from the point of view of the industry, the issue is certainly not as straightforward: apart from the investment/trade specificities underlined earlier, information-intensive services have one major specificity which relates to the organizational structures they have been helping to develop and which they now largely feed from, namely *networks*.

A network is essentially a continuum on which information flows. At certain points, this information can be collected, processed or stored. The capacity of a network to create value is tightly linked to its scope, architecture, and above all its ability to function in a continuous and uninterrupted fashion. This being kept in mind, it is obvious that for the operators of such networks balance-of-payments safeguards would be potential sources of disruption, and thus a threat to the totality of the operations of their network.

If Company A has been allowed to install and operate some network facility in Country B, this facility is most likely part of a complex organizational architecture whose profitability cannot easily be segmented between outlets and subsidiaries. If Country B invokes balance-of-payments reasons to stop information flows across its national borders by Company A, the consequent disruption of the networks will have important effects throughout the network, including other countries where Company A may engage in similar or related activities.

The issue of balance-of-payments safeguards is thus far more complex in the case of data services than in many other sectors. The economic and organizational specificities of the industry suggest that a different approach might be taken, which would allow the importing (or host) developing country to plan the payments (credits and debits) resulting from its choice to import foreign data services or to allow foreign investment in the sector. Such an approach would require extensive consultations between the private sector and the governments of developing countries: until now, such consultations have seldom been possible or even looked for.

PART TWO : PREFERENTIAL TREATMENT

Preferential Treatment in International Trade: Lessons from Experience

When the GATT came into being, most international trade transactions were taking place between industrialized countries or between these countries and their respective colonial empires. The specific case of developing countries was therefore not considered in the initial formulation of the General Agreement.

In the early sixties, developing countries emerged as a political force (the 'Group of Seventy Seven', formed at the first United Nations Conference on Trade and Development - Geneva, 1964 - held the majority in the General Assembly of the United Nations). Considering that the existing General Agreement was not adequate to render international trade mutually beneficial when such trade took place between unequal partners (in particular between developing and developed countries), they requested and obtained the inclusion in the GATT of the principle of 'Special and Differential Treatment' (S&D) for developing countries, which relies mainly on the so-called 'Generalized System of Preferences' (GSP). According to this principle, developing countries are not required to reciprocate the advantages they receive from their developed trading partners and are therefore not exposed to retaliation measures if, for instance, they invoke the necessity to protect some infant industry from foreign competition.

Such a system (see Appendix C 'Part IV' of the General Agreement) remains largely unsatisfactory for at least four main reasons:

- It relies on an 'accepted' list of developing countries, thus implying that any developing country might in principle 'graduate' at some point of its economic development to the status of a developed country. Given the absence of an 'objective' set of criteria that would define whether a country is 'developed' or 'developing', this issue is likely to create important political problems and tensions between trading partners.

- It consists of 'exceptional treatment' which is *granted* by the more advanced countries to their less advanced partners and can thus be denied unilaterally at any point in time. This element adds to the uncertainty of the environment of developing countries, while putting them in a position of beggars rather than of contracting parties.

- Few developing countries have proved able to take full advantage of existing preference schemes, suggesting that trade relationships between developing and developed countries are plagued with problems that 'S&D' does not address.

- Eventually, the erosion of GATT disciplines has contributed to a bypassing of the philosophy of Part IV, by allowing (or failing to contain) 'grey area' trade measures such as voluntary export restraints (VERs) and even institutionalizing them (as in the MutliFiber Arrangements, MFA 1,2,3 and 4).

Altogether, the 'S&D' experience of developing countries has been less than exhilarating. To some extent, the prospects of a multilateral trade negotiation on services can be seen as offering brighter perspectives.

Preferential Treatment in a Service Agreement: Beyond Part IV

As far as developing countries are concerned, the New Round of Multilateral Trade Negotiations can be considered as taking place in a more favorable context than previous Rounds: indeed, it is the first time in the history of such Rounds that the concept of development is given central priority in the discussions. This is particularly important in the area of services, where no cross-sectoral multilateral rules or principles currently exist.

Negotiators thus have the opportunity to build a coherent and balanced framework for the progressive and mutually beneficial liberalization of trade in services. The participation of developing countries in such a framework would be fully justified by a consistent and development-focused approach, as opposed to the 'patching up' exercise necessitated by the *ex post* addition of GATT's current Part IV. [12]

The best card in the hands of services negotiators is probably the fact that the Uruguay Round is not constrained by GATT rules, principles or philosophy. Thus, the granting of special and differential treatment (S&D) to developing countries should not mirror the past experience of GATT described earlier. No multilateral service agreement should "institutional-ize" the vision of developing countries "begging" exceptional treatment from their trading partners. On the contrary, a productive and mutually beneficial agreement on services should spell out 'ordinary rights' (and corresponding 'ordinary obligations') for all countries involved. One way of pursuing this objective (and not repeating past errors) would be first to secure consensus on a set of *basic obligations and disciplines* (e.g., 'transparency'), and then to open the possibility to all countries to negotiate bilaterally or within 'homogenous groups' some of the *more onerous obligations*. This 'positive approach' [13] would offer the advantage of flexibility and 'sectoral' adaptability: it is highly unlikely that any country would be ready to accept the same constraints and obligations as 'basic' in all service sectors. As far as information services are concerned, the char-acteristics underlined elsewhere in this paper (i.e., structural deficit of developing countries, dominant position of TNCs, importance of informa-tion as a key input to production and competitiveness) should be reflected in a careful consideration of the hierarchy to be established among such obligations.

The multilateral discussions on services seem to have now reached the point where no country would offer unconditional support to the mere concept of *'deregulation'* in international service transactions. The focus of discussions is now much more on concepts such as *'appropriate regulations'*, or *'negotiable regulations'*, or even on *'harmonization of existing regulations'*, in certain sectors.

As Gibbs and Mashayekhi note, the stakes for developing countries are particularly high in such sectoral negotiations. They write:

> At the level of the negotiation of the principles and concepts which could provide the basis for a multilateral framework on services, solutions could be sought which on the one hand would provide the basis for the negotiation of liberalization measures in the longer run, and on the other hand, recognize the legitimacy of measures applied as part of the essential national policy objectives and development strategies of developing countries. This would provide the developed countries with a negotiating framework within which to pursue

liberalization in specific sectors, whilst at the same time protecting the developing countries from claims that their development strategies in the service sector somehow constituted "unfair" or "unreasonable" trade practices. Thus, negotiations related to more specific issues or in individual sectors could take place in a more constructive atmosphere once the "Sword of Damocles" of possible retaliatory measures had been withdrawn. (Gibbs and Mashayekhi, 1988).

The Specificity of Information Services

The preceding general picture of international transactions in data services suggests that, for a liberal international framework to be acceptable to developing countries, it will be necessary that some of the most striking assymmetries in the current 'information economy' be counterbalanced in some way. However, the current relative economic situation of individual developing countries (which is not the one of the fifties or even the sixties), as well as the specific features of data services, give an authentically new character to this challenge. Negotiators will have to go "beyond Part IV" but they will also have to acknowledge the limitations of 'S&D' (special and differential treatment) in solving the complex problems ahead. The appropriateness of a "Code" (as opposed to a set of binding rules) will have to be examined in this context, as will the appropriate mix between national regulations and international rules.

Within this rather broad framework, the participation of developing countries in an international agreement on information services would be greatly facilitated if several aspects linked to 'preferential treatment' were seriously considered *ex ante*. Such aspects would include in particular (1) developing countries' *right to selectivity*, (2) the relationship between *market access and users' access* and (3) the proper institutional framework for a development-focused agreement on information services.

Right to Selectivity

Like most parties involved in ongoing discussions and negotiations on trade in services, developing countries could not subscribe to an international agreement which would increase the rigidity of their international economic environment. In the specific area of information services, these countries have important reasons to think that the 'spontaneous forces' of a deregulated information-dominated economy would not necessarily be 'naturally supportive' of the interest of developing countries. Therefore, one of the key elements developing countries might need to find in an international agreement on information services is that such an agreement would limit the influence of such forces rather than reinforce it.

At the same time, most developing countries would recognize that information services constitute a vital area for the resumption of growth in the world economy and thus for giving a new momentum to the development process in developing countries. Many would also recognize that market forces can contribute substantially to fostering quality/price ratios in this quickly expanding set of activities. Thus, developing countries would not, in principle, refuse to participate in an international agreement on information services as long as such an agreement complied with the philosophy enshrined in part II of the Punta del Este Declaration (i.e., that liberalization of international trade in services is not an end in itself but that it deserves international support if it contributes to growth and development). In other words, an international agreement on information services would probably gather the support of developing countries if it included guarantees on the recognition and protection of these countries' right to 'select' their commitments and their partners.

With regard to information services, the compromise between 'legitimate domestic regulations' and 'internationally acceptable regulations' would have to be sought with the objective of preserving the right of individual countries to select their commitments and partners in at least two specific contexts, namely

(1) foreign direct investment flows and
(2) transborder data flows.

As far as the first (FDI) is concerned, the on-going trade negotiations could benefit from the consideration of work under way in the United Nations towards the elaboration of a *Code of Conduct of Transnational Corporations*; [14] as regards the second (TDFs), a number of specific technical issues should be examined, [15] and specialized organizations such as the International Telecommunication Union (ITU) and its various foras (CCITT, WATTC) should play a more prominent role in these negotiations. [16]

Market Access and Users' Access

The points made in the general introduction to this paper about the new possibilities of 'fragmenting' the production process stressed the strategic importance of services in modern ways of creating value; at the same time, they underlined the vital importance of information and telecommunication services in more complex and 'de-concentrated' (as opposed to decentralized) production systems. Among the earlier proponents of international discussions on liberalizing trade in services, a number of large private companies have repeatedly underscored the importance for their

profitability and 'normal operating' of a liberal information environment.
[17] More recently, this accent on 'market access' has often been accompanied by an equally-strong emphasis on the 'rights of the users', and 'users access'. [18] It is quite surprising that, in most cases 'users access' is considered as a right that needs to be protected from the national regulations of host countries, as if these countries could not themselves be users of the same services. The point made earlier [19] about the relatively high proportion of intra-industry trade in services is particularly valid in the context of information services. Those developing countries which may be willing to offer a liberal local environment to foreign providers of information services would tend to consider it part of 'normal reciprocity' that their interests as users be protected. Seen from this point of view, the participation of developing countries in an international agreement on services immediately raises the issue of 'reciprocal access to networks' which is discussed below. [20] The balance between market access and users' access offers a productive area for discussions between developed and developing countries, as well as an area where 'preferential treatment' could partially be dealt with.

Institutional Framework

As mentioned earlier, the ongoing negotiations will have a better change to succeed (i.e., to yield a mutually beneficial set of agreements) if the best use is made of existing legal elements and organizations. [21] In the specific context of an international agreement on information services, one might think of GATT as a forum where trade policy is being dealt with and of ITU as a forum competent for telecommunication policies. However, developing countries might be reluctant to participate in an agreement that would be negotiated in a non-universal forum (like GATT) or in a forum where they would find it more difficult to relate technical issues to the broader context of their development policies. A third possibility could be identified of a more neutral institutional framework, in which more organizations than just GATT and ITU would be directly involved.

In any case, developing countries will probably show a great interest in 'watering down' some basic GATT principles with some information- and telecommunication-specific principles, since as Geza Feketekuty puts it,

> The strength of a regulatory approach to international telecom issues (as against a trade-oriented approach) is that it explicitly recognizes the need to protect the public interest, that it can address the impact of alternative policies on the operation of the telecommunications network, and that it can deal with broader social interests related to the provision of a public infrastructure service. (Feketekuty, 1988).

In this regard also, the U.S.-Canada Free Trade Agreement and the EEC 'Green Paper' include some important elements which could be of relevance in the context of preferential treatment to be granted to developing countries in an international agreement on services. [22]

PART THREE - RESTRICTIVE BUSINESS PRACTICES

RBPs: Definitions and Philosophy

The term 'Restrictive Business Practice' (RBP) designates essentially non-governmental measures taken by enterprises in order to strengthen their positions on a given market. Such measures can either be used by individual enterprises or by several enterprises acting in concert, so as to acquire, protect or reinforce what is generally called a 'dominant position of market power.' It is thus interesting to note that, from a legal point of view, the notion of Restrictive Business Practice implies the existence of an *intent* to distort the rules of normal competition. As underlined below, this element may not necessarily be relevant in the specific context of information services.

The practitioners of international trade have long been concerned with RBPs, since such measures constitute potential or actual distortions of international trade. Individually or collectively, many developed countries have taken measures to eliminate RBPs to the largest extent possible; such countries include the United States (Sherman Antitrust Act, 1890), and the European Communities (Treaty of Rome, Articles 85 and 86, 1957). From the point of view of developing countries, RBPs represent an even more threatening type of unilateral measure, since they hamper the 'collective wealth creation' mechanism which, according to the laws of comparative advantage, is supposed to function as a result of international competition and specialization. The international community as a whole was also rather prompt to consider RBPs a matter of concern. As early as 1948, the Havana Charter contained clauses aimed at regulating RBPs in international trade. However, contrary to the first part of the Charter (which gave birth to the GATT), its second part (which included provisions on RBPs) was never adopted. Nonetheless, a certain number of international instruments have later been designed to fulfill the same objectives.

Among such instruments, the *"Set of Multilaterally Agreed Equitable Principles and Rules for the Control of Restrictive Business Practices"* constitutes a crucial element. Adopted by the United Nations General Assembly in its resolution 35/63 of 5 December 1980, the 'set' is a voluntary code. Its institutional machinery is provided by an Intergovernmental Group of Experts on Restrictive Business Practices, established in UNCTAD.

RBPs in Services

Given the strategic role of services, any distortion in the functioning of services markets is likely to have important consequences for many other markets. In particular, restrictive business practices in producer services will trickle down to those producers for whom the services affected by such RBPs are strategic inputs.

There thus exists a need for a broader definition of RBPs, i.e., a definition which would take account of the pervasive effects that an RBP in a crucial service activity is bound to have on many other sectors. Thus, an upstream-onstream-downstream typology of services is fully applicable in the context of RBPs, and should yield a broader definition of what could be considered, in the specific context of services, a restrictive measure or strategy. [23] The following table suggests some such examples of 'trans-sectoral' restrictive business practices, along the lines of such a typology.

Restrictive Business Practices: a possible broader definition

---

'Stricto Sensu'	- Collusive tendering
In Upstream Services	- Restricted access to infrastructures
In On-Stream Services	-Restricted access to CRSs (airlines)
In Downstream Services	- Exclusion from distribution networks

---

It should be noted that any anti-RBP code in the area of services should be considered conditional and cross-referred with the concept of preferential treatment for developing countries examined above. This point was already clearly made in the Set of Mutually Agreed Equitable Principles and Rules for the Control of Restrictive Business Practices, which states that

in order to ensure the quitable application of the Set of Principles and Rules, States, particularly developed countries, should take into account in their control of Restrictive Business Practices, the development, financial and trade needs of developing countries, in particular of the least developed countries, for the purposes especially of developing countries in:

(1) Promoting the establishment or development of domestic industries and the economic development of other sectors of the economy; and

(2) Encouraging their economic development through regional or global arrangements among developing countries.

RBPs in an Information-Intensive World Economy

Given the monopolistic/monopsonic nature of most major data-services markets, developing countries should be expected to devote particular attention to RBPs in this area. Moreover, some analytical characteristics of information as a commodity (linked among other things to capacities of networks) tend to make RBPs an almost intrinsic component of corporate strategy in certain sectors. However, the results obtained as well as work under way constitute reasons for moderate optimism.

Like most technology-and-research-intensive activities, information services are characterized by the dominant market position of a small number of corporations. [24] Available evidence shows that the recent deregulation/globalization trend has helped considerably the oligopolistic nature of equipment markets to replicate itself in the area of service markets. [25]

Possibilities arise that such large groups might be tempted to consolidate their market power through the use of different restrictive practices. These could be 'vertical' (i.e., constraints imposed on their suppliers or consumers: refusal to deal, exclusive dealing, reciprocal exclusivity, resale price maintenance, tied selling, differential pricing, predatory pricing, transfer pricing, or concentration of market power through mergers, takeovers and joint ventures), or 'horizontal' (generally relating to the constitution of cartels, like collusive tendering for instance). [26]

A Conflict of Legitimacies?

As was recalled earlier, the generally accepted definition of RBPs suggests the *intent* to distort the normal play of competitive forces. The peculiarities of information as both a factor of production and a product are such, however, that the 'normal' (i.e., not intended to distort) actions of large users and large producers of information services may in fact have the same results as RBPs *stricto sensu*.). In other words, in information-intensive sectors, certain otherwise 'legitimate' corporate strategies could have the same impact on developing countries as restrictive practices.

The theoretical literature on information economics has long identified information as a 'public good', the provision of which to an additional user can be made at no extra cost, once the necessary network has been established. [27] This has important economic consequences: for instance, a number of information networks are *by nature* in an over-capacity situation. The complex problems of tarification that this raises, especially in terms of cross-subsidization between different kinds of services, call for original thinking when an international negotiation on services is envisaged. At least, it seems that information services deserve some priority (as an input to most other services) and a special treatment (given their economic peculiarity). For any company providing information services and wishing to make a profit out of it, the size of its distribution network is a key element: the intrinsic 'over-capacity' situation of such a network (at least in its initial stage) tends to confer on global strategies the status of 'ordinary business' in this sector. Given the considerable fixed and sunken costs associated with the building and operating of international information networks, the bigger these networks, the better the chance that such costs are quickly offset by profits. In such a context, economic realities are such that:

(1) only a small number of actors can enter the expensive and knowledge-intensive race for critical mass in information markets; and

(2) once some have been able to reach this mass, the 'public good' characteristic of information constitutes an economically unsurmountable barrier to entry for newcomers to such markets.

It is thus difficult to assess whether or not the formation of large information-services groups constitutes a restrictive business practice, since this state of affairs seems to be a direct consequence of the nature of the product involved. Moreover, at this still early stage of the negotiations, some corporate objectives may seem incompatible with some national objectives of developing countries. For instance, the fact that some developing countries tend to consider information a 'natural resource' and information networks a 'common infrastructure' may collide with some other notions that corporations would consider legitimate, such as 'intellectual property', and 'private use of private property'. The 'Industry View' recently reflected by the United States Council for International Business (1988), for instance, states that

> an international agreement for trade in services should include ten principles; these principles should be viewed as a package: (1) fair market access, (2) national treatment, (3) reasonable and transparent regulation, (4) fair treatment by government-sanctioned monopolies, (5) unrestricted movement of information, (6) access to and use of public telecommunication services, (7) conditional most-favored-nation treatment, (8) dispute resolution, (9) exceptions and safeguards, (10) standstill and rollback'. [28]

Through principles (5) and (6), such a business view makes information-services principles a necessary component of any services agreement. At the same time, it requests unrestricted access to local infrastructures without granting a symmetrical access to the information that such infrastructures would carry (as 'unrestricted movement of information' suggests). [29] However, other types of RBPs may be used by certain companies. When such practices are clearly identifiable, [30] they should be fought with all available legal instruments, including the *Set of Multilaterally Agreed Equitable Principles and Rules for the Control of Restrictive Business Practices* mentioned earlier.

PART FOUR - TECHNICAL ASSISTANCE

The Lessons of Experience: Trade-Related Technical Assistance

Given the complexities of multilateral trade negotiations, as well as the specific needs of developing countries in this regard, technical assistance has traditionally been a priority item on the list of requests by these countries. However, the needs of developing countries for technical assistance generally go far beyond mere assistance in the negotiations: very often, developing countries have to evaluate the impact of different trade scenarios on their own domestic economies in the absence of reliable and consistent basic economic data.

Trade-related technical assistance may thus include such diverse aspects as the building of data-collection and data-analysis systems and procedures, rationalization of customs administration, study of the projected import requirement of local industries under different trade-policy and specialization scenarios, evaluation of local trade-related infrastructures (transport system, telecommunications, storage facilities, etc.) and of possible regional arrangements (e.g., in the case of possible cumulation of preferences-related quotas). Most international organizations (especially those dealing directly with trade issues) are continuously solicited by developing countries for such technical assistance. It is to be expected that this demand will be growing as the Uruguay Round negotiations take momentum.

Technical Assistance in the Context of Services Trade

If (as is likely) consensus emerges in the GNS about the fact that participation of the developing countries in a services-trade agreement will require more exceptions and more time, then it immediately follows that technical assistance will constitute a most important element [31] in helping developing countries to accede progressively to 'more onerous' sectoral commitments (i.e., to participate in an agreement that would be more advanced than the General Framework). Such technical assistance will be of many different kinds, going from specific training to sectoral information to training on negotiating techniques.

A number of international organizations have been asked by individual developing countries to provide technical assistance in their efforts to analyze the role and the importance of services in their national economies. Among these institutions, UNCTAD, in pursuance of its mandate, [32] has been providing technical assistance to some twenty-five member countries over the last three years, mainly in the context of 'national studies' and often in collaboration with regional and sub-regional organizations and with financial support from the UNDP and certain donor governments. [33]

The experience accumulated by an organization like UNCTAD in this field shows that the need for a better understanding of the economic and statistical issues underpinning multilateral trade negotiations on services is deeply felt in developing countries. It also shows that the individual experiences of different countries often cast a new light on a number of service-related issues. In the particular case of information services, the technical complexity of the issues, as well as the specific terminology used, have contributed to the defensive attitudes of a number of actors *vis-a-vis* any kind of international arrangement in this area: in such a context, technical assistance can greatly help the negotiating process by clarifying the issues.

Future Needs: Technical Assistance and Information Services

In the short and medium term, technical assistance will continue to be an efficient way of equalizing the knowledge and awareness of governments, negotiators and decision-makers (including those in the private sector) with regard to a number of issues relating to information services. In particular, the role of these services in the development process, both as a crucial input in the production process and as a vital component of the competitiveness of local industries (both at home and abroad) could be analyzed with greater accuracy through specific 'national studies' of the type UNCTAD has been involved in.

Moreover, technical assistance should also be provided (bilaterally or multilaterally) in the form of *assisting developing countries in the negotiations directly*. The scope of such technical assistance should encompass not only negotiations in the GATT proper (i.e., in the GNS) but also more specialized discussions taking place in parallel (for instance under the ITU's auspices).

Eventually, technical-assistance programs should be provided to developing countries in their *dealings with transnational corporations*. In the specific case in which these TNCs happen to be major providers and/or users of information services, such programs would be particularly useful. The efforts already made in the past by different institutions probably offer a sound basis for further assistance to developing countries. [34]

Past negotiations show that significant progress can seldom be achieved until the different parties have acquired what they perceive as a 'common minimal knowledge' of the 'underlying issues' of the negotiation. In the case of services, developing countries have stressed repeatedly the need for adequate definitions and statistics. Technical assistance should be seen as a way of responding to this concern.

Information services are a case in point in this respect, since this is an area in which technology and terminology are moving at a rapid pace, thus making negotiators and decision-makers even more uncomfortable. Some have even been tempted to 'set information services aside' as a negotiation issue, until some progress is made on some more consensual aspects of services trade. The points made in this paper and elsewhere lead to the conclusion that, on the contrary, the intrinsic characteristics of information services [35] should give them the status of a 'priority area' in the present negotiations.

Conclusion

One might expect that the participation of developing countries in any kind of international agreement on information services will hinge on the conditions that they have spelt out since the GATT Ministerial Meeting of 1982 and which have been enshrined in the Punta del Este Declaration. The main one will be, of course, that 'trade liberalization' should not be considered an end in itself but should be seen as a way of contributing to the process of growth and development.

The specificities of information services may lead the international community to identify such services as a 'priority area' in the negotiations. In this particular context, some of the main concerns of developing countries will be that whatever agreement is reached, it:

- maximize the 'interlinkage effects' between 'imported' information services and the local economy;

- guarantee the host or importing country's access to the underlying technologies (especially through the training of local labor in the use of such technologies);

- guarantee the host or importing country's access to the international information networks involved.

The main motivation for an active involvement of developing countries in some kind of information services agreement would be that they have a major interest in the development of efficient and universally accessible information infrastructures, not only at the national level but also (and probably even more so) at the international level. This seems to be an objective suitable enough for a large international consensus.

ENDNOTES

1 Such an understanding will probably raise more fundamental issues such as those concerning the nature of information. Contrary to much of the business community in developed countries (for whom information is mainly a means and an output of their activity and should thus circulate freely across borders), some developing countries would rather consider information as a 'natural resource' and thus see as legitimate certain regulations aiming at guaranteeing their control over any information flow crossing their national borders.

2 Namely (1) Most-Favored-Nation (MFN) treatment, which is both automatic and unconditional, (2) nondiscrimination, which is basically the same concept as MFN, but neither automatic nor unconditional, (3) transparency and surveillance, which gives the GATT Contracting Parties the right to be informec and to criticize individual contracting parties' trade policies, (4) national treatment, which guarantees that trade concessions made at the border are not nullified by internal measures such as tax discrimination or locat content legislation, (5) multilateral reciprocity, (6) safeguards, (7) dispute settlement, or the ability to obtain redress against actions that nullify or impair any party's GATT rights, and (8) Special and Differential (S&D) treatment for developing countries.

3 Article XVIII specifies that 'no contracting party shall be required to withdraw or modify restrictions on the ground that a change in its development policy would render unnecessary the restrictions which it is applying under this Section' (Section B, paragraph 11). This point is currently the subject of quite lively debates between negotiators.

4 The stark indigence of available trade statistics for services hardly needs recalling here. In spite of their obvious inadequacies, IMF balance-of-payments data remain the best source for international comparable figures in this context. Ongoing discussions (including in the Group of Negotiation on Services - GNS - set up at Punta del Este) should help in the formulation of more appropriate definitions and data.

5 In 1986, 81% of total world imports (debits in the IMF balance-of-payments terminology) were going to industrialized countries and 86% of total world exports (credits) were coming from these same countries. Both figures are

even higher if one includes in the credits and debits considered the amounts corresponding to returns on investments abroad.

6 Large exporters of services happen also to be large importers of services, globally -- e.g., large exporters of banking services are also large importers of banking services. This suggests that certain countries have the necessary infrastructure to trade services both ways and that such trade is, in itself, a source of profit. The simple balance-of-payments arithmetic (exports are good, imports are bad) thus needs to be revisited in the case of services.

7 This situation is even clearer in the case of 'Other private services' (which include most advanced information-intensive services).

8 One could however remark that previous (goods) Rounds have not considered the availability of a definition of 'trade in goods' as a prerequisite for negotiating in this area.

9 This aspect will be examined below with regard to the special case of data services.

10 For instance, Japan has been posting deficit on 'Other private services' for the last five years.

11 This important notion of 'right of selectivity' will be developed in detail below (see Part Two). In the specific case of foreign companies wishing to provide services locally, the balance-of-payments objectives of the host country could be adequately pursued through a 'double substitution' policy: locally-extablished foreign companies would be encouraged to use domestically-produced services (substitution of Type1: and English bank established in Ghana for instance would be encouraged to use local advertising rather than 'import' Saatchi-&-Saatchi's services); at the same time, domestic enterprises would be encouraged to use the services provided by the foreign company whenever their own competitiveness (inward and outward) could thus be significantly stimulated (substitution of Type 2: an Indian bank might deal with a locally-established Canadian telecommunication company in order to access international financial markets and thus be able to compete in new markets). This point is developed from a more analytical point of view in B. Lanvin, 'Services Intermediaires et Developpement', *Revue d'Economie Industrielle*, No. 43 (1er Trimestre 1988), Paris.

12 As Gibbs and Mashayekhi put it, 'In constructing a multilateral framework for services it is to be hoped that the negotiators would take into account the experiences of the GATT system and , in particular, strive to avoid repeating the same errors. In the 1940s, development was not the main consideration of the countries most responsible for drawing up the GATT

96

framework for trade in goods. Consequently subsequent attempts had to be made to adjust the system so as to render it more compatible with the goal of global development through special derogations from what had been decided as the "norms" of the system in an earlier and different economic and political context. This "patching up" excersise provided somewhat unsatisfactory results, as is indicated by the current donfused debate on "graduation" and the so-called "integration" of developing countries within the multilateral trading system.' (Murray Gibbs and Mina Mashayekhi, "Services: Cooperation for Development", in Bressand and Nicolaidis, 1988).

13 As opposed to the 'negative approach' consisting in first adopting general principles and then 'carving out' exceptions.

14 The discussions and negotiations relative to the Code are being held by the United Nations Commission on Transnational Corporations .

15 For instance, the emergence of Integrated Data Services Networks (ISDNs) will make it virtually impossible for any user of such networks to exercise its *ex ante* right to selectivity in terms of types of flows (e.g., images as opposed to telephone messages).

16 In this regard, one might consider that the 'Principal Considerations' discussed at the Informal Consultations on WATTC-88 (held at the ITU on April 11-12 1988) do offer a fertile basis for further consideration.

17 This point will be reaclled and examined in more detail in Part Three below (Restrictive Business Practices).

18 This point has recently been developed both from the point of view of the ITU and from that of a national administration. See Richard Butler (1988) Interconnection and Trade: Priorities for WATTC-88 and for the International Community, Keynote Remarks at the ThinkNet Commission, Paris 13-14 June 1988 and Geza Feketekuty, "Telecommunications and Trade: Implications for GATT and ITU", Transnational Data and Communications Report, May 1988.

19 See Part One (Balance-of-Payments considerations).

20 See Part Three (Restrictive Business Practices).

21 This point is mentioned in part II of the Punta del Este Declaration.

22 References are (1) Schott, Jeffrey J. (1988) United States-Canada Free Trade: An Evaluation of the Agreement, Policy Analyses in International Economics 24, Institute for International Economics, Washington, D.C.: and (2) Commission of the European Communities, Green Paper on the Development of the Common Market for Telecommunications Services and Equipment, COM(87)290: Summary Report.

23 Actually, the scope of this broader framework would even extend beyond services: for instance, the Dresser-France case, a company found itself unable to deliver some sophisticated equipment because it had been denied access to the information stored in a database located in a foreign country. This is a case where limited or selective access to an upstream service (data used for the design of equipment) restricts the possibilities of a company to produce and deliver. Similar examples could be quoted for onstream services (maintenance) or downstream services (distribution and marketing).

24 Even innovation-intensive sectors, where small and medium-size enterprises had been competing in highly scattered markets (like personal-computer software), are increasingly being 'restructured' through mergers and acquisitions (including through vertical integration strategies of large firms from other sectors, like computer manufacturing).

25 This may appear as a paradox, since the initial effect of this trend was precisely the dismantling of a number of monopolies in informatics and telecommunications: however, the second step in this evolution was the necessityf for equipment services providers to reach the 'critical mass' (see below) they needed to operate profitably. Logically, then, the ultimate step in this process was the constitution of large global groups, whose competitiveness relied as much on equipments as services. For a well-documented description of this evolution, see Telecoms: le reveil des geants, Science et Vie Economie No 38, April 1988, Paris.

26 For a detailed discussion on collusive tendering and the ways to detect it, see Collusive tendering, Document TD/B/RBP/12/Rev. 2, UNCTAD, 1986.

27 The classical example is the one of a television or radio company, which broadcasts its programs within a certain geographical area: inside this particular area, the number of 'customers' of programs will not depend on the provider (if the quality of the programs is supposed to remain unchanged) but on the number of radio or TV receivers being used at a certain time in the area.

28 Similar principles had been spelt out before by the private sector. An interesting example can be found in two papers by E.J. Regan, namely, 'Telecommunications Policy Liberalization and User Needs' (presented at Interface 88', Chicago, March 1988), and 'Telecommunications Policy Liberalization and Electronic Banking Services' (presented at 'Deregulation in the 1990s', Paris, March 1988.

29 Actually, the point is made perfectly clear on page 3 of the USCIB document: 'Many firms are information based and thus rely upon unrestricted flow of information. Enterprises need to be assured of a free movement of information, consistent with the protection of individuals

privacy, intellectual property, public safety, and national security. National actions that directly impede unnecessarily the movement of information or create a need for the local duplication and storage of information are a serious disincentive to commerce. Countries should commit themselves to eliminating existing restrictions on the movement of information, to imposing no further restrictions in the future, and to creating an environment which promotes the exchange of information through actions such as the establishment of mutually-agreed international technical standards and the harmonization of intellectual property protection.

30 Such an identification should be understood as a country's conclusion that the practices of a particular company do not agree with the level of transparency and competition that the country considers adequate *vis-a-vis* its own socio-economic objectives. This means that any country may very well decide to 'accept' certain RBPs, either *'de facto'* (e.g., through joint ventures with 'restrictive' companies), or *'de jure'* (e.g., by reserving certain markets - especially through government procurement - to its own infant industries).

31 There has even been mention in some circles of the possibility of a 'Marshall Plan' to assist developing countries in developing their service sector.

32 The mandate given to UNCTAD at the thirtieth session of the Trade and Development Board (March 1985) included four parts: (a) consideration of the definitional aspects of services; (b) strengthing and refining the data base at the national, regional and international levels, together with methodological improvement in this field; (c) further in-depth studies of the role of services in the development process, to enable countries to analyze the role of the service sector in their economies and its contribution to all aspects of the development process; (d) assisting interesed Member States, upon request, and within available resources, in their analysis of the role of services in their economies. This mandate was confirmed in the Final Act of UNCTAD VII (3 August 1987), where UNCTAD's technical assistance mission is mentioned in the following way: "UNCTAD is requested to continue its programs of technical assistance to developing countries in the field of services. UNDP is invited to consider favourably the requests for the provision of adequate resources for this purpose."

33 Moreover, the developing countries requested UNCTAD to work out a program on technical assistance to improve their statistical basis on trade in services and explore the possibility of establishing a program of co-operation on services within UNCTAD as a mechanism for channelling financial and technical assistance to developing countries. The proposals of the Group of '77 relating to UNCTAD VII in the field of services were

reflected among the policies and measures that UNCTAD VII agreed upon on 3 August 1987 (See UNCTAD document TD/L.316/Add.4 and TD/350).

34 For instance by the Advisory Services of UNCTC, or by UNCTAD in the area of RBPs (See Restrictive Business Practices Information. TD/B/RBP/INF.19, UNCTAD, 11 November 1987).

35 In particular, their role as a 'common infrastructure' in the production and delivery of most other services. See B. Lanvin, "International Trade in Services, Information Services and Development", UNCTAD Discussion Paper No. 23, Geneva, May 1987.

GLOBAL TRADE IN SERVICES

A CORPORATE PERSPECTIVE ON TELECOMMUNICATION AND DATA SERVICES

James C. Grant[1]

Introduction

In recent years, there has been much discussion and analysis of the development of a "service" or "information" economy and, more broadly, the "post-industrial" society. While the terms used to describe this phenomenon vary, all analysts agree on the principal cause -- the alliance of communication and computer technologies or "information technologies".

The resulting impacts have been widely identified. They include:

- the collapse of traditional notions of time and space;

- the rise of services as the principle source of new employment in the "industrialized" world;

- a rapid decrease in the value of raw materials relative to information and technology in the selling price of finished products;

- the ever-decreasing cost of communications relative to transportation;

- the ever-increasing value of intellectual property -- patents, trademarks, copyright and industrial design -- relative to real property;

- the evolution of truly multinational production;

- the delinking of the financial economy from the real economy, with capital flows now being the prime determinant of exchange rates;

- the continuing fragmentation of former "mass markets"; and

- the acceleration of technological diffusion around the globe.

Information, once released, cannot be eliminated or contained. Like light, it knows no boundaries. Hence the forces unleashed by these technologies pose a major challenge to traditional concepts of national sovereignty - the power to control activity in a defined physical area. Technology is changing faster than bureaucrats can make decisions. The flow of information is therefore a revolutionary instrument of change and the major challenge to the *status quo*.

While the service sector already dominates the economies of all developed countries, international trade in services currently constitutes only 17% of total international trade. This relatively small percentage does *not* reflect the profound role of financial services in the global economy *or* the ever-increasing value of services in the final selling price of manufactured products. It can be expected to grow as telecommunication facilities allow the cross-border provision of services once thought to be exclusively local.

This growing role of services in international trade was formally recognized when signatories to the General Agreement on Tariffs and Trade -- the GATT -- declared their intention in September 1986 to work towards establishing a "multilateral framework of principles and rules for trade in services." Concurrent with these historic efforts are the approaching international deliberations, under the umbrella of the International Telecommunication Union, regarding the "rules of the road" according to which information technologies will transport their electronic cargo between countries.

Important as these efforts will be, it is also important to view this vital sector in a wider context. World sales of information technologies are approaching $500 (U.S.) billion per year, a major element of global merchandise trade. While trade in services is also growing in importance, the true value of information-intensive services can only be understood in terms of their role as an input into literally all economic activity -- the key facilitator of domestic and international commerce.

This paper will therefore attempt to explain the issues surrounding information services from the perspective of a corporation involved in the trading of services -- the Royal Bank of Canada. While many of the examples of services trade made possible by information technologies will be from the financial community, the key point is not the benefits to the bank or, for that matter, to its suppliers of telecommunication and data products and services. The real beneficiaries are *customers* -- individual, corporate and governmental. These issues therefore affect society as a whole.

The experience of several transnational corporations relying on information technologies will also be used to give insights into their true contribution to economic development. This corporate approach is intended to supplement the conceptual discussion in the papers that follow and to highlight both the economic opportunities and the policy challenges which the new technologies have created.

The Nature of Global Trade in Services

The subject of "trade in services" is conceptually more difficult to approach than trade in goods because of the amorphous nature of services. One must draw a distinction between "trade", which is the movement of services across borders as if they were goods, and "investment", which raises questions concerning the right of foreigners to establish a presence to provide services in a host country.[2] The latter may involve little actual transfer of services across national boundaries.

Services have traditionally been a matter of "investment". For centuries, individuals and firms have provided services through a place of business in a foreign country, repatriating the profits at some future date. The Royal Bank, for example, opened an office in Bermuda to finance international trade well before it established a presence in Toronto or Montreal - Canada's two leading financial centers.

Services have also been provided internationally by the consumer moving to the provider of services -- the physical act of attending a foreign university and paying tuition fees, seeking medical treatment abroad, or travelling as a tourist. Only in the maritime transportation sector could one say that services were "traded" in the strict sense of the word.

Information technologies have nullified the imperative of a physical presence and, in doing so, have opened up vast possibilities. Consider the following examples:

Agriculture

Information technologies are creating new opportunities for industries serving the international agricultural sector as well as expanding the access to information for farmers. Royal Bank agrologists, who specialize in farm lending, visit their rural clients carrying portable personal computers. These are used to study cash flows based upon estimated crop yields, weather and selling-price data that is accessed, *via* telephone lines, from distant data bases, located in Europe as well as in North America. This technology enables both the service provider and the farmer to make better decisions based on valuable information.

Education and Training

Corporations are using information technologies to educate their personnel across borders. The Royal Bank, like other corporations, retains some of the world's best consultants; they share their expertise with bank staff during four-hour seminars broadcast through an internal video network. Certainly, video conferencing not only shrinks time and distance, thereby often reducing the costs of conveying information, but it also allows people distant from the central organization to share in specialized expertise. In fact, those providing information in this manner to corporations are trading their services across borders and avoiding the complications of immigration restrictions.

Health

Canada is already a pioneer in making face-to-face medical expertise available to remote regions of the country *via* "Telemedicine". Several hospitals are accessing international medical databases to serve as diagnostic tools. This is another service that truly reflects the power of the marriage of computers with communications. The opportunities for sharing knowledge and creating trade in service markets in this area are unlimited. Rapid advances in fibre-optic and satellite transmission only magnify the application and reach of such efforts.

When the role of telecommunications is viewed in the broader context of enhancing access to knowledge and information, a country's communication policy environment takes on a new dimension. Cross-border electronic education will offer unique opportunities for both governments and private business.

Transportation

Transportation constitutes 30 percent of America's service exports. It is obviously also an essential component of international trade in goods. Airlines, trucking and shipping are all crucially dependent on information technologies. Federal Express is a highly successful American-based courier. While it boasts a fleet of aircraft to move parcels and envelopes, Federal Express's initial real market advantage could be attributed to an information system which was far ahead of its competitors'.

The driver carries a hand-held scanning device (25,000 of them are in use by Federal Express) which is used to scan a unique bar code strip affixed to each package at the time of pick-up. This information is then transferred to a unit in the truck outside and forwarded by mobile data communication technology over the Federal Express network to a mainframe computer in company headquarters at Memphis, Tennessee. The electronic system provides Federal Express and, most importantly, anxious customers with global up-to-the-minute status of all shipments. Information tracking a package's location has become almost as important as its swift passage.

One American financial institution tracks the movement of oil tankers around the world's seas and markets this information to its energy-related clients. The penetration of information technologies in the transportation sector is astonishing.

Trade in Financial Services

The recent acceleration of internationally traded financial services is directly caused by the application of computers and telecommunications. These technologies provide direct access to distant markets and information. This stimulates the volume of international transactions and traded services, which in turn creates new demands and greater reliance on the technologies. The cycle then continues.

In the post-recession 1980s, for example, corporate clients -- often enjoying better credit ratings than those of their banks -- have found it cheaper to raise money directly with institutional or individual investors rather than through their intermediary bank. In the case of Canadian companies, they developed an appetite for Canadian or U.S. dollar denominated instruments placed with foreign investors who were attracted by the higher interest rates compared with those available in their home currency. This investor demand permitted Canadian companies to pay slightly lower interest rates overseas than they would have incurred at home. Disintermediated from the deposit taking-borrowing process, banks began acting as arrangers of such issues overseas and developed products and services for which they were paid fees, which replaced the lost interest income from loans. At the same time, banks began breaking up their loans into negotiable securities which could be sold to the growing investor markets -- a process known as "securitization".

Increasingly, these investors could be found anywhere in the world. The importance of this phenomenon to Canada -- a net capital importer -- is clear. Among the principal purchasers of Government of Canada bonds are Japanese investors. In Edinburgh, a Scottish investment management firm is buying Japanese stocks on behalf of U.S. pension funds. Increasingly, companies seeking access to this international investor base are listing their shares on several exchanges around the world. For example, with the listing of the Royal Bank of Canada's shares on the Tokyo stock exchange in 1986, complemented by listings in London, Basle, New York and Canada, the bank's securities can be bought or sold virtually 24 hours a day. At the same time Canada, with its position as the world's fourth largest capital market, has attracted many firms seeking investors.

Information technologies have become so integral to banking that financial institutions are ranked among the largest purchasers and users of telecommunication services and data-processing equipment within their domestic economies. In Canada, The Royal Bank is the national carrier group's largest private enterprise customer. Worldwide, we spend over $80 million annually on our communication networks and have budgeted $2 billion over the next five years for information technology investments. This sector represents our fastest growing non-interest expense.

Euromoney recently predicted that:

> "The bank quickest to inform itself of the world's prices, and the most adept at making sense of them, will have the slickest product range. The bank with the most streamlined and cost efficient communications system will quote the sharpest prices. There will be a direct link between these factors and market share." (*Euromoney*, 1986)

Major fields of trade in international financial services include the following.

Foreign Exchange

Trade in both goods and services would not be possible without an active foreign exchange ("FX") market. Banks trade in currencies in order to manage their own positions (hedge against fluctuations) and on behalf of their corporate, institutional and governmental clients.

The volumes of FX transactions are staggering, estimated to average $425 billion per day (contrasted with $75 billion in the late 1970s). Largely due to better and faster access to moving rates and information affecting markets, FX rates have become extremely volatile, with monthly swings five or six times greater than they were a decade ago (Rivkin 1987: 2) This in turn increases the volume of trade as players scramble to hedge, speculate or just stay even.

For banks, serving client FX needs has become a lucrative business. Last year, the top eight American banks earned $2 billion in profits from this trading. *Institutional Investor* recently observed that money "...has become a protean mass of purchasing power, changing instantly at the press of a button as it ricochets through a global network of telephone and computer terminals".

The accuracy and timeliness of information is absolutely critical. In April, when the U.S. trade deficit figures were released, Reuters transmitted the numbers around the world and chaos immediately followed. Within *three minutes*, the U.S. dollar fell one and a half percent and only the immediate injection of $2.5 billion by the central banks stemmed the dramatic decline in world markets.

These essential services are all possible *only* through the application of information technologies -- to obtain the information that gives a competitive advantage, negotiate the best rates with markets around the world, place the orders and move the currency to settle completed transactions. Seconds can literally make or break a deal and a major extended communication failure in a bank's principal trading room could potentially threaten its stability. Information technologies have also enabled smaller markets to access and participate in the transactions of the world's three largest financial centres. In this regard, traders in even the most remote or economically disadvantaged countries enjoy enhanced access to market information and trading opportunities. Once the communication channel is established, it *does* operate in *both* directions.

Payment Systems

Another major financial traded service is international payments. The world's bank-payment systems settle all of the FX, credit, securities, and other international transactions. Through them, funds are transferred to complete these deals. As with other examples, these payment services, provided through linked telecommunication and computer networks, are not only valuable services in themselves - they are essential facilitators of international trade in general.

In a sense, the payment systems are nothing more than secure networks over which information, in recognized formats, is transmitted and acknowledged; but without them, international trade in its current form would end. In addition to proprietary bank networks, the Society for Worldwide Interbank Financial Telecommunications ("SWIFT"), founded in 1977, provides a global shared-payments system. Based in Belgium, with 1,500 member banks in 64 countries, SWIFT transmits international financial messages, including funds transfers, using standard formats. Payment and other messages are secure and economically conveyed. Last year volumes approached 1 million messages per day.

SWIFT is a perfect example of the domestic economic opportunities emerging out of the application of technology to trade in services. Many high-technology jobs have been created in Brussels to develop and operate this international payments system and others will follow. The direct benefits accruing to Belgium's telecommunication infrastructure are significant; tremendous indirect advantages accrue to the country hosting such a dynamic and leading-edge service industry and will have long-term implications for its economy and employment.

Volumes of payment transactions are surpassing increases in any economy's real transactions. Frankfurt, Germany's largest clearing centre, *daily* clears funds equivalent to one-quarter of Germany's annual GNP. In the U.S., large-dollar electronic payments amount to over $1 trillion per day. But tremendous risks are inherent in the payments system for any individual bank. Time zone considerations mandate that payments *follow* transactions and the gap in time can reach twenty-four hours, producing exposures because transactions are carried out on the assumption that payment will be received.

Cash Management

Perhaps one of the best examples of creating a new international financial service based upon a novel application of telecommunications and computers is to take existing client information, consolidate it and make it accessible to that client electronically around the world and around the clock. Through telecommunication lines and terminals on their corporate premises, treasurers can electronically access data around the world to control the domestic and international flows of funds between their subsidiaries and divisions, optimizing earning potentials. Cash management systems provide them with global balance reporting -- an instant view of the financial status of their company. Through the terminals, they are able to initiate FX and money market transactions, securities trades and funds transfers and to issue or amend international letters of credit.

Chemical Bank now markets its cash management systems to *other* financial institutions under the name "Banklink". In fact, most of its $250 million in revenues (1987) from non-credit services can be attributed to these cash management products. Banks will increasingly share their expertise in designing and operating information *systems*; these have already become tradeable commodities apart from the financial services which they support.

Retail Services

Under what conditions would a citizen of one country wish to maintain a banking relationship with a foreign bank that does not have significant physical presence in that country? This option is becoming a reality in many areas of the world. Through home videotext terminals and automated banking machines/networks, a foreign financial institution is able to extend its presence into a foreign country without maintaining substantial operations. The only barriers to such activity are local banking laws which may control the activities of foreign institutions. Opportunities to pursue a completely electronic banking relationship with foreign citizens will grow.

These networks are also helping travellers. A Japanese visitor to Britain is able to withdraw money from certain ATMs connected to the PLUS network. The electronic information is routed by the bank through its network from London to Toronto's data centre, then onto Denver, Hawaii and Tokyo and back again in under 20 seconds.

Home banking services are currently marketed in France, the U.K. and U.S.A., all relying on telecommunications to deliver their services. Soon, "Super Smart" cards, credit cards with imbedded computer chips, will allow customers to store and process information -- by no means limited to just money -- wherever they are. Many other innovations with transborder implications will follow.

Swaps

Interest rate and currency swaps allow clients to change rates in response to their altered view of rate directions. In an interest rate swap, banks act as intermediaries between two clients who wish to exchange obligations - a fixed rate for a floating rate. The payment streams from each obligation are swapped, permitting the client to achieve the desired effect in the balance sheet. In their simplest form, currency swaps permit companies to swap their home currency advantage for another's. A Canadian pulp and paper company can raise Canadian dollars from investors more cheaply than a German company, which can similarly raise Deutschemarks more economically at home. In fact both firms may desire funds in the currency of the other. Each raise the funds at their respective advantage and swap the payment streams. The world swap market, which started only in 1982, now stands at an estimated US $1 trillion and is growing at a rate of US $450 billion a year. The sophisticated qualitative and quantitative information required to reduce such cross-border flows to measurable risks is immense.

The fundamental point, however, is the one stated at the outset of this section. These services are the direct result of the merger of computers and telecommunications. They could not be provided without these two technologies. International commercial banks, by the very nature of their operations and size, have been among the first to exploit these services, to benefit customers and build business. Others are following - rapidly.

Access to international capital markets and investors is essential to most nations' economic futures - in both the developed and developing world. Can any country requiring capital afford not to be part of the emerging "electronic information circuit"?

To facilitate market demands that have *already arrived*, it is therefore vital that no country impose undue restrictions on the flow of information or on the electronic conduits carrying it. This is not only important to a country's participation in this new global economic order but also crucial to reducing risk in the global system overall. Regulators of financial services have been warned against creating uneven national regulatory barriers for fear of encouraging a form of "regulatory arbitrage". They have been called upon to create a common regulatory standard for markets around the world.

A move in this direction was recently made by the Bank for International Settlements which introduced common guidelines for capital standards for all OECD nation banks. Just as national regulators in the financial sector pursue the objective of regulatory conformity, a similar thrust must be made towards common "rules of the road" governing trade in information technologies.

Information Technologies and the Developing World

The impact of information technologies on the tradability of services is particularly relevant to many developing countries, some of whom regard open borders for services trade as an invitation to foreign multinationals to dominate their domestic service sector. These concerns must be addressed, both by developed-country governments and by multinational corporations using and providing information services across national borders.

The strategic application of information technologies, combined with the pursuit of niche service markets where a comparative advantage exists, will in fact present unique opportunities for developing countries. For developing and developed alike, there is a simple, stark choice: choose open borders and maximum market competition on an international basis -- or choose closed borders and opt out of the information economy and its immense benefits.

During the Industrial Age, for a time, protectionism was practised by a number of nations. We know with the aid of hindsight that the benefits were short-term and largely illusory -- but many nations tried this self-destructive course.

Now the world has changed. Expertise in telecommunications, computer hardware and software are not geographically dictated "natural economic advantages". They are *portable* and they are *temporary*. Technological generations are measured in months, not years; no nation, large or small, has any monopoly on inventive genius or creative adaptation; and the economic benefits accrue at least as much to users as to suppliers.

Closed borders, domestic preferences, supplier monopolies and cross-subsidized services are possible responses -- but they will condemn the nations choosing them to economic obsolescence. The challenge for policy makers, in the private and public sector alike, is to ensure that international aid and development programmes increasingly focus not just on the essentials of food production, health and education, but on the "third wave" technological infrastructures - telecommunications and computing.

Singapore, for example, is positioning itself as the gateway for international communications, attracting multinational data traffic through low rates and flexibility in an effort to build its own first-rate telecommunication infrastructure. This is an investment with which they country hopes to lure information-processing work and create local jobs.

Rather than "catching up" with the industrialized world in certain secondary and even primary industries, the inventive and selective use of information technologies could in fact propel some developing countries into an

Information Age in which even many developed nations have not yet positioned themselves.

In *Service-Led Growth*, Dorothy Riddle explores the impact of microcomputers and concludes that they offer greater access to information technologies for the developing world than the mainframes of the past. "We can anticipate a 'leap-frogging' effect, with developing economies able to move directly from paper-based to micro computer-based management and service delivery systems," she writes (Riddle, 1986: 122).

It is now possible for any country with an educated labour force to provide information service exports, spanning the spectrum between repetitive and labour-intensive data inputting to software development.

The Royal Bank and American Express, for example, are among many global traders who have purchased high-quality but inexpensive software from TATA Consultancy Services of Bombay, India. TATA employs more than 1,200 programmers. Boasting the third highest number of science and engineering graduates in the world, next to the USSR and USA, India has a pool of talent which companies like TATA are harnessing to create tradable services. Its New York office manager remarked, "Software is an ideal product for India because it requires good people and little capital." Today, 15 of the world's top 20 software corporations are in America. Tomorrow, that proportion may shift dramatically.

Another example of a developing country capitalizing on the comparative advantage of labour rates and time zones involves a New York law firm. The New York firm sends legal research assignments overnight *via* videotext to a Southeast Asian country. The research is done overnight by skilled lawyers and clerks trained in the common law, transmitted to the firm's London office for further value-added work and arrives in New York the following morning, eliminating the need for twenty-four-hour work days in New York. With current videotext technology, it is clearly possible to apply these strategies to such tasks as translation work, high volumes of word processing and other types of both clerical and professional tasks.

Not every developing country will be in a position to become a significant exporter of services but exports are only part of the potential. Even non-exporters must recognize how important information technologies will be to their entire domestic economy. For example, the World Bank reports that, in Nigeria, microcomputers have improved farm management surveys and agricultural profits as well as enhanced project monitoring and budgeting capabilities. Unrestricted and affordable access to global information affecting agriculture is essential for these services.

Information technologies also permit countries to participate in the emerging economic order without contending with immigration barriers and the capital needs of establishing significant operations abroad.

The New International Electronic Economic Order

Electronic Data Interchange (EDI) is revolutionizing international transactions and the movement of commercial information, streamlining the mechanism of trade and commerce in all goods and services. EDI, the electronic transfer of trade information, most of which is currently in paper form, has been developed out of a demand by clients confronted with escalating costs and the increased time demands involved in processing paper invoices, orders and other essential but routine trade data. General Motors, for example, already requires all of its 20,000 suppliers to communicate electronically using EDI or risk losing the auto giant's business. Banks are entering the field, initially to provide the electronic payment aspect of such transactions but eventually to serve as the medium for all information related to an order. From the perspective of a developing country, services like EDI create equality of opportunity. The inability to access such interchanges will be the equivalent of an absolute barrier to international trade.

The European Economic Community has recently made substantial financial commitments to information technologies by upgrading telecommunication infrastructures in some of its economically more depressed regions. It is even contemplating significant policy changes to create a new regulatory environment as recently articulated in its Green Paper. [3]

When recently asked how a European city could become a major financial centre, the Manager of Switzerland's Rothschild Bank AG replied:

> If you don't install a first-class telephone service you can give up all other efforts. Without an excellent telecommunications service, financial services are totally unthinkable. (INTUG, 1987: 122)

The Europeans are beginning to view information technologies as "propulsive factors" in economic development. Why?

- The technologies constitute a thriving business in themselves. They generate employment in high tech research and development, equipment manufacturing, and services operations and marketing.

- Computer and telecommunication equipment and services *facilitate* a wide spectrum of other economic activities, in both production and trade, of both goods and services.

W.G. Burns, Vice-Chairman of the Nynex Corp., recently said:

> Today, business throughout the world places a high value on telecommunications and information technologies. They do so because this technology gives them a powerful business tool in an environment

that is growing more and more competitive with each passing day. (Burns, 1988: 10).

For a few large telecommunication equipment manufacturers and network operators, trade in information-technology services may mean the freedom to build their own infrastructure within foreign countries. Most transnational corporations, however, merely wish to access domestic communication services on terms and rates available in their most liberalized markets. Their interest is to facilitate the movement of their information-based services. Few actually trade in these technologies.

So the issue of which services may or may not be *traded* between countries is often a separate question. If the domestic telecommunication policy environment does not encourage innovation, flexibility *and* low costs, then the complete liberalization of international trade in information technologies may not mean a great deal to many service traders.

Issues & Challenges

This paper has attempted to present a cursory exploration of the relationship between information technologies and enhanced trade in services, drawing many examples from the banking world. The availability of innovative, flexible and inexpensive information technologies throughout all markets, in both developed and developing countries, creates opportunities for *all* service industries. For services *and* for goods, these new inputs transcend the limitations of time and distance; they allow the pursuit of markets which were once only imagined. Those who possess the foresight and vision to recognize the impact of information technologies can position themselves to become market leaders.

However, these opportunities may be elusive, particularly in some developing countries, if certain issues and challenges are not addressed immediately. Many barriers to the efficient delivery of services *via* information technologies currently exist; still others will emerge. Because of the pivotal role which such technologies will play in facilitating trade and production in both services and goods, a country or enterprise which does not have access to the most innovative communication facilities available at the lowest cost possible will find itself at a competitive disadvantage. This applies as much in Indiana as in India, as much in Saskatchewan as in Singapore.

Although the international banking community, along with other multinational industries, currently faces these challenges, its early experience and formidable financial and technical resources have enabled most banks to adjust their operations on a market-by-market basis. If public data-network rates are too high or communication services limited in scope, we possess the technology skills to purchase bulk private lines and other facilities to create our own. Restrictions on transferring data across borders? We operate facilities locally or choose not to market our services there at all. The examples of our abilities to deal internationally with information technology issues are countless.

However, how will smaller service enterprises, such as those representing the majority of our clients, address these problems? What happens to those who wish to trade services globally but lack the expertise or desire to become information-technology engineers? For them, these issues become not just questions of marginal cost efficiencies but stark challenges to their very existence.

The question of how, if at all, trade in services will be liberalized internationally is currently in the hands of the Uruguay Round negotiators. If the declared objectives of the Uruguay Round are realized by the international community, it is clear that telecommunication and data issues must also be resolved in order for the benefits of information technologies to be equally extended to all who wish to take advantage of them. The following are several of the more pressing communication-related issues as they influence trade in services.

National Telecommunication Policies

A modern telecommunication policy environment is the most significant mechanism with which a government can influence the nature of trade in services delivered by information technologies.

The world's three key financial markets -- New York, London and Tokyo -- are all located in countries boasting liberal telecommunication policy environments where competition is nurtured. What are the communication policies of the countries with "second tier" financial markets - nations such as West Germany, Canada and Switzerland? Will they propel these markets forward or contribute to slippage into third-tier status?

Too few leaders of national governments understand the unique contribution of telecommunications to economic development and trade. Many fail to appreciate the international nature of information services and some who do appreciate it fear the consequences. They continue to shield their telecommunication carriers from competition, using them as seemingly unlimited sources of revenue with which to fund the national treasury. Innovative and flexible telecommunication services, the arteries of the Information Age, are not being nurtured. Restrictions on customer-premises equipment abound. The efficient resale and sharing of networks are prohibited in all but a few jurisdictions. Mr. I.P. Sharp, the founder of a very successful value-added network operating of a global scale, recently expressed his frustration with many PTTs when he said: "You can't argue or reason with someone who has a monopoly".

A lack of uniformity of policies and regulations characterizes the international telecommunication scene. Traders in services are forced to navigate through a sea of conflicting rules and service offerings. An example of these inconsistencies is the diversity of definitions of "basic" and "enhanced" telecommunication services. The distinction is important in those jurisdictions which allow full or even modest competition in enhanced services. However, no generally accepted approach has been adopted. For example, while Canada and the United States should be applauded for their efforts to create bilateral "rules of the road" in data services as part of the proposed Free Trade Agreement, Canadian and American interpretations of basic and enhanced services have recently diverged. This makes Canadian service providers *and* users uncertain of the future of the enhanced voice sector.

Just as Canada and the U.S. are recognizing the need to ensure a coordinated approach, the European community is also taking active steps by moving towards implementing many of the recommendations in the recent Green Paper. Seven percent of Europe's gross domestic product (currently 2 percent) and 60 percent of its employment are expected to depend largely on telecommunications by the end of the century. The Community has recognized the urgency of coordinating its policies and creating an environment that will respond to the demands of the trade-in-services explosion which will occur in a "Europe without frontiers" in 1992.

The time has come for all national governments to see information technologies in the context of their unprecedented contribution to *economic development.* In this regard, the construction of modern telecommunication infrastructures must be a premier objective of the strategies of less developed countries as well as of developed ones. As noted earlier, if the developed world wishes to benefit from a global, liberal trade-in-services regime, it must assume more responsibility for assisting in the developing areas. These systems are costly but only 1 percent of the World Bank's loan portfolio is in the area of telecommunications; by contrast, 23 percent has been invested in electrical projects. In 1970, developing nations spent 20 percent of their total capital investments on telecommunication infrastructure; by the end of this decade they are expected to devote 30 percent. With investment opportunities becoming more homogeneous in industrialized countries, perhaps it is time to look more closely at communication ventures in the developing world. Higher risk may be accompanied by greater rates of return in the long term. If progressive information-technology policies do not become key components of all national economic strategies, users will seek their own solutions and follow the paths of least resistance. "Technology and customer demand (in telecommunications) will outstrip every public policy that seeks to restrict them", concluded the Vice-Chairman of Nynex, a carrier which once operated in a monopoly environment but now prospers in a competitive marketplace.

Communication Costs

With communication tariffs between countries varying by a factor of up to 20 times, the cost of operating communication networks is increasingly relevant to trade in services, particularly as the information underlying certain kinds of service transactions will demand vast amounts of transmission and processing capacities. With a Free Trade Agreement recently struck by two of the world's largest traders, Canada and the United States, the discrepancy in telecommunication rates between the two neighbours (Canadian tariffs are up to double those of the U.S.) is causing great anxiety for many Canadian industries which will need to rely on inexpensive communications effectively to penetrate the American market and compete on an equal basis.

As an example, book distributors in North America rely on inexpensive telephone service to sell their publications. But while the catalogues of both Canadian and American distributors are very similar, U.S. companies are gaining a competitive advantage over their Canadian counterparts because of the differences in carriers' tariffs.

Likewise, a small company has developed a competitive PC-based software product on the west coast of Canada. The most effective method of marketing this particular software is through telephone sales, often referred to as "telemarketing". Through telemarketing, the company is successfully serving the Central Canadian marketplace and all of continental United States. However, its main competition, across the border in Western United States, enjoys a competitive advantage by accessing American long-distance services at about one-half the costs which the Canadian company must bear. How long can the Canadian firm resist relocating its marketing operations to the U.S.A.?

A country which continues to view business communication tariffs principally in the context of their contribution to government revenues or to subsidizing basic residential service does so at its own peril. It is handicapping its ability to attract or encourage information-intensive activity within its jurisdiction. It is failing to ensure that all of its industries possess the basis tools with which to produce, sell and deliver services and goods efficiently.

Standards and Reliability

Two of the most persistent obstacles to utilizing telecommunications internationally are inconsistent equipment and service standards and transmission protocols. Although a great deal of progress is being made within the ITU to harmonize differences, perhaps ISDN -- the Integrated Services Digital Network -- being the most recent example of a concerted effort, all transnational firms are confronted with these issues. Customizing electronic services to accommodate national differences is simply not practical, particularly when development and operational costs demand global economies of scale.

Many PTTs continue to insist on their own modems for dial-up services. The Royal Bank does not offer electronic services to clients in a number of countries because they are not permitted to use the Royal's standard equipment.

A related problem is the inferior performance quality of communication networks of some nations. This unreliability means that bank offices in some developing countries cannot access the Royal Bank's international computerized Asset Information System; the local communications are that bad. The bank is unable to provide the level of service to clients in other countries but the real loser is not the bank: it is the customer.

Vulnerability of Telecommunications Facilities

Gerald Corrigan, President of the New York Federal Reserve Bank, points to the tremendous reliance which the payments system places on telecommunications, moving over $1 trillion daily:

> Any major disruption in the large-dollar payment systems can quickly impair the workings of many institutions and the markets generally. (Corrigan, 1987)

A disaster at a key central switching office in New York, Tokyo, or Toronto that produces a prolonged failure in communication networks can literally threaten the financial stability and, over time, viability of some of the world's largest financial institutions.

Carriers throughout the world have not responded to the tremendous shift in the use of their facilities. That was acceptable when they were merely providing a business tool. It is not acceptable now, when they are serving as the arteries of the global information economy.

Most carriers continue to hide behind legislated limitations on the legal liability for network failures. Few allocate adequate resources to contingency planning, back-up systems and redundant switching sites. Governments must re-examine these limitations in the context of telecommunications' unique and critical role in facilitating trade in all services. The reliance of the world economy on their services demands measures which strengthen accountability -- not encourage inefficiency or neglect.

Restrictions on International Telecommunication and Data Services

Many countries maintain currency restrictions; others limit or prohibit the export of certain data or require a minimal level of information processing within their borders prior to export. Considerations of privacy, confidentiality and extraterritoriality justify many of these limitations on the flow of information. Yet in an economic context some are short-sighted and many be more harmful to a nation's long-term development interests.

While it may not be feasible, or even desirable, to develop a comprehensive code governing all aspects of data flow, these matters could be addressed separately. Privacy security, and computer crime are but a few broad issues affecting international telecommunication and data services which should be the subject of distinct multilateral "codes of conduct". While there are few current instances of impenetrable barriers to the flow of electronic information, uncertainty remains.

In 1983, Rowland C. Frazee, at the time Chairman and Chief Executive Officer of The Royal Bank of Canada, proposed the establishment of a framework governing trade in computer services between Canadian and American users and the harmonization of privacy protection. The "Frazee Initiative", as it became known, was a preemptive effort responding to concerns over vulnerability of information flows to sudden and arbitrary government restrictions. The Canada-U.S. Free Trade Agreement addresses these issues partially but much remains to be done.

With trade accelerating in all services, these issues must be dealt with, preferably at a multilateral level. The OECD has issued its own code in this regard but it extends only to a handful of nations and only partially addresses the issues. Both the GATT principals and the ITU have studied the issue but not addressed it aggressively. It may therefore be an opportune time for them to review these matters and assess their implications for trade in services generally.

National Policies Influencing International Trade

With the growing relationship between information technologies and economic development, all national policies and laws must be re-examined from the perspective of their impact on these technologies.

For example, restrictions on the authorized nature of a bank's business in Canada under banking legislation has effectively precluded the industry from developing information services which were a natural outgrowth of banking -- at its root, an information business. Given the absence of other Canadian-owned enterprises of similar scale and resources, the result has been a smaller and weaker Canadian service sector than would otherwise exist. American financial institutions, on the other hand, while restricted in the scope of their domestic operations by the separation between investment and commercial banking created by the *Glass-Steagall Act* and Article 65 of the *Securities and Exchange Act*, have not faced similar restrictions in "information services". Citicorp, for example, having recognized that its future competitors would be AT&T, IBM and Reuter, initiated diversification into the markets held by these information giants in the early 1980s.

Other policies have a large, if less direct, impact on the information economy. For example, Canadian authorities are contemplating a pioneering value-added tax on financial services, and have already imposed a sales tax on certain communication services. Research and development policies and anti-trust laws will also clearly affect the further development of information technologies. And intellectual property laws can act as an incentive or brake on the creative process. In short, national policy-makers who fail to take an integrated approach could unknowingly inflict severe damage on a company's or country's ability to exploit these modern technologies.

Trade in Services and Information Technologies in Perspective

This paper was not intended to serve as a comprehensive treatment of trade *in* telecommunication and data-processing services. Rather, it was intended to canvass the experiences of several industries, particularly financial services, in integrating information technologies with their traded services in pursuit of competitive advantage.

"The unhindered flow of information within and across national boundaries is of fundamental importance to business," declares the International Chamber of Commerce (International Chamber of Commerce, 1988: 3).

Information flows raise many issues, both economic and political, which must be explored before we can hope to achieve global trade in information technologies. Particularly, the concerns of the developing world must be addressed by those nations which possess a disproportionate share of such technologies. Strategic alliances, the pursuit of niche markets and technological aid will all be necessary to relieve the imbalances faced by developing countries.

Information services cannot be viewed as constituting just another "service industry" when their true place in multilateral trade-in-services (Uruguay Round) or regulatory (ITU) frameworks is considered.

While information technologies are in themselves traded and their producers include some of the world's largest and most sophisticated corporations, their greatest contribution lies in facilitating the trade of *other* enterprises' services and goods. Given this reality, it can only be hoped that the ongoing GATT and ITU negotiations prove fruitful.

ENDNOTES

1 The author wishes to acknowledge the substantial editorial contribution and assistance provided by Mr. George Horhota, Manager, Computer Communications, Policy and Regulation, The Royal Bank of Canada. Additional editing suggestions were provided by Mr. Peter Burn, Partner, Ottawa-based trade consulting firm, Grey, Clark, Shih and Associates.

Copyright to this paper is jointly held by the Royal Bank of Canada and the Atwater Institute, which specifically commissioned its preparation. Reproduction other than brief quotations for purposes of discussion requires the specific permission of both parties.

2 The "right of establishment" is discussed in some detail in Professor Balasubramanyam's paper in this volume

3 The Green Paper is discussed in the papers by Sidney Dell and Toshio Kosuge in this volume.

INTERNATIONAL VIEWS ON THE TRADEABILITY OF TELECOMMUNICATIONS

G. Russell Pipe

For more than a century telecommunication services were considered a public service, provided to residential and business subscribers on an essentially non-commercial, non-competitive basis. There was just one basic service, whether telegraphy, voice telephony or telex. The convergence of telecommunication and computing technologies in the 1970s made possible many new services by introducing computers into the telecommunication infrastructure and connecting computers to telecommunication terminal points on customer premises.

A policy ensuring *universal service* to all households and businesses has been the goal of governments of both industrialized and developing countries. Historically, universal service has meant the right of all citizens to have access to a telephone. Accordingly, government-owned monopolies were established to provide telecommunication, postal and other services. Since these PTTs were operated for the public good, their tariffs and charges and the sharing of such revenues between postal and telecommunication authorities were considered a reasonable way to conduct a *public utility*. In industrial countries, these practices have lately been undergoing serious re-examination due to advancements in technology which have resulted in telecommunication services having important commercial dimensions.

In a period of less than 20 years, the concept of what telecommunication services are has been dramatically transformed -- from a public good, to a contribution to national development, to a core service delivering many international services. AT&T is a company which has exhibited this transformation in its advertising messages. Until the mid-1970s, the company was a *telephone company* but from about 1980 it became a *communication company* and, since divestiture, AT&T considers itself an *information company*. This rapid transition that AT&T recognized has not, however, been fully understood or accepted in Europe or in many developing countries.

In parallel with technological developments and greater appreciation of the economic importance of telecommunication, there is a strong movement to deregulate traditional terms for ownership and provision of many of the new services which have been created. Deregulation, or re-regulation as it is known in some countries, is at least in part intended to provide commercial users with greater flexibility to utilize public networks and leased circuits, to purchase and attach terminal equipment, and otherwise to exploit these capabilities for internal operations and external marketing of products and services.

In initiation of formal trade negotiations on services, bilaterally between Canada and the United States and Israel and the United States, and multi-laterally in 1987 with the opening of the Uruguay Round, could have a considerable impact on Telecommunication Administrations and other operators, the equipment industry, new value-added and information services, and business users. Although trade-in-services negotiations have been under way for three years, the telecommunication community remains largely preoccupied with managing technological change and regulatory adjustments. Discussions between telecommunication experts and trade-policy experts have revealed a wide gap in understanding the terms and concepts of each other's field.

Given this situation, the Telecommunications Services Trade Project[1] undertook to learn the views of individuals with professional responsibilities in telecommunication and international trade policy as to their perceptions of the *tradeability* of telecommunication services. A questionnaire was sent to 502 individuals residing in 48 countries in June 1988. Their specialties and/or affiliations ranged from international organizations, national governments, business entities, higher education and research, to journalism and consultancy.

The objectives of the survey were to learn their views on potential benefits or disadvantages resulting from applying trade rules to telecommunication services, which services may be considered tradeable, what types of principles and general rules a multilateral agreement might contain, and how such a new regime might affect the ITU and be administered by the GATT.

The results are not intended to be a statistical portrait but rather to provide provisional indicators of how a sampling of informed observers and participants in the trade-policy process currently view a range of issues. No attempt has been made to disaggregate beyond the level of region and field of specialization.

A total of 197 responses were received, a 40% return. A little less than half were from Europe with a small number from the Middle East and Africa. A further 35% were primarily from North America and 15% from Japan. Trade negotiators at missions in Geneva were included in the European responses as well as representatives from several international organizations. 60% percent of those returning the form are involved in telecommunications as providers of services, equipment manufacturers or users of international services. Most of the remaining 40% are in trade policy, either with governments or corporations, and some are academics, journalists or experts.

The personal opinions of respondents were sought, not the positions of organizations or companies. Responses were anonymous. Difficulties due to lack of clear definitions of terms and concepts were recognized. Those responding were invited to apply their personal interpretations. For the purposes of the survey, trade in services was defined as 'services essentially produced by residents of one country and paid for and used by residents of another country.'

Participants were asked to consider several possible objectives of trade agreements covering telecommunication services. Some 75% from both the telecommunication and trade-policy areas saw the ability of users to acquire new services where they do business as the most important goal. They further viewed user access to new services as likely to be achieved under a trade-in-services regime. Other objectives looked upon as having almost the same importance were: (1) selling telecommunication services in foreign markets on an equitable basis; (2) accelerating the process of deregulating telecommunication services; and (3) expanding world trade.

Trade policy officials in Japan and the U.S. perceived a trade-in-services agreement as affecting deregulation more than did telecommunication providers and users. The former rated the relevance of a services agreement to deregulation as 75% and the latter 65%. More significant than these marginal differences was the broad agreement among the two groups on both the objectives and likely impact of including telecommunication services in a multilateral trade agreement.

A number of advantages and few disadvantages are envisaged if services accords covering telecommunication are established. Neither benefits nor risks are viewed as dramatic, with those involved in trade policy highlighting the advantages while telecommunication professionals express more concern over possible dislocations. Table I presents the average scores for all respondents who judged the possible results on a 10-to-1 scale, from extremely likely to extremely unlikely to occur.

Increased opportunities for new services, lower costs to users and improvements to existing services were predicted. Some Europeans, however, were less certain that lower costs would materialize. Slower economic growth, increased unemployment and destabilization of markets for services and equipment providers were viewed as progressively unlikely. Reduced national control over service sectors, the establishment of common rules of the road, disruption of national and international regulatory regimes were viewed on average as neither particularly likely nor unlikely to result from applying trade rules to telecommunication services.

Table I - Impacts of Trade Agreement Covering Telecom Services	
Opportunities for new services will increase	8
Lower cost of services to users	7
Reduced national control of service sectors	6
Establishment of common rules of the road	6
Opportunities for improved services will increase	7
Disruption of international regulatory practices	5
Slower Economic growth	2
Destabilization of markets for service and equipment providers	4
Growth in unemployment caused by market restructuring	3
Disruption of national regulatory practices	5
Reduced trade barrirs associated with widely different regulatory regimes	6
No significant *advantages*	3
No significant *disadvantages*	6

Tradeability of Telecommunication Services

Ascertaining opinions on which telecommunication services can be considered traded or tradeable was an important objective of the survey. It has been widely acknowledged that basic telephony is a public service because of the technology involved and because of its use by residential subscribers. Table II indicates how respondents ranked the tradeability of various types of services.

Table II - Tradeability of Telecommunication Services	
Basic telephony (transport services)	45%
Basic (in an ISDN environment	55%
Enhanced (value-added component)	82%
Enhanced (value-added information services)	84%

The viewing of basic telephony as tradeable by 45% of those responding was unexpected. Telecommunication professionals considered basic telephony less tradeable than did trade-policy officials, but it seems nearly all the academics, journalists and experts opted for its tradeability. However, telecommunication service providers and users were almost identical in their opinion. Since basic telephony was excluded from the Canada-U.S. Free Trade Agreement and the European Community considers basic transport service as reserved for public monopolies, these results suggest that some rethinking may be taking place.

In addition to the tradeability of particular services, a question was posed as to whether tradeability is affected by how services are provided or the structure of user organizations. Do jointly provided international voice, data or image services, handled by two administrations or operating companies, given that only exchange of traffic takes place, involve trade? Eighty percent evenly distributed between all respondents indicated that such services 'lend themselves to being traded.'

The tradeability of telecommunication services was viewed to some extent according to the way they are used. Intracorporate networks were seen by 50% as involved in trade, a figure higher than may have been expected given their internal nature and applications. Closed user groups, such as SWIFT and SITA, were considered engaged in trade in services by 62%; companies using EDI and other systems to communicate with customers and suppliers received a 76% rating; and online commercial information processing/retrieval services 90%.

If telecommunication services are provided by a monopoly rather than by multiple providers -- whether public or private entities -- they are less tradeable, according to 62% of those responding. In the context of multilateral trade negotiations, such as are currently taking place in the Uruguay Round, special rules over monopoly practices may be considered. These conditions would be designed to ensure fair treatment of suppliers and users, so even without competition an open environment may be prescribed.

Having identified the types of telecommunication service which may be tradeable, the survey sought to determine perceptions of the role of these services in international trade. When asked to choose between two different concepts of telecommunication services, over 60% viewed them as an intermediate service which supports others, such as aviation, banking or insurance, rather than as a clearly identifiable and defined sector. All respondents viewed the role of telecommunications in roughly the same way, except for the Japanese, who see them more as a clearly defined service sector. It is not easy to discern what this impression of telecommunications as an intermediate service may mean in the context of the Uruguay Round negotiations. It could well expose telecommunications to more scrutiny and inclusion in a framework of basic rules and principles being prepared by negotiators in Geneva.

Negotiations on Trade in Services

Telecommunication trade agreements are being prepared bilaterally, as is the case with the U.S. and Japan on international value-added network services (IVANS), regionally by the European Community with its single telecommunication market, and multilaterally in the Uruguay Round. While bilateral accords were seen as the most expeditious by 57% of the respondents, multilateral agreements were considered the most desirable long-term solution by 81%.

The Uruguay Round negotiations, launched two years ago, cover for the first time services, agriculture and intellectual property. A broad framework agreement rather than specific sector-by-sector codes was favored by 45% of survey participants. However, the sectoral approach was endorsed by 26% and a more elaborate annotated framework backed by 25%. A higher percentage of trade-policy officials supported the annotation approach, possibly because this may be a less controversial approach to giving specific meaning to principles set forth in the framework without having to negotiate separate codes for a number of sectors. Strong support, averaging 70%, was evident for three principles which have been introduced into the Uruguay Round negotiations: (1) enterprises should have the right of access to establish and operate in foreign markets; (2) national laws and regulations should not discriminate against persons, goods or services on the grounds of their origin; and (3) there should be progressive liberalization of trade practices combined with institutional mechanisms to achieve appropriate regulation of service sectors. The access-to-markets-and-establishment principle, supported especially strongly by private-sector respondents in North America and Japan, is controversial because it involves the right of investment and if adopted could result in foreign companies being treated more favorably than local firms.

There is concern in the telecommunication community that its representatives are not involved formally or informally in negotiations on services in the Uruguay Round, which could have significant impacts on their operations. A process exists for the formulation of international telecommunication policy in a number of countries whereby user groups can express their views to Telecommunications Administrations (TAs) and consultation mechanisms at the ITU. Seventy percent of the respondents support informal meetings and exchanges of views with trade-policy officials at the national level and with Uruguay Round negotiators. However, only 36% believe formal advisory bodies should be established. This may be due to the fact that the talks have been under way for some time and informal approaches seem the most timely and suitable.

ITU and GATT Relationships

Although the implementation of a services agreement covering telecommunication is unclear, its potential implications for the functions of the ITU have been the subject of considerable speculation. The overlapping or the blurring of jurisdictional lines was forecast by 40% of the respondents with another 29% expecting no major impact on the Union's standards-making responsibilities. Trade-policy officials registered even stronger opinions that the consequence of a trade regime will be an overlap rather than conflict. Telecommunication professionals, on the other hand, anticipated more conflicts, such as encroachment on the ITU's jurisdiction if contradictory decisions were to be taken under a future GATT dispute-settlement procedure.

The ITU should adopt measures in anticipation of a multilateral trade regime covering telecommunications according to 53%. The ITU Plenipotentiary Conference taking place in Nice, France during May/June 1989 'should address economic and trade issues and take the necessary steps to amend the Union's convention,' the majority of respondents recommended. Plenipotentiary action was considered necessary by 60% of telecom professionals. The internal structure and consultative mechanisms of the ITU, 25% suggested, can already be adapted to trade regimes without changing the basic instrument of the Union.

With regard to how GATT might be reorganized or reconstituted to administer a services agreement, 75% thought the necessary infrastructure could be created within the present institutional framework. GATT should be responsible for the overall supervision and dispute settlement, it was indicated, with technical and specialized expertise provided by existing international organizations. Only 12% supported the establishment of a new inter-governmental body to administer a services agreement.

The foregoing data suggest that whether telecommunication services are tradeable is no longer an open or unresolved question. Initiatives by several OECD countries to enter into bilateral trade-in-services agreements and the launching of the Uruguay Round have effectively resolved that issue. These survey results illustrate the new challenge: to define the conditions under which specific telecommunication service transactions constitute trade and to specify the rules by which such trade will be governed.

ENDNOTES

1 The Telecommunications Services Trade Project was launched in 1988 and will continue into 1990. It was designed to build understanding between the telecommunication and trade communities through informal meetings and exchange of information. Project sponsors have been provided a major research report on the implications of introduction of trade rules to telecommunication services.

CONCEPTS &
PRINCIPLES

INTERNATIONAL TRADE IN SERVICES

THE ISSUE OF MARKET PRESENCE AND RIGHT OF ESTABLISHMENT

V.N. Balasubramanyam

The origins of the debate on presence and right of establishment are to be traced to the continuing discussion on what constitutes a service as distinct from a good. The sizeable body of literature on the issue identifies two major characteristic features of services - non-storability or the intangible nature of services and the fact that production of services usually takes place in the presence of demanders of services (Hill, 1977). With these characteristics as a starting point, services are classified according to those which involve the movement of the producer to the locale of the consumer and those which involve the movement of the consumer to the locale of the producer. Jagdish Bhagwati has added to this list a third category of services which involve neither producer nor consumer mobility - the 'long-distance' services (Bhagwati, 1987). These include a broad class of services such as live music concerts, insurance transactions and banking, which do not essentially require the physical proximity of producers to consumers. These services can be transmitted 'over the wire' and the scope for such 'long distance' service transactions is likely to increase with the advance of technology. Bhagwati, however, notes that even in the case of such services physical proximity is likely to enhance efficiency and at times to allow for a wider range of transactions. It is this characteristic of services -- that they either require or benefit from proximity of producers to consumers -- that has brought to the fore the issues of 'presence' and 'establishment' in the context of the debate on liberalization of trade in services.

It is worth noting that the often-drawn fine distinction between tradeable and non-tradeable services may have little relevance for the debate on liberalization of trade in services. It has, for instance, been suggested that a criterion for trade is "whether or not the majority of the value added is exchanged between residents and non-residents" (UNCTAD, 1985). On this criterion a large chunk of service transactions including those associated with foreign direct investment would be excluded from the ambit of trade in services. The only tradeable services on the basis of this criterion of trade would be the long-distance services and it would, in fact, remove the issues of 'presence' and 'establishment' from the agenda. It is for this reason that some commentators prefer to talk in terms of service *transactions* rather than services trade. It is essential to recognize that most transactions in services involve mobility of factors of production across geographical borders and that 'presence' and 'establishment' thus involve a discussion of the nature and extent of factor mobility and the rules and regulations governing the operations of foreign entities in the importing countries.

The objective of this paper is an analysis of the issues of 'market presence' and 'right of establishment' of foreign firms frequently alluded to but rarely elaborated on in literature on trade in services. The first section of the paper analyzes the concepts of 'presence' and 'right of establishment'. The second section discusses the issues of 'presence' and 'establishment' in the context of international trade in general. The third section analyzes the issues in the context of liberalization of trade in services. Section four dwells on the implications of the growth in information-technology industries and transborder data flows for the issue of 'presence' and 'establishment'. The final section pulls together the main conclusions of the paper.

Conceptual Issues

Broadly defined, 'presence' and 'establishment' refer to the right of foreign producers of goods and services to engage in commercial operations and gain access to markets in the importing countries. There are, however, subtle differences in meaning between the two concepts. Establishment is usually associated with foreign direct investment (FDI). By definition, FDI involves ownership of capital and the setting up of a branch or a subsidiary by the investing entity in the host country, which gives the entity operational control over decision-making. Needless to say, FDI through the establishment of a branch or a subsidiary allows the investing entity to gain access to markets in the host country. In other words, establishment is a broad concept which implies not only 'presence' but also the power to exercise control over decision-making.

'Market presence' is a somewhat amorphous concept. It lies mid-way between pure trade and FDI. Pure trade involves the exchange of goods and services across national borders without a need for the physical presence of the producers in the markets of the consumers. As stated earlier, FDI involves the physical presence of the producer in the markets of the consumers in the form of a branch or controlled subsidiary. In between these two extremes are various organizational mechanisms through which foreign firms are able to gain access to overseas markets. Such mechanisms include joint business ventures, licensing agreements, management contracts, subcontracting arrangements, franchises, representative offices and agencies. All of these mechanisms provide for the presence of the foreign firm in the importing countries in one guise or another. They all facilitate commercial transactions between different national entities.

Joint business ventures involve the commitment of resources including funds, facilities and services by two or more legally separate entities to one enterprise for their mutual benefit (Tomlinson, 1970 and Balasubramanyam, 1973). There are no hard and fast rules specifying the share of the partners in the resources they commit to the enterprise. The significant aspect of this mode of organization though is its emphasis on the commitment of resources to the enterprise by all the partners to the venture for their mutual benefit. It follows that, in the case of joint ventures, none of the partners own capital to an extent that gives them exclusive control over operations. The foreign partners to the venture do, however, gain access to markets and a share in the profits of the venture.

Licensing agreements or technical-collaboration agreements are defined as agreements between foreigners and entities created under local law and owned by local public or private interests in which the foreigner provides management services, technical information, or both and receives payment in money (Fforde, 1957). The significant features of this arrangement are that the enterprise is owned by local entities, foreign ownership is precluded, and the payment received by the foreigner is in return for technical services rendered. This arrangement also allows foreign entities to gain access to overseas markets, albeit through the sale of technology and know-how rather than through final goods embodying such technology and know-how.

A management contract is defined as 'an arrangement under which operational control of an enterprise ... is vested by contract in a separate enterprise which performs the necessary managerial functions in return for a fee' (Balasubramanyam, 1973). Significant features of this arrangement are that it too, like licensing agreements, precludes foreign ownership of capital and operational control is vested in foreign hands by contract for a specified duration. This arrangement also enables foreign firms to gain access to overseas markets for the sale of managerial know-how.

Sub-contracting arrangement, franchises, and representative offices are somewhat more loosely knit mechanisms than the ones discussed above. But all of these mechanisms also provide foreign firms access to overseas markets and facilitate commercial transactions. Again the significant feature of these arrangements is that they all preclude exclusive control by foreign firms over decision-making.

In sum, all of the non-FDI mechanisms discussed above provide for 'market presence' without 'establishment'. They all preclude exclusive control over decision making by foreign entities. These features should be of appeal to both foreign firms and the importing countries. The growth in the number and extent of such arrangements in recent years suggests as much. But these arrangements are not without their problems. From the point of view of the importing countries, the absence of control over decision-making by foreign firms is often seen to hold only in theory. Foreign firms may be able to exercise effective control over operations because they hold the reins over technology and know-how which are significant inputs in the production process. Ownership of such inputs may enable them to influence the locally-owned firm's actions in charting its future. They could also exercise control over the operations of locally-owned firms through the imposition of a variety of restrictions relating to sources of input purchase, the type of markets serviced, and production procedures. In other words, foreign firms may be able to enjoy all the benefits of establishment including market presence without investment of funds or the ownership of capital.

For their part, foreign firms may find the business mechanisms discussed earlier imperfect and inadequate vehicles for the transmission of complex technologies and know-how. They are imperfect in the sense that they do not allow foreign firms fully to integrate the advantages of technology and the know-how they possess with the resource endowments of host countries. For a large part they have to rely on the ability of the locally owned firms to absorb and efficiently utilize the technology they provide in the production process: such abilities of locally owned firms may be limited. Such arrangements may also be inadequate vehicles of transmission in the sense that most modern technologies are inseparable from the corporate entity that owns them. They form an integral part of the firm and, in the absence of a branch plant or a wholly owned subsidiary which allows the firm to function as a fully integrated entity, it may not be able to transfer technology and know-how to the host countries. In other words, these mechanisms may not permit foreign firms fully to realize the returns on their investment in the production of technologies and know-how -- hence the desire for a 'right of establishment' on the part of the producers of goods and services.

These problems associated with business mechanisms other than FDI appear to be at the root of the current debate on 'market presence' in the context of trade in services. As discussed earlier, in the case of most services considerations of efficiency require the presence of the producers in the locale of the consumers. Frequently cited examples of such services include hospital services and the provision of complex software packages. In the case of the former, local establishment is intrinsically necessary; in the case of the latter, establishment may be necessary to facilitate adaptation of the packages to local market needs and conditions. In both cases establishment implies control over decision-making by the producers of services. Trade in services which requires establishment is designated in the literature as 'establishment trade' -- constituted by those transactions which emanate from locally established affiliates of foreign firms (Sauvant 1987).

Moreover, in the case of many services the distinction between trade and FDI is blurred. How are the operations of a travel agency providing travel services in the host country and relying heavily on the transnational computer communication systems of its parent to be defined? Is the agency to be classified as FDI because of its close links to its parent which enables the latter to exercise control over operations or is it to be classified as a mere operating agency of the foreign firm? There could be many such examples of services which defy classification. The point to note though, as Karl Sauvant puts it, is that "... the boundaries between FDI and trade are blurring in certain services, a development likely to accelerate given the growing complexity and rising data-technology content of modern products and production and the services and servicing requirements associated with them" (Sauvant 1987).

One implication of these characteristics of services for the debate on 'market presence' and 'establishment' is that fine distinctions between the two concepts may be academic. In practice, what matters is the institution of mechanisms, rules and regulations which permit suppliers of services to engage in the efficient delivery of such services. This in turn requires a broad interpretation of the concept of 'market presence'. It may not be judicious to confine the concept to business mechanisms which do not allow for foreign control over operations. This is not to say that licensing arrangements, management contracts and franchises should be eschewed in favour of FDI. These arrangements may suffice in the case of many types of services, especially those which can be disembodied from the entity of which they normally form a part. The revolutionary advances in the field of information technology may also increasingly render such arrangements a viable alternative to FDI. But in the case of many services, for the foreseeable future, considerations of efficiency may require the 'establishment' of the producer in the locale of the consumer. In this context 'market presence' needs to be interpreted broadly to encompass 'establishment'. Simply put, market presence is to be interpreted to mean the right of foreign firms to have a commercial presence in the importing country. As Karl Sauvant elaborates, right of presence in this context encompasses such component rights as the 'right to deliver' or the 'right to sell' a service; which means either that the service provider is permitted to have access to the market from abroad and can compete in it on equal footing with domestic firms or it means in addition that the service provider has a 'right of establishment', the 'right to connect' for instance with foreign affiliates, customers or brokers; the 'right to receive' services from suppliers abroad; 'the right to plug in' necessary equipment to the national telecommunication network; perhaps even the right to establish local marketing, sales and distribution systems needed to sell services and to use foreign employees to maintain these systems (Sauvant 1987).

All this no doubt amounts to a long list of rights for the providers of services - a veritable 'Bill of Rights'. These rights raise several contentious issues. First, does market presence interpreted broadly imply unimpeded entry of foreign producers of goods and services into the importing countries? Second, once entry is allowed for, what sort of regulatory framework should govern the operations of foreign producers of services? It could be argued that market presence and liberalization of trade in services by definition require unimpeded entry of foreign producers into the importing countries. But most importing countries, be they developed or developing, would find this interpretation sweeping. They would object to unimpeded entry on the grounds that it would be inimical to national sovereignty and national economic objectives. They would, more likely than not, favour an approach based on selectivity with regard to sectors and industries in which foreign producers are allowed to operate. This sort of selectivity with regard to entry, based on considerations of national security and the time-honoured infant-industry argument for protection, is frequently observed in the case of foreign direct investment in the manufacturing sector of host countries. Barriers to entry is one of the contentious issues inherent in the concept of 'market presence' broadly defined.

National Treatment

Related to the issue of entry, and equally contentious, is the principle of national treatment included in the broad interpretation of 'market presence'. Indeed, the broad interpretation appears to advocate no restrictions whatsoever in the interests of market access. The principle of national treatment, applied to producers rather than products, would require that there should be no discrimination between foreign-owned firms and locally owned firms in the host countries with regard to the rules and regulations governing their operations. The principle is often equated with the doctrine of free trade on the grounds that it places locally owned firms and foreign-owned firms on the same footing in their bid for markets. It would require host countries to do away with the variety of regulations and restrictions they place on foreign firms, referred to as performance requirements. The objectives of these requirements are the promotion of local employment, local value added and the growth of locally owned firms, and in general they favour locally owned firms and discriminate against foreign-owned firms.

The thesis, however, is unlikely to find favour with either the developed or the developing countries. Indeed, many of the developing countries are none too happy even with the suggestion that foreign direct investment should be included on the agenda for discussions on liberalization. The fundamental objection to the thesis, however, is that it not only provides for unimpeded entry but also deprives host countries of their right to protect and promote the development of locally owned firms with a potential for growth.

On the other hand, most services transactions, by their very nature, involve international factor flows and this more often than not implies foreign direct investment. The issue then is how best to forge a compromise between the demands of exporters of goods and services, principally the United States, for national treatment and the reluctance of host countries to accord such treatment to foreign firms. Is the principle sacrosanct? Is it vital for the promotion of efficient global resource allocation? These issues will be analyzed in sections II and III of the paper.

Reciprocity

Another controversial aspect of the debate on 'market presence' relates to the concept of reciprocity. Broadly defined, reciprocity refers to the reciprocal exchange of concessions between trading partners which neither party would wish to make in isolation. Reciprocity has been a feature of negotiations on trade liberalization under the aegis of the GATT. It has also figured prominently in the Uruguay Round negotiations on services. The developing countries are concerned that the developed countries would demand concessions on services in return for rollbacks and standstills on restrictions they impose on imports of goods from the developing countries. They argue that standstills and rollbacks should be granted as a right and not tied to negotiations on services. Hence their demand that negotiations on trade in services should proceed separately from negotiations on trade in goods - the so called 'parallel track' approach. The parallel track approach, whatever its perceived advantages, would only make sense, however, if services were distinct from goods. It is arguable whether services are distinct from goods in a sense relevant to trade policy. In any case, little progress may be made on rollbacks and standstills if developing countries continue to insist on a separation of negotiations on services from those on goods. Moreover, in the absence of access to imported services, many of the developing countries which are slowly beginning to tear themselves away from the pursuit of inward-looking development strategies could benefit very little from standstill and rollbacks. The high degree of complementarity that exists not only between goods and services but also between various types of services may render the implementation of reciprocity both impractical and inefficient.

There is, though, one specific category of trade in services in which developing countries may gain by insisting on reciprocity: one of the services activities in which developing countries possess an overriding comparative advantage is in services intensive in the use of unskilled labor, the exportation of which requires migration of labor from the developing to the developed countries. The former group of countries may be well advised to insist on reciprocity within the broad group of services. The concessions they offer on imports of services from the developed countries would be in return for concessions on exports of labor-intensive services. In other words, developing countries could insist on 'market presence' for labour-intensive services in return for granting the right of market access to developed-country services. Immigrant labor, for instance, would be guaranteed its earnings and employment; in the event of the contract coming to a premature end, labor would be compensated for loss of earnings, and for the duration of the contract immigrant labor would be allowed access to social services such as education and health. The Canada-US agreement on free trade contains provisions for 'temporary market presence' of skilled and professional workers, including visits by businessmen, essential for commercial transactions. The agreement could provide a model for negotiations on the right of temporary presence for unskilled labor. Indeed, the agreement could also serve as a model for providing market access to skill-intensive services in the importing countries including the developing countries.

Presence and Establishment in the Context of Trade in Goods

It is worth noting that goods and services are both produced by factors of production. As Sampson and Snape note "it is the 'services' of these factors which create value added or output. Goods are a physical embodiment of factor services while 'services' are more directly supplied by the owners of factors of production to their clientele" (Sampson and Snape 1985). In theory, factor services embodied in goods can be traded across national frontiers without the need for the presence of factors of production in the importing country. Indeed, in the theoretical literature, trade in goods is generally regarded as a substitute for the international movement of factors of production (Corden 1974). There is also the belief, with some support from empirical studies, that barriers to trade in the form of quotas and tariffs are a major motivation for factors of production to move into the importing countries (Huffbauer and Chilas 1974). The proposition is that a firm can penetrate foreign markets either by exporting or producing locally; faced with barriers to its exports, it would be forced to invest in the protected markets. Put differently, foreign firms faced with barriers to trade, are forced to seek 'presence' and 'establishment' in the importing countries.

This line of reasoning suggests that the issue of 'presence' and 'establishment' is irrelevant given free trade in goods. The need for 'presence' and 'establishment' arises only in the presence of barriers to trade. This view, however, may be much too narrow and myopic. It is likely that presence and establishment -- or more specifically foreign direct investment -- may in fact induce and promote trade. The contribution of foreign marketing agencies and buying houses in the importing countries to the promotion of international trade has been referred to earlier. The distribution of products from manufacturers to wholesalers involves relatively heavy overhead costs in the form of construction and maintenance of warehouses, control of inventories and handling of goods. Manufacturing firms can exploit the economies of scale inherent in these activities by pooling their resources for establishing such marketing and distribution facilities. An individual firm would, however, encounter problems in monitoring the performance of the distributors in promoting its products as opposed to those of other firms. For this reason, major multinational enterprises have tended to establish distribution facilities of their own in the importing countries. This tendency on the part of large manufacturing firms to combine manufacturing and non-manufacturing activities has implications for trade. The non-manufacturing distribution wing of the firm in the importing country would be in a position to assemble and transmit information concerning taste patterns, market trends and market conditions to the manufacturing wing of the enterprise in the exporting country. Such information obviously facilitates the promotion of increased trade. The consumers in the importing countries would also gain in terms of speedier access to products tailored to their tastes and preferences.

Several of the empirical studies which have detected a positive relationship between exports and foreign direct investment of the United Kingdom and the United States emphasize this aspect relating to distribution as one of the reasons for the positive relationship (Bergstern, Horst and Moran 1978; also Stopford and Turner 1985). These studies provide an example of the 'presence' of a service activity in the importing country promoting trade in goods.

The presence of foreign firms in the importing countries also generates trade through the demand of imported inputs these firms generate. Again empirical studies have suggested that such investment-induced trade in inputs could be substantial, especially in the case of technologically intensive industries. One of the noticeable examples of such trade relates to assembly operations of foreign firms. The assembly of imported parts and components may be for sale in the local markets or export markets. In the latter case, the presence of foreign firms generates both imports of components and exports of finished products. As is well known, such assembly operations are motivated by the presence of relatively cheap but efficient labour in the importing countries. The gain to the country from the presence of the foreign firms in this case would be the employment it generates. Available empirical evidence, however, is inconclusive on the issue of whether or not the trade in inputs generated by foreign direct investment tends to exceed the trade in final products which it displaces.

Another example of trade-generating foreign direct investment is furnished by export-oriented investments. Frequently cited cases of such export-oriented investments relate to the experience of newly industrializing economies such as Hong Kong, Singapore, Taiwan and, in recent years, Mexico and Brazil (Helleiner 1981; also Hughes and Dorrance 1986). Much has been written on the aspect of foreign-investment-related trade and we need note here only the salient points. First, the presence of foreign firms in these countries has not only provided them with the technology and managerial skills relevant for exporting but also marketing skills and market outlets. Second, 'presence' of foreign firms in these cases does not always consist of foreign direct investment. Foreign presence is also exercised through licensing agreements, management contract, and marketing contracts. While these sorts of arrangements may not involve investment of foreign capital they nonetheless provide for 'foreign presence'. Third, the major input that foreign presence contributes to exporting in these countries consists of know-how including marketing know-how. It is thus that foreign investment assumes the role of a service. Fourth, the experience of these countries suggests that freer trade or an outward-looking strategy of development may not necessarily impede inflows of foreign direct investment. In an environment free of barriers to trade, foreign direct investment may respond to the factor endowments and the climate for investment that the host countries provide.

Yet another relationship between trade and foreign direct investment relates to the phenomenon of *intra-industry trade*. This consists in the exchange of manufactures for manufactures and especially in the simultaneous import and export of manufactures from the same product line. In simple terms it refers to the growth of international trade in differentiated products -- for example, the export of large cars from the United States to the European countries and the import of small cars from European countries into the United States. A large proportion of such trade occurs between developed countries but the phenomenon is swiftly spreading to trade involving developing countries.[1]

The gains to trading partners from growth in intra-industry trade are obvious. Such trade provides consumers with a large variety of goods to choose from, it promotes increased specialization and the gains associated with such specialization, and it spurs innovation. One of the proximate causes of the growth in intra-industry trade is foreign direct investment. Firms endowed with technological and managerial skills invest abroad and establish production facilities for a variety of reasons. One such reason is their desire to exploit economies of scale in producing a particular variety of a product. Whilst they may be able to produce a particular variety of the product in one specific country they are able to sell the variety in all markets. Thus they tend to invest in the production of specific varieties of products in specific markets and sell different varieties of the products in all markets. The production activities of Ford of Europe provide an example. Specific plants of Ford in different countries specialize in particular models of cars but each plant services all consumers in Western Europe. It is thus that foreign direct investment or presence of foreign firms generates intra-industry trade (Greenaway and Milner 1986).

In sum, presence and establishment of foreign firms promote trade in several ways. The significant point to note, though, is that foreign direct investment in general is essentially in the nature of a service and it is this characteristic that contributes to the promotion of trade. This contribution of foreign investment to trade is significant in the context of the current debate on liberalization. Liberalization is not advocated as an end in itself: it is a means of achieving an efficient allocation of global resources, which in turn would promote the welfare of the trading nations of the world. Foreign direct investment is one method of promoting specialization in production and trade based on comparative advantage. Most nation-states acknowledge the contribution foreign direct investment could make to the realisation of these objectives; but they are concerned that the gains from foreign direct investment may not always accrue to their citizens or that the distribution of the gains may be heavily weighted in favour of the foreign investors. Hence the various sorts of regulations they impose on foreign firms, most of which are designed with the objective of enhancing the share of the gains from foreign direct investment accruing to the domestic economy.

In the context of trade and foreign investment the most significant of such regulations relate to trade related investment performance (TRIM) requirements. TRIM requirements include host-government measures designed to increase the local procurement of inputs by foreign-owned firms or joint ventures and/or to increase the exports of those investments (Moran and Pearson 1988). Moran and Pearson note that both the developing and developed countries stipulate TRIM measures and that the implicit performance requirements imposed on foreign firms by the developed countries are very much similar in nature to the explicit TRIM measures imposed by developing countries. In terms of numbers of countries imposing TRIM measures, though, they are more prevalent in developing countries than in developed countries. The incidence of such measures appears to be relatively high in specific industries such as automobiles, food processing, chemicals and petro-chemicals, and computers and office equipment.[2]

Theoretical analysis of TRIM measures suggests that they could prove to be counter-productive. TRIM measures requiring foreign firms to purchase a specified share of their inputs locally may inflate their costs of production and reduce the value added and employment in the production of the final good. They may also reduce their competitiveness in export markets with an unfavourable outcome for the trade balance of the host countries. On the other hand, they could have favourable effects. TRIM measures may compel foreign firms to seek relatively cheap and efficient sources of supply of inputs in the domestic economy, they could induce them to impart technology and know-how to local producers of inputs, and they may induce them to increase their competitiveness in third markets. In any case, available evidence suggests that the adverse consequences of TRIM requirements for trade and employment tend not to be significant. Moran and Pearson conclude, on the basis of available evidence, that "estimates of the extent to which TRIM requirements actually alter patterns of trade, displace production or cost jobs vary between industries, but consistently they suggest that TRIM requirements tend to have a small overall impact" (Moran and Pearson 1988). It is also interesting to note that entrepreneurs tend to view TRIM requirements with equanimity; their attitude is that they would have in any case sought local suppliers of inputs and promoted exports and that TRIM requirements only accelerate the implementation of their intentions.

TRIM requirements imposed on foreign firms, however, violate the principle of national treatment discussed earlier. But in view of the evidence that their adverse consequences are not significant and they quite often promote national objectives, it could be argued that strict adherence to the principle may not be necessary. There may be nothing sacrosanct about the principle. In so far as rules and regulations imposed by host countries do not interfere with the promotion of specialization and trade based on comparative advantage their right to impose such regulations should be conceded. The pragmatic approach would be to seek ways and means of mitigating the adverse consequences of regulations such as TRIM requirements rather than to urge their removal.

Host countries could be asked to invoke TRIM requirements only in the presence of evidence of an excessive bias on the part of foreign firms, unjustified by economic considerations of costs and efficiency, in favour of imported inputs. Foreign firms could be required to seek and promote efficient local suppliers of inputs with the proviso that failure to do so would result in the imposition of TRIM requirements. Another solution, which in essence would preserve the principle of national treatment, would be to subject all firms, irrespective of their nationality, to increased levels of taxation, with the proviso that all firms which purchase a relatively high proportion of their inputs locally and engage in exporting would be entitled to tax rebates. Firms which demonstrate an unavoidable need for imported inputs could also be accorded tax rebates. The problem with this scheme, however, is that it calls for a high degree of fiscal and administrative expertise, which many host countries may not possess.

This section of the paper has analysed the issue of 'presence' and 'establishment' in the context of trade-related foreign direct investment. It has underscored the need for a pragmatic approach to the principle of national treatment. Much the same sorts of issues arise in the case of services and the 'right of establishment' and 'presence'.

"Presence" and "Establishment" in the Context of Services

The debate on liberalization of trade in services is essentially a debate on the issue of 'presence' and 'establishment'. For, as argued earlier, most service transactions by definition involve proximity between producers and consumers of services. In large part such proximity requires 'presence' and 'establishment' of service producers in the locale of the consumers. The point has also been made earlier that services complement and promote the production and trade of goods.

The issue then is not so much the need for presence and establishment but the nature and extent of presence and establishment. Analysis of this issue requires discussion of the types and varieties of services. There is now a sizeable literature on the taxonomy of services (Sampson and Snape 1985; also Lanvin 1987) but for purposes of the discussion the following broad types of services are identified.

- Services which are inextricably intermingled with the production of goods

- Services which are essential inputs in the production of goods but are separable from goods for purposes of trade

- Services which aid production and trade of goods but are separable from production activities.

- Services which are in the nature of essential inputs in the production of other services and goods.

This classification is based on the nature and end use of services and not on their tradeability. As argued earlier all services are tradeable, they can be embodied in goods and transported across national borders or traded through the mobility of factors of production that produce them. The classification is designed to analyse the nature and extent of 'presence' and/or 'establishment' required for effective transactions in services.

The first category of services may require the establishment of foreign firms for the efficient production of goods. Certain types of technology and managerial know-how may be inseparable from the corporate entity which produces the goods. Such technology-intensive goods also tend to be subject to rapid product-and-process-oriented innovations. Efficient production of such goods would require continuous interaction between managers and plant-level workers and technicians. In other words, such production activities may require effective control over operations, which can only be derived from ownership of equity by the foreign firm. The automobile industry, which is experiencing wide-ranging process and production innovations, provides an example of an activity where managerial and technical services may be inseparable from the process of production. It is reported that most developing countries, which are recipients of foreign technology and managerial know-how in the industry, are conceding the need for effective control over operations by the multinational corporations investing in the industry (O'Brian 1988). Majority ownership of equity by foreign firms, or establishment, appears to be gaining in importance in the case of this industry.

Does establishment, however, necessarily imply national treatment in the case of this category of services? Regulations such as TRIM requirements, especially those relating to local content of inputs and export requirements, may constitute barriers to entry. But, as argued in section II, there are ways and means of preserving the spirit and objectives of TRIM requirements but at the same time minimizing their adverse consequences. In any case, host countries wishing to promote industrialization and exports based on technology-intensive industries would have to exercise discretion in implementing regulations such as TRIMs. For the demand for technological and managerial know-how associated with such industries tends to be relatively high and host countries can ill afford to place restrictions on the operation of foreign firms supplying these inputs.

In the second category of services, where services are separable from the production of goods, 'presence' or access to markets may suffice without the need for establishment. Relatively simple technologies can be embodied in blueprints, designs and drawings and transmitted to importing countries. Indeed, technological change, especially that associated with the information technology industry, has opened up a wide range of opportunities for transmission of services without the need for establishment. The contractual arrangements on the basis of which such transmission can take place are the management contracts and licensing agreements discussed earlier. These provide for 'presence' in the sense of 'market access' without establishment.

Such technology licensing agreements between firms in the developed countries and locally owned firms in developing countries have grown in extent and numbers in recent years. Brazil, India and South Korea have shown a marked preference for such arrangements as opposed to foreign direct investment (UNCTC 1980).

As stated earlier, however, these arrangements for the transmission of technological and managerial know-how are not without their problems. They too are subject to rules and regulations imposed by the importing countries. Such regulations include ceilings on royalty rates and fees, limits on the duration of agreements, and specification of industries and sectors which are eligible to enter into licensing agreements and management contracts with foreign firms. Most of these regulations are designed to conserve foreign exchange and delimit foreign control over the domestic economy. Such regulations, though, violate the principle of national treatment to the extent that they limit foreign enterprise participation and competition in the importing country. But more often than not the brunt of such regulations is borne by the locally owned firms importing the technology rather than by foreign firms which export the technology. The onus of making a case for the imports of foreign technology and for exemptions from the regulations rests on the importing firms.

Paradoxically, in the case of these arrangements, the principle of national treatment may be violated more often than not by the exporters of technological and managerial services rather than the importers. As stated in section II, technology-exporting firms frequently impose a variety of restrictions on exports of products embodying the imported know-how, on sources of purchase of inputs, and on dissemination of imported 'know-how' to other locally owned firms. All such restrictions are designed to gain control over operations and protect the markets for the goods and technology of the exporting firms. The point to note, however, is that such restrictions discriminate against locally owned firms and in favour of the foreign firms. They delimit market access for locally owned firms and influence their choice of inputs in favour of imported inputs supplied by the technology-exporting firms.

The problem merits serious consideration in view of the fact that the feasibility and efficiency of technology-licensing agreements and management contracts, as vehicles for the transmission of technology and human skills, are likely to be enhanced with the revolutionary changes occurring in information technology and related industries. Several attempts have been made by international institutions and host-country governments to ban the imposition of restrictive clauses in technology-licensing agreements. But foreign firms may resort to implicit rather than explicit methods of imposing such restrictions and regulations on the importing firms. It is to be noted that if the importing firms willingly accept such restrictions it is indicative of the strength of their need for imported know-how.

One solution to the problem would be to remove ceilings and limits on royalty rates and technology fees imposed by host countries as a *quid pro quo* for the removal of restrictions placed by foreign firms. Admittedly, such a move may increase the prices charged by the foreign firms for the technology they supply, but locally owned firms would gain freedom of operations with regard to sourcing of inputs and also access to export markets. It is also likely that the innovations occurring in information technology industries may generate increased competition for markets on the part of existing suppliers of technology and usher in new entrants to the market; both of which should result in a general reduction in prices charged for know-how and technology.

The third category of services relates to those that aid the production and trade of goods, but are separable from the production of goods. Examples of such services include banking, insurance, marketing and distribution. This category of services poses a complex set of issues in the context of liberalization of trade in services, most of which have been discussed in the sizeable literature on services. We discuss here the salient points in the context of the issue of 'presence' and 'establishment'.

There is no need to emphasize the importance of financial and related services in the promotion and growth of the goods-manufacturing sector. Such services range from the provision of bank finance to industry to the underwriting and placing of new issues of the manufacturing sector. Such services can no doubt take the form of long-distance services and be transacted 'over the wires'. But it is generally recognised that, in order to provide appropriate and efficient service, the physical presence of the provider of the service in the locale of the purchaser of the service is essential. It is also to be recognised that financial and related services encompass a wide variety and that the services rendered are highly differentiated and often tailored to the specific needs of the purchaser. Moreover, risk assessment and the evaluation of the financial viability of the project to be financed requires physical proximity between the producers and purchasers of the service. In essence, establishment defined to mean both market presence and ownership and control of the entity providing the services may be necessary.

It is, though, a widely noted fact that the principle of non-discrimination is rarely adhered to in the case of financial services. Most countries, be they developed or developing, impose a variety of restrictions on the scope, extent, and nature of the activities of foreign providers of financial services. These include market delineation, imposition of limits on assets foreign institutions can own, regulations including reserve requirements and capitalization limits, and stipulations requiring foreign firms to place foreign currencies in some proportion to the volume of domestic lending they undertake with the central bank of the country. These and other measures are essentially in the nature of quantitative restrictions or non-tariff barriers to trade in financial services (Walters 1985).

There is little doubt that such host-country restrictions and regulations inhibit the efficiency of operations in the goods-producing sector. They not only delimit access to sources of finance for the manufacturing sector but also raise the cost of finance. As Ingo Walter notes, protection of the financial sector reduces the degree of effective protection enjoyed by the manufacturing sector. In other words, it increases the costs of production and reduces the value added in the manufacturing sector and also denies the sector valuable advisory services foreign financial firms may be able to provide.

It is, however, unrealistic to expect importing countries to disband the various regulations they impose on foreign firms. Most countries, especially the developing countries, regard the financial sector as one of the commanding heights of the economy and would be loath to relinquish control over it. Also a policy of free trade in financial services may impair the promotion of domestic monetary policy objectives. The realistic solution to the problem would be to recognise the need for host-country regulations but negotiate for a gradual reduction in such regulations over time. A sectoral approach to liberalization, with due recognition of host-country objectives, would be much more realistic than an all-out bid for free trade. It is also worth noting that developing countries are likely to follow suit if the developed countries take the initiative in liberalizing the financial sector. The proposed unification of the financial sector of the EEC countries by the year 1992 may accelerate the process of liberalization elsewhere in the world.

The fourth category of services, those that are in the nature of inputs into goods and other services, raise policy issues which are much more complex than those raised by the other three categories. These relate to services and service-related activities in the area of information generation, information processing and information transmission. This sector of service activity is experiencing a radical transformation with the rapid technological change that has occurred in computer and telecommunication technologies. These developments have far-reaching implications for international trade in goods and services in general and for international trade in information and information-intensive services in particular. Section IV of the paper addresses this aspect in the context of the issue of 'presence' and 'establishment'.

International Trade in Information Services

The phrase 'information revolution' has now become common currency although the magnitude of the revolution is not always fully comprehended. The revolution has wrought significant structural changes in the economies of the industrialized countries and it may not be long before the developing countries also experience its impact. Information and information-related industries account for 50 to 60 percent of the GNP and for nearly 50 percent of the work force in the industrialised countries (Lanvin 1987). That information is an input into the production process of goods and services has long been recognised and the revolution has served to enhance its importance and visibility.

The information technology sector is a complicated amalgam of a number of sub-sectors. Broadly defined it consists of two sub-sectors: computers and telecommunications. The former includes hardware, software to be used in conjunction with the hardware, and data-processing services. Telecommunications not only include data-processing and transmission and retrieval of data, but also the production of telecommunication equipment including terminal equipment ,transmission equipment and switching equipment.

Technological developments in the industry have had a significant impact on trade in information. As Karl Sauvant notes, "modern telecommunication facilities have overcome time and distance as major obstacles to access to sophisticated computer services for the processing, storage, and retrieval of machine-readable data. The transnationalization of this process, in turn, has given rise to transborder data flows (TDF); international data transmissions over transnational computer-communication systems" (Sauvant 1983).

Available estimates show a rapid growth in transborder data flows. The United Nations Centre on Transnational Corporations noted in its technical paper on transborder data flows published in 1982 that "the volume of data flows (as measured by the number of transactions between data communication users) originating on an average working day in Western Europe will increase from approximately 136 million transactions in 1979 to almost 800 million in 1987; of these the share of international transactions is expected to rise from 10 to 15 percent during the time period" (UNCTC 1982).

The developed countries account for the bulk of these flows. Moreover, as the UNCTC report notes, all aspects of the market for data - from the manufacturing of the equipment to the transborder use of machine-readable data are a domain of the transnational corporations located in the developed countries, principally in the United States. More often than not, affiliates of these corporations in the importing countries, especially those in the developing countries, export raw data to the parent firms and import the processed data.

There is no need to emphasize the benefits flowing from the information revolution and the consequent growth in transborder data flows. It provides producers and users of goods and services with instant access to up-to-date information, facilitates decision making, promotes specialization and efficient global allocation of resources, and opens up new vistas to both producers and consumers in terms of technologies and products. The growth in transborder data flows that has occurred in recent years is only the beginning. By all accounts it is poised to grow further, both in terms of volume and geographical spread. And, with its growth and spread, existing trade and production patterns are likely to alter, the seat of corporate power and decision-making is likely to shift in favour of those entities which control the generation and dissemination of information, and the information have-nots are likely to be faced with difficult choices.

These developments cast a new light on the issue of 'presence' and 'establishment.' Two opposing tendencies are likely to emerge. One would render 'presence' without 'establishment' feasible, an outcome that importing countries are likely to welcome. The second is not only likely to render 'presence' without 'establishment' feasible but also preserve all the features of establishment, an outcome unlikely to find favour with the importing countries.

The first outcome is likely because of the ease with which complex data and information can be transmitted across national borders. Managerial and technological know-how can be separated from the production process and conveyed to the producers of goods and services in the importing countries. As managers in the exporting countries can monitor and guide operations from afar through recourse to telematic channels of communications there would be no need for their physical presence in the countries where the production takes place. For these reasons, management contracts and licensing agreements between foreign firms and locally owned firms may grow in importance as compared to foreign direct investment. And to the extent these arrangements permit foreign firms to participate in the markets of the importing countries they would enjoy 'presence' without 'establishment'.

There is, though, the opposing tendency towards increased centralization of operations that the information revolution is likely to promote. The ease with which data and information can be assembled, processed, retrieved, and transmitted may enable transnational corporations to wield effective control over operations of their affiliates abroad. Indeed, they could also exercise control over the operation of non-affiliates with which they may have forged technological and managerial links. As many studies on multinationals have noted, intra-firm transactions which bypass the market are the essence of the process of internationalization of firms. And the internalization of all transactions within the firm bestows on it increased power over decision-making in areas such as the pricing of inputs and products, the location of plants, and marketing. It is thus that the information revolution may endow foreign firms with all the benefits of 'establishment' and 'presence' without the need for their physical presence in the locales of production.

Another consequence of the information revolution relates to location decisions of manufacturing firms. Here again two opposing sets of tendencies may be at work. The hitherto observed tendency of multinational corporations to establish manufacturing plants in countries endowed with relatively cheap labour -- to farm out the labour-intensive segments of the manufacturing operation to such countries -- may tend to wane. This could occur because of the increased opportunities for mechanization and the substitution of capital for labour which the information revolution makes possible. This could result in the loss of market presence in the developed countries for the export-oriented developing countries.

It is, though, possible that the information revolution would in fact promote the location of labour-intensive manufacturing operations in the labour-rich countries. Such location choices could occur because of the ease with which managerial and technical know-how associated with labour-intensive activities could be swiftly and efficiently transmitted to the developing countries. It is hard to say which of these two opposing tendencies is likely to gain prominence. The outcome may well hinge on the receptivity of host countries to foreign-enterprise participation in their countries but these countries may be at a disadvantage in their ability to bargain with multinationals on the terms and conditions of foreign-enterprise participation.

Another significant aspect of 'presence' and 'establishment' relates to the location of information technology industries and services. This aspect, which has been the subject of intense debate, encompasses two issues. The first relates to the location of industries producing the hardware -- computers and related products -- and the second relates to the location of data-processing facilities.

The intense concern expressed by most countries, especially the developing countries, with regard to both these issues stems from the dominance of the developed countries -- and especially the United States -- in all segments of the information industry including the production of computers and the associated software, and data processing and transmission facilities. Much of the data-processing facilities are located at the headquarters of transnational corporations with their foreign affiliates linked to the central system through terminals. The obvious concern of countries in the lower divisions of the information-technology league is that the American dominance of the industry is not only inimical to the growth and development of local capabilities but also poses a threat to their political sovereignty and national economic objectives. The policy stances and policy pronouncements on the future course of production and trade in information technology reflect the prevailing distribution of economic power in the sector. As the UNCTC report on transborder data flows, cited earlier, notes, "a number of developed countries, most notably the United States, insist that the establishment of any framework for non-personal transborder data flows must be guided by the recognition of the principles relating to a free flow of information, free enterprise, free trade, and the adequate availability of appropriate telecommunication facilities and services" (UNCTC 1982). A number of other countries including Canada, the European Community, France, Sweden, and Brazil have not only advocated government intervention and regulation of the market for information but also instituted a regulatory framework. Among the developing countries, Brazil has taken the lead in instituting a national computer policy. Many of the regulations instituted by these countries are designed to protect and promote national capabilities in information technology and related industries. In general they delimit the extent and areas of activities of foreign-owned firms and hence violate the principle of national treatment.

The position of the United States cited above amounts to an advocacy of the right of establishment encompassing the principle of national treatment. While on the economic grounds of efficiency in trade and production in such a case may be strong, it is unlikely for obvious reasons to find favour with the other developed countries -- let alone the developing countries. The developed countries, however, are likely to face the perceived threat from the U.S. to their national objectives and the development of local capabilities through various measures designed to enhance the efficiency of their industries. These include cooperative research and development, mergers of existing production facilities with a view to achieving economies of scale, and the allocation of resources to areas of activity in which they possess a comparative advantage. Such pooling and allocation of resources are already actively taking place in the European Community; and the Community has expressed an interest in an administrative approach to the issue of national treatment which amounts essentially to a case-by-case negotiated approach instead of an all-embracing free trade compact (*Financial Times* 1987).

The developing countries, however, find themselves in a less fortunate position than the developed countries. Very few developing countries possess local capabilities in the production of computers and other hardware and countries such as India and Brazil which do possess such capabilities are faced with chronic problems of inefficiency associated with most import substituting industries. The dilemma facing them is that they can neither

152

afford to be passive bystanders in the information revolution nor can they actively participate in it. The web of regulations they have imposed on foreign firms, however, may prove to be counter-productive. Given the nature of the information-technology industry, in the absence of active cooperation and help on the part of the transnationals that own and control information technology, these countries are unlikely to succeed in developing local capabilities. In any case, the massive resources required to exploit the economies of scale inherent in most information technology industries may be beyond their reach.

One way out of the dilemma for the developing countries would be to recognize and accept the realities of the situation and seek manageable niches within the vast web of the information-technology industry. Several developing countries such as India and Brazil possess a comparative advantage in the production and export of software. The establishment of foreign producers of hardware in these countries may promote the demand for such software. Again, they may specialize in the provision of human skills and capabilities required for data-processing. They may urge the cooperation and assistance of transnational corporations in the promotion of the production of and trade in goods and services in which they possess a comparative advantage as a prerequisite for the right of 'establishment'.

The issues of 'presence' and 'establishment' in the context of transborder data flows, as opposed to the context of the production and distribution of hardware, are much more complex. Most developing countries at present have a relatively low involvement in such trade; in cases where it exists they are likely to be exporters of information to be processed in the head offices of transnationals. Admittedly, considerations of efficiency may require centralization of data-processing. But this is a segment of the industry which involves a relatively high degree of human skill with opportunities for learning by doing. It is also an area of activity in which developing countries are likely to possess a comparative advantage. The developing countries may be well advised to insist on 'establishment' rather than mere 'presence' in the case of this segment of the information-technology industry. In this context, 'presence' would amount to the installation of terminals linked to a central data-processing system, whereas 'establishment' would involve the presence of data-processing facilities and opportunities for training in the use of such facilities for nationals of the country.

In sum, the policy options open to developing countries with regard to 'presence' and 'establishment' in the context of the information-technology sector in general may be much more limited than those open to the developed countries. Even so, they may have room for manoeuvre provided they set their sights on objectives that are achievable rather than those that are only theoretically possible.

Conclusions

This paper has focused on the issues of 'presence' and 'right of establishment.' It has attempted to define the concepts and analyze the problems they pose for policy in the context of trade in goods, trade in services, and the emerging trade in information services. The thrust of the paper is to argue that little can be achieved by insisting either on the 'right of establishment' interpreted to mean a policy of *laissez faire* and national treatment or on a rigid commitment to a complex regulatory framework. Given the complex nature of trade in services in general and trade in information services in particular it may not be realistic to formulate all-embracing general guiding principles. There may be no alternative to a sector-by-sector approach to the issue, based on gradualism.

ENDNOTES

1 Available estimates show that in 1978 intra-industry trade accounted for 64 percent of trade between the developed countries, 48 percent of the trade of newly industrialized countries with the developed countries, 22 percent of the trade of developing countries with countries other than the newly industrialized countries, and 38 percent of trade between the newly industrialized countries.

2 Empirical evidence on the incidence of TRIM measures is scant, not because they are not prevalent, but because they are not reported either by host governments or foreign firms, and no official agency has a mandate to collect such information. The evidence reported by Moran and Pearce is culled from several survey-based studies.

"APPROPRIATE REGULATION" FOR COMMUNICATION AND INFORMATION SERVICES

Ester Stevers and Christopher Wilkinson

Introduction

The Concept of Regulation

Regulation, both as a legal and an economic concept, refers to the use of legal powers by public authorities in order to direct the conduct of actors in the market (Stigler, 1981:73; Bauer, 1987:3). The formal competence of regulators is based on a legal statute, e.g., a constitution, a law, an international treaty. Regulators' formal mandate to serve the "public interest" tends to be restricted by the meaning this expansive term takes from the purposes of the particular regulatory legislation involved (Supreme Court, 1976).

Regulatory measures are generally justified as being necessary to cope with market failure and there is a set of classical rationales for these measures (Breyer, 1982: 34-35). More sophisticated and comprehensive research has led to an increased knowledge of, and concern with, the costs of regulation. Three main sources of regulatory ineffectiveness may be distinguished:

1. organizational inefficiency of the regulatory body,

2. mismatch between regulatory measures and the characteristics of the economic processes in the market, and

3. the pursuit by regulators of objectives that are contrary to the "public interest".[1]

At present, a reassessment of the regulatory process -- its instruments and their consequences (efficiency and distributional effects) --is under way in an attempt to find a new balance between a fully regulated and a completely unregulated market.

A major concern in the regulatory debate at a national level is the competitiveness of national industries. Technical and organizational inefficiency in regulated industries and allocation inefficiency in the affected industries increase the pressure for regulatory change. The principal concepts in this so-called "deregulation debate" are: competition, liberalization and privatization.

Competition is often seen as the alternative to regulation. With liberalization, efficiency costs of regulation are expected to diminish and, especially when competition emerges, the necessary adaptation of the previously protected industries is likely to increase their efficiency and competitiveness. The liberalization process may involve the total or partial privatization or denationalization of the industry but it is not incompatible with public ownership. Moreover, competition need not by itself reduce the demand for regulation. The transition process of liberalization as well as new competitive market sectors as such may call for new and other forms of regulatory control. One has also to consider an increased danger of the abuse of a dominant position by a deregulated or private monopoly. Free entry may have negative effects on product and service quality and lead to increased externalities. A renewed demand for regulation can arise in reaction to distributional effects of liberalization, which effects may run counter to other policy objectives (e.g., regional development, anti-trust goals).

Since liberalization alone does not guarantee effective competition, a thorough analysis of the obstacles to competition and to (national) competitiveness will be essential. Fear of foreign entrants - especially during a first adaptation period -- can lead to protective regulation such as restrictive licensing.[2] The increased technological and economic interdependence may turn into greater dependence for the competitively weaker countries (Schulte-Hillen BDU, 1988: 22-25). In areas where international coordination and harmonization of regulation is mandatory (e.g., market-access conditions, network interconnectivity, environmental externalities) balances are sought between the benefits of increased cooperation and harmonized regulation on the one hand and the cost of growing dependence on the other.

The Effects of Regulation on Trade in Telecommunication and Data Services

The communication-and-information-services sector is subject to a wide range of regulations. Such regulations may create obstacles for trade in these services and/or divergent market-access conditions leading to international friction. The absence of regulation (e.g., in the field of privacy protection) and the lack of regulatory harmonization (e.g., in the case of usage conditions) and transparency may have trade-distortive effects.

Advances in technology and the growing commercial and strategic importance of telecommunications have led to pressures for regulatory change in this sector. Because of different responses to these changing conditions and different constitutional, legal and administrative structures, the market structure for telecommunication services has lost much of its homogeneity. These growing differences between regulatory regimes, especially with regard to market-entry possibilities, reinforce the need for a set of commonly accepted rules governing trade in communication and information services.

Moreover, the centrality of telecommunications to trade in services, the requirements of economies of scale and scope (Fuss, 1983), the demand for better international service provision and the risks of by-pass have increased the pressure for a multilateral effort to reach agreement on regulatory coordination and harmonization and to reduce regulatory obstacles to the development of trade in services.

In negotiations on a multilateral trade agreement for telecommunication services, the question of appropriate and inappropriate regulation becomes crucial. Each government has a right to determine its own regulatory regime in accordance with its objectives and circumstances. At the same time, each government must take into account the effects of its regulatory policies on common international goals such as the expansion of mutually beneficial trade and economic growth and development. The tension between the different objectives involved in creating a regulatory regime has to be reduced by reaching agreement on the appropriateness of regulations.

Appropriate Regulation and International Trade

Regulation may be judged to be appropriate in terms of its objectives (guaranteeing service, safeguarding privacy, cultural identity, and national security) or its means. Means are appropriate to the extent that they are effective in reaching the objective. A regulatory measure may thus be considered appropriate if it is relevant to its objective, not disproportionate in its means and minimally distortive in its effects (OECD/TC, 1987(2):12).

If appropriate regulation is described as the optimal balance between regulatory costs and benefits in furthering the public interest, then two major problems in establishing such regulation become apparent:

1. to the extent that "public interest" is related to space and time, the appropriateness of regulation cannot be determined in absolute terms and priorities have to be set and

2. the concept of appropriateness has to be operational: specific goals and concrete regulatory measures should be determined taking particular efficiency and distributional effects into account.

Multilateral negotiations on a regulatory framework imply the involvement of several countries whose "public interest" may require different sub-goals and regulatory measures. In order to determine the appropriateness of regulation, a hierarchy of priorities has to be decided on with regard to:

1. the "public interest" of one country or group of countries as compared to the "public interest" of other countries and

2. certain sub-goals and regulatory measures (means) as compared to others.

Acceptability to the negotiating partners may be taken as the criterion for the appropriateness of such a hierarchy of priorities as well as of the resulting regulations.[3]

The Uruguay Declaration which sets out the mandate for negotiations on trade in services (Part II) states as twin objectives the "economic growth of all trading partners" and the "development of developing countries". In so far as the Declaration does not rank-order the two objectives or the interests of countries or groups of countries (e.g., economic growth does not necessarily require the same regulations for each trading partner), the negotiating partners will still have to decide on their priorities. The appropriateness of these priorities and of the resulting regulations may be judged by their acceptability to the negotiating partners which in turn may be based on consensus or on an agreed-upon voting procedure.

Besides the above-mentioned twin objectives which may be considered the ultimate purpose of the negotiations, the Declaration sets out the subsidiary objective of achieving an "expansion of trade [in services] under conditions of transparency and progressive liberalization". Four categories of regulation may be distinguished with regard to this objective:

1. regulation which supports international trade (e.g., harmonized regulations on charging principles, rules on transparency) and is acceptable to the negotiating partners,

2. regulation inhibiting international trade but acceptable since it is considered justified by national or international public interest (e.g., national security, pluralism, privacy protection),

3. regulation supporting international trade but not acceptable to the negotiating partners (e.g., the regulation may distort the growth and/or development of a particular group of countries), and

4. regulation inhibiting international trade but not justified by other goals and consequently not acceptable.

In the light of the Uruguay Declaration, the first two categories are forms of appropriate regulation in so far as they further economic growth and development and the last two are forms of inappropriate regulation.

The Declaration gives priority to liberalization and transparency as means to reach the objectives. Other principles developed in international trade negotiations and especially in the GATT context may act as guidelines for selecting the means to achieve the declared objectives in an appropriate manner.

The Role of Regulation in the Communications and Information Sector

Convergence

At the basis of the current transformation of telecommunication, information and audio-visual sectors into an integrated whole, is the tremendous change in technology. The development and convergency of technologies from originally separate sectors are blurring traditional boundaries. Moreover, company strategies, user demands and regulations are themselves influencing technological change (Dosie, 1981) and are in constant interaction with one another. These developments are primarily responsible for the growing complexity of regulation in the communication and information area.

Technological Change and Services Development

The technological developments in transmission, switching and terminal functions and consequent changes in network economics have led to increased differentiation of network services and have blurred the boundaries between the roles of the different networks, between network and terminal functions and between telecommunication and electronic data-processing functions (European Commission, 1987 (COM)87)290):28-43).

Digitalization of signals carrying information allows for the operation of telecommunication functions -- both transmission and switching -- in a digital form and, furthermore, for the introduction of computer technology for network intelligence. Improvement of cable technology (coaxial cable, optical fibre) and microwave, and the development of satellite transmission together with the new network intelligence functions increase the transport capacity and reliability of telecommunication networks. The trend towards "neutral" digital networks capable simultaneously of combining and transporting different forms of information (sound, text, moving image) increases the potential for service differentiation and blurs the boundaries between these services.

Apart from their constituent components, networks are also different in configuration: e.g., switching networks, point-to- point networks, distributive networks. The incorporation of switching technology into cable TV networks enables operators to segment their services and to offer two-way services. Moreover, the use of fibre-optic cable will increase the capacity of the network. The rapidly growing use of satellites allows for even more flexibility in network configuration. The networks are now able to provide point-to-point, point-to-multi-point, and multi-point-to-multi-point services. Satellites can also provide transmission capacity for two-way transmissions. The increased flexibility in network configuration is another important factor in enabling the different existing networks to provide a larger range of mutually overlapping services.

The increased complexity of terminals has also contributed to the growing diversity and integration of telecommunication services. In terminal equipment, a trend towards integration of functions is developing. These functions may relate to network needs (e.g., routing control), the usability of the terminal (e.g., memory dialer), or even applications completely separate from the network (e.g., a clock in a telephone). The developments in multi-functional terminals and in digital multi-configurational networks are mutually reinforcing and blur traditional boundaries in service provision.

Furthermore, functions which were previously carried out inside the network can now be carried out outside the network by intelligent digital terminal equipment. This is blurring the distinction between network and terminal functions. Finally, the computerization of terminals and switches leads to the convergence of telecommunication and electronic data-processing functions.

The implications of technological change for network economics are also affecting service provision. Major changes in network economics are:

- the costs of transmission and bandwidth use have fallen;

- the costs related to distance have declined compared with the costs of connection time (the cost of using satellites is indeed independent of distance), and

- the costs to the user of terminal equipment is declining.

Company Strategy and Service Provisions

Technology, increasing user demands and regulatory change are strongly affecting company strategy and service provision in the communication and information market.

Convergence of technologies and network services and related increase in user demand have led to new entrants and new forms of collaboration in this market. At both international and domestic levels, firms predominantly active in the supply of telecommunication, information and audio-visual services, in computer and network equipment provision and even in relatively unrelated sectors, have been entering the expanding market for network services (Mansell, a.o., 1988:4). To span the full breadth of required competence, to overcome high investment costs (e.g., for hardware, software and marketing) and regulatory restrictions (e.g., on market access, right of investment, right of establishment), new strategic alliances have emerged. Differences among sectors, especially in technical culture, marketing and regulatory environment, are inhibiting firms from covering new parts of the communication and information market alone. Specific difficulties in this market concern the dependence on the developments in the network and equipment market, the need for a minimal viable customer base in order to profit from economies of scale and scope and the existence of dominant firms (official or de-facto monopolies) and strong vertical relations in the markets (Vanguard/U.K. Department of Trade and Industry, 1987). Moreover, uncertainty is caused by the difficulty of planning for changes in demand and regulation.

User demand for network services has been strongly stimulated both by the growing importance of information and communication in modern economy and by the increased diversity and superior quality of these services due to technological change. However, unstable demand and differences in user groups' interests and market power make it hard to evaluate the impact of user demand on company strategy and service provision. Large multi-plant companies might be expected to have a disproportionate influence in comparison to their actual number. Because they are major users, they express most strongly the need for cost-based, high-quality services and they are the most demanding regarding reliability and security. To the extent that public and/or private providers of network capacity and services are unable to cope with these requirements, development of private lines and in-house services (by-pass) and pressure for open market access and competition can be expected (Bar, and Borrus, 1987). However, given the high cost of these private services, the complexity of regulation and the difficulty of marketing spare capacity, [4] external networks and services will usually be preferred whenever they are adequate. Improvements of public networks (e.g., ISDN) and the emergence of multiple combinations of function packages (e.g., Managed Data Network Service (MDNS)) are likely to countervail by-pass trends. Small and medium-sized users (business or residential), in particular, depend on the public network and external services. Consequently, they have a major interest in the public network and services in terms of low costs, broad geographical coverage and diversity (adapted to specific needs of small user groups).

Ongoing re-assessment of and changes in regulation -- at the national as well as at the international level -- and the consequent uncertainty and lack of transparency are responsible for problems in market planning and reluctance in market entry (Taylor, and Williams, 1987). The kind of regulatory decisions which are important for company strategy include:

- market access conditions (competitive service provision, separation of regulatory and operational activities),

- usage conditions (e.g., shared use or third-party use for leased lines, resale of spare capacity of private lines),

- user charges (e.g., cost-related, usage-sensitive separation of transmission and value-adding functions),

- interconnectivity (e.g., clear definitions and publication of technical standards, charging principles, user conditions), and

- legal issues affecting the unrestricted flow of information (privacy protection, intellectual property, national security, cultural identity, advertisement, etc.).

Differences in company strategy may arise from national differences in market structure, the characteristics of the users and the regulatory environment. The resulting strategies determine, *inter alia*:

- preferential development of the market for services directed to specialist user groups,

- where and at what cost new services are available (especially at the international level),

- the degree of interconnectivity between different user systems, and

- developments in related sectors (e.g., hardware and software industry) and in the information-and-communication-dependent industries in general.

Convergence and Regulatory Change

Technological change and consequent developments in the equipment and service markets have led to strong pressures for regulatory change in the communication and information area.[5] The convergence of technologies and market sectors causes regulatory confusion at several levels. The issues cut across traditional lines of regulatory responsibility creating confusion among the regulatory bodies. This is aggravated by the growing comprehensiveness of these issues, rapid changes, and increased political interest due to the growing influence of this sector on society. Until recently, distinct markets (for example broadcasting and cable) have been subject to different regulatory principles. As these markets converge technologically, the interference between the regulatory environments is becoming a source of confusion (Sola Pool, 1983). Principles such as freedom of information, universal service, and cultural identity and pluralism have to be weighed against one another. Moreover, the crucial role of this sector for economic development and strong pressures from providers and users have led to a growing emphasis on economic and trade aspects and a shift in the policy framework from the national to the international level. Confusion also exists between regulatory categories. The growing technological integration of services makes it more difficult to draw practical distinctions. The attempts to categorize services (basic *versus* value-added, the different value-added services) and service providers (public *versus* private, common carrier *versus* specialized provider, recognized *versus* non-recognized) and to delimit network and terminal control functions are in this context fraught with difficulty. Moreover, the definitions should be unambiguous but should not inhibit the development of the market. In certain cases, exhaustive or indicative lists of services may be preferred. The fading boundaries and uncertainties in the regulatory framework indicate the importance of discussion and coordination at the national as well as international level.

Major regulatory problems in the communication and information area relate to market access conditions, usage conditions, tariff principles, interconnectivity, and information access and distribution (OECD/ICCP, 1987: 7-13).

The improvement of service provision and national competitiveness are major arguments for the opening up of the market. In order to decide which parts of the market should be open for whom and under what conditions, questions such as the following need to be raised and answered.

- Will the opening up of the market lead to new entries? What is the level of national competitiveness? Is (initial) protection by means of restrictive licensing desirable? What are the comparable market opportunities in other countries?

- Are dominant positions and possible abuse of dominant positions likely to exist (e.g., former national monopolies or emerging international conglomerates) and what means are available to control them?

- What regulations are needed for licensed monopolies which are also present in competitive markets?

The efficiency of regulation (e.g. on competition) and the distributional effects (e.g., on employment, wages, working conditions, geographical location, and coverage and costs of services) have to be balanced.

For example, usage conditions for leased lines include: maximum provision time, minimum contractual period, quality of service, maintenance and fault reporting, resale of capacity, shared use, third-party use, interconnection with public and private networks (Analysis and Forecasting Group (GAP), 1988: 30-31). A liberal policy towards leased lines may stimulate the development of network services (Mansell, a.o., 1988: 15). However, high investment costs and the need for a minimal customer base may at first call for restrictive licensing for the provision of some services. Moreover, the improvement of public networks and/or the convergence and substitutability of (low) value-added and basic services may reduce the number of entrants into the value-added services market (Vanguard/U.K. Department of Trade, 1987: 43-44). The allowance for private networks and eventually for resale of spare capacity may lead to substantial by-pass of public networks and service provision, although countervailing trends may exist as well (Mansell, a.o., 1988: 16). Another important aspect is the influence of private-network development on public control of network configuration, interconnectivity, and network access for service providers and users (Bar and Borrus, 1987).

Charging principles imply a balance between commercial considerations and universal service objectives. Changes in network economics (especially the lower cost of long-distance services compared to local services), in connection with cost-based pricing in basic as well as in enhanced services, may cause considerable distributional changes. However, cost-based pricing is likely to stimulate the development of new value-added services (e.g., safeguarding financial viability), to discourage resale of basic offerings, and to increase competitiveness at the international level (European Commission/Green Paper, 1987: 79-80).

Increased openness for network access in terms of well-defined and published conditions of supply, usage, charges and technical standards will facilitate market access for service providers. On the other hand, flexibility in technological and market development has to be guaranteed. Interconnectivity among network service systems, although a major advantage for the end-user, may have negative implications for competing supplier of network services, since it eliminates the necessity to subscribe to the other connected services as well (Vanguard/U.K. Department of Trade, 1987: 58).

Thus open architecture and common standards may prove to be an effective alternative to competition between network infrastructures.

Regulations restricting access to information involve a trade-off between economic, social and political objectives. National security, protection of personal and private information, protection of intellectual property rights, and other concerns will be invoked to justify the limits to deregulation. However, restrictive access to information may give a competitive advantage to national enterprises and help to overcome user resistance (e.g., commercial data protection) and lower the market-entry threshold (e.g., copyright piracy).

Restrictions on information distribution are mainly aimed at safeguarding pluralism, cultural identity, public order (e.g., protection of young people), and national advertisement revenues (TIDE, 1984). These objectives, however, have to be weighed against trade objectives, service provision growth and the principles of "free" flow of information and cultural exchange.

Regulation in the communications and information area is at the same time becoming more complex and more important to society. Both developments are likely to increase considerably the pressure on regulators and may lead to withdrawal from, and one-sided interpretation of, new information and evidence (Stevers, 1985). Complexity is not only growing in the objective or factual sense but also in the normative sense. Increasing conflicts between values and objectives call for a reassessment of priorities and of the appropriateness of regulation. Priorities set by regulators are not only likely to differ between countries or according to political orientation but also between different sectors (e.g., telecommunications, broadcasting, press, trade). Moreover, the specific characteristics of national situations (e.g., market structure, industrial competitiveness, demands from user populations, infrastructure, cultural diversity) also call for different measures to reach similar goals (van Tulder, 1987). In multilateral trade negotiations, priorities with regard to the interests of countries or groups of countries as well as with regard to different goals have to be determined.

Regulation and Trade in Communication and Information Services

As described above, there is a growing need for a set of commonly acceptable rules governing trade in telecommunication and data services. Although obstacles to trade in goods and services are linked, a number of problems specifically relating to trade in services have emerged. Major problems in the regulation of international trade in services generally, and for the communication and information sector especially, include the following.

1. Conceptual confusion over the demarcation between "goods" and "services" (Schulte-Hillen BDU 1988(2): 18-19. The problem of defining regulatory categories is especially complex for communication and information services (see: II.d above). Moreover, national differences have negative implications for international coordination and/or harmonization.

2. Definitional debate on the "tradeability" of services (Robinson, 1987: 372; Richardson, 1987: 14-15). Although any definition seems necessarily to include the condition that the producer and the consumer must be of different nationality and/or be in different countries when producing or providing the service, certain points still need to be clarified. In particular, the concepts of "foreign resident" and "foreign enterprise" have to be unambiguous when determining the nationality of the involved parties; the relationship between producer and provider, especially in the case of subsidiaries and parent companies of different nationality, also has to be specified in order to be able to determine the "essential" service supplier. However, specific problems and solutions are likely to arise when applying a general definition to an individual service sector. In the case of the communication and information sector, particular problems may arise with regard to the definition of "foreign firm" and the joint provision of international telecommunication and data services.

3. Related to these two conceptual problems is the lack of comprehensive, objective and comparable data in the service sector (Schulte-Hillen BDU, 1988(1): 18; OECD/TC, 1987(2): appendix I). Besides major differences in definitions of categories in balance-of-payments data, data about companies' presence in foreign markets are lacking. The extreme confusion about categories and the rapid growth in service applications aggravate the situation in the communication and information sector. Moreover, such parts of the market as intra-company data services and subscriptions to data banks are not included in trade statistics.

4. Trade in services is on the whole more regulated than trade in goods: a great majority of the obstacles to trade in services seem to derive from government regulation (Richardson, 1988: 6). This regulation is often linked to political and ideological issues which reduce the chances of achieving their abolition and concluding trade agreements. This may be even more true when regulation of different sectors and related ideologies start to interfere. The enormous impact of the communication and information sector on society as a whole

make this, at the national level, a highly sensitive area, even less susceptible to consensus, concessions and trade-offs at the international level. On the other hand, major pressures are at work to improve the market conditions for providers and users.

5. Finally, there is the question as to the extent to which the principles developed for trade in goods are really applicable to services. The principle of national treatment, for example, could still allow for different levels of market opening *between* the countries involved. The application of principles like MFN and reciprocity is likely to slow down the liberalization process, since existing differences in restrictiveness and in perception of appropriateness make general concessions extremely hard to achieve. The political sensitivity to development in the communication and information sector make this particularly likely with regard to this sector.

Proposed solutions to these problems involve:

- the need for a conceptual framework taking into account the specific characteristics of trade in services (OECD/TC, 1987(2); Office of the U.S. Trade Representative, 1987),

- the specific concepts, obstacles and ideology relevant in each service sector and the importance of sectorial considerations (European Commission - GNS, 1987),

- allowing for various levels of conditional MFN treatment, operating for different degrees of reciprocity and differences among countries in the speed and extent of deregulation of the services concerned (Robinson, 1987: 375), and

- the provision of complete, quantified and comparable data on international trade in services (OECD/TC, 1987(2): appendix I) by means of definitional and statistical efforts and coordination.

Specific Experiences

The European Community and the Member States

1. General trends in the Member States

With variations on the main theme, telecommunication policy in the EC countries has been conducted by Telecommunication Administrations.[6] They were also responsible for the provision and operation of the public network infrastructure, for provision and maintenance of network terminals, and for the provision of (basic) network services. They have also exercised

-- to differing degrees -- regulatory and standardization functions. However, the general movement towards deregulation is reducing the monopoly rights. How far this should go is viewed differently by different countries and seems strongly related to deeply rooted national traditions (Hills, 1984: Bauer, 1987). Nonetheless some major trends in the development of regulation with regard to network services can be discerned (European Commission/Green Paper, 1987 (COM (87)290):

- separation of regulatory and operational activities in order to prevent possible abuse of a dominant position where a Telecommunication Administration is competing with other operators;

- opening up of the value-added service sector (excluding voice telephony);

- continued provision and operation of the network infrastructure by Telecommunication Administrations;

- liberalization of the terminal market and opening network-equipment markets to greater competition;

- continued restrictive policy with regard to shared use, resale and interconnection with the public network for leased lines and private networks;

- adoption of more cost-related charges and introduction of elements of usage-based charges for leased lines in order to safeguard public service providers against cream-skimming;

- improving openness in network access and interconnectivity through the development of harmonized technical standards and principles for telecommunication charges and usage conditions (Open Network Provision (ONP));

- development, coordination and implementation of legal approaches to issues involving the free flow of information (e.g., privacy protection, intellectual property protection, safeguarding of cultural identity and pluralism).

These developments relate primarily to creating a single European market, but they will also progressively affect the Community's international relationships in the GATT, in the ITU and, bilaterally, with its principal international trading partners.

2. European Community and regulatory integration

Since the approval of an Action Programme for European Telecommunication policy by the Member States (17 December 1984), a dynamic and comprehensive Community telecommunication policy has come into being. Proposed positions and action lines are highlighted in a Green Paper published by the Commission (European Commission 1987 (COM(87)290)). It is emphasised that the progressive opening of the telecommunication equipment and services market is a major condition for achieving a competitive integrated domestic Community market. In addition to the broad consensus arising from the comments on the Green Paper, there is a substantial legal basis for Community action in this field furnished by the Treaty of Rome, the Single Act, decisions of the European Community and discussion on the scope of Art. 90(2). (See also Dang Nguen, 1986.)

In February 1988, the Commission released a communication which sets out a programme for action (European Commission, 1988 (COM(88)48)). This programme contains proposed directives (and deadlines for implementing them) which cover the major trends in the Community as described above. However, as the Commission points out (European Commission COM(88)48: 24), in some areas a comprehensive policy consensus still has to be worked out -- for example,

- defining a pro-active approach to develop Europe-wide compatibility and interoperability of telecommunication services (e.g., joint Community-wide service provision and network planning),

- a coherent European position regarding the future regulation and development of satellite communications in the Community,

- development of common principles for telecommunication charges in order to bring them closer into line with costs, especially internationally, and

- defining a common framework for restrictions on the flow of information.

3. The European Community and trade in telecommunication and data services

The Community's position on trade in telecommunication and data services is characterized by the following concerns:

- International trade agreements should support domestic objectives as set out in the Green Paper (in particular, the achievement of a competitive internal market).

- Trade relations with the rest of the world should be discussed in the appropriate fora such as GATT and ITU or, in certain circumstances, bilaterally. In the process of creating a single European market, weight is given to the interactive effects at the international level.

- Trade relations in other sectors should be taken into account during bilateral or multilateral negotiations (fair balance of opportunities).

- Particular attention should be paid to certain political, social and technical objectives including access to and security and confidentiality of data on international telecommunications network; cultural identity and pluralism, autonomy of the communications network and the crucial position of the telecommunications industry, and network integration and high-level standardization in order to ensure reliable international services and facilitate access.

The United States

1. The regulatory environment.

Telecommunication regulation in the United States is shaped by a multitude of governmental institutions which may differ in views and objectives. At the core of national regulatory authority is the Federal Communications Commission (FCC), an independent regulatory agency. The FCC actions are influenced by all three branches of federal government - depending on the issue. This has led to a process of permanent adjustment in the regulatory environment for telecommunications in the United States.

The FCC Computer II and III rulings are now the basic regulatory framework for the United States' telecommunication sector. Of major importance is also the Modified Final Judgment (MFJ), leading to the AT&T divesture under Judge Green. This judgment imposes structural separation requirements on AT&T and the Bell Operating Companies (BOCs) for the provision of enhanced services. Within the Computer III inquiry, the FCC decided in May 1986 to remove the structural separation requirements and to make the provision of enhanced services by AT&T and the BOCs dependent on their compliance with non-structural safeguards (such as the implementation of approved Open Network Architecture (ONA) plans). The FCC recognizes that its Computer III ruling is subject to agreement by Judge Green under the MFJ. In September 1987, Judge Green allowed the BOCs to compete in information services but they are still forbidden to provide the information content of services. The Court is currently considering the exact distinction between content and transmission.

2. *The United States and trade in telecommunication and data services.*

In the area of international telecommunications, the regulatory situation seems even more complex. Here, major roles are played by the State and Commerce Departments and the Office of the U.S. Trade Representatives.

The following principal concerns appear to motivate the different agencies which are involved:

- The Adminstration (mainly the U.S. Trade Representative) is pressing strongly for the liberalization of telecommunication goods and services, through bilateral talks and the GATT negotiations. It promotes deregulatory policies through international bodies like the ITU and the OECD (Pipe, 1987).

- The FCC is considering whether it should take actions that could limit access to the U.S. market on the basis of sectoral reciprocity. It has established a number of reporting requirements to collect information on the extent of participation of foreign firms in the U.S. market (Federal Communication Commission, 1987).

- The U.S. Congress adopted a Trade Bill which was subsequently vetoed by the President and which would have made foreign access to the U.S. market conditional on sectoral reciprocity. However, no clear access criteria or adequate definitions of telecommunication goods and services have yet been developed. The Administration was initially opposed to such measures but an amended Bill has now been adopted which still contains provisions relating *inter alia* to telecommunication trade which are unacceptable to the Community.

- In general, preference seems to be given to non-restrictive and flexible regulation, rather than to regulation furthering (international) network integration and harmonization of network access. Regulation on legal issues affecting the free flow of information seems to be strongly directed towards the safeguarding of national security and business interests, e.g., protection of commercial data, copying of computer software.

Japan

1. Liberalization and re-regulation.

Until recently, Japan's telecommunications were operated by NTT at the national and by KDD at the international level. Major telecommunication reform is based on the "Nippon Telegraph and Telephone Corporation Law", the "Telecommunications Business Law", and the "Law on Preparation of Enforcement of the Nippon Telegraph and Telephone Corporation Law and the Corporation Law and the Telecommunications Business Law" (OECD/ICCP, 1987: 272-280). The most important elements of the regulatory change, implemented as of April 1, 1985, relate to:

- privatization of NTT (initially the new NTT is owned by the government but up to one third ownership can be ceded),

- introduction of competition in all areas of telecommunications, domestically and internationally,

- division of telecommunication carriers into two classes: Type I, providing telecommunication services by establishing telecommunication circuit facilities or not and Type II (subdivided into special Type II (large scale), and general Type II),

- one third limitation of foreign ownership for Type I carrier; no foreign ownership limitation for Type II carriers.

This regulatory reform has led to new entrants and intensive competition in each carrier class (Pacific Research Group, 1987: 12-17).[7]

Major government institutions involved in the telecommunication sector are the Ministry of Post and Telecommunications (MPT) and the Ministry of International Trade and Industry (MITI). Market entry is subject to approval (Type I), registration (special type II) or notification (general Type II) through MPT. Service rates and changes must also be approved (Type I) or notified (special Type II) through MPT.

2. Japan and trade in telecommunication and data services.

MITI in particular is involved in negotiations on trade in data services. Major orientations and concerns of Japan in this context may be summarized by the following points:

- Strong interest into entry in foreign markets so as to let national companies profit fully from the new domestic competitive environment (Heronymi, A., 1987),

- *De facto* reluctance vis-a-vis foreign participation, especially in the Type I category (Office of U.S. Trade Representative, 1987(1)), and

- Weaker requirements for standards (standards are not going to cover interworking of services, except for telephony).

Brazil

1. Regulation and development objectives.

In the early sixties when the Brazilian telecommunication service industry faced a crisis, the adoption of the Brazilian Telecommunications Code (August 1962) provided for important changes. This law and later decrees form the legal basis for the regulation of telecommunication services in Brazil.

The growing importance of communications led to the creation of a Ministry of Communications in 1967. The Ministry performs its basic functions through three bodies:

- General Secretariat: in charge of administrative and financial planning, coordination and control,

- National Telecommunications Department (DENTEL): responsible for assistance, coordination, supervision and control with regard to the enforcement of laws, regulations and standards pertinent to telecommunication activities, and

- Secretariat for International Affairs: coordinating and supervising technical, economic, administrative, legal and political activities at the international level, in conjunction with the Ministry of Foreign Affairs.

A conglomerate of 35 companies providing nearly all public telecommunication services (the TELEBRAS System) is generally in charge of planning, implementing and operating the National Telecommunications System.[8] After the creation of TELEBRAS, a unified system for rate-setting was gradually adopted. The new method determines a percentage figure for each company in line with the total income received from calls it generated. In turn, each company's share in total revenues is determined in relation to its total income.

EMBRATEL -- a joint stock corporation and subsidiary of the holding company TELEBRAS -- is empowered to implement, expand and operate the interstate and international telecommunication systems. The EMBRATEL telecommunication systems are classified as domestic or international according to their scope. EMBRATEL provides services for both interstate and international public communication. It also provides these services privately according to user requirements.

The policy adopted by the Ministry of Communications with regard to the development of telecommunication services is based on the following twin objectives: increasing the availability of telephone service to wider segments of the population and increasing the sophistication and diversification of the range of telecommunication services for the more developed and economically productive segments of the country. In the second case, communications are treated as an essential production input rather than a consumer good.

2. Brazil and trade in telecommunication and data services.

The telecommunication policy of the Ministry of Communications is directed towards the promotion of autonomy and public control. For Brazil an imperative in trade-related policy is the maximization of exports and the limitation of imports. In the domain of telecommunication services, restricted market access, [9] limited foreign participation in the service industry and restrictions on the use of private funds and investment have been emphasized to achieve these objectives.

Related concerns at the international level with regard to the telecommunication sector are:

- securing external credit for the development of telecommunications in Brazil,

- technical and technological cooperation in the form of a technological absorption policy (a cooperation policy has been established with developing countries), and

- participation in international standardization agencies in order to secure the universal use of telecommunications and to facilitate the export of services and equipment.

An Appropriate Negotiating Context

ITU and WATTC '88

In 1982, the Plenipotentiary Conference of the ITU decided on the World Administrative Telegraph and Telephone Conference to be held in December 1988, to consider: "to the extent necessary...", "...proposals for a new regulatory framework to cater for the new situation in the field of Telecommunication services".[10] A Preparatory Committee for the WATTC '88 (PC/WATTC),[11] assisted by various Study Groups of the CCITT, released draft regulations and a working report in November, 1987.[12]

Regulations approved by WATTC '88 would be binding on all ITU members who ratify them; however, art, 77/16 of the Nairobi Convention provides for a delegation to enter reservations to a decision.[13] CCITT Recommendations are probably not part of a legal instrument having the force of an international treaty (Bruce, and Cunard, 1987: 12-13).

The draft regulations for WATTC '88 have become the subject of an intense debate. Differences in views relate to the scope of service providers and the services which should be covered by the new regulations. Current wording in the draft regulations leaves room for a very broad application (see: art. 1.7, 2.1, 2.2, and 4.2). Another point is the absence of any reference to preferential accounting procedures which are sought by developing countries (see: art.6).

The following questions need to be considered:

- Given that telecommunications technologies, markets and regulation are in a state of flux, how flexible must the international policy framework be to adjust to these developments?

- How much freedom should be left for national and regional differences?

- What would the effects be on the balance of interests at the national level?

- How will ITU regulations affect bilateral and multilateral trade negotiations? Could these regulations pre-empt the GATT negotiations? Will they be able to accommodate an open international trading environment?

- Will the new regulations give more clarity and certainty to countries still largely dependent on telecommunication developments in other countries?

- What will be their effect on market entry and the development of new services?

- How to solve the problem of defining regulatory categories? (This will be the harder the greater the scope of the regulation and consequent problems of international coordination and control may arise.)

- How will the regulations affect the position of dominant service suppliers and what will be the consequence for the quality and accessibility of telecommunication services?

- What types of services need or need not be regulated? (Compare the examples of the French Telepac and the pan-European digital mobile radio.)

- How may (voluntary) arrangements for network interoperability best be stimulated?

GATT and the Uruguay Round

In Punta del Este, Uruguay, the parties to the GATT decided in September 1986 to open a new Trade Negotiation Round: the Uruguay Round. The mandate established by trade ministers for the Uruguay Round covers for the first time trade in services as well as trade in goods. The negotiations on trade in services -- set out in Part II of the Uruguay Round Declaration -- are not part of the GATT. However, "GATT procedures and practices shall apply to these negotiations". A "Group of Negotiations on Services" (GNS) has been established and instructed to prepare a multilateral framework of principles and rules for trade in services, including the elaboration of possible disciplines for individual sectors.

Due to the growing importance of the communication and information sector for the international economy in general, and for trade in services in particular, this sector enjoys considerable attention. The exceptional complexity of regulation in this sector in the GATT context, is illustrated by the different GATT codes involved: the inclusion of the communication and information sector in a services code will have direct implications for its position with respect to a standards code, a procurement code and an intellectual property code. This means, in practice, that the following equipment and service issues have to be considered in relation to one another:

- customs tariff structures,

- technical standards, including testing and type approval,

- procurement policies,

- distinctions between 'reserved' and competitive services,

- restrictions on trade in information services,

- interconnectivity conditions (e.g., technical standards, tariff principles, usage conditions),

- effective safeguards regarding right of access to information, and

- protection of intellectual property rights to information communicated electronically.

Some questions with regard to GATT negotiations on the communication and information sector may be:

- How will the different codes relate to one another and what should they contain? (For example, should procurement by telecommunication administrations have its place in the Government Procurement Code or in special provisions which cover all licensed operating companies?)

- What will be the link between de-regulation of services (e.g., VAS, MDNS), and regulation on standardization?

- How can access to data in foreign data banks be ensured?

- How can a standardized level of protection for security and confidentiality of data be assured?

- What will be the consequences of communication and information service deregulation for the developing countries?

- To what extent will trade-offs between regulations on services and goods be acceptable?

- Should the communication and information sector be part of a general service code, or form a code of their own, within an agreed framework, covering the whole scope of issues related to this sector?

INTELSAT

The International Telecommunications Satellite Organization (INTELSAT) has 112 members, each holding an investment share based on its use of the system. Intelsat's main objective is the provision on a commercial and non-discriminatory basis of the space segment required for international public telecommunication services (e.g., telephone, telex, data, television). The Intelsat space segment may also be made available for other domestic public telecommunication services (e.g. IBS, Intelnet).

Currently, there is a growing pressure for more regulatory flexibility in the provision and use of satellite services, in order to increase competition and consumer choice. Permission for private ownership and operation of the following is under discussion (European Commission, 1987 (COM (87) 290 appendices): 107-110):

- receive-only terminal earth stations

- receive/transmit very small aperture (micro) terminals (VSAT)

- uplink hub earth stations (on a licensing base in order to prevent interference with other systems).

This would require signatories of Intelsat to submit applications for earth station approval and allotment of space capacity on behalf of third parties in their territory.

A further step has been advocated, notably by the United States: so as to allow direct access to space segment capacity, permit separate systems to compete with Intelsat. However, this would call for a common interpretation of the "economic-harm" provision contained in the Intelsat Convention, which is intended to protect Intelsat from diversion of traffic and revenue.

Some points to consider with regard to a more flexible regulatory regime may be:

- Will Intelsat be adequately protected and/or sufficiently competitive, to continue fulfilling its public service mission?

- How will this influence the availability of geo-stationary orbits for future use by developing countries?

- What will be the consequences for Telecommunication Administrations developing VSAT-networks?

- How will it affect the provision and use of terrestrial facilities?

- How will it affect the scope, coverage and price of services offered (e.g., low-data-rate services)?

- How will it influence other sectors -- e.g., the space industry, or the audio-visual sector?

- Would it support the control of worldwide service capability by massive service conglomerates?

- Can adequate and timely legal provisions be developed and adopted in order to protect intellectual property, privacy, commercial data, cultural identity, national security, and the like?

Appropriate Negotiating Fora

The way topics are distributed over the different negotiating fora is likely to influence considerably the direction and pace of multilateral negotiations.

Major considerations involved in the determination of an appropriate forum for discussing trade in communication and information services are: the nature and scope of its members, the available expertise and the binding power of agreements in its framework. Given the growing global inter-dependence (especially evident in the case of network-based services), a multilateral framework where both the North and South are properly repre-sented seems essential for the development of stable rules (Narjes, 1988: 25). Agreements with the binding power of international treaties may also contribute to stability. Furthermore, the complexity of regulation in the communication and information sector makes it necessary to consider all its aspects in a negotiating context which facilitates taking account of all these interrelationships.

It is arguable indeed that both the GATT and the ITU could be appropriate negotiating fora for aspects of trade in communication and information services but that the relationship between them should be clarified.

However, both organizations seem to be handicapped by "institutional unpreparedness" (Robinson, 1987: 371). One main reason is the rapid and fundamental change taking place in this sector. In particular, the ITU has largely confined its activities to more technical questions and may lack a feel for national regulatory policies (Richardson, 1986: 399) and trade policies. The GATT, on the other hand, is struggling with concepts and principles which can be applied to trade in services and, what is more serious, may be much too dominated by mere trade considerations. The enormous impact of the communication and information sector on society seems to justify a broader approach for the formulation of its policy reform (Narjes, 1988: 21).

Finally, we will indicate some essential conditions for progress on regula-tion with regard to trade in communication and information services:

- The involvement of several international and transnational organizations is inevitable for the coverage of the entire regulatory scope (e.g. GATT, ITU, OECD, WIPO, UNCTAD, INTELSAT). However, it is of major importance to ensure that international rules are developed consistently in the different fora involved. Careful timing is another pre-requisite, since it will influence the development of issues and priorities.

- National experiences (e.g., US, EC, Japan) indicate that progress is achieved incrementally; a similar process should be expected at the international level.

- With regard to some issues, the pressure for change will be especially strong.

The international community has to reach a broad consensus which allows for adaption to technological and market developments, assures the interests of users in developed as well as in developing countries, and accounts for national differences and accommodates, when appropriate, partial (bi-lateral, regional) and/or temporary solutions.

The incentives for an overall agreement are strong, and the costs of failure high. The absence of a balanced and flexible agreement will increase the attractiveness of independent bilateral and regional agreements. This would in turn undermine the possibility of reaching global agreement on appropriate regulation for trade in communication and information services.

ENDNOTES

1 Since the sixties there has developed a growing literature on political interest and the concept of regulation (Wilson, 1980; Posner, 1979).

2 An example may be seen in the licensing policy in the field of network operation and ownership in the U.K.

3 Their appropriteness might also be considered subject to objective rules of justice or still other criteria.

4 Resale of leased-line capacity is often restricted.

5 Besides sectorial developments, a general reassessment of regulatory costs and benefits is taking place (Bauer, 1987).

6 The phrase "Telecommunication Administrations" is used to mean any telecommunication operator providing public services with special rights and obligations.

7 International Telecommunications of Japan and International Digital Communications, are currently (1988) planning to commence international communication services.

8 Law No. 5792 of July 11, 1972 established a "Telecommunicacoes Brasileiras S.A. - "TELEBAS", the holding company of the TELEBAS System. The company is controlled by the Ministry of Communications on behalf of the Federal Government which holds 51 percent of its shares.

9 Brazil requires, *inter alia*, that data received from unrelated parties be processed within the country.

10 Resolution No. 10, International Telecummunication Convention - Nairobi, 1982, et 238-239.

11 The CCITT's VIIIth Plenary Assembly in October 1984, adopted Resolution No. 15, which established the PC/WATTC.

12 CCITT Circular No. 67

13 Reservations may only be made to decisions which are "of such a nature as to prevent its government from ratifying the Convention or from approving the revision of the Regulations."

MOST-FAVORED-NATION PRINCIPLE AND NEGOTIATING STRATEGIES

Henning Klodt

Introduction

The most-favored-nation principle (MFN) is the central rule of the General Agreement on Tariffs and Trade (GATT). According to Article I of the GATT treaty,

> "any advantage, favor, privilege or immunity granted by any contracting party to any product originating in or destined for any other country shall be accorded immediately and unconditionally to the like product originating in or destined for the territories of all other contracting parties."

By this rule all contracting countries are bound to grant to one another treatment as favorable as they give to any country in the application and administration of import and export duties and charges. No country is to give special trading advantages to another or to discriminate against it. In consequence, all parties share the benefits of any moves towards lower trade barriers.

The whole regulatory framework of the GATT treaty applies solely to trade in merchandise goods. By the Ministerial Declaration of Punta del Este of September 1986 it was decided to start work on an international agreement on trade in services. These negotiations on services are an integral part of the Uruguay Round that is due to finish at the end of 1990.

The discussion that follows begins with an analysis of trade generally (Part 2). The applicability of the principle to trade in services is examined in Part 3 and its applicability to trade in telecommunication and data services in Part 4. Part 5 is a summary of the preceding discussion.

The MFN Principle in International Trade

The establishment of the GATT was an immediate post-war reaction to the deterioration of the world trading system during the inter-war period and during World War II. It was felt that the great depression and perhaps even the war itself resulted, at least partly, from destructive national egoism in trade policy. Since the late twenties international trade was dominated by exchange-rate manipulations, increased tariffs, restrictive import quotas, and numerous bilateral preferential-trading arrangements. Most countries strived to promote their own exports and to reduce imports from other countries. International trade was not regarded as mutually advantageous but as beneficial especially to the exporting country.

After World War II several initiatives were adopted against beggar-my-neighbor policies. The system of Bretton Woods was intended to avoid artificial depreciations of national currencies and a proposed International Trade Organization (ITO) was to keep a strict eye upon unfair trade policies at the micro-level. In 1947 a provisional General Agreement on Tariffs and Trade (GATT) was signed by 23 countries, which was intended as a subsidiary agreement to the ITO. The ITO charter (Havana Charter) was, however, never ratified and the GATT was left as the only international agreement on trade rules (Jackson, 1984). Today, there are 96 contracting parties to the GATT and more than 30 countries which maintain a *de facto* application of the GATT. These countries are responsible for most of the world's trade.

The GATT treaty rests mainly on two fundamental principles: (1) the system of world trade should be based on internationally agreed and legally binding rules and (2) non-discriminating multilateral agreements should be preferred to bilateral trading arrangements. What is the background of this view and are the arguments in favor of it still valid?

Among most economists and policy-makers it is well understood that free trade will in general increase economic growth and welfare by fostering greater efficiency in allocating resources, lowering prices and increasing the variety of options for consumers and producers (see, for example, Corden, 1974). With no artificial barriers to international transactions each country would specialize in those activities in which it can make the best use of its production capabilities. An undistorted international division of labor would be beneficial even to those countries facing an absolute disadvantage against their trading partners (Samuelson, 1939). These are the major implications of David Ricardo's famous "theorem of comparative costs".

Given these properties of free trade, it may be asked if international consultations on the reduction of tariffs, quotas, export restraints etc. are really necessary. As free trade is expected to promote economic growth in each participating country, national governments would presumably adopt a liberalization strategy on grounds of self-interest. A reduction of trade barriers might emerge even without any supra-national agreements.

The empirical evidence, however, does not support such an optimistic view. Newspaper headlines are not dominated by success stories about trade liberalization but by "trade wars" in microelectronic chips, commercial aircraft, chickens and noodles. Obviously, many governments are still as reluctant to liberalize trade as they were in the twenties and thirties. They are still striving for increased protection of domestic industries instead of promoting market access of foreign competitors.

In general, today's protective measures are adopted for five major reasons:

- In some industries, it is argued, unhampered market forces would not generate optimal results. Considerations of national sovereignty or security, financial stability, natural monopoly and the protection of consumers from unfair pricing, fraud and other undesirable practices would require government restraints in order to compensate for market failures (for a critical evaluation see Baumol and Willig, 1981 and Baumol et al., 1982).

- The establishment of new lines of business may take some time. Young enterprises will probably start at a comparatively low level of economic efficiency, but their performance can be rapidly improved by learning-by-doing. On this view, the comparative advantage of countries is not a static concept but may change in the course of time. For this reason, it is often argued, "infant industries" need temporary protection in order to create a comparative advantage (for a comprehensive survey of the issues see Grubel, 1966).

- Some industries appear to be more profitable than others. As above-average profits are in general supposed to prevail in high-tech industries, the so-called strategic trade policy approach aims at increasing the share of these industries in aggregate output. The rationale of this strategy is earning monopoly rents at the expense of foreign producers and consumers (Spencer and Brander, 1983; Krugman, 1986).

- Increased competition from abroad may give rise to output reductions in specific industries. If the pressure for adjustment exceeds adjustment flexibility, governments tend to provide protective shelter in order to avoid structural unemployment. As structural change in international trade is a persisting phenomenon, many of these measures, intended initially to give temporary assistance, turn into permanent protection of inefficient industries (Lawrence, 1984; Klodt, 1988a).

- Finally, the benefits from protection are in general concentrated on specific subjects and are well-known, whereas the costs are spread over the whole economy and hard to identify. Political decision-makers often are tempted, therefore, to exploit this asymmetry in order to maximize votes. Perhaps the predominance of concentrated gains and distributed losses is the most important reason for the adherence of national governments to protective trade barriers (Stigler, 1971; Krueger, 1974; Buchanan, Tollison, Tullock, 1980).

A critical assessment of the soundness and validity of these arguments lies beyond the scope of this paper. It should be recognised, however, that they are a major influence on public discussion and that there is still no overwhelming tendency towards free trade. [1] International agreements on trade rules have obviously not lost their importance since the establishment of the GATT.

The case for a regulatory framework for international trade does not imply, however, a case for the specific rules of the existing GATT treaty, especially with regard to the MFN. Historically, this principle was introduced into post-war trade negotiations by the United States mainly in order to dismantle the preference system of the Commonwealth (Jackson, 1969, p. 251). It is a question whether the non-discriminating and unconditional granting of favorable treatment of imports is still an appropriate basic principle for international trade negotiations.

The main objectives of the MFN clause are: [2]

- to minimize distortions in the international division of labor, since it ensures that each country will receive its imports from the most efficient supplier;

- to free trade from as much government interference as possible, since it precludes protectionist practices against particular countries that could otherwise result from political tensions;

- to stabilize the world trading system, since it increases the transparency of trade policies and inhibits special preference deals between countries;

- to guarantee the access of newcomers and less powerful countries to world markets, since it generalizes favorable treatment achieved by large countries;

- to reduce administration costs and simplify customs procedures, since the treatment of imports does not depend on their origin.

On the other hand, it is argued that the resistance of domestic producers to *multilateral* trade liberalization is in general more pronounced than their resistance to *bilateral* liberalization. Hence, an adherence to the MFN principle would block the process of liberalization that could otherwise emerge from a number of bilateral steps. Moreover, the MFN principle opens world markets even to those countries that heavily protect their home markets. Such a free-rider strategy would call for country-specific retaliation.

Basically, the opponents to the MFN principle point out that the unconditional granting of favorable treatment gives insufficient incentives to liberalization and precludes the punishment of protectionists. They would prefer a bilateral reciprocity in trade policy that would discriminate against those countries which are not willing to open their home markets (see, for example, Goldstein, Krasner, 1984). This view is supported by recent work in the game theory that argues for the superiority of a "tit-for-tat" strategy (for a survey see *The Economist*, 1985). In the language of trade negotiations, tit-for-tat means strict reciprocity of liberalization, i.e., that favorable treatment of imports is to be accorded only to those countries that in turn open their home markets and that protectionist policies of other countries are to be retaliated against by means of countervailing trade barriers.

In real life, however, it is often impossible to decide if a specific protective measure is a "tit" or already a "tat". A misperception of trade policies of their countries could easily lead to escalating trade conflicts. For these reasons many observers still support an adherence to the MFN clause of the GATT treaty (Aronson and Cowhey, 1984; Donges, 1986).

An intermediate strategy between unconditional multilateralism (as established by MFN) and reciprocal bilateralism (as suggested by tit-for-tat) is the concept of open liberalization clubs (Giersch, 1985). Those countries that are prepared to adopt a liberal trade policy can grant each other preferential treatment. They discriminate against non-members but each country is invited to join the club. The only condition for becoming a member of the club is the acceptance of trade liberalization. This is the core of the so-called conditional MFN principle. [3]

There exist a number of liberalization clubs in international trade, e.g., the European Community (EC) and the European Free Trade Association (EFTA). But these regional trading arrangements, which are exempted from Article I of the GATT treaty by Article XXIV, are in general not open to new members. Hence, they tend to fortify discrimination and the segmentation of world markets. In a sense, the GATT itself can be regarded as an open liberalization club. Article I restricts favorable treatment to contracting parties but it is open to new members. The openness is demonstrated by the fact that the original 23 members have now expanded to 96 (Snape, 1988).

The establishment of such clubs is not permitted by the GATT treaty within the areas it covers with the exception of the regional trading arrangements mentioned above. This concept could be adopted, however, in areas not yet covered by the treaty. One of these possible areas is trade in services. In the following section, where the applicability of MFN to trade in services is discussed, the concept of conditional MFN will be examined in more detail.

Aspects of Liberalizing Trade in Services

It is still an unsettled issue what the main impediments to international trade in services are and how a substantial liberalization could be achieved. Simply extending the existing GATT rules to trade in services would obviously not be sufficient. The GATT is mainly concerned with border barriers (tariffs, quotas etc.). Such barriers are of very minor importance in services. Instead, government interventions are in general oriented at business activities within countries.[4] This form of protection needs new concepts of liberalization that may be analogous to but can not be identical to the liberalization of trade in goods.

The new issues that arise from the integration of trade in services into the Uruguay Round may be illustrated by the conceptual differences between goods and services. By definition, a good is a physical object that can be transferred between economic units. A service, by contrast, is an intangible change in the condition of a person or a good resulting from the economic activity of some other economic unite (Hill, 1977; Siniscalco, 1988). Due to this property most services cannot be stored and for the provision of some services even a physical contact between provider and customer is essential (factor-embodied services). Other service industries do not require the physical proximity of producers and consumers. Spatial movement of persons is replaced by flows of information. Examples are telecommunications or financial services (disembodied services).[5]

Of course, the border lines between embodied and disembodied services are somewhat arbitrary. Moreover and more important, they change in the course of time. Transaction costs in trading disembodied services arise mainly from information and communication costs. Due to rapid technological changes in transmitting and switching technologies, these costs have been and are being steadily reduced. It has become profitable, therefore, to replace factor-embodied services by disembodied ones (Stern and Hoekman, 1987). In finance, insurance and business services, in particular, many activities which once required spatial movements of economic units are nowadays provided in a disembodied manner. Technical progress has thus significantly increased the potential for international trade in services and international trade in non-factor services [6] might therefore have been expected to expand more rapidly than trade in goods.

As a matter of fact, however, the share of services in world trade decreased slightly in the seventies, whereas in the eighties it just kept pace with trade in goods. This discrepancy between potential and actual trade performance points to the existence of significant artificial trade barriers that impede an intensified international division of labor. The "classical" instruments of restrictive trade policies, tariffs and quotas, are almost non-existent in the service sector but there are numerous other forms of government regulation, notable market entry and operating restrictions. [7]

Differences in the nature of goods and services give rise to different impacts of government regulations on international trade. If *market entry* of foreign firms is prohibited, for instance, industrial production of foreign affiliates may be replaced by exports of goods to the regulating country. With trade in goods, therefore, restrictions on international flows of production factors may even create international trade. Due to the intangible nature of services, however, the presence of at least some representatives like branch offices or sales agencies is often a precondition for the provision of services in foreign markets. Many service firms that want to participate in international trade have to go multinational. Hence, restrictions of foreign direct investment and labor movement tend to destroy international trade in services. For this reason, the liberalization of trade in services is inextricably entangled with the liberalization of international capital flows and migration.

Similarly, *operating restrictions* are more damaging to trade in services than to trade in goods. Most of these restrictions are allegedly enacted to protect consumers. It may be argued, however, that some of them aim implicitly at deterring the entry of new competitors.

For whatever reason these regulations are adopted, most of them actually discriminate against foreign firms and impede international trade. Mandatory asset ratios in banking, funding restrictions in insurance, country-specific safety standards in transportation, technical controls in telecommunications and the like make it difficult to enter a foreign service market. As these regulations are often the result of lengthy and complex discussions between governments and national lobbying groups, they are in general especially attuned to the needs of domestic production. In consequence, they raise the costs of domestic firms less than they do those of foreign competitors, even if they are applied to both domestic and foreign producers (Hindley, 1988b).

In the Uruguay Round, the issues raised by protectionist operating restrictions in service industries could be negotiated on the basis of Article III of the GATT treaty which requires national treatment of imported goods (see the paper by Aronson in this volume). The issue of entry barriers, on the other hand, is concerned with cross-border flows of production factors, capital and labor, which are not covered at all by the GATT treaty (see the paper by Balasubramanyam in this volume). Negotiations in this area need concepts that are completely new to trade talks associated with the GATT.

With respect to MFN, all of these topics can be negotiated either on an unconditional or on a conditional basis. In a sense, MFN is the rule behind the rules that is concerned with all aspects of liberalizing international trade. It is a matter of decision whether new agreements are legally binding obligations on all contracting parties of the GATT or only on a subset of countries that are ready to open their service markets.

Obviously, there is a trade-off between substance and coverage. If the agreement on services is to be signed only by a limited number of countries, it could include liberalization steps that are not acceptable to others. On the other hand, such a conditional approach would probably be achieved at the expense of less powerful countries and could bring about a substantial distortion and segmentation of world service markets.

In order to get the current talks moving the government of the United States proposed a three-step procedure (Group of Negotiations on Services, 1988a):

- Phase one of the negotiations would involve general rules and disciplines that could be incorporated in an umbrella agreement on trade in services.[8]

- Phase two would be concerned with the sectoral coverage of the agreement. It should result in a list of service industries subject to the framework and it should include national reservations to the framework agreement.

- Phase three would involve negotiations on the national reservations and on those industries that are not covered by phase one and two.

The results of phase one and two could lead to an agreement on the basis of unconditional MFN. The subjects of phase three can either be deleted from the agenda of the Uruguay Round or be negotiated on the basis of conditional MFN.[9]

The opponents to this approach point out that trade liberalization within the Uruguay Round is a "package deal". The opening of markets in each specific service sector would inevitably depend on the negotiation results in other service sectors or even in merchandise trade. Developing countries, in particular, have pointed out that all negotiations within the Uruguay Round are "integral parts of a single political undertaking" (Group of Negotiations on Services, 1987c).[10]

Regulatory barriers to trade are very different in specific service industries. And sector-specific regulations require sector-specific negotiations. They do not, however, necessarily imply sector-specific agreements. The results of the negotiations could be integrated into an enforceable general framework as suggested by the Japanese government (Group of

Negotiations on Services 1988b). According to this approach, the principle of unconditional MFN could be extended to the whole service sector.

Alternatively, the general framework could serve as a standard model for specific sectoral agreements as suggested by the Scandinavian countries. The sectoral agreements could be conceived on an unconditional MFN basis. This approach would also allow a restriction of unconditional MFN to some service sectors and conditional MFN agreements with varying country coverage in others (Baldwin, 1985).

All in all, it must be recognized that trade in services will never be as free as trade in goods. Since many trade restrictions flow from deliberate policy objectives, liberalizing trade in services is a much more ambitious task than liberalizing trade in goods. Perhaps the Uruguay Round can be no more than a first step on a long road.

Due to the complexity of the subject, no straight-forward negotiating strategy seems feasible. Each service industry deserves its own attention and concrete moves towards free trade will require a patchwork approach with special consideration of industry-specific regulations. One of the most important parts of the patchwork will be the liberalization of trade in a young and rapidly expanding industry -- telecommunication and data services.

Negotiating Strategies in Telecommunication and Data Services

Telecommunication and data services are at the top of the agenda of the Group of Negotiations on Services in the Uruguay Round. This high priority corresponds to their growing importance in economic activity. In many countries, the share of communication industries in total output is rising and even traditional manufacturing industries are becoming more and more information-intensive. Rapid technical progress in information and communication technologies is substantially reducing the costs of transferring information over long distances and facilitating the world-wide organization of production processes (Sauvant, 1986a,b).

Data services are a typical example of disembodied services. Inherent barriers to trade are comparatively low and, due to new developments in microelectronics, continuously declining. There is thus a high potential for rapidly increasing international trade in data services.

As in other service industries, however, international trade is hampered by government regulation. In the past, telecommunication services were almost everywhere concentrated in state-owned PTTs (Post, Telegraph and Telephone administrations) or government-controlled monopolies. The rationale of this strong form of government regulation is the supposed "natural monopoly" in telecommunication networks. According to this argument, the existence of competing networks in one region is impossible, since with rising output average costs would infinitely decline and only one provider could survive in the long run. As this provider would have strong market power, customers must be protected from monopolistic exploitation. Network supply thus needs, on this view, to be supervised by government or provided by state-owned companies (for a critical evaluation of this proposition see Baumol and Willig, 1981 and Baumol et al., 1982).

The natural-monopoly approach was extended from networks to services and equipment, since uncontrolled use of networks is expected not to be technically feasible. The market position of public or government regulated providers of telecommunication services was increasingly eroded, however, by the emergence of new information and communication technologies. In the United States, for example, the monopoly position of AT&T in telephone networks was circumvented by private suppliers of wireless communication equipment. And in West Germany the public monopoly in television was endangered when private suppliers from Luxembourg announced the installation of a geo-stationary TV satellite above the West German territory. Since the late seventies the discrepancy between traditional PTT policies and technical opportunities has widened substantially. Moreover, the growing importance of transborder data flows for international production and trade has created new demands for more flexible and differentiated telecommunication services.

It is increasingly difficult, therefore, to maintain a public monopoly in these services. It would require the permanent extension of government controls to technologies capable of replacing traditional modes of telecommunication services. Most European governments have actually adopted such a strategy. In a few countries, on the other hand, governments have reacted to the increased competitive pressure from new communication technologies by liberalizing telecommunication service markets.

This new approach started in the United States, where the deregulation of telecommunications culminated in the divestiture of AT&T in 1982. In recent years a similar deregulation policy has been initiated in Japan and in Great Britain. These three countries are striving for a liberalization of telecommunication service markets in other countries as well, in order to facilitate the access of their private firms to foreign markets. The lack of consensus among national governments on appropriate regulations in data services still prevents a more rapid progress towards liberalization of international trade.

It was in 1982 that the U.S. government proposed, for the first time, multilateral negotiations on trade in telecommunication services. This proposal was rejected not only by developing countries but also by the European Community, where public PTTs were defending their monopoly position. The European Community has since changed its position and an increasing number of countries are interested in opening up telecommunication service markets.

Three important topics are on the agenda of trade liberalization in data services:

- network competition and competition in basic services,

- competition in enhanced or value-added services, and

- competition in telecommunication equipment.

For the Uruguay Round, the possibilities of negotiating the first of these topics are rather limited. The number of countries that would accept foreign competition in *networks and basic services* is very low. It should be recognized, however, that high fees or restricted access to basic telecommunication services can create substantial barriers to trade, especially in information-intensive industries. It would be worthwhile, therefore, to think about an international agreement on national treatment with regard to access to the networks. Such an agreement would involve the unrestricted use of domestic basic services by foreign enterprises at fees equal to those charged to domestic enterprises. There appear to be no major difficulties in negotiating this agreement on an unconditional MFN basis. Of course, it could also be negotiated on a conditional basis.

The most important area is competition in *value-added services*. [11] These services may be offered either on regular networks or on private leased lines. The reluctance of national governments to open these markets arises from various considerations: the protection of domestic producers, of privacy, of security and even of national sovereignty. An agreement on the access of foreign-controlled affiliates to value-added network facilities would require the dissolution of various government regulations concerned with these activities.

As the regulatory systems concerned with value-added services are very different among different countries, the above-described trade-off between substance coverage and country coverage in a liberalization agreement is extremely important. An agreement according to the conditional MFN principle could pull together countries with similar regulatory systems and could bring about considerable liberalization in separate regions. Such an agreement could be quite harmful to those countries that do not join, since they would probably be cut off from the main streams of information in world markets. On the other hand, an agreement covering all members of the GATT would probably be a rather vacuous one, since it would almost be impossible to cover the various regulatory systems in one multilateral agreement.

The Commission of the European Communities has proposed an approach that avoids struggles with particular regulations in the first round and that nevertheless rests upon unconditional MFN: instead of negotiating the derogation of specific regulations, the contracting parties could agree on the constitution of a permanent Regulations Committee (Group of Negotiations on Services, 1987d; see also the paper by Stevers and Wilkinson in this volume). Each country would be obliged to notify the Committee of regulations that affect international trade in services. The Regulations Committee would decide whether these notified regulations were 'appropriate' or 'inappropriate'.[12]

This approach would require an agreement on a series of criteria for the examination of particular regulations. For instance, they could include the criterion that regulations adopted for specific policy objectives should have a minimum impact on trade. Hindley (1988b) has suggested a rule of thumb for the identification of appropriate regulations: According to welfare analyses in international trade theory, a regulation that provides a cost advantage to domestic producers is superior to regulations that provide cost disadvantages to foreign suppliers or restrict market entry. Perhaps this proposal could serve as a guideline for identifying inappropriate regulations.

The proposal of the European Community is addressed to the whole range of service negotiations. It could be argued, however, that it is especially suitable for value-added network services since the differences in national regulatory systems are comparatively high. A framework agreement on appropriate and inappropriate regulations could probably preserve some elements of unconditional MFN in this highly complex area without blocking substantial progress towards liberalization.

The third aspect of trade liberalization in telecommunications is concerned with telecommunication equipment. Imports of services are often hampered by restrictive practices in the public procurement of telecommunication monopolies. According to Article XVII of the GATT treaty, the MFN principle of non-discrimination is also to be observed by state-owned companies. They are obliged to make purchases solely in accordance with commercial considerations and to afford foreign suppliers adequate opportunity to compete. The rules on public procurement were further specified in the Tokyo Round concluded in 1979.

Despite these commitments most state-owned PTTs are still favoring "national champions". The discrimination of foreign suppliers is achieved mainly by restrictive technical standards that preclude imports of telecommunication equipment. In the Tokyo Round, an agreement was also signed on non-discriminatory norms and standards (Standard Codes). But these rules are obviously ineffective in telecommunication service markets (Sapir, 1986).

A supplementary agreement on telecommunication equipment could avoid a fragmentation of world markets and the obstruction of trade in telecommunication services. It could include criteria for minimum technical standards that are concerned with the avoidance of harm to networks, the avoidance of interference between different users and the protection of privacy of transmitted information. An over-extensive consideration of optimum standards would probably freeze technical progress and prevent the diffusion of innovations in communication technology (Roseman, 1988). According to this approach, the customers could decide which equipment would suit their needs best. And foreign suppliers of data services would no longer be hampered by prohibitive restrictions on data-transmitting and data-processing technologies.

As an alternative to such a technical standards agreement, these issues could also be dealt with by the above mentioned permanent Regulations Committee. In this field, the obstacles to an application of the unconditional MFN principle appear to be less severe than in value-added services.

Finally it should be recognized that data services play a dominant role in international trade in the entire service sector and even of information-intensive manufactured goods.

If the Group of Negotiations on Services adopts the approach of a general umbrella agreement that is supplemented by various industry-specific codes, telecommunication and data services need not necessarily be subject to an industry code. Since an agreement on transborder data flows would facilitate international trade in most other sectors it might be appropriate to include data services in the umbrella agreement itself.

Summary

In past GATT rounds the main elements of the MFN principle, multilateralism and non-discrimination, have been extended to several non-tariff barriers to trade in goods such as export subsidies, dumping practices, and public procurement. As the potential for international trade in services has increased significantly, a liberalization agreement on services could contribute to a further international division of labor and could promote economic growth and welfare in all participating countries.

For a regime of free trade in services, however, a simple extension of existing GATT rules to services would not be sufficient. In contrast with trade in goods, trade in services is strongly affected by government controls within countries that are in general not covered by the GATT treaty. Concessions by national governments necessary for trade liberalization are therefore much more significant in service markets than in goods markets.

For this reason and because of considerable differences in national regulatory systems, a multilateral agreement on liberalizing trade in services is hard to achieve. There is a strong trade-off between substance and country-coverage of such an agreement and the unconditional MFN principle is but one possible guideline for the negotiations. Insisting on this principle, it is argued, could block the entire process of liberalization. Others point out that bilateral and reciprocal arrangements would probably result in discrimination against less powerful countries and especially against the developing world.

Telecommunication and data services are certainly in the centre of international trade in services. They not only constitute a rapidly expanding industry with promising prospects for further growth but also provide important inputs for international trade in many other industries. Therefore, these services should probably be included in an umbrella agreement on trade in services instead of a separate industry code.

Trade liberalization in data services is concerned with three fields: networks and basic services, value-added services, and telecommunication equipment. An application of the unconditional MFN principle seems feasible especially with regard to agreements on the access of foreign-controlled companies to basic services and on technical standards for telecommunication equipment. The main difficulties will probably arise from liberalization of trade in value-added services. Here, an approach incorporating the concept of 'appropriate regulations' and the institution of a Regulations Committee probably provides a strategy for establishing or maintaining the unconditional MFN principle.

As the liberalization of trade in services is often considered a threat to national regulatory systems, many governments are reluctant to join a multilateral non-discriminatory agreement. Hence, some observers argue that progress could only be made by conditional trading arrangements. The historical evidence suggests, however, that discrimination facilitates the rise of protectionism and that greater progress towards free trade is achieved by the unconditional MFN principle.

ENDNOTES

1 Bhagwati (1984) even states that "trade negotiations are unfortunately conducted on the perverse assumption that one's tariff reductions are a loss rather than a gain." And Aho and Aronson (1985, 6) conclude, that "unless forward momentum is maintained, the trading system, like the bicyclist, will tumble over."

2 For a survey see Jackson, Davey (1986, 432ff.); Hesse (1988).

3 Sometimes this concept is also referred to as 'optional MFN' (Group of Negotiations on Services, 1987a).

4 One possible explanation for the different forms of government interventions in goods markets and services markets is that many services are "experience goods" rather than "inspection goods." "Hence, regulation of the output of services industries is difficult. It is less costly for governments to regulate the quality of inputs into the provision of services." (Hindley, 1988a).

5 This taxonomy was originally developed by Bhagwati (1984). It is very similar to the approches of Sampson and Snape (1985) and Gray (1988).

6 In official balance-of-payments statistics labor and investment income from abroad are also treated as trade in services. If trade in services is analyzed in analogy to trade in goods, this item must be excluded. The remaining items are non-factor services.

7 For a brief survey of government regulations in different service industries see Klodt (1988b) and the references cited therein. See also Hindley (1988b).

8 For a more detailed description of the possible content of this framework, see Group of Negotiations on Services, 1987b.

9 The U.S. government would obviously prefer the latter alternative (see Feketekuty, 1985). Some U.S. enterprises suggested a conditional MFN approach even to phases one and two (The Coalition of Services Industries, 1988).

10 See also Randhawa (1987) and Bhagwati (1987).

11 For a discussion of the boundaries between basic services and value-added services see OECD, 1988.

12 This suggested procedure is very similar to the control of national subsidies by the Commission of the European Communities according to Articles 92 to 94 of the EEC treaty (see e.g. Schina, 1987).

INSTITUTIONAL ASPECTS

Francis Gurry

Introduction

The decision to launch negotiations on trade in services, as part of the present Uruguay Round of Multilateral Trade Negotiations, set the aim of establishing "a multilateral framework of principles and rules for trade in services" (Appendix A of the present volume). Much attention has been directed at the content of the rules of substance which need to be evolved to facilitate trade in services and it is tempting to regard the establishment of these rules of substance as the major task of the negotiations. Equally important, however, will be a set of institutional arrangements designed to regulate the relations between contracting parties with respect to the implementation and further development of the rules of substance.

Such a set of institutional arrangements involves much more, of course, than considerations of an administrative nature. At stake is what may be compendiously described as the credibility of the multilateral framework, a matter which depends less on the formal adoption of the rules than on the practical implementation of the adopted rules in the trading practices and policies of the contracting parties. If the system of rules which emerges from the negotiations is to provide a viable framework for trade in services, the mutual concessions needed to reach agreement on the rules must also find expression in a satisfactory level of compliance with the rules. The role of institutional procedures is to provide, through appropriate mechanisms, the assurance of sufficient compliance with the rules to maintain the confidence of the contracting parties in the system.

Traditional Difficulties

While credibility is essential to the survival of any system of rules, its achievement in the context of international instruments has been a notoriously difficult and persistent problem. States have traditionally been reluctant to commit themselves to institutional procedures which involve supervisory or enforcement mechanisms, since such procedures involve a commitment to a higher level of international integration. They require a concession on the part of States which is of a higher order than that needed for mere agreement with a rule of conduct. Where mere agreement with a rule of conduct is required, the State retains the autonomy to control the implementation of the rule in accordance with its perceptions of domestic political and economic needs and pressures. Agreement to an institutional procedure designed to supervise or enforce compliance with a rule of conduct, in contrast, involves a loss of measure of autonomy to control the implementation of the rule and, thus, a loss of power to deal with perceived domestic needs and pressures.

The difficulty presented by the traditional reluctance of States to concede any part of their autonomy to choose how best to implement international rules is compounded by the characteristic generality of such rules. Typically, multilateral rules result from long and often difficult deliberation and negotiation. Their final form may reflect a balance of the interests expressed during the negotiation process and a compromise between certainty of operation, on the one hand, and sufficient flexibility to encourage widespread adhesion, on the other. The breadth of subject matter covered also often requires a concentration on matters of broad principle, rather than on details of implementation. The resultant generality of the rules discourages the concession to an external authority of the power to interpret the rules and to determine whether the rules have been implemented domestically, not the least because of a fear that such a process of interpretation may create new obligations which were not understood to be included within the meaning of the rules when adopted.

The Context of Trade in Telecommunication and Data Services

The traditional difficulties associated with reaching agreement on effective institutional procedures are in no way less compelling in the context of trade in telecommunication and data services. There are, in addition, a number of particular features of the environment of trade in these services which need to be taken into consideration in the design of institutional procedures in this context.

The first pertinent feature to be noted concerning trade in these services is its essentially international character, which results from the mobility given to information by existing technology for its storage, retrieval and transmission. Whether the trade relates to access for remuneration to a data base, the design and supply of systems or operating software, the supply of engineering or systems-analysis services in connection with computer and telecommunication systems, or the use of the telecommunication network, this trade is characterized by evolution in the context of the global marketplace and is, in many instances, designed specifically for such a marketplace. This international character, which creates interdependence, suggests that trade in data services is an area which is particularly appropriate for an attempt to achieve a high level of international integration.

On the other hand, in a historical perspective, trade in data services is a relatively new phenomenon. Several relevant consequences flow from this novelty. The first of these is a relative lack, compared to trade in goods, of factual and statistical information on the extent of such trade, the ways in which it occurs, national regulatory practices and the impact of such practices on international trade.

A second consequence, aggravated partly by the lack of available factual information and partly by the speed and extent of technological change in the modalities of trade in data services, is the lack of an agreed conceptual and definitional framework for dealing with the regulation of trade in data services. Conceptual and definitional problems affect the area of trade in services in general and it has often been suggested that a sectoral approach, which aims at negotiating rules separately for each possible sector of services, may assist in overcoming this difficulty. While such an approach would certainly contribute to making the notion of services less amorphous and unmanageable, it remains the case that the sector of data services raises its own particular definitional problems. For example, print, broadcast and telephone and telegraph were once considered discrete spheres, subject to different regulatory considerations. Electronic publication and the various types of services and methods of delivery in electronic publication, however, cross these traditional categories. Teletext, a one-way distribution system of pages or units of information, can be transmitted by television broadcast signals. Videotexts, an interactive two-way system for the request and retrieval of information from a data base, is commonly transmitted over telephone lines. The conceptual difficulties which such new technologies have produced have not always been resolved on the national level, so that the establishment not only of international rules but also of international mechanisms to regulate the national implementation of such rules may be considered by some premature.

The view that it may be premature to attempt a high level of international integration is also supported by the special problems which trade in data services may raise in connection with one area which States most frequently seek to reserve from international jurisdiction: national security. National security is, or can be made to be, a peculiarly compendious term. Matters which it is sought to incorporate within the term include, for example, the strategic importance of self-reliance in information capacity, so that a country's industries are not reliant on external data bases and information resources. Such an argument is not necessarily distinguishable from self-reliance in respect of any raw material, or from arguments in respect of the need to allow restrictions for infant industries. National security may, however, be more identifiably in question when the data services are capable of military application, since export restrictions on items having such an application are already widespread. [1]

A further facet of the newness of some of the technologies involved in trade in data services which is pertinent to the design of institutional arrangements is the unevenness of the development of data services internationally which results from differences in technological capacity, particularly between the industrialized countries and the developing countries. Because of their relatively limited experience with such services, the regulatory issues involved may be less familiar to some developing countries. In consequence, such countries may feel that they are being placed in a position where they are required to resolve issues internationally before having adequate opportunity to examine the national implications of such issues.

Key Elements of a Framework

The particular features of the environment of trade in data services, coupled with the traditional difficulties associated with achieving international agreement on institutional arrangements which touch on national autonomy to oversee the implementation of internationally agreed rules, underline the need for realistic expectations and gradual progress in the design of institutional procedures. It cannot be expected that States will suddenly shed traditional inhibitions, especially in an area subject to rapid evolution where the subject matter is being submitted to international agreement for the first time. Any move towards a higher level of integration should, accordingly, be presented in manageable steps which permit gradual evolution. To this end, it would also seem desirable that the different procedures which might possibly be implemented should be segregated in the negotiation process.

In general, there are four such procedures, namely those which are directed at:

- the *surveillance* of national practices through a reporting or information-gathering mechanism;

- the *settlement of disputes* arising between two or more contracting States over the non-observance or violation of existing rules;

- the further *development of rules* through a mechanism for the revision of existing rules and for the adoption of new rules; and

- the *enforcement* of compliance with a rule in circumstances in which it has been established that the rule has not been observed or has been violated.

Surveillance or Monitoring (Transparency)

The surveillance or monitoring of the national implementation of international rules suggests a very highly developed form of international integration. The usual modalities of surveillance or monitoring in multilateral agreements, however, are less radical than the words "surveillance" or "monitoring" imply.

The basic objective of surveillance or monitoring is to achieve transparency through the provision of adequate information on national regulations and practices which affect trade in the relevant sectors. The obligation to provide such information imposes a form of self-discipline on the contracting party, which is thereby required to assess the ramifications of any measures which it adopts on the functioning of the multilateral rules to which it has agreed. The information so provided contributes to the establishment of a factual and statistical base for the evaluation of the effectiveness and appropriateness of international rules.

Three stages may be considered in the design of a surveillance or monitoring procedure:

(1) At the first level, there may be an obligation on the part of contracting parties to furnish information on any national measure (whether in the form of a law, a regulation under a law, or a defined administrative practice) which is directed at or affects the operation of an agreed international rule. Such an obligation may apply either after the establishment of the relevant national measure, or, more effectively, in advance of the implementation of the measure and immediately after an intention has been formed to implement the proposed measure. The requirement of advanced notification obviously allows for the theoretical possibility of a modification to any proposed measure, and certainly leaves less room for a State to claim that modification is impossible owing to the adoption of changed practices in its market.

(2) A second stage, consequent on the first, is the distribution of the information reported to all other contracting parties. At this stage also, it would obviously be desirable to foresee an administrative function in the collation and analysis of the information reported and the publication of the collations and analyses.

(3) The third and most advanced stage would be the establishment of an Advisory Committee comprising delegates from the contracting parties. The function of the Advisory Committee would be to examine reported information and to advise the Council or Governing body of the contracting parties on any inconsistencies between

national measures and international rules. Such advice could form the basis for bringing into operation other provisions in the overall agreement with respect to enforcement.

Existing mechanisms for reporting and information-gathering in multilateral agreements are somewhat undeveloped. Article 10 of the GATT provides for the prompt publication, "in such a manner as to enable governments and traders to become acquainted with them," of laws, regulations, judicial decisions and administrative rulings of general application relating to customs and imports and exports. In particular, Article 10 requires that no measure increasing a rate of duty or other charge on imports under an established and uniform practice, or imposing a new or more burdensome requirement on imports, shall be enforced before official publication. In addition, Article 10 requires each contracting party to maintain its own system of tribunals or procedures for the review of administrative action relating to customs matters.

The notification requirements of Article 10 are confirmed in the Understanding Regarding Notification, Consultation, Dispute Settlement and Surveillance adopted by the Contracting Parties of GATT in November 1979 (IBDD, Supplement No. 26, 231 ff.) which also adds an undertaking, to the maximum extent possible, of *advance* notification of trade measures affecting the operation of the GATT. In addition, the Understanding contains a provision whereby the Contracting Parties agree to review trade measures notified. The operation of the system, however, remains primarily one of notification and publication, and the evaluation of notified information for the purposes of identifying inconsistencies with obligations under that GATT is left rather to the domain of dispute-settlement than actively pursued through a more disinterested review by the Contracting Parties.

The existence of a review mechanism operating through an Advisory Committee is more easily applied in the context of bilateral trade agreements, where examples can be found in the form of the Canada-United States Trade Agreement, or of the Joint Committee under the China-EEC Trade and Economic Cooperation Agreement. In such contexts, the smaller volume and less diversified forms of trade (in comparison with global trade) render the task of monitoring easier.

In the context of multilateral trade in data services, the conceptual difficulties associated with the definition of such trade and the rate of technological change in the modalities of such trade, as well as the relative lack of available factual and statistical information, need to be taken into account. These factors may suggest that institutional procedures relating to surveillance and monitoring should initially be limited to a reporting obligation, as well as a procedure for the publication of collations and analyses of the information reported. The function of these procedures, at this stage, would thus be to advance understanding of national practices and to create a more reliable base of factual information concerning the issues in trade in data services, thereby assisting the future evolution of any system. The further stage of the establishment of an Advisory Committee to identify inconsistent national practices might be considered premature until greater experience has been gained in the functioning of any new rules which emerge from the negotiations and in the ways in which national measures impinge on trade in data services.

Dispute Settlement

An effective mechanism for dispute settlement lies at the heart of a framework of institutional procedures. Whereas a surveillance mechanism aims at preventing or bringing to light national measures which may be inconsistent with agreed rules, the existence of a dispute indicates the perception by a contracting party that the non-observance or violation of an obligation has already taken place and has caused or is causing prejudice. Unless the friction caused by the dispute can be satisfactorily eliminated, disillusionment with the system of rules is likely to develop quickly.

In the context of international commercial relations and transactions, a reasonably well-developed institutional environment exists both for disputes which occur between States and for disputes arising in transactions or dealings between private parties or economic agents of different national origin. Disputes between States concern the framework agreement of international commercial and economic relations and raise considerations which relate to the constitution or structure of the system within which individual transactions and dealings should take place. Disputes between private parties or economic agents, on the other hand, are concerned with the individual transactions or dealings which are conducted within the framework.

There are legal reasons for the separation of these two spheres of disputes. It is a truism of international law that States cannot be compelled to submit their disputes to a settlement procedure. A submission to such a procedure can occur only in so far as the State has agreed to an obligation and to a mechanism to discuss or resolve differences relating to the existence or operation of the obligation. An individual transaction between private parties, on the other hand, will take place in one or more jurisdictions which will accept or assert the authority to rule on differences or disputes arising in connection with the transaction.

More important, however, than the legal reasons for the distinction drawn between the two types of dispute is the difference in objectives between procedures designed to resolve disputes in the two spheres. Dispute settlement in the State sphere is not necessarily directed at attributing fault or blame. More commonly, its aim is to preserve or restore the often delicate balance of concessions and obligations which has emerged from the long negotiations leading to the agreed framework of a regulatory system.

Dispute settlement in respect of individual transactions between private parties or economic agents, on the other hand, is concerned more with the transaction itself, without reference to the larger considerations of the system as a whole. Its objective is to achieve a workable solution that will facilitate the continuation of the economic activity envisaged by the transaction and avoid the sterilization of the resources which have been committed to the transaction. Consequently, the terms of settlement or remedies are likely to differ in the two spheres. In the State sphere the terms of settlement may seek an adjustment for the future in national measures which affect the structure of the system. In the sphere of the individual transaction, the remedy may be directed at the payment of compensation in respect of a past wrong or failure to fulfill the agreed terms of the transaction, as well as a workable solution to achieve the future consummation of the transaction.

The Institutional Environment of the State Sphere

Three principle models of pacific dispute settlement between States exist in international affairs: diplomatic procedures, conciliation and arbitration, and judicial resolution.

1. Diplomatic Procedures

The diplomatic procedures used as part of an institutional procedure for dispute resolution range from an obligation to consult, often coupled with an obligation to provide information relating to the subject matter of the complaint or dispute, to the use of mediation in some form, such as the good offices of a third party.

Consultation is a desirable preliminary mechanism. It may serve the purpose of limiting frivolous complaints and clarifying the issues in dispute by encouraging dialogue between the parties. Where coupled with an obligation to furnish information concerning the matters raised in a complaint, consultation can be a valuable means of identifying the extent and effect of any prejudice being caused by the complaint.

While useful, however, an obligation to consult has significant limitations as a procedure for dispute settlement. It leaves the issue in question as a matter between the parties themselves, without any objective assessment of the question, and thus does not contain a safeguard against the disproportionate exercise of economic or negotiating power on the part of the stronger party. Dispute resolution through consultations or negotiations also typically results in a private settlement without detailed published reasons explaining the terms of settlement. Negotiated settlements therefore contribute less to the evolution of the system through the development of a known body of acceptable norms and practices.

Mediation involves the continuation of consultations under the guidance, direction or supervision of a third party. The introduction of the third party is seen as a means of crystallizing the issues between the parties through the focus of an outside party who is able to provide a dispassionate view and, thus, direction as to the key issues. The outside party can further serve the role of providing the parties with insights into the likely way in which an impartial adjudicating authority would view the merits of the respective positions of the parties should the dispute proceed to a form of arbitration.

Mediation is, however, non-binding and, may thus be criticized as time-consuming and involving the commitment of resources with the risk that no concrete result will emerge. It has also been said that, if there is a will on the part of the parties to find a satisfactory resolution to their dispute, they will be able to do this without the intervention of a third party (Plank, 1987). Mediation is more suitable to disputes which are inherently political, where progress is expected to be slow and the purpose is to defuse tension, than to economic ones, where the emphasis will be on the need to find a pragmatic solution in the shortest period possible to enable the continuation of economic activity without further prejudice to the principles of the system regulating the activity.

2. Arbitration

Arbitration is a method of dispute resolution in which the parties choose, or approve the choice of, the judge or arbitrator, the place and forum in which the proceedings will be conducted, and the law and procedure which will be applied in those proceedings. [2] In contrast to consultations, arbitration involves an objective assessment of the issues by an outside party, thus reducing any advantage enjoyed by a disputant with greater economic or negotiating power.

Arbitration is sometimes preceded by an obligatory procedure for conciliation. Conciliation, while tending to be subject to more formal and pre-conceived procedures than mediation in general, raises the same considerations as mediation and thus will not be discussed further.

Arbitration has a long history in international affairs as a method of settling *ad hoc* disputes between States. It is also a feature of the institutional procedure for dispute settlement within international systems regulating particular activities, such as the GATT, discussed below.

Arbitration has a number of advantages over judicial resolution before the International Court of Justice as a method of dispute settlement between States. Generally, it tends to be less adversarial and less likely to suggest that the dispute has become an *affaire d' etat*, involving all of the consequent rigidity of position which national pride insinuates into such affairs. Arbitration tends to be less concerned with the attribution of fault and the allocation of blame, and more directed towards finding a pragmatic solution which the parties themselves have been unable to reach agreement on. In contrast to judicial proceedings, arbitration also tends to be quicker, less subject to procedural formalities, more accessible to an effective array of remedies, and can confer the often paramount attraction of the conduct of the proceedings in confidentiality.

3. Judicial Resolution

Resort to the International Court of Justice as a means of dispute settlement between States in relation to economic affairs has few advocates. In 1944 Manley O. Hudson observed that "a conviction seems widespread that judicial settlement is not the best way of handling economic disputes" (Hudson, 1944, 213). The same reasons which make arbitration attractive suggest that judicial resolution, with its relatively lengthy and formal proceedings, and adjudication by generalists rather than specialists, is inappropriate.

Where disputes arise in the context of a multilateral agreement seeking to regulate activity in a specific area, judicial resolution seems particularly inappropriate. In such a context, the principal concern is the preservation of the balance of concessions and obligations contained in the system. Resort to judicial settlement may have a shocking effect on this balance and may introduce an ossification of the issues, rather than a gradual evolution of a definition of acceptable norms and practices.

4. The Example of GATT

Most of the modes of dispute settlement referred to above, with the exclusion of judicial resolution, are utilized by the GATT. Indeed, its liberal use of various modes constitutes the basis of one of the criticisms leveled at the GATT dispute-settlement machinery, namely, that it is too complex and contains too many options.

The GATT procedures are principally contained in Articles XXII and XXIII. As pointed out by Professor Jackson (Jackson, 1969, 164-165), however, Articles XXII and XXIII can scarcely be considered to contain the only dispute-settlement apparatus in the GATT. There are, for example, seventeen other Articles in the GATT which contain an obligation to consult, mainly as a prophylactic measure designed to prevent disputes through negotiation.

Article XXII envisages a procedure for consultations in respect of "any matter affecting the operation of [the] Agreement". (See Appendix C to the present volume.) It requires, in the first place, bilateral consultations. Failing a satisfactory solution through such consultations, it prescribes multilateral consultations among the Contracting Parties. Article XXIII (Appendix C) is directed at the nullification or impairment of any benefit accruing directly or indirectly under the Agreement, or an impediment to the attainment of any objective of the Agreement. It also requires consultations as the first stage of any settlement of the dispute, followed by, in the event that the consultations fail to effect a "satisfactory adjustment" between the relevant parties, a reference of the matter to the Contracting Parties.

These Articles contain only a skeleton framework. An extensive practice concerning the management of disputes has, however, developed since the adoption in 1952 of a proposal for a panel procedure to deal with complaints. Pursuant to this procedure, experts are empanelled to receive and hear submissions from the parties to a dispute, conciliate between the parties, and perform a quasi-arbitral function in making recommendations to the Contracting Parties concerning the dispute. The practice concerning panels in dispute settlement was codified and adopted by the Contracting Parties on 28 November 1979 following the Tokyo Round of Multilateral Trade Negotiations in the Understanding Regarding Notification, Consultation, Dispute Settlement and Surveillance. The Understanding has since been subject to some amendment, particularly in the Ministerial Declaration of 29 November 1982 (IBDD, Supplement No. 29, 14-16).

Perhaps the most important point to be noted concerning the GATT dispute-settlement procedures is, as set out in the Understanding, that the objective is "to settle disputes not by decisions of a legal nature, but by recommendations designed to re-establish the balance of concessions and advantages between the disputing parties". Sanctions have generally been considered by the Contracting Parties to be inappropriate following a reference to them of a dispute, and have been authorized in only one case, in 1955. [3] Rather than re-establishing the balance of concessions and advantages, sanctions can have the effect of defeating the very purpose of the Agreement, namely the liberalization of trade.

Individual International Transactions

The ever-increasing volume of transactions and dealings that have characterized international trade and commerce in recent decades has been accompanied by significant developments in the institutional structure for dispute settlement between private parties in international commercial transactions.

The modes of dispute settlement which are available in respect of disputes between States exist in parallel in the sphere of individual international commercial transactions, namely, consultation and negotiation, arbitration and judicial settlement. Consultation is often specifically required in international contracts and often encouraged through a requirement of notification to a defaulting party of an alleged default, followed by a designated waiting period before taking other action. Since the parties to a contract will usually be in constant contact, consultation is also perhaps more easily implemented in this sphere than between States. Arbitration and judicial settlement, however, are the usual means adopted to resolve disputes, the latter being determined by a national court accepting or asserting jurisdiction in respect of the dispute through an application of the ordinary rules of private international law.

The greatest strides towards developing an institutional mechanism with widespread acceptance in international commercial transactions have been made with respect to arbitration. There are a number of well-known advantages that arbitration offers, mirroring the advantages of arbitration over judicial settlement in the State sphere, that account for this.

Perhaps most importantly, arbitration is often preferred in international commercial transactions between private parties in order to avoid any advantage which might be seen to accrue by resort to the judicial system of the country of which one party is a national. The choice of a neutral forum and law and procedure places both parties on an equal footing, neither enjoying greater familiarity with the institutions, procedures and legal culture pursuant to which the dispute will be resolved.

This basic function fulfilled by arbitration has been increasingly recognized by national legislatures through the enactment of Arbitration laws, and by many national courts, which have progressively revised their traditional hostility to arbitration clauses which, through the designation of an outside forum and law, were once regarded as ousting the courts' proper jurisdiction. Thus, the Supreme Court of the United States stated in *The Bremen* v. *Zapata Off-Shore Co.*

"For at least two decades we have witnessed an expansion of overseas commercial activities by business enterprises based in the United States. ...The expansion of American business and industry will hardly be encouraged if, notwithstanding solemn contracts, we insist on a parochial concept that all disputes must be resolved under our laws and in our courts. ...We cannot have trade and commerce in world markets and international waters exclusively on our terms, governed by our laws, and resolved in our courts." (407 US 1 (1972))

Resort to arbitration as a method of dispute settlement has also a number of perceived advantages over State litigation systems. The civil litigation system in many countries is burdened with a large volume of work which can produce what are seen by the business community to be inordinate delays in the prosecution of a case. Costs of an arbitration are generally lower than litigation within a State system and procedure is more flexible, leaving less room for the tactical manoeuvering which is common in litigation in a State system.

A further significant reason for increased resort to arbitration is the scale and complexity of the technical issues raised by disputes in areas subject to rapid technological development. In such a context of advanced or rapidly developing technology, the technicality of the issues may call for judgment by an expert in the relevant field rather than by a generalist. The technology often also precedes its legal regulation, so that the additional powers of an arbitrator to act as *amiable compositeur* and to decide on just measures in accordance with the circumstances may be desirable.

Arbitration is often also said to be more sensitive to the needs of the business community. This view is based partly on the attitude which leads to the choice of arbitration rather than litigation and partly on the flexibility of arbitral proceedings and the range of remedies available to an arbitrator. The choice of arbitration, rather than litigation, may reflect a desire to achieve a workable solution to a problem which has arisen in a commercial relationship. The arbitration may thus be conceived as a continuation of the business relationship, with the assistance of an outside umpire, rather than a hostile, adversary proceeding.

Many of these considerations can be seen in the Order and Remarks of the Arbitrators in the arbitration between IBM Corporation and Fujitsu Ltd, decided in 1987. [4] This arbitration concerned a complex and long dispute over the alleged violation by Fujitsu of IBM's copyright in certain operating system software. In the words of one of the Arbitrators, the Order of the Arbitrators was "a framework - a blueprint - for constructing a workable way for both companies to maintain their principles, protect their customers, and compete vigorously in the marketplace. ...It is because both companies preferred to devote resources to marketplace competition rather than copyright and contract battles that this Order is possible." [5] The Arbitrators' Order included, accordingly, remedies directed at the future business relationship of the parties, such as the Secured Facility regime, pursuant to which specified personnel of a party were to be given access in a Secured Facility to programming material of the other party from which they might derive and place on survey sheets certain interface specifications and other information, in return for compensation. The information so extracted could then be used by a different programming team of the company granted access for the purposes of developing software. The Secured Facility regime was said to bring "certainty to both companies and their customers in an area which has been marked by uncertainty and a great deal of suspicion."[6]

The great increase in the use of international commercial arbitration, explained by the foregoing advantages, has brought about a developed and stable institutional environment for arbitration. This well-developed structure for the conduct of international commercial arbitration consists of three main components - arbitration centres, rules for the conduct of arbitration and provisions relating to the enforcement of foreign arbitral awards.

Among the many centers which have been established to provide a facility for the conduct of international commercial arbitration, particular mention may perhaps be made of the American Arbitration Association (AAA); the Arbitration Institution of the Stockholm Chamber of Commerce; the Inter-American Commercial Arbitration Commission (IACAC); the International Chamber of Commerce (ICC) Court of Arbitration; the London Court of Arbitration; and the Regional Center for Arbitration at Kuala Lumpur.

Each of the afore-mentioned centres has issued a standard clause for inclusion in contracts in which the parties wish to submit their disputes to arbitration administered by the centre. Each has also adopted a set of rules for the conduct of arbitration. Significant progress towards the adoption of a common framework of arbitration proceedings was also made with the formulation of the Arbitration Rules of the United Nations Commission on International Trade Law (UNCITRAL). [7] The UNCITRAL Rules were adopted by the General Assembly of the United Nations in 1976, [8] pursuant to a Resolution which recognized "the value of Arbitration as a method of settling disputes arising in the context of international commercial relations" and which expressed the conviction that "the establishment of rules for *ad hoc* arbitration that are acceptable in countries with different legal, social and economic systems would significantly contribute to the development of harmonious international relations".

A key component in the development of the structure for international commercial arbitration was added by the 1958 Convention on the Recognition and Enforcement of Foreign Arbitral Awards. Fifty-six States have ratified the Convention, which seeks to secure the recognition and enforcement of arbitral awards "made in the territory of a State other than the State where recognition and enforcement is sought". The Convention facilitates the enforcement of a foreign arbitral award by simplifying formalities required to enforce an award and by limiting the grounds on which the enforcement of a foreign arbitral award can be refused. Experience subsequent to the adoption of the Convention has shown that the general tendency of courts has been to grant recognition and enforcement under the Convention wherever possible (Sanders, 1979, 269-287).

Interaction Between the Two Spheres

There are signs, still somewhat sporadic, of interaction between the once discretely separated spheres of disputes between States and disputes between private economic agents.

It is not uncommon to find in bilateral treaties directed at setting the framework of trading relations between the relevant States a reference to arbitration of disputes arising between the economic agents operating within the framework set by the treaties. The commercial treaties of the United States, for example, have provided since 1950 for the reciprocal enforcement of arbitration agreements and awards in respect of disputes between nationals and companies of either party, regardless of the place of arbitration and nationality of the arbitrators. The Trade Agreement of 7 July, 1979 between the United States and China went much further than mere recognition and enforcement of arbitral awards. Article 8 contains quite elaborate provisions in respect of trade-related disputes between the firms, corporations, companies and trade organizations of the respective contracting parties, prescribing consultation, conciliation and, ultimately, arbitration in China, the United States or a third country.

Provisions in treaties such as those mentioned in the preceding paragraph are significant for reaching beyond the relationship of obligations and concessions between the States themselves to the economic agents which are intended to operate within the framework of these obligations and concessions.

There are also signs that States or their agencies are increasingly involved directly in arbitration with private parties. It was estimated that in 1987 one sixth of the parties to arbitration before the ICC Court of Arbitration were States or State agencies (Jarvin, 1986, 15).

The most significant development in this respect has been the establishment of the International Centre for Settlement of Investment Disputes (ICSID), which was created by the Convention on the Settlement of Investment Disputes between States and Nationals of Other States (ICSID Convention). The Convention came into force on 14 October 1966. As of 30 June 1987, eighty-eight States had ratified the Convention.

The ICSID Convention is remarkable, in particular, for two matters. First, it provides for an arbitration procedure -- subject, like any other arbitration, to the consent of the parties -- between a Contracting State or "any constituent subdivision or agency of a Contracting State", on the one hand, and a national of another Contracting State, on the other hand. It thus provides for an institutional procedure bridging the two traditional spheres of arbitrations between States and arbitrations between private parties.

Secondly, the jurisdiction accorded to the ICSID by the Convention extends "to any legal dispute arising directly out of an investment" (Article 25). Nowhere in the ICSID Convention, however, is the term "investment" defined. The Convention thus addresses the problem of international investment not by setting obligations and providing for a mechanism for regulating disputes between States in relation to those obligations, but by taking international investment, State intervention in such investment, and disputes as matters of fact. The difficulty of achieving agreement on a multilateral basis about standards and obligations in relation to international investment is thus avoided. Rather, international cooperation is directed at resolving disputes and, therefore, permitting the continuation of activity in this important domain.

Resort to the arbitration facilities of ICSID was infrequent at the start. The first dispute submitted to ICSID arbitration was in January 1972, five years after the entry into force of the ICSID Convention. Since that time, however, activity has intensified. The 1987 Annual Report of ICSID records a total of twenty-three disputes having been submitted to ICSID arbitration or conciliation.

The Context of Trade in Telecommunication and Data Services

In addition to the particular features of trade in telecommunication and data services described above, which are pertinent to institutional arrangements in general, there are several other features of such trade which are of special relevance to the design of an appropriate dispute-settlement mechanism.

The first cluster of features is the often instantaneous nature of trade in these services and the continuity of relationship between supplier and customer in such trade. The interest of an enterprise or agency using a data base located in a foreign country is instantaneous, or near instantaneous, access to the data base, and the confidence that the service provided by access to the data base will continue without disruption. A legislative or administrative measure introduced in either the country of the user or the country in which the data base is located, which affects in some way the user's access to the data base, will have an immediate impact on trade. In contrast, in the case of most goods, a legislative or administrative measure affecting trade in goods will not have such an immediate impact. It may be possible for any adverse effects of such a measure to be absorbed by adjustment of the quantity of goods produced, by stock-piling, or by using production time to locate an alternative market. The instantaneous and continuous nature of trade in data services underlines the importance of a dispute-settlement mechanism which is efficient in the sense that it is able to produce resolutions to disputes within a time-frame which is related to, or takes account of, the immediate impact of a disruptive measure.

Secondly, more so than in respect of trade in goods, a disruption in trade in telecommunication and data services has a potential for ramifications or consequences beyond the immediate act. This potential derives from the very notion of a service as an aid, help or assistance to some other function. Thus, if access to a data base is disrupted, or the use of the telecommunication system is impeded, the damage is not just felt in the use of the data base or the telecommunication system, but penetrates into all of the ancillary services and acts which depend on the utilization of the data base or the telecommunication system. Restrictions that interfere with the availability of data services may, therefore, significantly disrupt many other national and international commercial and financial operations.

Because of the use of the air waves and common-carrier transmission facilities, such as the telephone system, disputes in respect of trade in data services are also likely to involve a mixture of juridical personalities. The State's role in the provision and regulation of common-carrier facilities has been prominent. Disputes are likely to involve States, State agencies with varying degrees of independence from the State, and corporations or trade associations. The independence of the spheres of disputes between States and disputes between private parties may therefore be called into question.

Elements of a Possible Structure

In designing a possible structure for the resolution of disputes, it is necessary at the outset to define clearly the objective sought to be achieved through a dispute-settlement mechanism. This objective, it is suggested, should be the provision of an efficient and impartial or de-politicized mechanism which enables any preceived non-observance or violation of a multilaterally agreed obligation to be corrected in the shortest possible time, thus restoring the original balance of concessions and obligations which has been adopted in the negotiation process.

In order to implement this objective, it would be desirable to provide several different procedures which allow for the different treatment of disputes of friction between contracting parties, according to the perceived gravity of the dispute. However, the introduction of different procedures gives rise to the possibility, much criticized in the present dispute-settlement system in the GATT, of procedural manoeuvering and delay. It would seem essential, therefore, that, while different procedures be provided, a clear demarcation should exist so as to favor the possibility of the quick resolution of a dispute through the choice of a clearly defined route.

Given the desirability of providing clearly separated procedures, it is suggested that an efficient dispute-settlement mechanism might comprise the following three elements:

(1) The first element would be a consultation procedure, whose aim would be twofold -- first, to provide a mechanism for the resolution of friction or minor irritants arising in the operation of the agreed rules, but not constituting a clear case of non-observance or violation of the rules; and, secondly, to provide at the *option* of a contracting party, a preliminary procedure to an arbitration.

Obviously, the contracting parties cannot be prevented from consulting amongst themselves and, as a matter of practice, bilateral consultations on trade matters of mutual interest take place constantly. The objective of a consultation mechanism should be, therefore, to encourage the conduct of such consultations in the environment most consistent with the nature of the framework, namely, a *multilateral* framework for the conduct of trade. Thus, consideration might be given to the provision of a forum in the headquarters of the secretariat for the administration of the agreement on a regular (for example, annual) basis, Within this forum, bilateral consult-ations, which might otherwise take place in the capitals, could be held in a multilateral atmosphere. The advantages of such a forum would be that the resolution of bilateral disputes might take greater account of the multilateral implications of any settlement. Moreover, the application of superior economic or political power on grounds unrelated to the dispute would be less likely to pass unnoticed by disinterested parties.

(2) The second element in a possible structure would be the provision of an arbitration mechanism, compulsory in the sense that all con-tracting parties would submit to its jurisdiction. Such a mechanism, of course, exists in the present procedures in the GATT, but the opportunity could be taken to seek to improve certain of its most commonly criticized features.

The first feature generally found to be deficient in the present procedures of the GATT is the possibility for one party to inject excessive delay into the proceedings. In order to overcome this difficulty, it may be considered desirable to provide that each of the procedures which precedes an actual decision should take place automatically, in the absence of the exercise by a disputant of a right with respect to each procedure. Thus, each disputant would have a right to select one arbitrator in a panel, to submit evidence and so forth as under the existing procedures of the GATT. Defined time periods could be set for each procedure and a party would forgo its prerogative in respect of the procedure in the absence of compliance with the time period. Such a discipline would seem particularly appropriate in the context of disputes concerning trade in data services, in view of the immediate disruption which a national measure might introduce in such trade and in view of the ramifications for other forms of trade which such a measure might bring about.

A further feature of existing procedures under the GATT which might be re-considered is the nature of the decision which emerges from an arbitration. Under present procedures, a panel decision is in the form of a non-binding report which must be considered by the GATT Council. The removal of the decision to the Council has often been criticized on the basis that it opens the possibility of politicizing the dispute and consequently favors disputants with greater economic and political power. Consideration might therefore be given to making a decision on an arbitration binding on the disputants, thereby lessening the delays in implementing the decision and rendering the arbitration proceedings less open to political influences.

While the above-mentioned suggestions of strict time limits and the binding nature of an arbitration tend to increase the jurisdiction of an arbitration procedure, it may be considered desirable to restrict in another way the present jurisdiction for conciliation and arbitration procedures in the GATT. Article XXIII of the GATT operates on the basis on a nullification or impairment of a benefit accruing under the General Agreement. Such broad language introduces the possibility that arbitration proceedings might be used to create new obligations through a process of interpretation by filling gaps in the Agreement. While such a process of interpretation does not create difficulties for contracting parties whose legal system is compatible with an actively interventionist judicial or quasi-judicial role (the common-law jurisdictions), it clearly creates difficulties for certain legal traditions. Thus, an early communication from the EEC Delegation to the Negotiating Group on Dispute Settlement stated that the "machinery cannot and must not be used to create, through a process of deductive interpretation, new obligations for contracting parties, or to replace the negotiating process" (MTN. GNG/NG 12/W/12.) It may be considered desirable, therefore, to replace the notion of the nullification or impairment of a benefit with a narrower concept, such as the non-observance or violation of an existing obligation. Such a narrowing of the jurisdiction may encourage greater submission to a compulsory, binding procedure.

(3) A further element in a dispute-settlement structure might seek to establish a procedure for the resolution of disputes between economic agents in connection with the trade regulated by the framework agreement. In the preparatory session in 1947 leading to the GATT, a proposal to establish a procedure for direct complaints by in-

dividuals to an international trade organization was rejected (Jackson, 1969, 187-189). Much, however, has happened in the past 40 years to call for a re-consideration of this matter. International trade and commerce and economic inter-dependence have intensified, largely through the action of private economic agents, and the structure of international commercial arbitration has matured.

In many ways, the issue presented by the inclusion of non-State parties is a test of the relevance of regulatory systems established between States. For as long as non-State entities are excluded from the direct application of the systems, there is a risk that such systems will remain arcane to many of the principal agents of international trade and commerce. This may tend to encourage parallel structures operating in relative isolation -- one structure between States, little understood by private organizations, and another between the private economic agents, seeking pragmatic and non-political solutions to commercial problems which allow the continuation of the economic activity through which the dispute has arisen.

There are three main ways in which some form of access to dispute-settlement procedures could be granted to non-State parties. First, obligations under a multilateral agreement could be made self-executing, with the further obligation (for those constitutional systems which do not recognize the direct application of international obligations) of adopting the substantive obligations in national law. This method, however, requires a clarity and specificity of obligation which often escapes the conclusions of multilateral negotiations. It also carries the danger of introducing unnecessary rigidity into a system in which technology indicates that the nature and type of trade is in evolution, so that the obligations themselves may require time for development and modification.

Secondly, non-State parties could be accommodated by being allowed to make submissions directly in the course of dispute-settlement procedures between States. This method has the advantage of heightening awareness of the multilateral framework among the agents of trade, and of bringing first-hand experience and information to the dispute-settlement proceedings. It may, however, introduce into the proceedings, which are designed to preserve the balance of concessions and advantages in the multilateral system, considerations more relevant to issues connected with an individual transaction.

The third method is to concentrate on a facility designed for disputes relating to individual transactions within the multilateral framework, whether they be between private parties or private parties and States acting in a commercial capacity. Thus the framework could encourage the use of arbitration by recognising the validity of arbitration clauses, including such clauses submitted to by States; by establishing a new or designating an existing arbitration centre for the conduct of disputes arising in connection with the trade in question, as well as settling rules for the conduct of arbitration; and by providing for the enforcement of the awards made pursuant to the arbitration.

Rule Development and Evolution

In view of the rapid evolution of the modalities of trade in data services, it would be desirable that the review of existing rules should be institutionalized so as to ensure the adaptation and continued relevance of the rules to changing circumstances. This would seem to be particularly necessary also on the basis that any rules which emerge from the present round of negotiations will represent a first attempt at multilateral agreement on the subject matter.

In considering appropriate procedures for institutional review of the existing rules, two matters in particular require attention -- (1) the need for an advance commitment to regular negotiations for the review of existing rules; and (2) the possibility of allowing for higher levels of integration, not inconsistent with the basic agreement, amongst particular contracting parties or groups of contracting parties.

In respect of the regular periodic review of rules, it is possible that a commitment in this respect might be included in any framework agreement for trade in services in general which may emerge from the negotiations. Consideration might nevertheless be given to the inclusion of a specific obligation in this regard in respect of any sectoral agreements and, more particularly, any agreement relating to trade in data services, on account of the pronounced technological basis of such trade and of the rapidity with which change in that basis is taking place.

The possibility of permitting special agreements between particular contracting parties allowing for a higher level of integration or more specialized or detailed rules may be confronted with the possible criticism that such specialized agreements might have the effect of excluding or disadvantaging countries with less developed data services. If it is ensured, however, that any provision allowing specialized agreements is expressed in such a way that such agreements must not contravene the provisions of the basic agreement, an acceptable compromise might be reached whereby no disadvantage is incurred by non-participating countries. The failure to participate in the more specialized arrangements might then involve forgoing additional benefits accruing from the specialized arrangements, but the possibility of enjoying such additional benefits would remain open to all contracting parties wishing to submit to the more rigorous conditions in the specialized arrangements.

Enforcement

A procedure for the enforcement of obligations presents perhaps the most thorny issue in the design of institutional arrangements.

The question of enforcement would arise once it had been established pursuant to a dispute-settlement mechanism that a contracting party had failed to observe or had violated an obligation. In a more highly developed system, it could also arise pursuant to a finding of an Advisory Committee conducting a review of reported information.

Once non-observance or violation has been established, however, it remains to be decided what measures should be taken. Sanctions or the withdrawal of benefits in respect of the party in default is one form of measure, but, as has been frequently pointed out, sanctions have the effect of defeating one of the purposes of the framework rules, namely, to remove restrictions to free trade. It has, accordingly, been suggested that "the first objective of (dispute-settlement) procedures...is not to decide who is wrong and who is right or to establish the liability of a State, but to so arrange matters that violations...are only temporary and can cease as rapidly as possible" (Malinverni, 1974, 106--author's translation) On this basis, the objective of enforcement is to achieve the implementation or the re-instatement of the obligations contained in the framework rules, and not to punish or to deter through punishment.

A procedure for enforcement might therefore operate on the basis of a decision of an arbitration establishing the non-observance or violation of an obligation, and require the withdrawal of the infringing measure or the implementation of the obligation which has not been observed within a specified period of time. The possibility of imposing sanctions or withdrawing benefits could be reserved for situations in which an enforcement order is not complied with and for situations of recurrent violation of rules.

In accordance with this approach, the possibility of obtaining a form of compensation would be left to arbitral proceedings between the economic agents conducting activities under the framework agreement, pursuant to any international arbitration facility sponsored by the framework agreement for such economic agents.

ENDNOTES

1 The role of the International Coordinating Committee on Strategic Trade with Communist Countries (COCOM) may be noted here. Fifteen countries are members of COCOM, whose function is to establish a list of items of military significance which it is agreed should be subject to restrictions or prohibitions on export to prohibited countries.

2 Cf. the definition of arbitration given in Article 37 of the Hague Convention on the Pacific Settlement of International Conflicts of 18 October 1907: "International arbitration has as its object the resolution of disputes between States by judges of their choice and the basis of respect for law."

3 The Contracting Parties authorized the Netherlands to impose, for one year, a quantitative restriction on imports of wheat flour from the United States as a result of prejudice suffered from restrictions on the importation of dairy products imposed by the United States (IBDD, Supplement No. 4, 35).

4 Case No. 13T-117-0636-85 of the American Arbitration Association. The Opinion of the Arbitrators, delivered on 15 September 1987, is reprinted in (1987) 6 *Software Protection* (Nov.) 11-19). The Arbitrators' Order is reproduced in (1987) 6 *Software Protection* (Dec.) 3-15.

5 Remarks of Arbitrator Robert H. Mnookin (1987) 6 *Software Protection* (Dec.) 18.

6 Ibid. 19.

7 Adopted by UNCITRAL at its ninth session, Official Records of the General Assembly. Thirty-First Session, Supplement No. 17 (A/31/17), chap. V, sect. C.

8 Resolution 31/98, 15 December 1976.

TELECOMMUNICATION & DATA SERVICES

TELECOMMUNICATIONS

Toshio Kosuge

Introduction

As national economies develop and their industrial structures become increasingly interdependent, they rely increasingly on telecommunications to collect, exchange and transfer information. The effective use of information and information technologies has become one of the most important factors in the production of goods and services. Telecommunications are thus essential to modern industry and to the smooth functioning of the global economy. It is critical for corporate enterprises which want to remain competitive in national and international markets to improve productivity and efficiency through the effective use of telecommunications.

Telecommunications have also become the main distribution channel for trade in information-based services. The new telecommunication and information technologies make it possible for service companies to contact distant markets as easily as domestic markets. The effective use of telecommunications has thus become a driving force in world competition in the service industries.

For this reason, policies or practices that create barriers to the flow of information or to the use of telecommunication services should be accorded a special place in any trade-in-services negotiations. A relatively unrestricted flow of information, a relatively free use of telecommunications without regulatory constraints and the provision of telecommunication services under reasonable terms and conditions are all essential on both the national and the international levels. Telecommunication systems which incorporate these features will enhance the prosperity of participating nations and promote international trade in goods and services. It is the premise of this paper that the changing telecommunication environment has enormous significance for international trade.

New Developments in Telecommunication Technologies

Digitalization

Telecommunications have developed very rapidly since the introduction of the telegraph by Morse in 1845 and of the telephone by Bell in 1876. Within a hundred years of these innovations, service became almost universal in the U.S. and Europe. The technologies which support telecommunications are also changing (from conventional analog to digital). Digital technologies make the fusion of telecommunication and information-processing technologies possible. Accordingly, digital technologies bring development and expansion of data communications. For example, AR-PANET, the first U.S. public computer network, has adopted the packet exchange system which is more appropriate for computer communications than the line exchange system.

Digital technologies also make it possible to develop multimedia telecommunication systems by adding facsimile and video telephone to conventional voice services. The narrow-band Integrated Services Digital Network (ISDN) is currently making practical use of these possibilities by integrating voice, image and data communication media under 64Kbs (Kilobits per second).

Modern telecommunication networks, unlike conventional telephone networks, allow man-to-machine and machine-to-man communication. They have the ability to process information by computer both in exchanges and in terminal equipment. Such sophisticated services as triparty conversation, identification, virtual leased networks, security management and network management are made possible by digitalization.

Digital technologies have had a great impact on exchange, transmission and terminal equipment technologies. "Exchange" is the very important intelligent part of the network and exchange equipment and transponders; "transmission" involves the transmitting of information via optical fibre, coaxial cable and microwave facilities; "terminal equipment" is equipment on customer premises, like telephone and data terminals. The functions of all these aspects of the telecommunication network have developed in accordance with digitalization.

Exchange Systems

Exchange systems have moved from manual switch exchanges with human operators, through crossbar and electronic (analog) exchanges, to digital exchanges. Digital exchange with VLSI (Very Large Scale Integration) and many microprocessors is possible as with a computer. This improves cost performance in comparison with the analog exchange. Wide-band exchange technology will be necessary for the development of multimedia exchanges for video and images.

Transmission

There are two kinds of transmission: cable and radio. "Cable transmission" covers optical-fibre and coaxial-cable transmission; "radio transmission" covers satellite, microwave and cellular communication systems. Optical-fibre cable has several characteristics of light, with greater band width in comparison with conventional cable transmission. And its larger carrying capacity makes it possible to reduce the cost per channel. For satellite communication as for cable transmission, it has become possible to reduce the cost per channel by increasing numbers of transponders and by the use of VSATs (Very Small Aperture Terminals).

Terminal

The development of technology in information processing has led to the development of intelligent terminals with information-processing capacities.

Impact of New Developments in Telecommunication Technologies on the World Economy

Introduction

The development of telecommunication technologies has had a great impact on the world economy. In order to improve international trade and accelerate industrial developments, to manage corporations efficiently and to get quick information on consumer demand, the development of telecommunication technologies is vital.

The following are among the important issues in this regard:

- the possibility of a global telecommunication network with low-cost, diversified communication media;

- the expansion of the new communication services which combines telecommunications and information processing;

- the increasing importance of software in the software: hardware ratio; and

- the possible widening of the gap between developed and developing nations as we approach the twenty-first century and the pace of development of telecommunication technologies accelerates.

The development of global networks and the activities of multinational corporations in transportation and telecommunications have diluted the significance of national borders. Along with international interdependence has come severe competition between nations. Each nation tends to promote its own views and interests. It is important that these be harmonized.

Telecommunication Policies

A review of telecommunication policy has been going on in many countries, especially in the developed world. The liberalization of telecommunication markets and deregulation in the U.S. have had a major impact on telecommunication policies in the U.K. and Japan. Canada, France, West Germany and the North European countries have also been reviewing their telecommunication policies with regard to opening up markets to competition in terminals, the liberalization of enhanced or Value-added Network Services (VANs) within a specified framework, and decreased regulation of basic services provided by monopolies.

In the developing countries, on the other hand, telecommunication services are still not universal. Developing nations have therefore been slow to review their telecommunication policies. Some Asian NIEs (Newly Industrializing Economies) have, however, accepted open market policies with respect to terminals as well as the introduction of enhanced services.

The U.S., with the largest telecommunication network in the world, has introduced competition through deregulation, the relaxation of various restrictions, and the application of anti-trust laws. Recently, the U.S. has evolved telecommunication policies aimed at improving its national security and making it more competitive internationally. According to the Computer III decision, the U.S. retains the original classification of basic and enhanced telecommunication services. There is some ambiguity, however, in the U.S. definition of services regarding, for example, voice mail or protocol conversion. The Computer III decision might be viewed as an attempt to enable AT&T and the BOCs to strengthen their domestic and international positions by a relaxation of restrictions under anti-monopoly conditions.

European nations have developed new telecommunication policies, including deregulation, at various rates. There appears to be a general consensus on the relaxation of restrictions in some areas. European countries are gradually opening up their terminal equipment market with some conditions regarding type approval. There is no similar trend in Europe in the area of basic services except in the U.K., where competition in basic services like voice communication may be introduced. It is generally agreed in Europe that enhanced services like VANs might be liberalized. These services are already deregulated in the U.K. and in France.

Green Paper of the European Community

The following proposed positions in the Green Paper may be one way of understanding the emerging consensus in the EEC.

- Special or exclusive rights for the Telecommunication Administrations regarding provision and operation of network infrastructure. Where a Member State chooses a more liberal regime, either for the whole or for parts of the network, the short- and long-term integrity of the general network infrastructure should be safeguarded.

- Special or exclusive rights for the Telecommunication Administrations regarding the provision of a limited number of basic services, where such rights are considered essential at this stage for safeguarding public service goals. Exclusive provision must be narrowly construed and must be subject to review at specific intervals.

- Free provision of all other services (competitive services, including in particular value-added services) within and between Member States (in competition with the Telecommunication Administrations) for own use, shared use, or provision to third parties, subject to conditions for the use of the network infrastructure yet to be defined.

- Clear definition by Community Directive of general requirements imposed by Telecommunication Administrations on providers of competitive services for use of the network, including definitions regarding network infrastructure provision. This must include clear interconnect and access obligations by Telecommunication Administrations towards trans-border service providers in order to prevent Treaty infringements.

- Separation of regulatory and operational activities of Telecommunication Administrations. Regulatory activities concern, in particular, licencing, control of type approval and interface specifications, allocation of frequencies, and general surveillance of network usage conditions.

Developing Countries

There are still many countries in Africa and Asia where the diffusion rate of telephone service in under 1%. However, in the so-called Asian NIEs, such as Taiwan, Korea, Hong Kong and Singapore, telecommunication services and the export of telecommunication equipment can rapidly be improved. In these countries the first step -- the wide provision of a basic service like the telephone -- has been accomplished. Apart from these countries, however, most of the developing world is still in the process of securing and improving upon basic services.

In order to develop a telecommunication infrastructure, these nations urgently need sophisticated equipment and facilities, supported by skilled human resources. Long-term planning for the promotion of telecommunication services and co-operation from the developed countries on many levels, including technology transfer, are crucial for the developing countries.

Telecommunication services in the developing countries have usually been provided by the government, which has maintained network management. However, the trend towards deregulation in the U.S., the U.K. and Japan has affected telecommunication policy in the developing countries as well, especially with regard to the relaxation of restrictions in the area of enhanced services and investment in telecommunications by the private sector.

Telecommunication Service Providers

Digitalization

The digitalization of telecommunications could improve the cost performance of conventional services and permit the development of multimedia and intelligent communication systems. Therefore, telecommunication providers have tried to digitalize their networks, including relay transmitters and exchanges.

Restrictions

In countries where competitive measures have been introduced, telecommunication providers still differ from each other in their attitudes to the changing environment. In some cases, non-symmetrical restrictions on business rates or services have been imposed on those telecommunication providers which customarily provided service on a monopoly basis. This is evident in restrictions on cross subsidies between local and long-distance services, rate calculation methods, entrance into enhanced services, and hardware manufacture.

Internationalization

Telecommunication service providers are expanding their spheres of action overseas in response to deregulation. They intend to develop their business in response to a global market, with homogeneous service and global users. However, at the present time, telecommunication service providers are still more regulated than telecommunication equipment providers. Services providers are therefore developing their business in the areas of international cooperation, consulting services and equipment manufacturing. In the future, as with the global digitalization network plan of Cable & Wireless, the internationalization of telecommunication services may expand as a result of competition in international telecommunications.

Restructuring

In order to cope with digitalization, deregulation and internationalization, telecommunication service providers are now trying to restructure. They intend to control the increase in the number of employees in the field of basic services and to transfer more employees to enhanced and new services.

Telecommunication Users

In the changing environment of telecommunications, users need to be aware of various issues, especially on the international level.

Information and Telecommunications as Management Resources

The cost of information and telecommunications has been increasing rapidly every year for users, especially bigger users in the fields of finance, insurance and transportation, which have advanced telecommunication systems. (The increasing cost of telecommunications is more evident in data than in voice communication.) Users are also introducing new services like electronic mail, facsimile and teleconference. It is appropriate for corporations as users of telecommunications services to regard information and telecommunications as strategic resources as well as business management tools.

Network Management

Developments in telecommunication technologies have important effects on networks. The big users now use networks based not only on public circuits but also on leased and private circuits. In the U.S., before digitalization, telecommunications were developed and offered by the provider on a monopoly basis. Services offered to big business subsidized those offered to small business and home users with cross subsidies and big business users were always dissatisfied with the relatively high service rates they paid. They have therefore tried to create private networks in high-density traffic areas, using digitalized, cost-efficient equipment. They have preferred ISDN leased circuits with large volume, VSAT and bypass systems. To cope with these developments, telecommunication providers now offer special services to big business users with lower long-distance rates. Since big business users can easily construct private networks, which divert traffic from the public networks, telecommunication providers are eager to develop new services, including ISDN. (Private networks are not under the network management of the providers and require the establishment of their own management systems, including cost and security management systems.)

The Telecommunication Services Market

Telecommunication service issues did not come to the forefront as quickly as telecommunication equipment issues but new trends in the telecommunication services market make these issues very important and they need to be dealt with.

Competition Between Satellite and Cable

On the inception of INTELSAT, the U.S. supported the Balanced Loading Policy in the U.S. ratio between international satellite and cable circuits with other member countries. However, in the 1980s the U.S. has relaxed its Balance Loading Policy to promote competition among different providers of telecommunication facilities. In March 1987, the U.S. proposed a more deregulated policy including the abolition of the Balanced Loading Policy.

Competition Among Nations to Become International Telecommunication Centres

With the globalization of industrial activity, an increasing number of corporations have their own telecommunication networks. Severe competition is emerging among countries to host these networks. In Europe, the U.K. has the lead but France and West Germany are not far behind. In Asia, there is competition among Japan, Hong Kong and Singapore.

Competition in International Value-Added Network Services (VANs)

Bilateral agreements exist between the U.S. and Japan, the U.K. and Japan and the U.S. and Canada on international VANs (in the U.S., 'international enhanced services,' in Japan, 'special second-type services'). Several other bilateral agreements are under negotiation between Japan and The Netherlands, the U.S. and the U.K.

It will be very helpful for us to look into the bilateral free-trade agreement negotiated between Canada and U.S. for possible indications of future treatment of telecommunication services in the multilateral negotiations on trade in services. The Canada/U.S. agreement contains the following three main provisions:

- non- discriminatory access to and use of the basic telecommunication transport services, including: the lease of local and long-distance telephone services; full-period, flat-rate, private-line service; dedicated inter-city voice channels; public data services for the movement of information including intra-corporate communication; the sharing and reselling of basic telecommunication services; and the purchase or lease of terminal equipment;

- maintenance of existing access to the telecommunication networks for the provision of enhanced telecommunication services and computer services within and across the borders of both parties; and

- assurance that the provision of enhanced services by the providers of telecommunication facilities does not benefit from unreasonable cross-subsidization or other anti-competitive practices undertaken by these providers in virtue of their monopoly position. Appropriate safeguards, such as separate accounting records, sufficient structural separations and disclosure are to be put in place.

There may be a more competitive market in international VANs after appropriate international legal frameworks have been developed. In some countries, like the U.S., Canada, the U.K. and Japan, new entrants in this field are already free from restrictions. With increased demand for international telecommunication services, data communication services will be very important not only for VAN providers but also for public telecommunication-service providers. There might be therefore more competition between public telecommunication-service providers and international VAN-service providers in meeting the greater and more sophisticated demands of future users.

WATTC-88 and Telecommunications Services

The World Administrative Telegraph and Telephone Conference (WATTC-88) is to be held in Melbourne, Australia in November 1988, where new Telecommunication Regulations will be discussed and adopted in place of present Telegraph and Telephone Regulations.

According to Resolution No. 10 at the Plenipotentary Conference in Nairobi 1982, the World Administrative Conference is to be held for consideration of proposals for new regulatory regimes in response to the growing number of new telecommunication services being offered. In consequence, in 1987, the Preparatory Committee of WATTC produced draft proposals of New International Telecommunication Regulations. However, there were differing opinions between the U.S. and the U.K. on the one hand and many other countries on the other on the question of suitable proposals.

These proposals raise several important issues.

Which telecommunication services should be covered by the Regulations?

The draft proposal defines international telecommunication services offered to the public. There were some opposing views on the definition of "public" and on the inclusion of "services offered to the public." The United States insisted that the new regulations should apply only to common carrier services but not to enhanced services. In the drafting process, Western European countries succeeded in adding the definition of "public," which is defined as the general population or any person, including governmental and legal bodies, within the whole or part of the territory of Members. These countries insisted that any services offered to anyone in their territories could be deemed services offered to the public. Since the initial disagreements, attitudes in Europe have changed as the broader policy implications of the draft proposals have come to be recognized.

To which objects shall the Regulations be applied?

According to the draft, the Regulations should apply to Telecommunication Administrations and to Recognized Private Operating Agencies (RPOAs) which are regulated under the present regulations and also to any entity which offers international telecommunication services by using the international telecommunication network. Japan supported this provision because Japan wanted international VAN service providers to be recognized under the regulations. The European countries, for their part, wanted fair competitive conditions among telecommunication service providers. Therefore they supported the provision to include all entities which provide international telecommunication services. The United States, however, was strongly opposed to the provision because of concerns about increasing restrictions and extending regulations to entities not currently regulated. These initial attitudes also changed with increasing understanding of the wider implications.

Is it necessary to specify the international telecommunication services to be covered?

Developing countries and East European Countries demanded specific service lists in the regulations. They intended to check unilateral changes by developed countries and to affirm the ITU's responsibility for the worldwide diffusion of new services. Developed countries, on the other hand, preferred a more general conception of telecommunication services because it is very difficult to differentiate traditional services from value-added ones.

There is thus much debate about the new telecommunication regulations. In the U.S., the enhanced service providers, like IBM and the data-processing industries have expressed strong opposition to the draft regulations. User groups, such as the financial institutions and multinationals generally also oppose the draft. In April, the International Chamber of Commerce (ICC) sent a circular to member committees which was concerned about the new regulations restricting international business and the development of telecommunication services.

It is clear that the present Telephone and Telegraph Regulations are out of touch with new developments in telecommunication services. This is the reason for the revision of regulations now under way. However, in the ITU there are complicated disagreements among members and the diversification of telecommunication services has increased immensely through their merger with information processing. Telecommunication policies are thus being intertwined with industrial policies, the national interest generally and the interest of enterprises in each country. The increasing number of telecommunication service providers and users, unlike the RPOAs, have not been able to express their opinions in the CCITT (the ITU's International Telegraph and Telephone Consultative Committee). There are also great differences among the member states of the ITU in the liberalization of telecommunication services and the development of telecommunication infrastructures.

Thus there are many disagreements about the draft proposals for new telecommunication regulations. The General Secretariat held informal consultations on the issues in April 1988 and an alternative draft was created which was more flexible and used more permissive language. These new proposals establish general principles which apply to international telecommunication facilities and services generally available to the public and recognize the right of members to make special arrangements for specialized telecommunication networks, systems and applications, including the underlying means of international telecommunication transport.

It seems that member states might prefer to implement their new services not only through multilateral but also through bilateral arrangements. It would be appropriate for each state to consider new international telecommunication regulations on the basis of the following principles suggested in the new informal draft.

Supplementing the Conventions

The International Telecommunication Regulations are intended to supplement the Convention which covers telecommunications of all kinds.

Accommodating Individual National Needs

The regulations must accommodate an environment which allows sovereign countries to establish and operate their telecommunication facilities to meet their individual national objectives and yet allow for interconnection with the facilities of other nations. This creates a complex international environment and the regulations should permit the different infrastructure arrangements that might be necessary.

Providing a Flexible Framework

The major purpose of the regulations is to provide a flexible, general framework for global interconnection and interoperability.

Services Generally Available to the Public and Specialized Needs

The regulations should clearly encompass telecommunication services generally available to the public. Equally, they should cover other forms of international telecommunication transport, which are different from those normally related to services for the public.

Coping with Technological and Other Changes

Changes in the telecommunications environment are occurring every day and the regulations must be flexible enough to cover another decade of such changes. During the past year, since the PC/WATTC Group completed its work in May 1987, there have been significant changes in technology, service provision and national telecommunication infrastructures and many others are envisioned.

The Emergence of New Service Providers

No longer is the provision of international telecommunications the domain of the conventional operator alone, e.g., administrations or RPOAs as we have known them in the past. A study of current national legislation shows that already there are authorized organizations (and, indeed, perhaps persons) who have been given the authority to provide international interconnection arrangements with other parties. Even if, at this stage, there may only be a limited number of countries involved, it is important that the International Telecommunication Regulations of the ITU accommodate this diversity.

Relation of New Regulations with the Convention

Because the new International Telecommunication Regulations supplement the Convention, they should rely on and extend the terms and concepts contained in the Convention.

Distinction Between Recommendations and Regulations

The recommendations have no binding force and are not at a treaty level like regulations. Care must therefore be taken in the regulations regarding unintended and inappropriate linkages with recommendations that would in effect give the recommendations the status of a treaty. Instructions were introduced in the 1973 Regulations to identify those items which, *inter alia*, were not dealt with at a treaty level and which, in the common interest of interconnectivity, were to be the subject of "best intent" for introduction and application. While instructions are not binding provisions, they have proved a useful means of recognizing interconnectivity arrangements on certain matters.

Encouragement of a More Liberal Environment for Trade in Telecommunication Services

In order to create a more liberal environment for trade in telecommunication services, the following principles are suggested for consideration in any negotiations on trade in services. Achievement of these objectives will benefit the manufacturing, processing and service sectors.

Free Flow of Information

International business activity, particularly that of the service industries, is information-based and thus relies upon the free flow of information *via* telecommunications.

Non-discriminatory Access to and Use of Telecommunication Services

Requirements for telecommunication services vary greatly among service industries, depending upon a number of considerations, such as whether data processing is centralized or decentralized, how different offices are linked and what degree of back-up or redundancy a firm chooses to have. Firms vary in their sensitivity to price, quality and security considerations and in their technological levels. Access to a variety of telecommunication services with a minimum of restrictions or qualifications is important. Individuals and firms operating in foreign countries need to obtain and use telecommunication services on reasonable terms and conditions. Regulations governing access to and use of telecommunication services need to be clear and should be applied fairly and equally to both national and foreign citizens. At the same time, governments may give special treatment to official, non-commercial communications, such as those regarding national defense or public safety. However, governments should not use these exceptions as non-tariff barriers.

Freedom to Choose Customer Premises Equipment

Telecommunication services include both transport services and terminal equipment. In many cases, service firms need to use a specific type of equipment to make full use of telecommunication services. Certain kinds of equipment and the service they provide are often inseparable. Firms may also need to ensure equipment compatibility throughout their organization. For example, the delivery of a particular service may require specialized equipment and this may mean that that particular type of equipment must be used in all of a firm's locations worldwide.

Individuals and firms need freedom to connect telecommunication and computer equipment required by their needs and applications to telecommunication networks. Procedures for approving the attachment of such equipment need to be simple, expeditious and non-discriminatory. The criteria for approval need to be kept to a minimum, i.e., that there is no harm to the network or to network personnel; that transparency is ensured with respect to the establishment of technical standards and approval procedures; that fair treatment of equipment manufactured in other countries is ensured. Countries will have to work towards the harmonization of national standards, with the ultimate goal of achieving international agreement or reciprocal recognition on equipment approval among countries.

Transparency of Regulations and of the Regulatory Process

In order to plan ahead for what is often a major investment in telecommunication equipment and facilities, corporations need to know the rules for telecommunication services and any contemplated changes in these rules. Moreover, user opinion needs to be reflected in telecommunication policy-making. Governments will need to ensure that the regulatory process is transparent, that proposed changes are clearly and openly stated, and that an opportunity for comment is provided to all parties affected by a change in the rules.

Issues for Further Consideration

As more countries introduce competition into their telecommunication industries, another set of issues will require serious consideration:

Opening the Telecommunication-Services Market to Foreign Entities

Compared with other service-related sectors, the telecommunication sector has the unique problem that many governments prohibit the firms of other countries from entering the field in their countries. While it must be recognized that it would be difficult for governments to open their markets unconditionally for the provision of telecommunication networks or transport services, it is necessary for foreign firms to gain market access in order to provide enhanced or VAN services under reasonable national telecommunication regulations.

Deregulation of International Circuit Usage

In many countries, the use of international leased circuits is subject to restrictions that are the result of efforts to protect the interest of the existing telecommunication entities. These restrictions sometimes cause inconveniences to users and make the international provision of value-added services difficult. It is desirable that the restrictions set forth in the ITU Regulations and Recommendations be reviewed in a broader perspective.

Telecommunication Charges

Given the fact that telecommunication charges now constitute a large portion of the cost of producing goods and services, a reduction in these charges would help to accelerate economic activity. Competition tends to lower prices. In cases where competition does not exist in the provision of telecommunication products and services, actual costs should be reflected in the setting of tariffs.

Participation of Users in the Policy-Making Process

Since telecommunications have traditionally been managed as a government monopoly in many countries and since this management has required sophisticated technical expertise, user opinions have not been well reflected in the policy-making process. Due consideration should be given to how users can participate more actively in the formulation of telecommunication policy.

MARKET ACCESS AND TELECOMMUNICATION SERVICES

Jonathan D. Aronson

This paper reviews issues relating to market access that need to be considered during trade negotiations involving telecommunication and data services. This raises two questions. What is meant by telecommunication and data services? What does market access for telecommunication and data services entail?

This paper focuses on what the Organisation for Economic Co-operation and Development (OECD) calls telecommunication network-based services (TNS). Given the lack of generally accepted definitions of the boundaries and categories of telecommunication services, the OECD never defines TNS but notes that the TNS concept is flexible and dynamic. "TNS can include all services that combine information, production, manipulation, storage facilities and software functions...TNS can be based on circuit, packet, message, switched or leased circuit networks. TNS can be provided by public communication operators, information service vendors, closed-user groups, and private intra-firm information transfer and/or services" (OECD 1988, 4). To oversimplify, this paper deals with the new, sophisticated services made possible by computers and other recent technological breakthroughs. This is a small, fast growing and potentially critical sector. The paper does not deal with on the international exchange of basic transport services such as telephone and telex and ignores trade in broadcasting services.

The concept of market access as it applies to trade negotiations and TNS services is complex and is spelled out in some detail. Distinguishing the concepts of national treatment, market access, market presence and the right of establishment from one another is difficult because the boundaries have blurred. Traditionally, national treatment and market access were viewed as trade concepts while market presence and the right of establishment were generally associated with investment issues. This *de facto* segregation worked reasonably well while trade negotiators bargained over trade in goods.

Today it is trickier because it is harder to draw a line separating trade and investment in services. Until recently, most services were provided and regulated within national borders. To provide services abroad suppliers needed to establish an office and put people on site to provide the service.

Today, in contrast, there is growing acceptance that services are becoming ever more tradeable. The emergence of a global communication infrastructure makes it possible to sell telecommunication and data services from afar. It is also possible to trade financial services, insurance, education services, professional services, health services, architecture, drafting, design and other services over the telecommunication network.

The rules, principles, and procedures that countries use to manage the world economy were formulated more than four decades ago. Today, they are out of date. They were designed for a less interdependent, industry-based world economy where the lines between goods and services and between trade and investment were clearer. The Uruguay round of negotiations is one important step in the effort to update and reform the ways in which nations deal with each other in the realm of international commerce. The negotiations on services are central to this effort and TNS are at the heart of the negotiations.

Boundaries are indistinct. To clarify the issues, this paper focuses on the evolving meaning of market access and relates it to the concept of national treatment. Elsewhere in this set of papers, Professor V.N. Balasubramanyam examines issues of market presence and right of establishment related to telecommunication and data services. In addition, Anne Wells Branscomb concentrates on one type of access -- access to data. Some overlap is inevitable but for the most this paper does not deal with these issues.

Defining Key Concepts

It is useful to discuss national treatment and market access as they are used in the GATT, as they might apply to trade in services, and as they might apply to TNS in particular.

National Treatment and Market Access in the GATT Articles

As it applies to trade in goods, the goal of national treatment is presented in Article III of the GATT which is entitled "National Treatment of Internal Taxation and Regulation." "The contracting parties recognize that internal taxes, ... laws, regulations are requirements ... should not be applied to imported or domestic products so as to afford protection to domestic production." In short, once a foreign product has overcome the barrier of the border it should be treated just like a domestic product.

In contrast, market access is nowhere discussed in John Jackson's definitive 1969 study, *World Trade and the Law of the GATT*, or in Gilbert Winham's excellent overview of the Tokyo Round negotiation. (Jackson, 1969 and Winham, 1986). Market access is not a legal principle established under the GATT. If a country does not want to import goods from abroad, that is its right.

National Treatment and Market Access in Trade in Services

Trade in services was launched as an issue in the early 1970s.[1] The United States raised the issue during the Tokyo Round negotiations, but little was accomplished.[2] In 1980, the United States persuaded the Trade Committee of the OECD to examine service issues. When William Brock became U.S. Trade Representative in 1981, he put services high on the U.S. agenda, catapulting services to center stage in the trade arena. Services was one of the three most important and contentious agenda items at the GATT Ministerial meeting in Geneva in late 1982.

National treatment and market access for foreign services are new concepts under consideration by negotiators. Countries extending national treatment to foreign services would treat domestic and foreign providers of the same service in the same way. When, from time to time, identical treatment becomes impractical because of differences in institutional structures or regulatory regimes, countries would impose equivalent regulations on domestic and foreign service providers. When variations in treatment prove necessary, governments would be obliged to show that equivalence was real.

Nobody really knows what market access means in the context of services. It is broader than national treatment but narrower than the right of market presence. National treatment applies to goods (or services), not to the producers of those goods (or services). Market access for services implies the right to do business in a host country but it falls short of guaranteeing foreign service providers the right to establish operations and compete with local service providers -- the right to invest. As with goods, market access for service involves restrictions applied at and within national borders. If trade rules are to be extended to services this will require innovation, flexibility and commitment on the part of negotiators. It will be impossible to apply existing GATT Articles and Codes, designed to deal with trade in goods, mechanically to trade in services. Thus, given the intangible, invisible nature of services supplied from abroad, if countries decide to provide market access for foreign services, market access will need to be applied more broadly for services than it is for goods.

Views on this issue vary. Countries like the United States contend that to safeguard the existing trading system and update its rules and principles requires providing some form of guaranteed market access to service providers in some sectors. Although there is some attempt to downplay the fact, this would mean that all countries, developed and developing, which accepted this new principle would have to accept that their domestic sovereignty and national regulatory autonomy would be restricted to some extent. Market access would be more intrusive than national treatment into domestic decision-making. In short, participating countries would have to acknowledge that there is no way to revolt against economic interdependence.

Countries such as Brazil and India which are critical of the services initiative believe this exercise is unnecessary, unwarranted and undesirable. They do not believe that a total overhaul of the system is needed and suspect that efforts to promote freer trade in services will help developed countries and hurt them (Nayyar, 1986). They worry that new trade rules for services which might include guarantees of market access to foreign service providers are unneeded and perhaps detrimental to their influence and development prospects.

National Treatment and Market Access for Telecommunication Services

Insurance, construction, aviation and shipping were initially at the center of the services discussions. Over time, telecommunications came to the forefront because of the rapid growth of the sector, its ability to make other services tradeable, and its importance for making manufacturing sectors competitive.[3] Most of the attention has been focused by users and suppliers in industrial countries on value-added and information services, now increasingly designated as telecommunication network-based services or TNS. Trade in basic telephone, telegraph and telex services is not likely to receive much attention in the current round of trade talks. Neither has trade in broadcasting services -- films and television programs -- received much attention (Wildman and Siwek, 1988).

As TNS gained prominence in discussions concerning trade in services, the potential importance of the issue of market access increased. Telecommunication suppliers of TNS argued that, when dealing with domestic monopolists, national treatment was not enough. They claimed that unless they could provide their services abroad, they could not compete. Heavy users of TNS, an increasingly vocal and organized international lobby, supported this position. Not only did the focus on TNS push market access on the trade agenda, it also required a far more detailed understanding of how the concepts of national treatment and market access might be modified and applied to services.

National treatment of TNS would require, according to a recent OECD study, "that laws, regulations, requirements and advantages affecting the sale, provision or distribution of telecommunication network-based services shall apply identically to national and foreign services alike, and therefore allow foreign service providers ... to compete on an equivalent basis with national providers" (OECD, 1988, 16). National treatment would not require countries to harmonize their telecommunication policies. Indeed, extending beyond TNS, it would be difficult to envision wide granting of national treatment for the basic services provided by the public switched telephone networks.

In the same paper the OECD defined market access for telecommunication network-based services to include "cross-border delivery of services, which implies the *right of non-establishment*, and *the right to interconnect*. Market access also may require *commercial presence, right of establishment*, and *investment*. ... Access also includes fair and equitable terms for interconnection to public networks, the provision of leased lines by telecommunications administrations, and the right to connect equipment which meets appropriate requirements to the network" (*ibid.*)

Two new concepts that are fundamental to the goals of those wishing to liberalize trade in telecommunication services are introduced in this definition. The right of non-establishment suggests that countries should not make establishment a condition for providing services. If a country decides to purchase foreign services, the service supplier should be entitled to provide its services from inside or outside the buyer's borders. The location of the service provider should be irrelevant. In contrast, some countries currently insist that foreign service suppliers invest in the country before they can provide services. [4] Suppliers and users of data services seek the right to provide those services from offshore. In other cases, the opposite demands are made of TNS suppliers. Before they can provide services they must put equity and technology into a country.

The right to interconnect, sometimes also referred to as the right to plug in, is another new concept. Foreign service suppliers do not, or are generally not allowed to, provide a full range of telecommunication services in most countries. Yet they need to be linked to the underlying facilities of the dominant service suppliers. The dominant supplier can eliminate competition by denying foreign firms the right to interconnect with its network. Most users and foreign suppliers of services favor facilities competition. In the absence of such competition, foreign TNS suppliers seek assurances that they will be allowed to interconnect with the dominant carrier and use the basic transport services it provides in a manner that is fair and does not impede their ability to compete. This request rankles many telecommunication administrations which seek to offer these new services and perhaps extend their monopoly to cover these services.

Background

How central is market access for TNS? In 1985, the Service Policy Advisory Committee of the Office of the U.S. Trade Representative (USTR) advocated including market access for telecommunication services in the framework agreement covering services during the Uruguay Round negotiations (Service Policy Advisory Committee, 1985). Access to the marketplace for service providers is also central to a draft proposal for a multilateral agreement on trade in services put forward in June 1988 by the Coalition of Service Industries and endorsed by the Business Roundtable and the United States Council for International Business (Coalition of Service Industries, 1988). Many in the U.S. government wish to make market access for TNS central to the new negotiations. Other negotiators are not convinced of the wisdom of extending the GATT in such a dramatic fashion.

Until recently, market access in the telecommunication sector was not a major issue. In the key markets, there was limited international competition in telecommunication equipment. In the United States, AT&T supplied its own needs but did not export its equipment. In other key markets, local manufacturers closely linked to the local monopoly dominated. [5]

Traditionally, market access was not an issue for basic services either. International telephone, telegraph and telex services were seen as "jointly provided services." In effect, control of the information was passed from one domestic telecommunication monopoly to another at the mid-point between the two countries. The sender paid his own telecommunication monopoly. At intervals imbalances were settled among the parties. The bargain was akin to the one struck among post offices around the world so that the sender need only put domestic stamps on international mail. [6] International trade in TNS is a new phenomenon. It is still so small that until recently nobody worried about the trade implications of TNS.

In the past, the technology on which telecommunication services were based changed relatively slowly, the same services were generally available everywhere, and these services were easily distinguishable from each other. (Communication computer and broadcasting services were discrete and separate.) The same basic range of communication services was provided in all countries and was subject to similar regulatory provisions (Reid, 1985, 16-25).

Today, in contrast, technological breakthroughs and deregulatory surges are bringing fundamental changes to the telecommunication, finance, transport and other sectors and eroding barriers within and among service sectors. Policy-makers can no longer concentrate just on trade, investment or monetary issues and let their counterparts worry about the others. The management of the world economy is more difficult and market access, particularly with regard to TNS, is much higher on the policy agenda.

Most countries now accept that many services are traded over the communication infrastructure. To sell these services abroad, vendors need access to foreign markets. Large domestic and multinational users support the vendors' position, wanting cheaper, more varied and more efficient international services. The United States and some other industrial countries are supporting their users and suppliers of TNS services.

Issues

The OECD paper and the United States agree that the "central principle for trade in telecommunications network-based services is market access."[7] Without access to and use of the basic transport system it is impossible for foreign suppliers of TNS to sell their services. This is why access has taken on such a critical role that the U.S. Coalition of Service Industries embeds market access within an expanded definition of national treatment for services, which would include "access to and use of distribution and delivery systems, including telecommunications networks" (Coalition of Service Industries, 1988, 6.)

What are the issues? Broadly, if the overall goal of liberalizing trade is to make it easier to sell to customers abroad, then in the evolving world economy market access must also be related to the broad concepts of non-establishment and the right of interconnection (the right to "plug in"). First, should TNS providers have the right to sell their services through a commercial presence or through establishment or from afar (non-establishment)? Second, should TNS vendors be guaranteed access to and use of the underlying telecommunication transport system? On this last issue the OECD distinguishes among access to facilities, access to networks and access to markets.

Establishment and Non-Establishment: The Source of the Services

The freedom of the service provider to locate its equipment and network as it pleases is a big issue. The service providers, users and advocates of liberalization argue that the provider should be free to choose locales from which they supply services. They want to configure their network and locate their equipment in the most efficient and profitable way. They seek a "right of non-establishment" which would guarantee their ability to sell their services on a cross border basis. They also want to be able to establish a commercial presence abroad. This might involve taking local partners, setting up offices, installing their own equipment or, more dramatically, engaging in full establishment in a host country. Suppliers and users, in effect, want to be able to decide where to place their investment and how to run their network without interference from domestic authorities. They seek the ability to supply TNS, often in competition with local monopolies, to domestic or multinational users from near or far.

It is technically possible to supply TNS from abroad but only if local authorities cooperate. Skeptics doubt that the technical possibility should automatically be translated into a "right of non-establishment." Many governments with high ambitions of their own do not trust foreign service suppliers, many of which are giant multinational firms. They may feel more protected from possible abuses if they impose investment requirements on foreign service providers so that they can keep a close eye on the providers, making sure that they are effectively regulated. By forcing countries to invest before they provide services, countries may also hope to gain new jobs and the transfer of technology and to minimize the risk of a new round of transfer pricing that works against them. Privacy and security interests may also persuade some countries to demand that data bases containing sensitive national data be stored within the country.

At the other extreme, some countries seek to restrict entry into their markets, preferring to adopt an infant-industry strategy to encourage their existing monopoly or local entrepreneurs to establish their own TNS operations. They oppose calls for what is tantamount to a "right to invest" in leading edge sectors in their economies. They do not want foreigners in their countries to undermine their domestic regulators and telecommunication providers. They would rather do without some sophisticated services in the short-term so that their own nationals can acquire the technology and provide those services further down the road. They also oppose the creation of new rules that would extend the reach of GATT into the area of investment.

Thus the idea of creating and implementing a "right of non-establishment" for the benefit of TNS providers is controversial. Operationally, such a right would speed the creation of a more integrated and efficient world economy. But many countries fear that their interests could be undermined and want no progress until they are convinced that they will benefit. However, the champions of market access for TNS and the right of non-establishment, particularly in the United States, the United Kingdom, and Japan, are powerful and impatient. These liberalizers would prefer that agreement be as broad-based as possible but are likely to proceed alone among themselves if a wide-ranging agreement proves impossible.

Access to and Use of the Telecommunication Transport System

Very few TNS providers have any desire to build their own facilities. However, they cannot operate unless they are interconnected with the existing basic transport facilities and basic transport services are made available to them on a reasonable basis. In most countries, the government regulates and runs the basic transport infrastructure. The telecommunication monopoly may see foreign TNS vendors more as competitors than as customers. By restricting access, or more subtly by setting attachment policies, standards and pricing to their own advantage, the facilities' operators can tilt the playing field as much or as little as they choose. Furthermore, the terms on which foreign TNS providers are or are not granted access to these facilities and facilities services determines whether or not they can operate and be profitable. Advocates of liberalization are therefore seeking new rules and principles in the current negotiations that would guarantee their ability to do business in an environment that is not rigged against them. Or, alternatively, they would be content with fewer, looser rules, if they could choose among two or more competing facilities providers. [8]

Critics respond that such rules and principles would impinge on their domestic sovereignty and regulatory freedom. Most developing countries have no intention of undercutting their existing telecommunication monopoly and no desire to channel their limited funds into creating a new network of facilities that overlaps with the one already in place. Many countries see these fancy new services as expensive extravagances that divert them from more important concerns and are secondary to their future development. At the same time, they are concerned because the United States is making such a fuss about TNS. If TNS are indeed critical, they do not want to foreclose their own prospects. They want to ensure that there will be an opportunity for late-comers to compete. They fear that industrial countries and multinationals might keep them at the periphery in the development of a sector critical to their future growth, jobs and development.

The United States seems to be most concerned that foreign providers of TNS be allowed to buy the various high-quality, state-of-the-art telecommunication transport services they need internationally at prices that reflect the cost of providing the services. It is also seeking flexible attachment policies that permit TNS suppliers and users the freedom to choose their own equipment to the maximum extent possible. The United States is also concerned about the fairness of the standard-setting process and particularly wants to make sure that suppliers are permitted to use their own proprietary protocols for the provision of TNS over private networks. [9]

Not surprisingly, skeptics worry that such rules would benefit the rich, the large and the powerful. (It is notable, however, that some smaller countries that do not have plans to develop their own independent industries could live with these rules. They believe the advantages of being tied into the global economy outweigh the potential loss of automony.)

The OECD paper refines and puts into perspective the objectives of access to the network more fully. It distinguishes among access to facilities, access to networks and access to markets.

Access to Facilities

The paper notes that there is a trend toward greater facilities competition. A few countries, notably the United States, the United Kingdom and Japan, permit facilities competition and, although all countries limit foreign ownership of domestic facilities, other countries including the Netherlands and Hong Kong are considering sanctioning facilities competition. There is also increasing competition in the provision of international satellite facilities which has until recently been limited because of INTELSAT. New, competing fiber-optic cables across the Atlantic and Pacific Oceans are being installed which are likely to divert some traffic away from Intelsat. In March 1988 the United States withdrew its "balanced loading requirement" which directed AT&T, MCI and US Sprint to send half their transoceanic traffic by satellite. PANAMSAT and other alternative providers of international satellite services are poised to begin service. And Very Small Aperture Terminal ground stations are now available which can bypass terrestrial facilities and provide end-to-end services.

It is very unlikely that all countries will open up facilities competition. But the evolving mixed system means that reciprocity is impossible to achieve between those countries which permit facilities competition and those which do not. In countries that prohibit facilities competition, recognized facilities owners/operators, acting as common carriers, can use their dominant position to deny or undercut competition in the provision of TNS. This implies that operating agreements must be standardized both bilaterally and internationally. Otherwise carriers are likely to provide underlying transport services to themselves on a more favourable basis than to other would-be competitors in the provision of TNS.

Privileged access to the facilities structure can also affect the provision of internal communication operations of firms and specialized groupings with special network needs. The OECD suggests that negotiators will need to address "the issue of regulation of private networks and the imposition of operational performance requirements on such networks" (OECD, 1988, 11.) The OECD also suggests that in view of the emergence of ISDN it might be a good idea to regulate only the underlying transmission structure and have the ITU retain its authority over technical administrative and transactional formalities between common carriers , while service negotiators craft new rules covering service providers.

Access to Networks

Just as there is a trend towards facilities competition, many countries are beginning to allow service providers and end users more flexible access to their networks. For example, France and some other countries have regulations requiring the basic service supplier to meet interconnection demands. (This may be construed as equivalent to the right of non-establishment.) However, few providers of TNS provide end-to-end international services. As the OECD paper suggests, "the right and ability to interconnect is therefore a key element for suppliers and users of telecommunication-network-based services."

Those providers that meet certain requirements might be guaranteed the ability to interconnect. If it is agreed to allow fair competition, more guarantees would be needed to minimize the temptation of domestic monopolies to subsidize their own TNS offerings. Access to the network would depend on the availability, price and quality of leased lines; the ability to share and resell leased lines; and guaranteed interconnection between public and private networks and between leased circuits and the public switched network. Although possible, designing standards and rules for achieving access and interconnection could be very expensive and complicated as the experience in the United States with Open Network Architecture and in Europe with Open Network Provision demonstrates. In particular, if developing countries agree to provide access to their networks, outsiders seeking interconnection might be called on to contribute technical and financial assistance.

Access to Markets

Access to markets, according to the OECD, should also cover "the availability of capacity, conditions of investment, establishment, equipment attachment and non-discrimination." If sufficient capacity exists, it should be made available to users that need it. Ways of allocating capacity between leased lines and public switched networks need to be addressed. Questions about attaching equipment to the network by suppliers of TNS or by users will also need to be considered.

Past Precedents

No existing agreement has tackled market access for TNS with as much ambition as the Uruguay Round negotiations. But some limited measures to deal with market access for telecommunication services have been explored in recent bilateral talks between the United States and Israel, Canada and Japan. These are touched on briefly here.

The U.S.-Israel Free Trade Agreement

On April 22, 1985, the United States and Israel signed a Declaration on Trade in Services in conjunction with a Free Trade Agreement covering trade in goods which established a set of principles for trade in services between the two countries. The effort devoted to this exercise was in large part meant to help define issues that would need to be addressed in broader negotiations on trade in services.

The Declaration covered broad principles including market access and national treatment. Subsequently the United States and Israel entered into negotiations on three sectoral annotations covering telecommunications, tourism and insurance. The discussions continue on the telecommunications annotation. [10] The conceptual work begun here in a rudimentary way was applied, in part, by the United States to its negotiations with Canada and could contribute to reaching an agreement during the GATT negotiations.

U.S.-Canada Free Trade Agreement

On October 4, 1987, U.S. and Canadian negotiators agreed to a comprehensive trade agreement. Enhanced telecommunication services are an important element of the pact. But, it should be noted, the telecommunication portion of the negotiations nearly floundered when Bell Canada sought to emulate the U.S. model and pursue its largest customers abroad. [11] Canadian negotiators demanded a unilateral right for Canadian firms to build facilities or resell long-distance services in the United States but would not offer U.S. firms a reciprocal privilege.

U.S. negotiators resisted Canadian demands to include international basic services in the bargain. The agreement covers only TNS. American providers of TNS services were granted access to the Canadian telecommunication infrastructure on a national treatment basis. (Canadian firms received identical guarantees in the U.S. market.) Canada excluded the provincial market for TNS (about 30 percent of the total) from the deal.

Market-Oriented Sector-Selective (MOSS) Talks with Japan

The U.S. goals in the Market-Oriented Sector-Selective (MOSS) talks on telecommunications in the early 1980s included greater transparency in Japanese rule-making and standard-setting processes, fewer standards, and easier access for foreign terminal equipment to the Japanese market. To ease access to the Japanese market U.S. negotiators sought simpler licensing and approval procedures, broader opportunities for foreign companies to provide third-party services, and acceptance of foreign test data. Follow-up talks in 1987 focused on international value-added network services between Japan and the United States.

MOSS negotiations simplified application and approval procedures for terminal equipment and granted foreign firms the right to own value-added networks. The follow-up talks led to modification of Japan's Telecommunications Business Law to allow international value-added services between the United States and Japan. [12] Some of the technical work done in these negotiations may carry over to the Uruguay Round negotiations.

Trade-offs

This paper was intended to highlight the issue of market access for TNS -- not to judge the merits of the argument or to predict the likely outcome of negotiations in the GATT, the ITU, UNCTAD or elsewhere. But it may be worthwhile to highlight some of the trade-offs that negotiators might confront when dealing with this issue in a descending order of generality.

Managing the World Economy

If successful, negotiations on trade in services and TNS will help improve the management of the interdependent world economy, but they will also limit national sovereignty and regulatory autonomy. If unsuccessful, the likelihood for trade wars and even the fragmentation of the trading system will increase, but national autonomy would be better preserved.

Trade in Services Negotiations

Trade in services is important and growing. No integrated set of rules and principles exist for this trade. They are needed. However, time and people committed to services cannot focus fully on other important trade issues, many of which are larger than services in volume.

Forum

The ITU has the most technical expertise. But is trade in services and particularly telecommunication services too important to be left to communication experts? If some developing countries block progress in the GATT, industrial countries led by the United States might turn to the OECD, negotiations of the like-minded, or bilateral negotiations.

Telecommunication Services

Transportation and financial services are bigger. But telecommunication services are the key because they make other services tradeable.

Telecommunication-Network-Based Services

Trade in TNS is relatively small but it is growing rapidly. Vendors and users want new trade rules desperately. Telecommunication authorities are reluctant to allow the Uruguay Round to deal with telecommunication services at all but are more protective on basic services because they generate huge profits. Dominate carriers in liberal settings such as AT&T, British Telecom and Japan's KDD are more leery of liberalization of basic services than other common carriers (such as MCI, US Sprint, and Mercury). But unlike the PTTs, AT&T and other carriers in liberalized settings worry that unless there is more competition, their main corporate users will bypass them.

Market Access for TNS

Trade in other services requires market access for TNS. But countries would have to accept new obligations in granting market access for TNS.

Non-Establishment

The acceptance of the right of non-establishment would probably lead to aggregate growth and efficiency and advance the evolution of the world information economy. The distribution of benefits might, however, be skewed.

Access To and Use of the Transport System

One rule of thumb for judging "fairness" in national rules for TNS might be: The greater the degree of competition in the provision of infrastructure and infrastructure services in a country, the more latitude the country should have in setting rules concerning prices, access to the network, and technical standards.

An Alternative Model

Another alternative would be a competitive approach for TNS that resembles the airline carrier model. This system could emerge slowly among the United States, the United Kingdom and Japan which already permit domestic service competition. Countries would regulate TNS but not obstruct or undermine the development of new rules regarding international

TNS. The movement of facilities and services between signatory countries would be covered by international rules. Communication traffic might be picked up and delivered between "ports of entry" inside of signatory countries.[13]

Participating countries would decide how foreign carriers could serve their markets, bargain over ports of entry and agree to pricing rules. Local interconnection for international carriers would be provided and foreign carriers might be allowed to establish domestic infrastructure facilities necessary to deliver their services. Foreign carriers would pay an "access fee" for using the local national network. In short, these rules closely resemble the one evolving in the international airline market.

Under this scenario, most business of the local monopoly remains untouched. The reform could be almost invisible to most consumers who use international services infrequently. Access fees from international carriers and continued national control over the domestic market would provide ample room for continued cross-subsidies. And large users, international service providers and large electronic firms at the center of the telecommunication reform coalition would benefit.

ENDNOTES

1 For a short history of the rise of trade in services as an issue see the appendix to Geza Feketekuty, *International Trade in Services* (Cambridge: Ballinger, 1988). The early literature on trade in services includes Brian Griffiths, *Invisible Barriers to Invisible Trade* (London: Macmillan for the TPRC, 1975) and Hugh Corbet, "Prospects for Negotiations on Barriers to International Trade in Services," *Pacific Community* (April 1977), pp. 454-470.

2 To the extent that trade in services complemented trade in goods, it was covered under several of the Tokyo Round codes. For details see Ronald Kent Shelp, *Beyond Industrialization: Ascendance of the Global Service Economy* (New York: Praeger, 1981).

3 Much of the material here is drawn from Jonathan David Aronson and Peter F. Cowhey, *When Countries Talk: International Trade in Telecommunications Service* (Cambridge: Ballinger, 1988).

4 For example, Canada requires that data bases containing financial records on Canadian citizens be maintained in Canada. U.S. banks would prefer to maintain all of their North American records at a single location in the United States.

5 For example, Western Electric, a subsidiary of AT&T, provided essentially all of AT&T's equipment and Japan's NTT relied heavily on its family of four domestic providers. On the workings of AT&T over time see Gerald

Brock, *The Telecommunications Industry* (Cambridge: Harvard University Press, 1981). The best description of the breakup of AT&T is Peter Temin with Louis Galambos, *The Fall of the Bell System* (New York: Cambridge Unersity Press, 1987).

6 Indeed, in many countries post and telecommunication authorities were part of the same monopoly. As telecommunications overtook the post office, pressure to seperate post and telecom arose in almost all industrial countries. For a description of the settlement mechanism employed by International Telecommunication Union, see George A. Codding, Jr. and Anthony M. Rutkowski, *The International Telecommunication Union in a Changing World* (Dedham, Mass.: Artech House, Inc., 1982).

7 OECD, Trade in Telecommunication Network-based Services, p. 9. The following section draws heavily on the OECD report.

8 For an integrated, broad-ranging view of possible rules and principles for trade in value-added and information services that might emerge from the Uruguay Round negotiations, see Jonathan D. Aronson and Peter F. Cowhey, *When Countries Talk: International Trade in Telecommunications Services* (Cambridge: Ballinger, 1988), Chapter 9.

9 Private conservation with a U.S. government official.

10 The draft annotation sets out both supplier interests and users interests and seeks "to distinguish between the interests of small and large users and suppliers. The most important definitional issue, however, has ...been the dividing line between basic telecommunications services and value-added telecommunications services." Geza Feketekuty, *International Trade in Services: An Overview and Blueprint for Trade Negotiations* (Cambridge: Ballinger, 1988), pp.182-183.

11 Bell Canada recently purchased a pipeline transmission company that has holdings in the United States as part of a diversification program. Although the economics must have looked good, observers noted that Bell Canada was also buying valuable rights of way over which they could establish transmission facilities. If Bell Canada entered the U.S. long-distance or value-added market successfully, it would force a re-examiniation of all other arrangements governing both the equipment and services markets.

12 Entities wishing to operate in international VAN business in Japan are required to (1) register themselves as international Special Type II telecommunications carriers; (2) conclude agreements with foreign partners concerning the provision of international VAN services, which must be approved by the Government; (3) submit notifications of their service tariffs to the Government; (4) acquire non-tariff-based circuits from international Type I telecommunications carriers, who have obtained approval of the

contract on the provision of circuits from the Government. "New Regulatory Framework in Japan Concerning the Provision of International Value-added Services," Delayed contribution by Japan to the ITU's CCITT Working Party III/5, Question 21/III, D-146, Ottawa, 21-23 October 1987.

13 To illustrate, a U.S. international carrier such as AT&T could carry a conference call (or any form of telephone or computer service) from New York to Tokyo. Parties in Osaka and Kyoto could be added to the conference call, and later parties in London could be connected as well. Under this model, AT&T could run the conference call entirely over its own facilities without local partners, so long as traffic moved only between points in the United States and "ports of entry" in other signatory countries. However, to interconnect the call to a non-port, say Kobe, AT&T would need to use a local partner. The local Japanese carrier would have to offer AT&T comparable terms to those afforded Japanese international carriers on the connection to Kobe. That would be Japan's only international obligation.

INTERNATIONAL NETWORK COMPETITION IN TELECOMMUNICATIONS

Geza Feketekuty

Introduction

Technological change has led to a new phenomenon in telecommunications - competition. Until recently, telephone and telegraph services were the exclusive domain of national telecommunication monopolies in most countries. Over the past ten years, however, new telecommunication technologies and expanded demand for telecommunication services by business have so altered supply and demand conditions in the telecommunication sector that is has become economically rational to allow competition in the provision of many telecommunication services.

Competition in telecommunications first emerged in so-called value-added telecommunication services. With powerful computers, it has become possible to use the telephone system to transmit, store, and distribute electronically encoded information. These same computers can also be used to control the switches that route information through a network, providing the possibility for far greater control over the routing of a telecommunication signal than in the past. Computers have thus opened the door to a wide range of sophisticated, new telecommunication services. These services are called enhanced or value-added telecommunication services because they add value to the basic telecommunication service, which is to provide the physical means for transmitting an electronic signal from one point to another.

Since the computers that produce the wide range of value-added telecommunication services can be located anywhere, as long as they can be connected to the telecommunication network somewhere, competition in the provision of these services is eminently feasible. It is equally desirable when one considers that monopolies are not very good at thinking up a hundred new ways of changing old habits. The economic case of competition in the provision of these new computer-based, value-added telecommunication services is so strong that a majority of developed countries have decided to permit competition in these new services.

Powerful computers, space rockets and new materials have also expanded the means for transmitting telecommunication signals. They have taken us beyond copper wires to microwave transmitters, communication satellites and fibre optic cables. The emergence of these new technologies posed a new choice for the authorities regulating telecommunications: Should the development of these new technologies remain the responsibility of the telecommunication monopoly or should the development of these new technologies be open to anyone prepared to take the initiative and shoulder the risks involved? Confronted with this choice, U.S. regulatory authorities decided to allow competition in long-distance transmission facilities, while the U.K. and Japan have decided to allow a limited degree of competition in all transmission facilities.

The new computer technology has also revolutionized business use of telecommunications. Automation of production, management, and distribution systems has created the need for business computers to communicate with each other, both within the premises of a single business facility and among the various facilities owned by an enterprise. This has given rise to the development of private networks that serve the internal communication needs of an enterprise.

Since private networks are largely self-standing systems and since each of these systems needs to serve the unique needs of an individual enterprise, it makes a great deal of economic sense to allow each business to develop its own system, at least within the confines of its own buildings. While individual national regulatory authorities have reached different conclusions with respect to the autonomy individual businesses should have in developing private networks, and the geographic scope of such networks, a majority of countries now allow businesses to establish such private networks. Since not every business has either the capability or interest in building and/or operating its own private network, it again makes economic sense to allow competition in the provision of the services necessary to build and operate these private telecommunication networks.

The new policies in favor of competition in the provision of some telecommunication services has led to greater competition in international as well as domestic telecommunication services. Since international telecommunications are the joint responsibility of the two countries served by an international telecommunication link, at least two different regulatory authorities have to agree on the degree of competition that should be allowed and the terms and conditions under which it should be allowed. This requirement for agreement between at least two independent regulatory authorities has slowed the spread of competition in international communications.

As a result of the negotiations that have been carried out among national authorities, as well as between competitive providers of telecommunication services in some countries and the relevant foreign regulatory authorities, a complex set of arrangements have emerged over the last few years. Under these arrangements, international telecommunication traffic originating in countries that permit competition is provided on a competitive basis, while international telecommunication traffic originating in countries that do not permit competition continues to be the exclusive domain of the national telecommunications monopoly. Where both the country originating a call and the country receiving the call permit competition, competition takes place in both directions, but in each direction the competition is only among local enterprises authorized to provide telecommunication services in the country involved. Since the United States, the United Kingdom, and Japan also allow competition in international telecommunications, the last few years have seen a steady trend towards greater competition in the provision of international telecommunication services across the Atlantic and across the Pacific.

The emergence of competition among domestic enterprises in the provision of telecommunication services has raised the far more delicate question of *international* competition in the provision of telecommunication services. Each country needs to decide to what extent it should allow foreign as well as domestic enterprises to provide telecommunication services within its own borders. Up to now, the transition from domestic to international competition has been even slower than the transition from domestic competition in domestic telecommunication services to domestic competition in international telecommunication services. Nevertheless a considerable degree of international competition has emerged among developed countries in the provision of value-added telecommunication services, and a limited amount of international competition is emerging in the provision of basic telecommunication services across the Atlantic and across the Pacific.

It is conceivable that some time over the next few years, a few countries could allow full international competition in both domestic and international communications by telecommunication enterprises authorized to offer telecommunication services on both sides of a border, as well as across the border. In fact, in the years ahead, we could witness the emergence of multinational telecommunication companies that can offer a wide range of domestic and international telecommunication services on a competitive basis in a number of countries.

The emergence of international competition raises questions about the ground rules that should apply to competition between domestic and foreign suppliers of telecommunication services. Competition has to take place under certain agreed ground rules if it is to lead to the most efficient economic allocation of resources and if it is to be acceptable to everyone.

As national regulatory authorities introduced a degree of competition in their individual countries, they also found it necessary to apply domestic competition laws and to establish rules for fair competition between the traditional monopoly providers of basic services and the new suppliers of competitive services. Similarly, the emergence of international competition makes it necessary to develop appropriate international ground rules for that competition. At issue are not only questions about fair competition but also questions about mutual commercial advantage. The first set of questions has to do with the establishment of a level playing field for competing firms and the need to make sure that foreign firms do not derive special advantages from a possible monopoly position in their own country or an ability to transfer subsidies from a protected home market to the foreign market. The second set of questions has to do with the ability of domestic firms to obtain commercial opportunities in foreign markets that are equivalent to the commercial opportunities foreign firms are able to obtain in the domestic market.

The first part of this paper describes the type of competition that is emerging in the telecommunication sector, why a competitive market structure is displacing a monopoly structure in major segments of the telecommunication system, and the public policy goals that lie behind the pro-competitive regulatory policies that have been adopted by an increasing number of developed countries.

On the basis of this background material, we will examine the extent to which domestic competition is leading to international competition, the likely evolution of international competition, and the kind of issues that will arise as a result of international competition in the telecommunication services and the new international rules that have to be developed i) to guide competition among countries that choose to permit such competition and ii) to interconnect the telecommunication networks of countries that permit competition with the telecommunication networks of countries that do not.

In the final part of this paper, we will examine the relevance of trade-based rules to guide international competition among telecommunication networks. As indicated above, two sets of issues need to be considered - the need for rules to define the terms of competition and the need for rules to define reciprocal access.

The intent of this paper is not to advocate domestic policies or international rules to support greater competition but rather to examine the implications of the competition that is in fact emerging for international rulemaking in telecommunications. The traditional rules in this area have been based on the assumption that telecommunication is a monopoly activity. This is no longer universally true and the rules have to accommodate the changed facts.

The Domestic Telecommunication Network

We are used to thinking of telecommunications as a single activity. Actually, what we normally consider a single service can be broken down into a number of separate telecommunication services - the provision of transmission facilities such as copper or fiber-optic cables, microwave transmitters and receivers, communication satellites and earth stations and the electronic switches that interconnect them, the provision of network management facilities to control the flow of messages through the network of transmission facilities, the provision of information about telephone subscribers (directory assistance) and about local businesses (yellow pages), and retail distribution of specific telecommunication services to individual subscribers (including the marketing, selling, maintenance and billing activities associated with a typical retail "store").

While all of these functional activities associated with telecommunications have traditionally been carried out by the same entity, namely the local telephone monopoly, they need not be performed by the same entity. In fact, as we will describe below, a number of factors have lead to a growing degree of specialization and competition with respect to many of the activities traditionally associated with the delivery of telecommunication services.

Another way of looking at the provision of telecommunication services is as a "production" process that involves a series of intermediate stages of production. At each stage of the production process, additional service inputs are combined with a more basic service product to yield a more sophisticated, higher-valued service product. Thus the existence of transmission facilities makes it possible to send an electronic signal from one point in the network to another but that does not, in itself, enable an individual user to use the system for a specific purpose like sending a fax, connecting two computers, obtaining information about the weather, or making a long-distance call with a credit card. Various service inputs in addition to the provision of basic transmission facilities are required to create a useful service for a household consumer or a business user and to assure efficient utilization of the basic transmission facilities.

While the traditional communication companies maintained a monopoly on the production of intermediate as well as final telecommunication services, they have never been totally self-sufficient in the production of intermediate service inputs. Telephone companies have gone to outside vendors to purchase such intermediate service inputs as software development, computer processing of bills, printing of telephone books, etc. In recent years, most telecommunication companies have increased their purchases of inputs from outside vendors, either because the rapid changes in technology have made it difficult for many of these companies to maintain a state-of-the art capability within the firm or because they thought someone else could do it better or more cheaply. At the same time, even partial deregulation, and the competitive pressures it has generated, have made it more imperative even for the telecommunication monopolies to improve their productivity with state-of-the art hardware and service inputs. One area of competition, therefore, concerns the production of service inputs used by telecommunication companies.

In order to understand the emergence of competition in the telecommunication industry, we have to examine what has been happening with respect to all of the major activities associated with the provision of telecommunication services -- in other words, one has to examine each stage of the production process. For the purposes of this paper, the activities that can be performed with respect to a telecommunication network are divided into five categories. The five categories are:

1. The provision of basic transmission facilities. This category covers the cables, amplifiers, satellite circuits, and microwave transmitters -- sometimes referred to as communication "pipes" -- and the electronic switches that interconnect them. The technology underlying each type of transmission facility results in major differences in the quality of transmission (static, interference, echo, degradation of signal strength, etc.), the type of electronic signals that can be transmitted and the range of frequencies that can be utilized for the transmission, the ability to maintain the confidentiality of the message transmitted, the speed of transmission, the total amount of information that can be transmitted through each line, and the cost of providing particular services. As we shall see later, this dispersion in technical performance characteristics and the large number of trade-offs that have to be made between cost and various performance characteristics is the principal reason a number of countries have decided to allow a degree of competition with respect to transmission facilities. Exploring these trade-offs requires a large degree of innovation and a flexibility of approach, neither of which is a characteristic of any monopoly.

2. The provision of networking facilities. This category covers the computer hardware and software that enables a user to route calls or messages through a specific set of transmission facilities to establish a communication channel with a desired capacity, with specified performance characteristics, and a desired usage pattern.1 Control over the route taken by a message is accomplished through computerized control of the electronic switches that interconnect the various transmission facilities that constitute the network. The computers that control a network can be located at the network switching facility or at a more distant location in another part of town, in another city, or even in another country as long as the computer that controls the network is electronically connected to it. The computer hardware and software that controls the switching of facilities is often referred to as the"network intelligence."

The need for greater control over the routing of messages by individual business users arises from the development of new, specialized telecommunication-intensive production, marketing, and management systems by many business enterprises. Each specialized business application of computer and telecommunication technology creates a unique set of desired performance characteristics for the transmission facilities linking a firm's computers. For some applications, businesses need to be assured of available capacity at all times, while for other applications businesses need to be able to minimize telecommunication costs by pushing as much data through a line as is technically possible. For still other applications the emphasis may need to be placed on security, accuracy of transmission, the band width of the signal that can be transmitted or the total capacity of the circuit.

The demand for greater control has led to the introduction of private networks, made up of owned transmission facilities installed within the premises of the firm and leased transmission facilities between geographically separated premises. The provision of a network management capability gives firms the capacity to control the performance of the whole network and to optimize the performance of the network with respect to various business applications, including management information and control systems, production and inventory control systems, internal information-retrieval and data-processing systems, and systems for distributing information-based services to employees or customers.

3. The provision of electronic messaging services. This category govers facsimile, electronic mail, voice mail, and videotext. In order to provide these services, a firm must have access to the transmission facilities covered by category 1 and to computer hardware and software for temporarily storing and/or distributing messages to a user-defined list of addresses. The routing and storage of messages involves the use of a computer connected to the network. In fact, the same computer could physically perform the network management functions covered by category 2 and the massaging functions covered by category 3, though there may be any number of commercial reasons why an enterprise might choose to specialize in one type of service or another.

4. The provision of services other than telecommunication services through a telecommunication network. This category covers electronic data banks, data-processing services, electronic banking services, electronic shopping services, and entertainment services. Generally, any service that can be made available through the transmission of information can be distributed electronically through the telecommunication network. These

information-based services should obviously not be classified as a part of the telecommunication sector but the firm that produces these services often also provides the necessary telecommunication access to its customers, and it is this telecommunication component that is classified here as a category 5 telecommunication service.

The telecommunication network that is dedicated to providing access to a particular service is usually referred to as a VAN, a Value-Added Network. Telecommunication access is provided either by buying the underlying services from the entities that produce the telecommunication services covered by categories 1, 2 and 3, by leasing the facilities involved from the owners of these facilities, or by establishing the facilities necessary to produce these services within the firm. The choice depends, first, on the regulations established by the relevant authorities and, second, on commercial considerations.

The provision of electronically distributed services is so dependent on the cost and availability of communication facilities that the economic viability of such services is often closely tied to the regulation of private networks and the services involved are often treated as telecommunication services by analysts and regulators, despite the fact that the services involved fall into a totally unrelated sector of the economy.

5. The retail distribution of telecommunication services to individual subscribers. This category covers the marketing, selling, and maintenance of telecommunication services falling under either categories 1, 2, 3 or 4 to individual households or business enterprises and the billing for services provided. (Each of the activities carried out by a retailing firm is listed separately because in many cases the company that sells a service will subcontract the performance of billing, marketing or maintenance actvities, thus creating separate market niches for these service inputs.)

Using an analogy from the manufacturing world, we could consider category 1, 2, 3, and 4 activities as the "production" of telecommunication services, and category 5 activities as the "retailing" of the services produced under the preceding categories. The local telephone company sells access to the transmission facilities covered by category 1. A vendor of electronic mail services sells access to transmission facilities covered by category 1 and computer hardware and software capable of storing and disseminating messages, which are functions covered by category 2. A company that agrees to provide a private network for a global firm is probably selling access to transmission facilities covered in category 1 and computer hardware and software designed to provide the network management functions covered by category 2.

Each of the five categories can be viewed as successive layers of an onion, where the next higher category adds additional value. Category 1 provides the basic capacity to transmit a message from one access point in the network to another. Category 2 gives the user the capability to control the route over which the message is tranmitted. Category 3 provides the additional cpacity for accessing specialized input and output terminals and storing messages for later retrieval. Category 4 provides additional value by providing access to a broad range of services like information services, electronic banking services, electronic insurance services, computer shopping services, and electronic booking services. Category 5 adds the customer relations and account management function to the services produced under all the preceding categories.

The establishment of any classification scheme in the telecommunications area is fraught with difficulty because there are no clear boundaries in the real world. Every service that is produced in the telecommunication sector is closely linked to every other service that is produced in the telecommunication sector and most enterprises in this sector produce a wide range of telecommunication services that span any number of categories one can define. Moreover, each new advance in computer technology makes it possible to build more intelligence into both the terminals on customer premises and the centralized computers that control the network, thereby constantly changing the nature of the telecommunication business.

The changes in technology and the market reponse to those changes also lead to a continuing change in regulations and the categorization of telecommunications activities for purposes of regulation. Each national regulatory authority has developed its own classification scheme to separate regulated from unregulated activities and each national classification scheme is constantly evolving in response to technological change and the resulting market pressures.

In contrast with the classification system proposed in this paper, most of the current literature would divide the same set of activities into two categories - basic telecommunication services and enhanced or value-added services. This distinction has its origins in regulatory decisions to permit competition in some telecommunicaiton services labeled "enhanced" telecommunication services in the United States and "value-added" telecommunication services in many other countries -- while maintaining a monopoly structure for so-called "basic" services.

In general, the activities covered by category 1 and the related activities in category 5 have been treated as basic services subject to the monopoly and those under categories 2, 3 and 4 have been treated as enhanced or value-added services by regulatory authorities that have decided to permit a degree of competition. In practice, the definition of basic and enhanced telecommunication activities differs signficantly from country to country. Thus some countries treat messaging services such as fax (category 3) as a basic service, while other countries treat these services as enhanced services. The relevant definitions have also evolved in each country as the underlying domestic regulations have changed, leading to total confusion over the definition of these categories.

The categories used in this paper are not tied to any particular regulatory regime but are based on differences in the activities being performed and the emerging differences in market structure. The objective in establishing the various categories is to provide a basis for analyzing the economic characteristics of individual segments of the telecommunication industry and in particular, to examine the extent to which competition is emerging with respect to each segment.

The emergence of competition and the nature of that competition,in turn, have major implications for the principles and rules that have to be developed to guide such competition internationally, both the assure a level playing field and mutual commercial advantage among countries.

The Nature of Competition in the Telecommunication Sector

The level of competition that has emerged in the telecommunications area differs for each of the five areas of activity identified above. This is true in the United States, as well as in other countries. At the same time, it needs to be recognized that the five categories do not fully reflect all the differences in the degree of competition that can be found within the telecommunication sector. Each of the five categories could be subdivided into subcategories, either to reflect differences in regulations or differences in the degree to which market forces have led to competition. Thus, for example, public long-distance telephone service has been opened up to competition in some countries but local telephone service has not been so opened up. Moreover, in a number of areas, services associated with the operation of private networks have been opened up to competition but not the equivalent services associated with the operation of the public telecommunication network.

It is beyond the scope of this paper to provide detailed information by country and by type of service on the amount of competition permitted by national regulations. Generally, the United States, Japan, and the United Kingdom permit the widest degree of competition, while most industrial countries have agreed to provide some competition with respect to private networks and value-added networks.

For the purposes of this paper, the existence of competition in even a handful of countries creates the need for new international rules to accommodate that competition and to establish a basis for managing the relationship between countries that permit competition and those that do not.

While keeping in mind all the caveats mentioned above, one could summarize the competition that is emerging in each of the five categories identified here as follows:

1. The provision of transmission facilities (category #1) remains largely a monopoly in most countries. Competition has nevertheless emerged in key segments of the global communication network. In fact, there is probably more competition today in basic transmission facilities than most people realize.

The provision of transmission facilities for public telecommunication purposes largely remains a monopoly in the vast majority of countries. The major exceptions are the United States, which permits open competition in the provision of long-distance telecommunication facilities, and Japan and the U.K., both of whom allow a limited degree of competition in the provision of both local and long-distance public transmission facilities. The policies pursued by the United States, Japan and the United Kingdom have also led to a growing competition in the provision of public transmission facilities across the Atlantic and the Pacific oceans.

The widest degree of competition in the provision of transmission facilities has arisen with repect to the establishment of private networks, which serve the internal communication needs of individual firms, and with respect to the establishment of value-added networks, which provide vendors of services such as data-processing companies and banking the capacity to deliver these services electronically. These private networks combine private transmission facilities, installed within the premises of an enterprise, with public transmission facilities leased from a telecommunication company.

A fairly large number of countries permit firms to acquire internal transmission facilities, installed within the premises of the firm, from any competitive supplier. A somewhat smaller number of countries permit firms to acquire their own equipment for transmitting and receiving telecommunication signals *via* communication satellites. The United States also permits firms to establish any other facility for long-distance communication.

Generally, most countries that permit firms to establish private networks will also permit a certain degree of competition in the provision of the private transmission facilities installed within the premises of the firm. With respect to off-premises transmission facilities, countries that do not allow competition in public transmission facilities also generally do not permit competition in the provision of public facilities leased by a business in connection with the establishment of a private network or value-added network. Countries that permit some degree of competition in public transmission facilities generally also permit an equivalent degree of competition in the provision of facilities leased by businesses for private networks and value-added networks.

The rapid growth in the number and size of private networks and value-added networks has lead to growing pressure from the businesses that own and operate these networks for the right to sell excess capacity to other business users. In addition, smaller firms that cannot afford to establish their own private networks have argued in favor of the right to establish shared-use networks, whereby several firms jointly have a right to establish and operate a private network for their use. Most national regulatory authorities, with the exception of the United States, have resisted these pressures to date, though they are likely to find it more and more difficult to resist these pressures because it will adversely affect the competitive position of their firms in world markets.

2. The provision of network management services (category #2) gives operators of private networks and value-added networks control over the routing of messages through public and private facilities. Remote switching makes it possible to control the routing of calls from a computer located on the customer's premises or on the premises of a third-party vendor of network management services, thus giving businesses considerable control over the performance characteristics of a circuit, including cost, speed of response, quality of transmission, security, availability and capacity.

Generally, the provision of network management services is fully competitive wherever firms are allowed to establish private networks for intra-corporate communications and value-added networks for the distribution of information-based services. Since the growth of telecommunication traffic in private networks now exceeds the growth of traffic through the public network, the vigorous competition in this area is likely to put increasing pressure on public telecommunication monopolies to offer business customers greater control over swtiching without the necessity of establishing a private network.

In fact, despite the fact that the regional Bell operating companies retain a monopoly position in local telephone services, a number of them are exploring how they might unbundle transmission from switching services and offer business customers a broader choice with respect to both. The more farsighted leaders in the industry have clearly seen the handwriting on the wall and they want to develop the necessary competititve skills before they are forced to do so in the wake of regulatory responses to market pressures.

At the same time, the companies that have developed their own private networks or value-added networks will put increasing pressure on regulatory authorities to give them the right to resell excess capacity in their network. Many of these same firms have gone into the business of helping other enterprises to develop and operate private networks. In fact, so many firms have gone into the business of planning, building, and operating private telecommunication networks for enterprises that a highly competitive global market has emerged in the area of network management services.

3. **The provision of electronic messaging services such as videotext, fax, electronic mail and voice mail** (category #3) is treated as a competitive activity in a large number of countries. In fact, the initial regulatory impetus for the establishment of a new category for enhanced or value-added services came from a desire to encourage competition in this area.

There are three basic reasons why competition has emerged with respect to electronic messaging services:

First, these are new services that were not within the traditional mandate of the telecommunication monopolies and it was therefore possible to allow competition without taking anything away from the monopolies.

Secondly, anyone who could connect a computer to the public communication network could offer these services economically to anyone with access to the necessary terminal equipment. It was therefore difficult to argue that these services had the characteristics of a natural monopoly.

Thirdly, it has become increasingly feasible to build the capacity to provide these services into customer-premises equipment and third-party equipment, as well as network equipment. Thus, where the authorities have decided to limit competition in the provision of public electronic messaging services, we are likely to see a growing tendency to incorporate the capacity to generate such services in equipment installed on customer premises. With respect to some messaging services this has been happening in any case, as we have witnessed in recent years with respect to the rapid growth in the number of businesses and even households that now own fax machines in the United States.

There is a general trend in most industrial countries towards allowing competition in this area, a trend that has become clearly established with the publication of the European Community's Green Paper on Telecommunications.

4. **The provision of telecommunication-dependent information, data-processing, banking, shopping and entertainment services** (category #4) is clearly seen by most developed countries as a competitive activity. The difficulty arises with respect to the telecommunication component of the full services package that is offered to customers. As indicated earlier, a growing number of countries permit a certain degree of competition in the establishment of so-called value-added networks that serve as specialized communication channels for the distribution of information-based services. Most of these countries, however, view these networks as a public telecommunication activity that should be regulated in much the same way as other

public telecommunication services. One of the problems that arises in this context is a conflict between the sectoral regulations that apply to the production and sale of the services involved and the regulation of the communication component. The United States, as in other aspects of communication policy, allows the widest degree of competition and provides the widest degree of regulatory flexibility in the establishment of these value-added networks.

5. The retail distribution of telecommunication services to individual households and businesses (category #5) is generally within the mandate of the telecommunication monopolies, in so far as the provision of the services involved is subject to the monopoly. Thus the sale of transmission services to the general public is normally covered by the monopoly, while the sale of enhanced or value-added services is subject to competition.

It is conceivable, however, that over time some countries might permit a degree of competition with respect to the sale of "basic" transmission services, while retaining the monopoly on the provision of the underlying transmission facilities. This could occur if regulatory authorities decide to allow businesses with private networks to resell excess capacity in the network to other businesses while maintaining the monopoly on the provision of public tranmission facilities. Only a few countries now permit owners of private networks to resell capacity to other businesses but, with the growth in the number and size of private networks in other countries, the pressure on regulators to permit resale in these countries is undoubtedly going to grow.

The Changing Rationale for Competition in Telecommunications

The basic rationale for competition in the provision of telecommunication services, as in the provision of other goods and services, is that it spurs suppliers to produce the services consumers want at the least cost. The results of a lack of competition in telecommunications have been all too visible: lack of consumer choice and high prices.

Two key reasons are usually given in support of a monopoly structure in telecommunications: first, that the provision of telecommunication services is a natural monopoly and, second, that the provision of telecommunication services is a public good.

Installing the cables, microwave transmitters and switches that constitute the basic communication grid is a capital-intensive activity that benefits from significant economies of scale. For most households and businesses, a single telephone cable provides all the telecommunication capacity that is needed, and so having more than one network to serve households and a majority of businesses seems wasteful. This is the natural-monopoly argument that underlies the traditional communication monopoly.

General public availability of communication services results in advantages to a community over and above the advantages which individual households and businesses derive from having access to the telecommunication system. It leads to more frequent communication among citizens, therefore assuring a better-informed and a more harmonious citizenry. It enables many people to reach many employees, voters and neighbors who might otherwise not be able to afford a telephone. It also allows individuals to notify authorities promptly of any natural disasters, accidents and other emergencies that can affect the public at large. In short, the argument is that telecommunications are a public good that deserves to be subsidized.

The need for a subsidy, in itself, does not provide a rationale for a monopoly structure. The link to the monopoly is provided by the ability of a monopoly to subsidize universal access to local telephone service by charging households less than the cost of production for local access charges and charging them more for long-distance services, which have less social value. Similarly, the monopoly can charge businesses the same rates as households, even though the higher volume of telecommunication traffic generated by business leads to higher-capacity utilization rates and therefore lower costs for providing telecommunication services to businesses.

Until fairly recently, these arguments were generally accepted and telecommunication was largely the province of national monopolies. This has changed, in part, because a technological revolution in telecommunications and exponential growth in the telecommunication traffic generated by businesses has made telecommunications less of a natural monopoly. At the same time the disadvantages of a monopoly structure in terms of lost economic opportunities have become much more pronounced than in the past.

New technologies like communication satellites have reduced the capital cost of installing satellite transmitters and receivers to the point at which even individual companies can afford to establish their own satellite-based telecommunication networks and indeed find it cheaper to do so than to pay the rates charged by the public telecommunication companies. This nullifies the argument that telecommunications is a natural monopoly. At the same time that it has become cheaper build satellite-based networks, the volume of telecommunication traffic has expanded to the point at which the market can easily support competitive systems in heavily used segments of the market, further undermining the natural-monopoly argument.

The natural-monopoly argument can still be made with respect to the local network that serves individual households and smaller businesses and this then leads to the key question whether the expansion and operation of the local network should be subsidized through the preservation of a monopoly structure for the long-distance network and for the intra-corporate and inter-corporate network. Those who favor the continuation of a monopoly structure answer this question in the affirmative. Those who support competition either argue that no subsidies are necessary or that there are other ways of subsidizing the local network, such as direct government subsidies and access charges imposed on anyone who accesses the local network from a long distance-network or private network. Those who support competition also point to the growing costs of a monopoly structure in the form of lost economic opportunities.

The disadvantages of a monopoly structure are that it tends to reduce the variety of telecommunication services available to users and makes it too expensive to introduce many new telecommunication-based services. It also increases the production costs of national enterprises, reducing their competitive position in international markets. The technological explosion in electronics (computer chips), materials (fibre-optic cables), and space transportation (communication satellites) has vastly increased the opportunities for innovation in telecommunications, both with respect to the provision of a much wider range of telecommunication services and with respect to the installation of more efficient hardware and software. No matter how well run a monopoly is, it is bound to resist change.

Economic growth in the most advanced economies today is tied to innovation in telecommunications. This is because many of the productivity improvements in both manufacturing and services today depend on the installation of new computer systems that tie together widely dispersed production and marketing facilities. Moreover, many of the most innovative new products in services involve the electronic distribution of information-based services through value-added networks. In both of these areas, progress depends on the adaption of the new technologies to fit the requirements of these systems and a reduction in communication costs. It is impossible for any single organization such as a telecommunication monopoly to develop all the necessary technology even if it had an incentive to do so.

In summary, what has changed is that technological advances have led to the multiplication of potential channels for transmitting telecommunication signals (copper cable, fibre-optic cable, satellite, microwave), for switching signals (electro-mechanical switches as against advanced computer switches) and for transforming a client's message into an electronic signal (telephones, fax machines, modems) and this multiplication has made it possible to offer different types of services by linking together different facilities and equipment. The range of these potential services is so broad that a single organization can no longer be expected to meet all the specialized customer needs.

The Regulation of Domestic Competition

Countries that have decided to allow competition in some segments of the domestic telecommunications network have found it desirable, and indeed necessary, to separate the regulation of telecommunication activities from the management of the national telecommunication monopoly. In the United States, the two functions have always been separated to some extent, because ATT was a private company. Even in the United States, however, ATT established all the regulations on what could and could not be connected to the network. In most other countries, where the national telecommunication monopoly was part of a government ministry, the monopoly itself wrote all the regulations.

With the establishment of competition in some segments of the telecommunication system it could no longer be assumed that the managers of the monopoly could also act as neutral and objective arbiters of regulations that would affect telecommunication enterprises competing with the monopoly. It has therefore become necessary to create new regulatory agencies to establish even-handed regulations.

One of the priority objectives of regulatory authorities in these situations is to ensure that newly established enterprises that seek to compete with the old monopoly are not overwhelmed by the old monopoly before they have had a chance fully to establish themselves. Inevitably, the old monopoly is able to maintain a dominant position in the market and can use its very considerable resources to drive new competitors out of business before they have been able to acheve a certain degree of financial stability. There is, moreover, a continuing need to ensure that the old monopoly does not cross-subsidize its competitive activities from profits generated by monopoly activities and that it does not use its position as the exclusive supplier of certain basic transmission facilities to disadvantage competitors dependent on such facilities.

Another priority regulatory objective in a competitive environment is to ensure the orderly development and implementation of standards that will guarantee the interconnectability of the competing networks. As long as the monopoly had exclusive control over the whole telecommunication system, it could set the standards for all systems equipment as well as customer-premises equipment. In the context of a competitive environment, that standard-setting function has to be performed by an entity that can act as an honest broker, leading to the developing of standards that do not prejudice the position of any of the competing telecommunication enterprises. It has also become apparent that the standards-making process should also fully take into consideration the needs of users.

International Competition

The emergence of domestic competition in telecommunications has also created the possibility of international competition in telecommunications, i.e., competition among enterprises from different countries. For purposes of analyzing the extent to which such competition has emerged and the likely evolution of such competition, we need to look at international competition in international telecommunication services separately from international competition in domestic telecommunication services. In the first case, firms from different countries compete with each other in providing telecommunication services that involve the transmission of a message from one country to another. In the second case, firms from different countries compete with each other in providing telecommunication services that involve the transmission of messages within national borders.

International Competition in International Telecommunication Services

International telecommunications typically require the cooperation of at least two telecommunication entities - a telecommunication entity in country A, where a telephone call or telegram originates and a telecommunication entity in country B, where the telephone call or telegram is received. Telecommunication services between countries have therefore typically been provided jointly by the national telecommunication monopolies of the two countries involved. The cables and other facilities linking national telecommunication systems tend to be owned and operated by joint ventures, with major participation by the telecommunication companies of the two countries involved. Each national monopoly is responsible for the transmission of the message on its side of the border. Billing is handled by the company that originates the call and revenues are split on the basis of an agreed formula.

The same economic forces that have led to greater competition in many domestic telecommunication systems have also led to increasing competition in the international telecommunication system -- in all five categories of activity identified earlier in this paper. Since different countries have responded to the new economic forces in different ways and at different speeds, the international telecommunication system today has become a complex mosaic of competitive and non-competitive elements.

1.**International Telecommunication Facilities.** The introduction of new communication technologies, such as satellite communications and fibre-optic cables, along with a rapid expansion of traffic, has led to the installation of competitive communication facilities between key areas of the world, particularly across the Atlantic and Pacific oceans. The introduction of satellite communication systems, for example, created a form of competition between cable facilities and satellite facilities. Until recently, however, few people recognized that there was any competition between the two systems, because there was a close link between the management of INTELSAT, which owned and operated the global satellite communication system, and the managers of the various national telecommunication monopolies.

More recently, efforts made by PanAmSat and Orion to obtain operating rights for competitive satellite communication systems, however, have led to a more competitive stance by INTELSAT. Moreover, the recent decision to grant PanAmSat international operating rights has introduced a more direct form of competition, from an entity not controlled by the traditional telecommunication monopolies.

Competition has also emerged in international cable facilities as a result of the decision by Cable & Wireless to put in place competitive cable systems across both the Atlantic and Pacific oceans. Over the years ahead, we should expect to see increasing competition among companies providing international communication facilities.

2. International Network Management Services. International competition in the provision of international network management services first emerged as a result of the establishment of international private networks, which serve the internal communication needs of multinational corporations, and international value-added networks, which provide the means for delivering information-based services such as data processing and banking electronically to other countries. These international networks, like their domestic counterparts, integrate private facilities with leased public facilities. While these private intra-corporate networks and value-added networks do not directly compete with public networks for the business of individual users, the option of large users to set up their own network will obviously affect the rates and services that will be offered by public networks to business users.

Private international networks have been established by many multinational corporations such as EDS/General Motors, General Electric, IBM, Volkswagen, Citibank, American Express, et al. International networks have also been established by a number of industry associations to support certain common communication needs of an industry. Examples are SITA, established by international airlines for exchanging information about air reservations, and SWIFT, established by the banking industry for check-clearing purposes.

3. International Message Services. A number of companies offer international message services such as electronic mail and voice mail. Generally, a wide degree of competition exists in the provision of international message services to individual companies for intra-corporate communication and to closed user groups for inter-corporate communications.

Some efforts have also been launched to offer international messaging services to the public at large. The technology that has been most widely adopted is the fax technology, which has been growing rapidly in popularity. The intelligence for sending fax messages is largely built into customer-premises equipment, however, and the issue of competition is largely determined by regulations that spell out what equipment can be attached to the public network.

With respect to other international electronic messaging technologies, the policies of various national governments differ widely. Some permit open competition, as long as public transmission facilities are used. Others insist that the national telecommunication monopoly participate in the establishment of local computer and terminal facilities associated with such services. In some countries, a highly restrictive regulatory environment has made it impossible to offer these services at all. Generally, there is much less competition in the provision of these services to the public at large than to individual corporations or closed user groups.

4. International Value-Added Networks. International value-added network services are just beginning to emerge. Often these services are provided by corporations who seek to use their private internal networks to deliver specific services in data processing, banking, insurance, etc. to customers in other countries. For example, Citibank offers its customers around the world, where permitted by local regulations, access to bank accounts maintained in any Citibank branch around the world. Many companies like Control Data, EDS, and General Electric use their internal networks to give customers around the world the ability to access data banks located at centralized locations in the United States and elsewhere.

The central issue with respect to the provision of these services is whether companies should be allowed to use their private networks to deliver these services or whether the regulatory authorities insist that local subscribers access the foreign network through the public international communication network. The debate on this issue, however, is usually posed in more arcanc technical terms, namely as an issue over whether the corporation involved has a right to interconnect its private network with the local public-switched network. To the companies who seek to establish international value-added networks and to their potential customers, the basic issue is one of cost and the economic viability of the service being offered. Electronic access to foreign data bases generally makes economic sense only if the cost of telecommunication access can be reduced. To the national telecommunication monopolies, the basic issue is one of lost revenues if growth in telecommunications is diverted to private networks. Since the postal monopolies generally cannot provide an economically viable alternative, however, the net effort of their policies is to discourage the introduction of new telecommunication-based services.

In summary, competition in the provision of telecommunication-based services is hampered in many, if not in most, countries, by regulations that make it difficult to establish an international value-added network. At the same time, most public telecommunication monopolies have not established an economically viable alternative based on the public-switched telecommunication network. At the rates charged for regular telephone traffic, the cost of electronic distribution is too high, particularly at the low transmission speed that is typical for equipment owned by households. The general trend in this area, however, is towards greater competition in most developed countries and some of the more advanced developing countries.

5. Selling international telecommunication services to users. This category deals with the sale of international telecommunication services to individual household and business users, as against the provision of the facilities that "produce" such services. This is the same subtle distinction between "retailing" and "production" that was covered in the discussion of competition in domestic telecommunication services. As a general rule, the same firms that provide the facilities will also sell to individual subscribers the various finds of telecommunication services that can be "produced" with those facilities.

The real purpose in focusing on the retail distribution of telecommunication services to subscribers, as against the provision of the facilities, is to highlight the resale issue. The question is whether firms that lease telecommunication lines from a provider of transmission facilities have a right to sell a part of that capacity to other users. Generally, countries that do not allow competition in the provision of facilities also do not allow resale, while a country like the United States that allows considerable competition in the provision of facilities also allows the resale of leased capacity.

If competition eventually becomes widely accepted among a number of key countries, which is highly likely, many of the private networks are likely to become major vendors of international telecommunication services to other businesses. In the data-processing industry, many of the largest users of data-processing services are also some of the largest suppliers of data-processing services to other businesses (e.g., Boeing, General Motors, General Electric, Citibank). There is no reason why the same pattern could not emerge in the telecommunication area, after an appropriate lag due to regulatory resistance. For the moment, however, competition in public international telecommunication services is still in its infancy.

International Competition in Domestic Telecommunication Services

International competition in the provision of domestic telecommunication services can take place inside a country between national networks owned and operated by domestic enterprises and national networks owned and operated by foreign enterprises (or enterprises owned jointly by foreign and domestic enterprises.) International competition in the provision of domestic telecommunication network services is more a conceptual than a real issue today, though it is conceivable that the countries that now permit domestic competition in the provision of long distance transmission facilities could decide to allow firms from other countries to establish such facilities on a reciprocal basis.

At some point we might see the emergence of what I would call transnational telecommunication companies - joint venture companies that have operating rights within as well as between key countries. Cable & Wireless is well on its way towards becoming such a company. It could well evoke a competitive response from the more established carriers, who could decide to form joint ventures of their own, capable of supplying an integrated set of services across a range of countries. The recent formation of competing international joint ventures in air reservation systems could well be a harbinger of future trends in international telecommunication systems.

Negotiating New International Rules in Telecommunications

The emergence of competition has reduced the utility and relevance of many of the existing international rules and agreements in the telecommunication area. These rules were written at a time when all domestic telecommunication services were provided by national monopolies and international telecommunications were the joint responsibility of the national monopolies involved. Typically, each national monopoly negotiated bilateral operating agreements with its counterparts in other countries, agreements which spelled out technical standards for the interconnection of national networks and economic arrangements for the sharing of revenues and costs associated with the provision of international services. These bilateral agreements were entered into under the umbrella of guidelines and recommendations negotiated in the International Telecommunication Union (ITU).

The emergence of international competition in the provision of international telecommunication services creates the need for new rules that can deal with that competition. New rules are needed to define the terms under which firms from different countries that permit competition can compete with each other. New rules are also needed to define the terms under which countries that permit competition can provide international telecommunication services to countries that do not permit competition and vice versa.

For the foreseeable future, the market structure in global communications is likely to be a patchwork of market segments, some with very considerable competition, some with limited competition, and others with no competition. Each country will make its own choices with respect to the level of domestic competition it is willing to allow in each segment of the market and the extent to which it is prepared to allow foreign firms to participate in markets opened up to domestic competition. Quite aside from the level of competition the authorities are willing to authorize, certain markets will only support a limited number of competitive firms and this is turn creates the need for a different regulatory approach than might be appropriate in a market that can support a large number of competitive firms.

Over time, a more homogeneous market structure might emerge in most countries but it is likely to take a long time before that becomes apparent. For now, any system of international rules for telecommunication services must accommodate differences in the level of competition between countries and between different market segments within countries. One of the principal objectives of a new system of rules, therefore, has to be to establish the terms under which competitive telecommunication firms, operating in competitive segments of the global telecommunication system, will interact with telecommunication monopolies. Since the competitive and noncompetitive segments of the global telecommunication system form a tightly woven web of economic relationships, each market segment cannot be treated as an isolated market.

For example, in order to establish an international telecommunication link between country A which permits competition and country B which does not, the competitive firms from country A have to negotiate an operating agreement with the monopoly in country B. These arrangements spell out how the interconnection is to be achieved technically and how the revenues generated by the resulting telecommunication traffic are to be shared. Similarly, vendors of competitive telecommunication services such as videotext typically have to lease basic transmission facilities from the monopoly supplier of such facilities. All such negotiations between competitive buyers and a single, monopoly, seller are inherently unequal, as are similar negotiations between competitive sellers and a single, monopsonist, buyer.

It is a well-known theory in economics that negotiations between competitive buyers and a monopoly seller or between competitive sellers and a monopsonist buyer result in an outcome that is skewed in favor of the monopolist and the monopsonist. Therefore, any negotiations that have to be carried out between monopolist or monopsonist on one side and competitive firms on the other side have to be subjected to some degree of government involvement to offset the imbalance in market power. While each country will want to adopt its own way for handling this problem, the international rules need to mirror national efforts to balance negotiations between firms in competitive segments of the telecommunication system and firms which dominate other segments of the system.

Another important issue with respect to the relationship between competitive firms and monopolies concerns the terms under which the monopoly suppliers of basic transmission facilities should be permitted to compete with other firms in supplying value-added telecommunication services, i.e., telecommunication services that have been classified as competitive by the regulatory authorities. A monopolist in one segment of the market can easily develop excessive market power in competitive segments by using monopoly profits from the monopoly segment of the market to subsidize sales in the competitive segments of the market, thus gradually driving the competitive firms out of business. A monopolist could also use its power to grant or deny interconnection rights to win a favorable position in competitive segments of the market. In order to prevent such abuses, the governments involved have to develop rules that will force the monopolies to establish an arms-length relationship between their monopoly activities and their competitive activities.

Another question concerns the process by which standards are established for interconnection and interoperability. In order to make it possible to pass a signal from one segment of the system to another, it is clearly necessary to establish some common standards. It is equally crucial, however, that the process for establishing such standards not be dominated by firms that control monopoly segments of the telecommunication system. Telecommunication monopolies have a tendency to enforce an excessive degree of uniformity, cutting off possibilities for innovation based on different technical standards.

In order to keep open possibilities for the creative application of telecommunication technology, it has become essential to give careful consideration to the process for establishing standards. Not only is it desirable to ensure that the process is not dominated by monopolies as against competitive firms but it is also important to ensure that it is not dominated by suppliers as against users and by established firms as against firms that want to introduce new technology. This calls for a more open and more flexible process for establishing standards than has been typical in the past, one that recognizes that there are differences in the degree of standardization required in performing different functions and in providing different levels of service.

Another set of issues concerns requirements for achieving a balance in the creation of mutual commercial opportunities among countries. Greater competition in telecommunications opens up the possibility for international as well as domestic competition. Most countries, however, are going to be unwilling to take the step from domestic to international competition unless they are able to assure their own firms equivalent opportunities abroad. A country may well have a right to preserve a monopoly market structure for major segments of the telecommunications system. By the same token, other countries that decide to permit competition have a right to determine how wide that competition should be and how far firms from other countries should be allowed to participate. International rules can help to establish common expectations about the rules of the game in this area.

In those telecommunication services where international competition is becoming a reality, namely in the establishment and operation of value-added networks, additional rules are needed to assure a market-based outcome to the competition. Governments have many different ways in which they can advantage domestic firms at the expense of foreign firms, including the payment of government subsidies to domestic firms, the establishment of tax provisions that benefit domestic firms, discriminatory government purchasing procedures, the development of discriminatory standards, and the promulgation of regulations that discriminate against foreign firms. In each of these areas, international rules can help ensure a level playing field among firms from different countries that are forced to compete with each other in the provision of particular telecommunication services.

The Relationship Between Trade Rules and Telecommunication Rules

In order to be productive, an international effort to define new rules of the game for telecommunication services must encompass both trade officials and officials responsible for telecommunication policy. The challenge faced by trade officials in constructing a set of viable trade rules for services and the challenge faced by telecommunication officials in constructing new guidelines for enhancing cooperation among national telecommunication officials are closely connected.

What is the difference between an international telecommunication agreement and an agreement on international trade in telecommunication services? What is or should be the mandate for each set of negotiations? Where and how do we draw the line between international trade policy and international telecommunication policy?

While the boundary cannot be drawn in concrete, and while there will always be areas where responsibilities overlap, one should be able to identify the core issues that need to be addressed by each set of negotiations. International trade negotiations and international telecommunication negotiations are aimed at different policy objectives. GATT agreements and ITU agreements serve different governmental purposes. Each set of rules constitutes, in effect, an extension of national policies in a particular policy sphere to the international level and is based on a distinct set of assumptions that underpin national laws and regulations in each respective policy area.

By analyzing the objectives, underlying assumptions, and the role of trade policy as against that of telecommunication policy, we should obtain a fair idea of how negotiations in the GATT on international trade in telecommunication equipment and services and negotiations in the ITU on international telecommunications can best complement each other.

Discussions are currently under way in the ITU with respect to the revision of ITU guidelines and recommendations, with the objective of bringing them up to date. These negotiations are taking place under the aegis of WATTC 88, the World Administrative Telephone and Telegraph Conference of 1988. Negotiations are also taking place under the auspices of the Uruguay Round of Multilateral Trade Negotiations on the development of a system of rules for trade in services, including trade in telecommunication services.

The fact that two separate international organizations are tackling the development of new international rules or guidelines in telecommunication services has been the subject of considerable controversy. The two organizations, however, can play complementary roles in the development of new rules, as is explored below.

The Principal Objectives of Trade Negotiations

The principal objectives of international trade negotiations are to establish fair and mutually beneficial rules for trade among commercial enterprises operating in a market environment, the reciprocal reduction of barriers to mutually beneficial trade, and the establishment of principles and procedures that will minimize the extent to which domestic regulations distort trade.

The GATT rules for multilateral trade are based on the underlying assumption that trade based on market competition is generally both fair and mutually advantageous and that government intervention in commercial transactions based on market criteria should be kept within agreed limits. The GATT system of rules gives competing enterprises from different countries considerable flexibility and freedom to carry out commercial transactions within the limits established in trade agreements.

Where multilateral trade rules cannot provide adequate solutions, countries can negotiate bilateral agreements and understandings that directly address the trade issues created by domestic policies and regulations. Bilateral trade negotiations thus provide the means for pursuing commercial interests where trade rules based on an assumption of competition are not adequate.

In summary, the strength of a trade-policy approach is in its emphasis on mutual commercial advantage, competition on a market-oriented basis and the reciprocal removal of obstacles to mutually beneficial trade. Trade officials have a dual role in the government: to act as guardians of the country's general commercial interest and simultaneously to act as guardians of a system of trade rules that permits market-based competition among enterprises from different countries.

The Principal Objectives of Telecommunication Negotiations

The principal purpose of international negotiations in telecommunications should be to facilitate the interconnection of national telecommunication networks, regardless of the regulatory philosophy of the countries involved, and to facilitate the introduction of new international telecommunication services.

The interconnection of national communication systems is partly an issue concerning technical standards and partly an issue concerning the sharing of revenues generated by international traffic. The issue of technical standards is an issue that transcends questions of market structure. Issues related to the sharing of revenues, however, are very much related to market structure.

The guidelines adopted for the interconnection of national telecommunication systems must reconcile conflicts among national regulations that apply to international telecommunications. Since telecommunication services have long been provided by national telecommunication monopolies, the underlying assumption of ITU recommendations and guidelines has been that international telecommunications are a public utility provided jointly by national telecommunication monopolies and that the international rules of the game should support the achievement of domestic regulatory objectives in telecommunications. If ITU guidelines and recommendations are to become more relevant, this basic assumption will have to be altered.

In a world where all international telecommunications were in the hands of national monopolies, the ITU was able to play an important role in the development of international guidelines for the equitable sharing of revenues. In the more competitive and diverse environment that is emerging in the telecommunication area, it makes less sense to establish formulas for the sharing of revenues or to spell out detailed terms and conditions for the provision of international telecommunication services. The role of the ITU with respect to the economic provisions, therefore, needs to be redefined, in order to better enable the organization to serve the needs of all its member countries, regardless of their regulatory system. In recasting that role, governments should take fully into account the particular strengths of the ITU as an organization that can foster cooperation among telecommunication managers and officials from around the world.

The strength of a regulatory approach to international telecommunication issues (as against a trade-oriented approach) is that it explicitly recognizes the need to protect the public interest, that it can address the impact of alternative policies on the operation of the telecommunication network, that it can deal with broader social interests related to the provision of a public infrastructure service, and that it can meaningfully address the complex technical issues involved in interconnecting national networks. Telecommunication officials responsible for international issues in national administrations, in effect, have the dual role of acting as guardians of national regulatory objectives in telecommunications and simultaneously acting as guardians of the international telecommunication network as a public utility.

Sorting Out the Relationship

It follows from the discussion above that telecommunication officials are best equipped to deal with issues that relate to the establishment of cooperative arranagement among telecommunication enterprises and officials for the purpose of facilitating international telecommunications and for achieving common regulatory objectives. In contrast, trade officials are best equipped to deal with issues that relate to the establishment of rules for international competition in the competitive segments of the international telecommunication sector and the development of guidelines that will minimize the extent to which telecommunication regulations distort trade in services dependent on the telecommunication network. In short, trade officials are best suited to deal with issues that relate to national regulatory objectives and the operation of the global telecommunication system.

There are obvious areas of overlap. First, the responsibility of telecommunication officials to establish internationally recognized technical standards for the interconnection of national networks will overlap with the responsibility of trade officials to develop rules for minimizing the use of standards as trade barriers. Second, efforts by the ITU to harmonize conflicting national regulations with respect to international telecommunication services will inevitably overlap with efforts by the GATT to establish rules designed to minimize the trade-distorting effects of national regulations. Third, the traditional role of the ITU in developing economic provisions for the interconnection of national telecommunication networks will overlap with the role of trade officials for sorting out commercial conflicts between competitive firms and communication monopolies.

Telecommunication officials responsible for the negotiation of international telecommunication agreements and trade officials with the responsibility of negotiating new rules for trade in telecommunication goods and services will obviously have to work closely with each other. Both the trade officials and the telecommunication officials work for the same national governments, and these governments should expect them to discharge their responsibilities in a complementary manner. Rules developed in the ITU and the GATT therefore can and must be reconciled.

The road to cooperation will undoubtedly cross a difficult terrain and will not be traversed without passionate arguments over objectives and bureaucratic infighting over turf. Inevitably, we can expect a certain amount of competition between national telecommunication officials and the ITU secretariat on the one side and national trade officials and the GATT secretariat on the other. Competition need not be a negative factor, however, if it leads to a competition in new ideas and proposals for removing regulatory barriers to the expansion of international telecommunications and a parallel expansion of international trade in telecommunication-based services.

There has been a growing dialogue between trade officials and telecommunication officials on issues of common interest but the challenge we confront will require a substantial expansion of the scope, depth and quality of that dialogue in the future.

ENDNOTES

1. Most companies that provide the public transmission facilities, of course, maintain their own capability to manage and control the public network. For purposes of the paper, we could classify this internal network management function as a part of category 1, since it is an integral part of managing the transmission facilities, or we could classify it as part of category 2, since competition in the provision of private network management services inevitably will create a competitive impact on the internal capability maintained by the firms providing the transmission facilities.

LEGAL RIGHTS OF ACCESS TO TRANSNATIONAL DATA

Anne W. Branscomb

Introduction

In an information-oriented economy access to information is crucial to the operation of that economy. In a global economy, access to information, regardless of where it resides within that global context, becomes a matter of high priority. In transnational trade, transfers of information are the oil which lubricates the system -- expediting orders, arranging shipments, locating resources, diagnosing difficulties, deploying personnel, and effecting payments. Indeed, trade in information services -- e.g., economic data, national statistics, company profiles, weather predictions -- constitutes a considerable proportion of world trade. There were 514 "on-line" data bases publicly available worldwide in 1986. [1] Since 70% of such data bases were U.S.-based in 1985, giving rise to a market worth an estimated 1.9 billion dollars and growing at approximately 14% *per annum*, the worldwide market can be estimated to be approaching four billion dollars in 1988. [2]

If information is power, as is generally conceded, then access is the key to power. What then are the legal rights of access to proprietary data?

In this paper the subject is limited to legally enforceable rights to access data stored in computer memories not access to information generally. The paper also makes no effort to justify a civil or human "right to communicate". Thus we limit the area to individual, corporate, or national rights to access information gathered, processed, stored, and transmitted *via* computer communication systems across national boundaries.

Access, according to the dictionary, means the right to enter or use. Thus the mandate of this paper is to delineate the parameters of a legal right to enter and use data stored in a computer memory which resides beyond the political boundaries of the country in which resides the legal entity seeking to exercise such a right.

In an interdependent global economy, legal rights to access data stored in computers are critical to the normal operations of the economy. The right to unencumbered transit across national boundaries is a fundamental aspect of the infrastructure of that global economy. Today no such right is guaranteed. National laws are just that, national in orientation and application. Telecommunication systems are also by and large national in scope, operation, and regulation. Only by consensus and treaty do nation-states give up their national sovereignty over information stored within and transiting across their boundaries.

There exists a long tradition that messages contained in diplomatic pouches are subject only to the laws and control of the national sovereign sending and receiving such messages [3] unless it is clear that they are acting in contravention of the laws or best interests of the host nation. [4] There is also a generally recognized principle that private messages sent through the telecommunication systems are to remain private. [5] Yet there are no generally recognized principles governing access to data stored within or in transit across national boundaries.

The Organisation for Economic Co-operation and Development (OECD) issued a declaration on Transborder Data Flows in 1985 urging that all nation-states take care not impede such traffic. The purpose of this exercise is to identify where positive steps might be taken either within the Uruguay Round or elsewhere to guarantee legal rights of transmission in a computerized environment.

Importance of Access to Users

It is easy to go through the various economic sectors which are relying more and more upon access to information across national boundaries. The first and foremost is the transit of money or financial instruments across national boundaries. The computer network of the Society for Worldwide Interbank Financial Telecommunications (SWIFT), through which more than 2000 banks worldwide reconcile their accounts, is said to move close to a trillion U.S. dollars daily. Some financial markets around the world now operate on a twenty-four-hour basis and the fluctuations of value of yen, mark, pounds sterling, florins, dollars and francs depend upon access to the data flowing through money markets throughout the globe.

The oil industry is dependent upon access to data flowing to and from dispersed locations in many countries from the middle east to the North Sea to the Indonesian islands. Ships must be loaded and dispatched to the appropriate ports. Equipment and supplies must be sent to offshore oil rigs. Remote-sensing satellites record data which permit geologists to determine where oil deposits can be found. All of the far-flung activities of oil companies as well as the oil emirates and oil-producing countries rely upon high-speed data communication systems with access to data stored and processed in multiple locations for multiple purposes. Atlantic Richfield, for example, was one of the first oil companies to put into place a very sophisticated private network to control its very complex system of operations. A visit to the oil facilities at Prudhoe Bay, on the North Slope of Alaska, will reveal a control panel which would be the envy of any producer of a 21st-century science-fiction film. To block the access of the oil industry to any of these data would cripple the industry.

Similarly, the global system of disaster tracking depends upon access to weather data which is collected from thousands of locations worldwide and shared by all nation-states through a complex system of treaties. Worldwide weather tracking also uses the memories of the most advanced computers available. To share the data collected worldwide requires an uninhibited flow of data across many national boundaries. Both the data and the weather ignore national boundaries as snowstorms, typhoons, cyclones and tidal waves sweep across the face of the globe unaware of the territorial claims of political entities.

Man-made disasters are equally important to the world community when they transcend national boundaries. The recent nuclear meltdown at Chernobyl is a good example of a disaster where access to the data was crucial to appropriate responses by Western European nations over which the nuclear radiation clouds accumulated. Equally important is access to information about a disaster such as the disastrous 1985 earthquake in Mexico City. Although contained within only one nation-state, information about the earthquake was essential to the peace of mind of relatives living outside Mexico.

Health care is another area in which epidemics have no respect for political confinement. Access to data concerning the nature and characteristics of infectious diseases claim a high priority for rapid circulation throughout the global health-care community. Viruses and bacteria traverse the globe as jet travelers carry their medical problems with them. Access to the most recent data available is critical to the research community as well as to the policy-makers who must decide what actions to take to fight the physical devastation which occurs. The rapid spread of AIDS is a good example of a disease in which the sharing of data globally is critical to the health of the world population. It is also a good example of the conflict between access for public purposes and protection for the individual.

Clearly global transportation cannot function without access to data stored in computers belonging to airlines, shipping companies and railway systems. The International Air Transport Association (IATA) represents 160 airlines from over 100 nations all over the world. These airlines carry some 150 million passengers internationally every year and earn more than 45 billion dollars from international service alone. [6] SITA, the airline reservation exchange system serving the major world airlines, is one of the earliest and longest-functioning private networks. It serves 12000 airline offices in 800 cities in 154 countries. [7]

Airline reservation systems such as SABRE, APOLLO, ESTORAL, SMART, and START are also essential to the tourism industry. Transnational telephone and data reservation systems also serve major hotel chains and travel agencies worldwide which now rely upon computer terminals for a major portion of their business.

An ancient industry which may be thought to be without a need for access to sophisticated data systems is the fishing industry. However, fishermen now depend upon the data they are able to access *via* satellites which gives them information about where schools of fish can be found which they seek to catch, what the world markets are paying for their catch, where to take their catch to get the best price, and when the weather is inclement or optimum for fishing. Thus fishermen have become dependent upon access to remote-sensed data as well as to the financial markets for the success of their business activities.

Data-processing companies supply a shared resource which can be accessed by nations and companies which can more efficiently and economically lease services and facilities rather than provide their own computer capabilities. Educational programs and training programs as well as diagnostic software can be run more reliably and economically from a central computer at company or institutional headquarters. To deny access to such facilities can cripple the economies of developing countries and add unnecessarily higher costs to the transactions of developed economies.

Law enforcement agencies require access to data concerning the identity and movements of terrorists and transnational criminals. Illegal activities know no national boundaries and drug runners rely upon sophisticated data banks and telecommunication systems to manage the transport of their goods and services. Thus the right to enter and access data sources for the purposes of law enforcement is as pungent an issue as the protection of the data stored therein from access by unauthorized parties.

Religious institutions operate transnationally. The Catholic Church relies upon access to data worldwide to operate the far-flung activities of Papal mandates and as many as 23 satellites deliver television messages to an audience of a billion or more in their churches and homes worldwide. The Mormon Church has one of the most sophisticated data systems tracking the location and heritage of all Mormons worldwide. Some churches have problems with privacy laws which may differ from country to country and may act as a deterrent to accessing Church records transnationally.[8]

Scientists are perhaps the most voracious users of data systems worldwide, not merely for the purpose of exchanging scientific data but keeping up with the proliferation of scientific literature which doubles every four years. Access to the data systems operated by the International Institute for Applied systems Analysis (IIASA) in Vienna has created problems for the U.S. government which perceives this node in a computer system which is the only direct access from Eastern to Western scientists, as an opportunity for the hemorrhaging of technology transfer. [9]

Software programs are used transnationally to operate industrial plants or to design buildings and to transmit data back to home offices for analytic and diagnostic purposes. To block the transfer of such data, used in computer-aided design and computer-aided manufacturing, can inhibit what is becoming a truly global engineering system. The number of joint ventures in the manufacturing sector is increasing with the ease of telecommunications and the cost of doing business in a global economy.

Finally, national accounts and statistics and national assets are stored or processed offshore create vulnerabilities which are intolerable should they be blocked by the host nation from access by the owner nation. Thus during times of crisis or political unrest, host governments need to pledge to forgo actions which would prevent non-combatant users' access to their proprietary data. Otherwise, nations will be reluctant to use offshore facilities for the management of governmental departments and their data.

Types of Access

Access to Proprietary Data Processed and Stored in Non-National Data Banks

Normally economic efficiency would dictate that data should be processed and stored in the location which offers the most attractive price at the highest quality. Thus shared access to central computers can be advantageous especially to the large number of countries or companies which would find it prohibitively costly to install and maintain their own computer systems. Moreover, as the business day usually encompasses only 7-8 hours, there are two shifts which are available for use when the computer would be lightly loaded or not used at all while workers are sleeping. In order to make the use of shared facilities and services attractive or viable, however, the users must be assured that they will be able to access the data whenever they need it. They must be reasonably secure in the knowledge, except for unforeseen criminal acts or natural disasters, that their data will not be destroyed or sequestered or beyond their control. This type of access is a necessary component of doing business as a nation-state, a corporate entity, an institution, or an individual. It has not yet become a major concern in negotiating international agreement, but could become a *quid pro quo* for obtaining concessions within the Uruguay Round of Multilateral Trade Negotiations now under way.

Access to Leased Lines for Corporate Users Wishing to Reach Data in Affiliated Offices

As suggested above, transnational businesses rely upon the availability and interoperability of telecommunication lines linking their corporate offices and their business and retail outlets. A wide variety of businesses operate such leased lines in countries which make them available. The security of such lines is critical for some industries and not so vital to others. For banking it is of prime importance. The SWIFT system insists upon control of its own hardware, software, and longlines. Indeed, Korea has run into a stumbling block trying to decide whether or not to permit its banking system to join the SWIFT system for the very reason that the Korean Government insists upon control of all telecommunication lines within Korea and SWIFT will not tolerate such control.

Many countries place onerous or expensive restrictions on the use of private leased lines, preferring to route messages through the public network. Rather than lease lines for private use, some carriers offer something called a virtual private network. Whether technically the line is an actual leased line, dedicated solely to the use of specific company, or a virtual private network, operating through the public or shared system, common sense dictates that there is needed a legal status which describes the privacy, security, and availability which the company may expect. This may be determined through contractual relations between the parties involved. However, if the host nation can ignore this contract and tap into the lines or require deposit of the encryption keys or otherwise monitor the transmissions, it may inhibit if not deter potential users. Thus some kind of legal assurance of protection as well as authorized access will be essential in many cases and in all cases would seem highly desirable. This type of assurance might be negotiated in exchange for other concessions within the context of the Uruguay Round.

Access of Media Corporations to Information Having Transnational Consequences

The business of news collection is especially vulnerable to blockages of access to information sources. Aside from the normal physical access of journalists to the situs of disaster areas (which is beyond the scope of the present paper), there is another aspect to the disaster which has transnational consequences. If we take the Chernobyl incident as an example, the information that such a nuclear meltdown had taken place came from two sources outside the Soviet Union. One of these was the monitoring of nuclear radiation in Western European nations and the other was data from remote-sensing satellites.

The news media in other countries picked up pictures of the area and were able to disseminate information gleaned therefrom to readers worldwide. In this respect they act as agents of individuals, corporations, and governments in distributing data essential to their well-being and business or personal interests. There has been some talk, since the Chernobyl incident, of a "MEDIASAT" to serve the news media primarily, so that photographs of such areas could be made available immediately to news media around the world. However, it is quite costly to launch a satellite solely for the purpose of serving the media. Furthermore, there is substantial doubt that governments will agree to permit private news organizations to launch such a satellite. Under existing United States statutes, licenses will not be granted if "national security and foreign policy would be jeopardized". [10] There is doubt that such restrictions could withstand a constitutional challenge based upon the first amendment. However, access of media corporations to sources of news is fraught with such complexity and controversy that it is unlikely to become a subject for negotiation within a trade context.

Sharing data with other users should be quite satisfactory and more economical, so long as the media and the affected nation-states were not prevented from gaining access to the data gathered by others.

Another way of assuring distribution of information which may affect nations and individuals beyond the national boundaries of the nation in which the disaster occurs, would be to require, under international law, that such nations disclose data which may have an adverse effect upon their neighbors. Indeed, many Europeans decried the delay of the Soviets in sharing information concerning the Chernobyl plant until it became obvious that they could not continue to clothe the incident in shadows or deny its consequences. Heads of government attending the economic summit held in Tokyo in 1986 were concerned enough to issue a statement urging timely disclosure of such threatening circumstances. [11] Furthermore, the United Nations Committee on the Peaceful Uses of Outer Space (CUPOUS) recommended in 1986 that "remote sensing shall promote the protection of mankind from natural disasters" and that such data be transmitted to the affected states promptly and without delay. [12]

Access of Subject Nation to Data from Remote-Sensing Satellites Owned and Operated by Other Nations or by Private Companies

Another aspect of remote sensing involves the legal rights of sensed nations to data concerning matters lying solely within their national boundaries. Although technically a sensed nation cannot block the sensing unless it has the capability of destroying the satellite as it passes over its sovereign territory, many nations, especially Colombia, have claimed a legal right to prohibit use of such data without their permission. There is no practical way of assuring (let alone enforcing) compliance with such a legal right. To be recognized, such a right must arise from consideration of the equities by provider nations and companies.

Notwithstanding the difficulties of compliance, in 1986, after twelve years of discussion, the United Nations Committee on Peaceful Uses of Outer Space (CUPOUS) adopted a consensus principle recommending that "as soon as the primary data and the processed data concerning the territory under its jurisdiction are produced, the sensed state shall have access to them on a non-discriminatory basis and on reasonable cost terms." CUPOUS also recommended that remote-sensing activities not be "detrimental to the legitimate interests of the sensed state" but did not go so far as to recommend a right to prohibit remote sensing.[13]

Access to Non-National Data Bases for the Purposes of Litigation

Legal systems are nationally limited as jurisdiction can only be exercised by the national court system or by a cooperating jurisdiction which chooses to apply the laws of that nation state. Thus transnational application of national laws depends upon reciprocity, as in the case of extradition, or the strength of force whenever extraterritorial jurisdiction is claimed by virtue of nationality of citizens living or traveling abroad. In some cases, nations attempt to extend the force of their law beyond their borders by virtue of commercial activities of legal entities operating under the protection of their national laws.

We must consider how courts obtain access to the evidence which is necessary to enforce domestic laws, when the evidence resides beyond the boundaries of the state in which litigation occurs. Take, for example, the case of the Canadian law which prohibits circulation of racially offensive literature. A computer bulletin board operated by the Aryan Nations Liberty Net, located in Hayden Lake, Idaho, Fayetteville, North Carolina, and Dallas/Fort Worth, Texas, promoted white supremacy and was reported to contain a list of target names for extermination.[14] These messages, which contravened Canadian but not U.S. law, were readily available over the interconnected long lines operating between the United States and Canada. Presumably, potential Canadian prosecutors could avail themselves in this case of the open lines to tap into the neo-Nazi bulletin board and download or print out the messages in the same way that Canadian callers could. However, they could not obtain jurisdiction over the bulletin board operators without obtaining an order of extradition, nor could they obtain an injunction against the bulletin board without the cooperation of the U.S. authorities, nor could they require the U.S. or Canadian telephone companies to deny access to that number without the risk of inhibiting the normal business use of such lines for other purposes. Perhaps they could obtain the cooperation of host country authorities to require bulletin board operators to post a message stating that accessing data from this bulletin board contravenes Canadian law.

This is not a situation to be taken lightly. There are already reported to be more than 1500 public access bulletin boards in the United States and 300 verified free-access bulletin board telephone numbers worldwide, [15] operated by individuals and small organizations. These are easily accessed by a transnational telephone call over normal lines without operator intervention where direct dialing is permitted. Most bulletin boards are quite innocent in content. Others are quite outrageous or, in fact, contain messages which promote or lead to illegal activity in one jurisdiction or another. This is especially true of copyrighted computer software which has often been made available for downloading. Indeed, one such computer bulletin board, Pirate's Cove, operated on Long Island by a person identified as "Black Beard", originally boasted that it was the largest electronic board devoted solely to software piracy. [16] Whether such bulletin boards consist of private messages which are entitled to privacy laws protecting their content or operated as public electronic information systems subject to regulation remains unsettled. Which countries' laws are to be applied to such transnational data base operations is also in doubt.

Another situation is exemplified by two cases involving the Bank of Nova Scotia, a multinational bank with over 1200 branches in 46 countries. [17] A Miami branch of the Canadian bank was subpoenaed by a U.S. federal district court to produce financial data contained in subsidiary banks domiciled in the Bahamas, Cayman Islands and Antigua. No documents were found in the Antigua branch and the law in both the Bahamas and the Cayman Islands prohibited disclosure of the data held by those branches. Nonetheless, the Miami Court mandated its production, with a $25000-a-day fine for nondisclosure. Thus the cost of obeying two sovereigns may become very high (in this case the total levied was $1.8 million). As such transnational storage of data and conflicts of laws increase, some established principles for the production of evidence seem timely and, indeed, necessary.

Another situation in which transnational access to data was critical was that of the Swiss banks in disclosing information about the secret bank accounts of ex-President Marcos to the Philippines government, of ex-President Duvalier to the Haitian government, and of Lt. Colonel Oliver North. The secrecy of the numbered Swiss accounts has been a prime attraction of the Swiss banking system which manages some $600 billion in deposits. However, in the case of the claims of the Philippines and Haiti, national assets had allegedly been siphoned off by their national leaders for personal purposes and sequestered in these secret accounts. The disclosure of details was a matter of much controversy within the Swiss banking community. Ultimately, the decision was disclosure -- but for the first time in the history of the system. [18] More recently Switzerland agreed to cooperate with the U.S. Securities and Exchange Commission in its investigation of insider trading cases. The Swiss have passed a new law which makes insider trading a crime in Switzerland in order to permit divulging records of the bank accounts of alleged offenders. Swiss law permits divulging information to foreign investigators only when the act being investigated is a crime within both the seeking and disclosing countries' jurisdictions.[19]

Access of Host Country to Non-governmental Data Bases Residing within its Confines for Purposes of Enforcing Political Sanctions

Another concern is that data residing outside the state of its origin will be subject to political turmoils beyond the control of its owner. Assurances concerning the treatment of data by commercial data-service providers within countries experiencing political confrontations and upheavals could be discussed within the Uruguay Round. For example, Iranian assets were frozen by the U.S. Government during the Iranian revolution and hostage crisis. [20] Panamanian assets have been frozen as a device for forcing Noriega to leave office and U.S. companies mandated by the U.S. government not to pay taxes lawfully assessed under Panamanian law. [21] When the Soviets invaded Afghanistan, the United States prohibited Dresser Industries from supplying data from a U.S.-based computer to their French subsidiary which was supplying pipeline equipment to the Soviet Union.[22]

In the case of national assets, it may be assumed that the political situation, in some cases, both requires and justifies the use of economic sanctions. However, it can also be argued that the stability of the world economy demands some rules of the road so that innocent bystanders will not be injured and critical industries can be permitted to continue operations.

Negotiations concerning the treatment of proprietary data of non partisan and non-national users could take place within the Uruguay Round.

Access to Technology for Economic Development

There are a variety of ways in which technology is transferred from one country to another. It may be placed in the public domain by the inventor or discoverer as Arthur C. Clarke published all of the information concerning the geostationary orbit for communication satellites, because he felt it was a matter of global concern not to be monopolized by any single party or interest. It may be transferred by licenses from the holders of the patent or copyright with payments negotiated by the parties or royalties mandated by a statutory license. It may be pirated without the permission of the legally entitled owner. Industrial piracy is rampant, copyrights are ignored, and computer software is especially vulnerable to copying without permission of the originator. Clearly the interests of those who develop intellectual property and those who wish to use it diverge.

There are a number of efforts under way to clarify the substance of intellectual property laws with respect to the new information technologies as well as to determine where and under what circumstances these laws can be enforced across national boundaries and what rights of access may be exercised by newly industrializing countries. These efforts are going on within the World Intellectual Property Organization (WIPO), the General Agreement on Tariffs and Trade (GATT), the European Economic Community (EEC), and the United Nations Conference on Trade and Development (UNCTAD) as well as through bilateral negotiations between interested governments and interest groups. The difficulties which UNCTAD has experienced in attempting to reach an agreement on an international code of conduct for the transfer of technology to developing countries[23] merely presages the complications which the GATT will experience in attempting a similar undertaking concerning intellectual property rights in the Uruguay Round.

However, access *via* advanced telecommunication systems to transnational data bases for the purpose of disseminating scientific and technical literature, computer-aided manufacturing and design, artificial intelligence systems, and diagnostic software portend the greatest advancements in shared resources for economic development in history. The challenge to legislators and lawyers to come up with mutually agreeable codes of conduct is enormous but critical to the global economy.

Vulnerabilities

There are clear advantages in sharing computing resources across national boundaries. For transnational corporations and institutions doing business in many countries, there is an absolute necessity of interconnecting their farflung activities. For government institutions it is critical to obtain access to information originating outside their areas of influence which have important effects upon them. However, such access is vulnerable in obvious ways. Blockages can occur as a result of natural disasters, terrorism, pranks, political sanctions and judicial proceedings.

Vulnerability to Natural Disasters

There can be no legal provision which would provide absolute protection against natural disasters. Certainly the tradition in tort and contract law is to exempt from liability damage which occurs as a result of "acts of God".

Nonetheless, users can insure against the damage or delays caused by natural disasters and providers can offer redundancy of alternative channels of communication or storage. Two or more satellites can be in place. Secondary sites of central computers can be available for storage and processing. What is to be considered normal practice and what is to be considered negligence is a prime consideration in undertaking computerized transactions which transcend national boundaries. There is certainly a high priority for clarification of standard practices which can be relied upon by users, providers and insurers worldwide.

Vulnerability to Terrorism

Although there is no assurance that terrorism can be contained, there is certainly a need for nations which expect to participate in the global information economy to band together to fight computer terrorists like other terrorists. Although there have been few instances of computer terrorism in the past, as terrorists become more computer-literate the opportunities for damage will become more apparent. Already there have been reports of "worms" and "viruses" inserted into computer software.[24] These are self-propelling programs which enter into existing software and continue to cause destruction or distortion throughout the system. Clearly, the cost of such "terrorism" is exorbitant, in terms of lost time, lost business, and efforts to restore the system to normalcy. These damages which can be inflicted upon computerized systems have created a great deal of concern among computer users and have stimulated the development of a new form of computer software program to diagnose the "viruses" and "vaccines" to inoculate against them. Still, cooperation in an effort to contain and punish such "terrorists" is of high priority.

Vulnerability to "Hackers"

"Hacking" differs from "terrorism" in degree rather than kind. Terrorists are motivated by the desire to destroy, whereas "hackers" are motivated by curiosity or determination to prove their computer skills. Indeed, many "hackers" think they are improving the state of the art or identifying vulnerabilities. There is a fascinating book which describes a network of blind telephone "hackers" or "phreakers", in the 1920s, who take over the Bell telephone system with their own network.[25] Although they gain unpaid access to a critical resource for their own sociological satisfaction, their purposes are not deleterious and the leader attempts to help the Bell Company understand and guard against its vulnerabilities. Another recent book, *Hackers*, gives a factual account of the early development of personal computers when sharing of computer software and hardware was the predominant ethic of young and gifted computer programmers.[26]

Thus, contending with the "hacker" problem is mainly a matter of public relations, education, and an underlying social ethic that "hacking" is improper and should be punished. This level of understanding has not yet been reached, although the laws in many countries are being changed to clarify that such unauthorized entry into and use or destruction of computerized data bases is unacceptable behavior. Until the enactment of the Electronic Communication Privacy Act in 1986, the United States statutes contained no prohibition against wiretapping or eavesdropping on data communication circuits. Clearly a standardized and internationally harmonized definition of what is and what is not acceptable access to transnational data is highly desirable.

Vulnerability to Political Sanction

War is usually excluded from circumstances which can be guarded against on the grounds that it is as unpredictable and uncontrollable as "acts of God". Perhaps it is futile to suggest that rights of access to data should be protected from sequestration during wartime. However, there are wars and wars. Some are devastating and some are containable; some, indeed, seem to last forever. Also some users and providers are combatants; others are not.

It cannot be expected that all combatants would respect rules of law promulgated to protect against political sanctions. Nonetheless, it would be conductive to normal economic relations if some clear rules were established concerning rights of passage and access during periods of political stress. Innocent parties and companies should not suffer the consequences of national actions in which they are not involved and with which they have no concern.

Vulnerability to Judicial Proceedings

There are a number of circumstances in which data may be subject to subpoena for use as evidence in court proceedings.

- The host country, in which the data owned by a non-national resides, may desire access to the data in order to enforce local law against the transnational user.

- The transnational user may desire access to the data stored in another country in order to pursue rights of action against third parties in the user's country, the host country, or yet another jurisdiction.

- Third parties may desire access to data stored outside their national jurisdictions for the purpose of proving some point of law which is critical to the litigation in which they are involved. For example, a person wrongfully accused of a crime in country X may need to obtain access to data stored in country Y to prove an incorrect identification. This might occur in the case of a former oil company employee operating as a private entrepreneur who needed access to company files for litigation in a nation in which the company had no offices and in which the country of litigation had no jurisdiction.

- Countries of transit of data may desire access to data which they consider a violation of their national laws. Or countries of transit might engage in the tapping of telecommunication wires as a service to enterprising investigators without the protections afforded by either the host country's territorial jurisdiction or the transnational user's territorial jurisdiction.

Vulnerability to Distortion by Negligence of the Custodian

In most cases liability of the custodian of the data will be spelled out in contracts signed by the parties. However, such contracts can vary enormously and create uncertainties concerning the exposure to users and providers of the data. Clearly, there are cases in which negligence can be generally assumed to exist and others in which there can be agreement that no liability should accrue. Thus, to the extent that clearly established norms of custodial behavior can be achieved, the efficiency of the information economy will be improved.

Vulnerabilities Regarding National Sovereignty or Cultural Identity or Economic Independence

Many nation-states fear loss of sovereignty over their territorial domains through the erosion of control over the private interconnections across national boundaries. Others fear a diminution of cultural identity and loss of ethnic integrity. Many fear a loss of control over their economic futures from the rapid proliferation of transnational data traffic which may reflect values which better serve the nationals originating the traffic than those on the receiving end. These concerns have been expressed most eloquently by the Swedes in their study of vulnerability, by the Canadians in their numerous studies of computer/communication trends and policies, by the

Brazilians in the actions taken in pursuit of their informatics strategies for maintaining a tight control over the development of the Brazilian computer market, and by the French in their massive investments in information technology.

Nonetheless, the pressures for an integrated global economy are quite strong. Many nations around the world, both large and small, developed and developing, are restructuring their national telecommunication systems to adapt to a more competitive international environment. An issue facing all governments is the extent to which they are willing to modify their own national laws, their own operating facilities, and their own cultural habits in order to reap the benefits of an integrated and interdependent global information economy. Participating in this emerging economy could conceivably involve some dilution of absolute political sovereignty, cultural distinctiveness, and economic independence but these possibilities must be carefully weighed against the opportunities gained for economic growth, cultural diversity, and global security.

Conflicts of Interest

Many of the various rights of access which might be considered for promulgation will conflict with rights of access claimed by others. For example, the right of a nation-state to protect its security may be paramount. However, it will necessarily conflict with the right of a corporate entity to protect the privacy of its data. This is the situation in which there is a stand-off between the Korean government and the SWIFT banking system, where each maintains that it is essential to reserve ultimate authority to control the software and hardware.

A conflict of interest is also apparent in the case of nation-states which operate their own state corporations and therefore have some incentive to learn about the corporate strategies of their global competitors. Thus, the right of the state to monitor transmissions and computer memory would have to be very strictly written and interpreted, if the right to maintain secrecy of data is to be afforded corporate users.

The right of individuals to obtain access to data concerning themselves would conflict with the right of law enforcement officers to collect data concerning criminal activity. Common law systems consider it a matter of due process for persons accused of criminal activity to see or hear the evidence upon which the accusation rests. However, to permit criminals access to information obtained for the purpose of investigation would impede the investigative process and inhibit containment of criminal activities. Thus, rights of individual access need to be as carefully delineated as they are for non-computerized information.

The rights of the media to access data collected by remote sensing satellites might conflict with:

- the rights of sovereign states to protect their security,

- the interest of corporate entities in protecting proprietary data, and

- especially with the rights of individuals to seclusion and privacy.

Consequently, an excursion into the drafting of rights of access to transnational data must be begun with much caution, understanding the murky waters from which such rights must emerge and comprehending the limited goals which can be attained.

Conclusions

No effort has been made in this exercise to be comprehensive or conclusive. the purpose is merely to suggest the paths which may be selected by those who reach for a more rational, lawful and harmonious information economy. There is no rainbow at the end of the path. There are many stepping stones which must be laboriously put into place before even a cobblestone street can be erected -- and many well-worn cobblestones will precede a smooth legal highway system. Herein are a few rough stones to begin with.

ENDNOTES

1 Cudra/Elsevier, *Dirctory Of On-line Data Bases*, v. 7, no. 3.

2 Office of Technology Assessment, U.S. Congress, *Trade In Services,* p.72 (Washington, DC: U.S. Government Printing Office, September 1986).

3 Vienna Convention on Diplomatic Relations, April 18, 1961, Arts. XXVII, XXIX 23 U.S.T. 3227, 3239, 3240, 500 U.N.T.S. 95, 108, 110.

4 18 U.S. C.A. Sec. 2511 (3) repealed by Foreign Intelligence Surveillance Act of 1978, Pub. L. 95-511, 92 Stat. 1797 (1978), replaced by Exec. Order No. 12,333, 46 Fed. Reg. 59,941, (Sec. 2.5) Dec. 8, 1981.

5 The International Telegraph Convention of Paris, May 17, 1965, 9 Recueil des Traites de la France 254.

6 Monssen, W., "Airline Industry Takes Data Protection Seriously", *Transnational Data And Communications Report*, January 1988, p. 17.

7 "SITA: A Worldwide Telecommunications Service for Airlines:, *PTC Quarterly*, December 1985.

8 Burton, R.P. and Malmrose, R.D., "Impact of Privacy Laws on Religious Bodies", *Transnational Data And Communications Report*, June 1987, 5-9.

Stepp, L.S. "Pope Uses Space Technology to Spread an Age-Old Message; Prayers Reach Worldwide Audience Estimates at 1 Billion". *Washington Post*, June 7, 1987, Sunday, Final Edition, A-28.

9 Labadi, A. and I. Sebestyen, I. "IIASA TPA-70 Gateway-Network Promotes International Flows of Scientific Information", *Transnational Data Report*, vol. VD, no. 1, January/February 1982, 41-47.

10 *Transnational Data And Communications Report*, September 1987, p.2; The Media Institute, 3017 M Street, NW, Washington, DC, 20007, USA, has established a remote sensing archive to collect information about satellite sensing to serve news organizations. The Federal Communications commission may not grant licenses to any alien, or foreign government, nor any corporation of which any officer or director is an alien. "The entire entry is controlled for national security reasons" See, 47 C.F.R. 25.390. See also "Free Speech in Space: Satellite Images for News Media", *Transnational Data And Communications Report*, August 1987, p.9.

11 "Texts of the Statements Adopted by Leaders of 7 Industrial Democracies", *New York Times*, May 6, 1986, A-12.

12 Xinhua General Overseas News Service, via NEXIS, June 13, 1986.

13 American Institute of Aeronautics and Astronautics, Inc., December 1986; UN Chronicle, August 1986, via NEXIS.

14 Piernchiak, R.T., "White Supremacists See Computers as Revolutionary Key, AP 03/03/85 via NEXIS; Green, S. "Neo Nazis go High-Tech", UPI, 03/09/85, via NEXIS.

15 *American Banker*, September 8, 1986; ONLINE COMPUTER TELEPHONE DIRECTORY.

16 Lasden, M. "Of Bytes and Bulletin Boards", *New York Times*, August 4, 1985, Sec. 6, 34, c.1; Goncharoff, K. "Bulletin Boards go Electronic", *New York Times*, November 18, 1984, Sunday, Late Edition, Sec. 11 Long Island, p 1, c2.

17 United States v. Bank of Nova Scotia, 69 F. 2d 1184 (11th Cir. 1982); 740 F.2d 817 (11th Cir. 1984), 84-2 U.S. Tax Cas. (CCH) P9802; The logic of the court was that "the confidentiality laws of the Cayman Islands should not be used as a blanket to encourage or foster criminal activities...and even if the Cayman Islands had an absolute right to privacy" which it could bestow upon its own citizens, "this right could not fully apply to American citizens", who could not be insulated against a criminal investigation since they are required to report such financial transactions as were in question pursuant to 31 U.S.C. Sec. 11221 and 31 C.F.R. Sec. 103.24 (1979). The court also relied upon the fact that the disclosure was to a grand jury

304

investigation in itself a privileged and confidential proceeding. See also Burnett, J.T., "Information, Banking Law and Extraterritoriality", *Transnational Data And Communications Report*, January 1986, 17-18.

18 Dow Jones News Document, 860404-400, *Wall Street Journal*, April 4, 1986. 10.

19 "New law may make Swiss bank accounts a lot less secret", *USA Today*, June 24, 1988, p.8B.

20 On November 4, 1979, Iranian militants occupied the U.S. embassy in Tehran and took hostages. As one response to this indignity, President Carter declared a national emergency and froze all Iranian assets subject to the jurisdiction of the United States. Pursuant to this authority, the Secretary of the Treasury promulgated Iranian Assets Control Regulations, 31 C.F.R. Sec. 535.101-904 (1979) Numerous cases were filed by claimants to these assets, see, e.g. Malek-Marzban v. U.S., 653 F. 2d 1213 (4th Cir. 1981), Itel Corp. v. M/S Victoria U (Ex Pishtaz Iran) 710 F. 2d 199 (5th Cir. 1983), Behring International Inc. v. Imperial Iranian Airforce et al., 712 F.2d 45 (3d Cir. 1983), 36 Fed. R. Serv. 2d (Callaghan) 391.

21 Tweedale, D., "U.S. Businessmen Complain about Sanctions against Panama", UPI, April 15, 1988 BC Cycle via NEXIS.

22 After the Soviet Union placed Poland under martial law, the United States government attemed to disrupt the construction of the Soviet gas pipeline from Siberia to Western Europe by placing an embargo on U.S. originated products and technology. This affected Dresser Industries which relied upon data the United States.

23 "UNCTAD Meeting on Technology Transfer Fails to Reach Agreement on Code of Conduct", BNA, Inc, Daily Report for Executives, June 7, 1985, DER no. 10, L-8.

24 "Saboteur's deadly 'virus' threatens computers, *The Gazette*, Montreal, January 8, 1988, A-12; "The Scourge of Computer Viruses", *Science*, April 8, 1988, 133-134.

25 By Harvard Biology Professor, McMahon, T., *Loving Little Eqypt*, (New York, NY: Viking Penquin, 1987).

26 Levy, S., *Hackers* (Garden City, NY: Anchor Press/Doubleday, 1984).

ABOUT THE EDITORS
AND CONTRIBUTORS

Jonathan D. Aronson is Professor at the School of International Relations and the Annenberg School of Communication of the University of Southern California. He is the author of numerous books, articles and monographs on issues relating to international trade and telecommunications. He is also Co-chairman of the Academic Advisory Committee on Trade in Services to the Office of the U.S. Trade Representative.

V.N. Balasubramanyam is Head of the Department of Economics at Lancaster University, U.K. He has written on foreign direct investment and technology transfer and is the author, among other works, of *The Economy of India* (Weidenfeld and Westview, 1985) and *Multinationals in the Third World* (Trade Policy Research Centre, 1980).

Anne Wells Branscomb is President of the Raven Group, Adjunct Professor of International Law at the Fletcher School of Law and Diplomacy of Tufts University, and Research Affiliate of the Harvard University Program on Information Resources Policy. She is the author of numerous articles on legal questions raised by the growth of communication and information technologies.

Sidney Dell is Senior Fellow at the United Nations Institute for Training and Research (UNITAR). From 1982 to 1984, he was Executive Director of the United Nations Centre on Transnational Corporations (UNCTC). He has published both books and articles on trade, finance and the international monetary system.

Geza Feketekuty is Counselor to the U.S. Trade Representative, where since 1976 he has developed and coordinated U.S. trade policy, including trade in services. His most recent publication is *International Trade in Services: An Overview and Blueprint for Negotiations* (Ballinger, 1988).

Vishwas P. Govitrikar holds a Ph.D. in English from the University of Pennsylvania and a Ph.D. in Philosophy from McGill University. He has been Director of Operations & Research at the Atwater Institute since 1985, where he is responsible for project development, financial planning and administrative coordination.

James C. Grant is Executive Vice-President, Systems & Technology, of The Royal Bank of Canada. He has represented Canada in a number of organizations and has been the Canadian delegate to the Paris-based International Chamber of Commerce Commission on Computing, Communications & Information and the Business & Industry Advisory Committee (to the OECD) on Technology and on Information, Computing and Communication policies.

Francis Gurry is Head, Industrial Property Law Section, Industrial Property Division, World Intellectual Property Organization (WIPO) in Geneva, Switzerland, where he has worked since 1985. Dr. Gurry is the author of a book on the law of trade secrets and confidential information: *Breach of Confidence* (Oxford University Press, 1984).

Henning Klodt is Head of the Research Group on "Technology and Growth" at the Kiel Institute of World Economics, Federal Republic of Germany, where he has worked since 1987. His research focuses mainly on international trade, growth and structural change, new technologies and technology policies.

Toshio Kosuge is Professor of International Law and Telecommunications at the University of Electro-Communications in Tokyo, Japan. He has served as advisor to the Government of Japan on international telecommunication policy and written extensively on domestic and international telecommunication issues.

Bruno Lanvin is an economist in the Office of the Secretary-General of the United Nations Conference on Trade and Development (UNCTAD), Geneva, Switzerland. He has published numerous articles and co-authored several books on international trade in services.

G. Russell Pipe is founder and publisher of *Transnational Data and Communications Report (TDR)*, a monthly magazine covering economic, trade and strategic developments in the evolving international information economy. He is currently directing a research project on the implications of introducing trade rules into the field of telecommunication services.

Peter Robinson is Special Advisor on International Informatics in the Canadian Department of Communications. He chaired the OECD Working Group that drafted the OECD Declaration on Transborder Data Flows of 1985. In recent years, he has become well-known as a speaker and writer on policy questions related to the implications of developments in computers and communications.

Karl P. Sauvant is Acting Assistant Director, Policy Analysis & Research Division, United Nations Centre on Transnational Corporations (UNCTC). He has written widely on the economic, political, social and legal impact of transnational corporations and transborder data flows. Dr. Sauvant is the author of Volume 1 in The Atwater Series on the World Information Economy, entitled *International Transactions in Services: The Politics of Transborder Data Flows* (Westview, 1986).

Ester M. Stevers is a researcher, currently writing a dissertation on European policy-making and telecommunication developments at the European University Institute in Florence, Italy.

Christopher R. Wilkinson has been Head of Division, Strategy for Information Technology and Telecommunications, Commission of the European Communities, Brussels, Belgium, since 1983. He was formerly Head of Division, Directorate General for Internal Market and Industrial Affairs of the European Economic Community.

R. Brian Woodrow is Associate Professor in the Department of Political Studies at the University of Guelph in Ontario, Canada. He has published primarily on Canadian politics and public policy, including communication and environmental policy, and has acted as consultant to several government departments and private-sector organizations.

APPENDIX A

Uruguay Round Declaration on Trade in Services

(Source: *GATT FOCUS*, 41, October 1986)

Meeting in Punta del Este (Uruguay) from 15-20 September on the occasion of the Special Session of the GATT Contracting Parties, minister of GATT member countries adopted a Declaration launching a new round of multilateral trade negotiations -- the Uruguay Round. The Declaration falls into two parts.

As contracting parties, the ministers adopted Part I of the Declaration regarding trade in goods. It establishes the objectives and principles of the negotiations, and the launch of issues on which negotiations will take place. The Declaration provides for a standstill and rollback on trade restrictive or trade distortive measures under which governments undertake not to increase existing levels of protection and to phase out their existing breaches of GATT disciplines.

As representatives of governments meeting on the occasion of the Session, the ministers further decided to launch a negotiation on trade in services, and adopted Part II of the Declaration in that regard. It has been agreed that these negotiations will not be placed within the legal framework of GATT, but that GATT practices and procedures will nevertheless apply to them.

Ministers then adopted the Ministerial Declaration as a whole as a single policy commitment launching the Uruguay Round. The negotiations are to extend over four years.

PART II -- NEGOTIATIONS ON TRADE IN SERVICES

Ministers also decided, as part of the Multilateral Trade Negotiations, to launch negotiations on trade in services. Negotiations in this area shall aim to establish a multilateral framework of principles and rules for trade in services, including elaboration of possible disciplines for individual sectors, with a view to expansion of such trade under conditions of transparency and progressive liberalization and as a means of promoting economic growth of all trading partners and the development of developing countries. Such framework shall respect the policy objectives of national laws and regulations applying to services and shall take into account the work of relevant international organizations.

GATT procedures and practices shall apply to these negotiations. A Group of Negotiations on Services is established to deal with these matters. Participation in the negotiations under this Part of the Declaration will be open to the same countries as under Part I. GATT secretariat support will be provided, with technical support from other organizations as decided by the Group of Negotiations on Services.

The Group of Negotiations on Services shall report to the Trade Negotiations Committee.

APPENDIX B

Declaration on Transborder Data Flows

Adopted by the 23 member governments of the Organisation for Economic
Co-operation and Development (OECD), Paris, 11 April 1985

(Source: *International Information Economy Handbook*, ed. G. Russell Pipe and
Chris Brown, Springfield, VA: TDRS, 1985)

Rapid technological developments in the field of information, computers
and communications are leading to significant structural changes in the
economies of member countries. Flows of computerized data and information are an important consequence of technological advances and are
playing an increasing role in national economies. With the growing
economic interdependence of member countries, these flows acquire an
international dimension, known as transborder data flows. It is therefore
appropriate for the OECD to pay attention to policy issues connected with
these transborder data flows.

This Declaration is intended to make clear the general spirit in which
member countries will address these issues.

In view of the above, the Governments of OECD member countries:

Acknowledging that computerized data and information now circulate, by
and large, freely on an international scale;

Considering the OECD Guidelines on the Protection of Privacy and
Transborder Flows of Personal Data and the significant progress that has
been achieved in the area of privacy protection at national and international
levels;

Recognizing the diversity of participants in transborder data flows, such
as commercial and non-commercial organizations, individuals and governments, and recognizing the wide variety of computerized data and information, traded or exchanged across national borders, such as data and
information related to trading activities, intra-corporate flows, computerized information services and scientific and technological exchanges;

Recognizing the growing importance of transborder data flows and the
benefits that can be derived from transborder data flows, and recognizing
that the ability of member countries to reap such benefits may vary;

Recognizing that investment in trade in this field cannot but benefit from transparency and stability of policies, regulations and practices;

Recognizing that national policies which affect transborder data flows reflect a range of social and economic goals, and that governments may adopt different means to achieve their policy goals;

Aware of the social and economic benefits resulting from access to a variety of sources of information and of efficient and effective information services;

Recognizing that member countries have a common interest in facilitating transborder data flows, and in reconciling different policy objectives in this field;

Having due regard to their national laws, do hereby declare their intention to:

- promote access to data and information and related services, and avoid the creation of unjustified barriers to the international exchange of data and information;

- seek transparency in regulations and policies relating to information, computer and communications services affecting transborder data flows;

- develop common approaches for dealing with issues related to transborder data flows and, when appropriate, develop harmonized solutions;

- consider possible implications for other countries when dealing with issues related to transborder data flows.

Bearing in mind the intention expressed above, and taking into account the work being carried out in other international fora, the governments of OECD member countries:

Agree that further work should be undertaken and that such work should concentrate at the outset on issues emerging from the following types of transborder data flows:

- flows of data accompanying international trade;

- marketed computer services and computerized information services; and

- intra-corporate data flows.

Governments of OECD member countries agree to cooperate and consult with each other in carrying out this important work, and in furthering the objectives of this Declaration.

From the official OECD press release:

This Declaration represents the first international effort to address economic issues raised by the information revolution. It addresses the policy issues arising from transborder data flows such as flows of data and information related to trading activities, intra-corporate flows, computerized information services and scientific and technological exchanges. These flows are playing an increasingly important role in the economies of member countries and in international trade and services.

In adopting this Declaration, the governments of OECD member countries expressed their intention to promote access to data and information, to develop common approaches for dealing with transborder data flow issues. They agreed to undertake further work on the main issues emerging from transborder data flows.

APPENDIX C

Relevant Parts of Articles of the General Agreement on Tariffs and Trade Cited in the Foregoing Text

(Source: *The Text of the General Agreement on Tariffs and Trade*, GATT, Geneva, July 1986)

PART I

Article I

General Most-Favoured Nation Treatment

1. With respect to customs duties and charges of any kind imposed on or in connection with importation or exportation or imposed on the international transfer of payments for imports or exports, and with respect to the method of levying such duties and charges, and with respect to all rules and formalities in connection with importation and exportation, and with respect to all matters referred to in paragraphs 2 and 4 of Article III, any advantage, favour, privilege or immunity granted by any contracting party to any product originating in or destined for any other country shall be accorded immediately and unconditionally to the like product originating in or destined for the territories of all other contracting parties.

Article II

Schedules of Concessions

1. (a) Each contracting party shall accord to the commerce of the other contracting parties treatment no less favourable than that provided for in the appropriate Part of the appropriate Schedule annexed to this Agreement.

(b) The products described in Part I of the Schedule relating to any contracting party, which are the products of territories of other contracting parties, shall, on their importation into the territory to which the Schedule relates, and subject to the terms, conditions or qualifications set forth in that

Schedule, be exempt from ordinary customs duties in excess of those set forth and provided for therein. Such products shall also be exempt from all other duties or charges of any kind imposed on or in connection with importation in excess of those imposed on the date of this Agreement or those directly and mandatorily required to be imposed thereafter by legislation in force in the importing territory on that date.

(c) The products described in Part II of the Schedule relating to any contracting party which are the products of territories entitled under Article I to receive preferential treatment upon importation into the territory to which the Schedule relates shall, on their importation into such territory, and subject to the terms, conditions or qualifications set forth in that Schedule, be exempt from ordinary customs duties in excess of those set forth and provided for in Part II of that Schedule.

PART II

Article III

National Treatment on Internal Taxation and Regulation

1. The contracting parties recognize that internal taxes and other internal charges, and laws, regulations and requirements affecting the internal sale, offering for sale, purchase, transportation, distribution or use of products, and internal quantitative regulations requiring the mixture, processing or use of products in specified amounts or proportions, should not be applied to imported or domestic products so as to afford protection to domestic production.

2. The products of the territory of any contracting party imported into the territory of any other contracting party shall not be subject, directly or indirectly, to internal taxes or other internal charges of any kind in excess of those applied, directly or indirectly, to like domestic products. Moreover, no contracting party shall otherwise apply internal taxes or other internal charges to imported or domestic products in a manner contrary to the principles set forth in paragraph 1.

4. The products of the territory of any contracting party imported into the territory of any other contracting party shall be accorded treatment no less favourable than that accorded to like products of national origin in respect of all laws, regulations and requirements affecting their internal sale, offering for sale, purchase, transportation, distribution or use. The provisions of this paragraph shall not prevent the application of differential internal transportation charges which are based exclusively on the economic operation of the means of transport and not on the nationality of the product.

8. (a) The provisions of this Article shall not apply to laws, regulations or requirements governing the procurement by governmental agencies of products purchased for governmental purposes and not with a view to commercial resale or with a view to use in the production of goods for commercial sale.

(b) The provisions of this Article shall not prevent the payment of subsidies exclusively to domestic producers, including payments to domestic producers derived from the proceeds of internal taxes or charges applied consistently with the provisions of this Article and subsidies effected through governmental purchases of domestic products.

Article X

Publication and Administration of Trade Regulations

1. Laws, regulations, judicial decisions and administrative rulings of general application, made effective by any contracting party, pertaining to the classification or the valuation of products for customs purposes, or to rates of duty, taxes or other charges, or to requirements, restrictions or prohibitions on imports or exports or on the transfer of payments therefor, or affecting their sale, distribution, transportation, insurance, warehousing, inspection, exhibition, processing, mixing or other use, shall be published promptly in such a manner as to enable governments and traders to become acquainted with them. Agreements affecting international trade policy which are in force between the government or a governmental agency of any contracting party and the government or governmental agency of any other contracting party shall also be published. The provisions of this paragraph shall not require any contracting party to disclose confidential information which would impede law enforcement or otherwise be contrary to the public interest or would prejudice the legitimate commercial interests of particular enterprises, public or private.

Article XII

Restrictions to Safeguard the Balance of Payments

1. Notwithstanding the provisions of paragraph 1 of Article XI, any contracting party, in order to safeguard its external financial position and its balance of payments, may restrict the quantity or value of merchandise permitted to be imported, subject to the provisions of the following paragraphs of this Article.

2. (a) Import restrictions instituted, maintained or intensified by a contracting party under this Article shall not exceed those necessary:

(i) to forestall the imminent threat of, or to stop, a serious decline in its monetary reserves, or

(ii) in the case of a contracting party with very low monetary reserves, to achieve a reasonable rate of increase in its reserves.

Due regard shall be paid in either case to any special factors which may be affecting the reserves of such contracting party or its need for reserves, including, where special external credits or other resources are available to it, the need to provide for the appropriate use of such credits or resources.

(b) Contracting parties applying restrictions under sub-paragraph (a) of this paragraph shall progressively relax them as such conditions improve, maintaining them only to the extent that the conditions specified in that sub-paragraph still justify their application. They shall eliminate the restrictions when conditions would no longer justify their institution or maintenance under that sub-paragraph.

3. (a) Contracting parties undertake, in carrying out their domestic policies, to pay due regard to the need for maintaining or restoring equilibrium in their balance of payments on a sound and lasting basis and to the desirability of avoiding an uneconomic employment of productive resources. They recognize that, in order to achieve these ends, it is desirable so far as possible to adopt measures which expand rather than contract international trade.

4. (a) Any contracting party applying new restrictions or raising the general level of its existing restrictions by a substantial intensification of the measures applied under this Article shall immediately after instituting or intensifying such restrictions (or, in circumstances in which prior consultation is practicable, before doing so) consult with the CONTRACTING PARTIES, as to the nature of its balance of payments difficulties, alternative corrective measures which may be available, and the possible effect of the restrictions on the economies of other contracting parties.

5. If there is a persistent and widespread application of import restrictions under this Article, indicating the existence of a general disequilibrium which is restricting international trade, the CONTRACTING PARTIES shall initiate discussions to consider whether other measures might be taken, either by those contracting parties the balances of payments of which are under pressure or by those the balances of payments of which are tending to be exceptionally favourable, or by any appropriate intergovernmental organization, to remove the underlying causes of the disequilibrium. On the

invitation of the CONTRACTING PARTIES, contracting parties shall participate in such discussions.

Article XVIII

Governmental Assistance to Economic Development

1. The contracting parties recognize that the attainment of the objectives of this Agreement will be facilitated by the progressive development of their economies, particularly of those contracting parties the economies of which can only support low standards of living and are in the early stages of development.

2. The contracting parties recognize further that it may be necessary for those contracting parties, in order to implement programmes and policies of economic development designed to raise the general standard of living of their people, to take protective or other measures affecting imports, and that such measures are justified in so far as they facilitate the attainment of the objectives of this Agreement. They agree, therefore, that those contracting parties should enjoy additional facilities to enable them (a) to maintain sufficient flexibility in their tariff structure to be able to grant the tariff protection required for the establishment of a particular industry and (b) to apply quantitative restrictions for balance of payments purposes in a manner which takes full account of the continued high level of demand for imports likely to be generated by their programmes of economic development.

3. The contracting parties recognize finally that, with those additional facilities which are provided for in Sections A and B of this Article, the provisions of this Agreement would normally be sufficient to enable contracting parties to meet the requirements of their economic development. They agree, however, that there may be circumstances where no measure consistent with those provisions is practicable to permit a contracting party in the process of economic development to grant the governmental assistance required to promote the establishment of particular industries with a view to raising the general standard of living of its people. Spacial procedures are laid down in Sections C and D of this Article to deal with those cases.

4. (a) Consequently, a contracting party the economy of which can only support low standards of living and is in the early stages of development shall be free to deviate temporarily from the provisions of the other Articles of this Agreement, as provided in Sections A, B and C of this Article.

Section A

7. (a) If a contracting party coming within the scope of paragraph 4 (a) of this Article considers it desirable, in order to promote the establishment of a particular industry with a view to raising the general standard of living of its people, to modify or withdraw a concession included in the appropriate Schedule annexed to this Agreement, it shall notify the CONTRACTING PARTIES to this effect and enter into negotiations with any contracting party with which such concession was initially negotiated, and with any other contracting party determined by the CONTRACTING PARTIES to have a substantial interest therein.

Section B

8. The contracting parties recognize that contracting parties coming within the scope of paragraph 4 (a) of this Article tend, when they are in rapid process of development, to experience balance of payments difficulties arising mainly from efforts to expand their internal markets as well as from the instability in their terms of trade.

9. In order to safeguard its external financial position and to ensure a level of reserves adequate for the implementation of its programme of economic development, a contracting party coming within the scope of paragraph 4 (a) of this Article may, subject to the provisions of paragraphs 10 to 12, control the general level of its imports by restricting the quantity or value of merchandise permitted to be imported; *Provided* that the import restrictions instituted, maintained or intensified shall not exceed those necessary:

(a) to forestall the threat of, or to stop, a serious decline in its monetary reserves, or

(b) in the case of a contracting party with inadequate monetary reserves, to achieve a reasonable rate of increase in its reserves.

Article XXII

Consultation

1. Each contracting party shall accord sympathetic consideration to, and shall afford adequate opportunity for consultation regarding, such representations as may be made by another contracting party with respect to any matter affecting the operation of this Agreement.

2. The CONTRACTING PARTIES may, at the request of a contracting party, consult with any contracting party or parties in respect of any matter for which it has not been possible to find a satisfactory solution through consultation under paragraph 1.

Article XXIII

Nullification or Impairment

1. If any contracting party should consider that any benefit accruing to it directly or indirectly under this Agreement is being nullified or impaired or that the attainment of any objective of the Agreement is being impeded as the result of

(a) the failure of another contracting party to carry out its obligations under this Agreement, or

(b) the application by another contracting party of any measure, whether or not it conflicts with the provisions of this Agreement, or

(c) the existence of any other situation,

the contracting party may, with a view to the satisfactory adjustment of the matter, make written representations or proposals to the other contracting party or parties which it considers to be concerned. Any contracting party thus approached shall give sympathetic consideration to the representations or proposals made to it.

2. If no satisfactory adjustment is effected between the contracting parties concerned within a reasonable time, or if the difficulty is of the type described in paragraph 1 (c) of this Article, the matter may be referred to the CONTRACTING PARTIES.

PART IV

TRADE AND DEVELOPMENT

Article XXXVI

Principles and Objectives

1. The contracting parties,

(a) recalling that the basic objectives of this Agreement include the raising of standards of living and the progressive development of the economies of all contracting parties, and considering that the attainment of these objectives is particularly urgent for less-developed contracting parties;

(b) considering that export earnings of the less-developed contracting parties can play a vital part in their economic development and that the extent of this contribution depends on the prices paid by the less-developed contracting parties for essential imports, the volume of their exports, and the prices received for these exports;

(c) noting, that there is a wide gap between standards of living in less-developed countries and in other countries;

(d) recognizing that individual and joint action is essential to further the development of the economies of less-developed contracting parties and to bring about a rapid advance in the standards of living in these countries;

(e) recognizing that international trade as a means of achieving economic and social advancement should be governed by such rules and procedures -- and measures in conformity with such rules and procedures -- as are consistent with the objectives set forth in this Article;

(f) noting that the CONTRACTING PARTIES may enable less-developed contracting parties to use special measures to promote their trade and development;

agree as follows.

2. There is need for a rapid and sustained expansion of the export earnings of the less-developed contracting parties.

3. There is need for positive efforts designed to ensure that less-developed contracting parties secure a share in the growth in international trade commensurate with the needs of their economic development.

4. Given the continued dependence of many less-developed contracting parties on the exportation of a limited range of primary products, there is need to provide in the largest possible measure more favourable and acceptable conditions of access to world markets for these products, and wherever appropriate to devise measures designed to stabilize and improve conditions of world markets in these products, including in particular measures designed to attain stable, equitable and remunerative prices, thus permitting an expansion of world trade and demand and a dynamic and steady growth of the real export earnings of these countries so as to provide them with expanding resources for their economic development.

5. The rapid expansion of the economies of the less-developed contracting parties will be facilitated by a diversification of the structure of their economies and the avoidance of an excessive dependence on the export of primary products. There is, therefore, need for increased access in the largest possible measure to markets under favourable conditions for processed and manufactured products currently or potentially of particular export interest to less-developed contracting parties.

6. Because of the chronic deficiency in the export proceeds and other foreign exchange earnings of less-developed contracting parties, there are important inter-relationships between trade and financial assistance to development. There is, therefore, need for close and continuing collaboration between the CONTRACTING PARTIES and the international lending agencies so that they can contribute most effectively to alleviating the burdens these less-developed contracting parties assume in the interest of their economic development.

7. There is need for appropriate collaboration between the CONTRACTING PARTIES, other intergovernmental bodies and the organs and agencies of the United Nations system, whose activities relate to the trade and economic development of less-developed countries.

8. The developed contracting parties do not expect reciprocity for commitments made by them in trade negotiations to reduce or remove tariffs and other barriers to the trade of less-developed contracting parties.

9. The adoption of measures to give effect to these principles and objectives shall be a matter of conscious and purposeful effort on the part of the contracting parties both individually and jointly.

Article XXXVII

Commitments

1. The developed contracting parties shall to the fullest extent possible -- that is, except when compelling reasons, which may include legal reasons, make it impossible -- give effect to the following provisions:

(a) accord high priority to the reduction and elimination of barriers to products currently or potentially of particular export interest to less-developed contracting parties, including customs duties and other restrictions which differentiate unreasonably between such products in their primary and in their processed forms;

(b) refrain from introducing, or increasing the incidence of, customs duties or non-tariff import barriers on products currently or potentially of particular export interest to less-developed contracting parties; and

(c) (i) refrain from imposing new fiscal measures, and

(ii) in any adjustments of fiscal policy accord high priority to the reduction and elimination of fiscal measures, which would hamper, or which hamper, significantly the growth of consumption of primary products, in raw or processed form, wholly or mainly produced in the territories of less-developed contracting parties, and which are applied specifically to those products.

APPENDIX D

Telecommunication and Data Services in the Services Economy

R. Brian Woodrow

It is widely acknowledged that the major advanced industrial nations have become "services economies" over the past 20 to 30 years and fit, with some variation, a pattern which distinguishes them clearly from other countries. Table I provides data on services as a percentage of Gross Domestic Product (GDP) as well as on the percentage of labour force employed in services both for selected countries and for broad groupings of countries:

TABLE I - Services as a Percentage of GDP and Employment, Selected Countries and Group of Countries				
	Services as % of GDP		Services as % of Employment	
	1965	1984	1975	1984
Industrial Market Economies				
United States	59	66	72	76
Japan	48	56	61	66
United Kingdom	56	62	65	72
Sweden	53	66	65	72
Canada	61	72	72	75
Upper Income Developing Economies				
Argentina	42	50	-	-
Brazil	48	52	47	54
India	31	38	-	-
High Income Oil Exporting Economies[a]	n/a	25	25	35
Low Income Economies[a]	25	31	14	15
[a] - figures for 1960 and 1982 respectively				

Source: James R. Basche, *Eliminating Barriers to International Trade and Investment Services* (N.Y.: Conference Board Research Bulletin, 1986) and

Juan Rada, "Information Technology and Services" in O. Giarini (ed.), *The Emerging Service Economy* (N.Y.: Pergamon, 1987).

In domestic and structural terms, then, advanced industrial nations represent highly developed services economies while many other countries throughout the world are clearly moving in that direction.

The extent to which services are traded worldwide among nations and the importance of this trade *vis-a-vis* other indicators, however, is more problematic. According to available balance-of-payments data, total world exports of services were reported in 1984 to be $357 billion, although other estimates which take into account the systematic underestimation of services trade would put the figure for the same year as high as $700 billion [Shelp, 1987: 70]. Table II places the official figure in perspective *vis-a-vis* merchandise exports, foreign investment income, and world GDP:

TABLE II - Total World Export of Services and Merchandise, Investment Income, and GDP Selected Years and Annual Growth Rates

	Value in 1984 ($ billion)	Average Annual Growth Rate 1970-80
Service Exports	357	18.7
Merchandise Exports	1,545	20.4
Investment Income	244	22.4
GDP	11,891	14.2

Source: Robert Stern and Bernard M. Hoekman, "Issues and Data Needs for GATT Negotiations on Services", *World Economy* (March, 1987).

Internationally traded services continue to represent about 20% of total world trade; rates of growth through the 1970s and into the 1980s were comparable to those for merchandise trade and foreign investment income; in overall terms they make only a minor contribution to total world GDP.

The relationship between domestic services economies, international trade in services and foreign direct investment requires more careful attention. Table III presents summary data on this relationship for advanced industrial economies. As developed and analyzed by Karl Sauvant, this data -- with the serious reservations about some of the measurement problems involved, and recognition that it applies primarily to the early 1980s -- can be used to demonstrate several points:

- "The internationalization of services through trade has increased but at a slower pace and at a consistently lower level than for industrial production". Only 11% of services production in 1980 (up from 7%

in 1970) was traded internationally compared with 45% of agricultural production and 55% of industrial production.

| | Exports of services, 1980 | Foreign Direct Investment | | | | Sales of foreign service affiliates, 1982 |
Country		Stock Total, 1981	Services, 1981	Outflows, 1981-83 (yearly averages) Total	Services	
USA	35	226	63	9	5	178
UK	34	66	13	6	3	32
FR Germany	32	46	11	4	1	27
Japan	19	45	18	8	5	44
Canada	7	26	6	-	-	14
Total Above	127	409	111	27	14	295
Other developed market econs.	165	128	35	9	5	86
Developing countries	66	18	5	-	-	12
World Total	358	555	151	36	19	392

TABLE III - Estimated World Trade and Foreign Direct Investment in Services ($ billion)

Source: Karl P. Sauvant, *International Transactions in Services: The Politics of Transborder Data Flows*, (Westview Press, Boulder, CO 1986).

• "While the proportion of what is traded varies from country to country, the overall pattern is consistent: the proportion of services trade is considerably lower than that of goods" . The U.K. exported 11% of services and 60% of goods in 1980 compared to Japan at 4% and 35% respectively, the United States at 3% and 19% respectively, and Canada at 8% and 28% respectively.

• "The top 10 exporters of services in 1980 were all advanced industrial nations as were 16 of the top 20". The U.S. led with $35 billion followed closely by the U.K., France and West Germany and Canada at $7 billion while the largest importers of services were these same advanced industrial nations plus oil-rich nations like Saudi Arabia, Iran, Mexico (although this probably does not hold for this latter group in recent years).

- "Foreign direct investment -- rather than services trade -- has been the principal vehicle for the major developed countries through which services have been delivered to foreign markets". The accumulated foreign direct investment stock in services had reached a quarter of the world's total foreign direct investment stock of $555 billion in 1980 while the annual FDI outflows for services of the major nations listed in Table III accounted for $14 billion of the $27 billion in total FDI outflows that year.

- "Services transactions effected through transnational corporations are considerably more important than trade in services both overall and particularly for the principal capital-exporting countries". For example, the services exports of the countries listed in Table III amounted to $127 million in 1980 while the total sales of foreign services affiliates were more than twice as high at $295 million in 1982.

- "Not surprisingly, most of the world's largest service TNC's are headquartered in the principal capital exporting countries". The United States and Japan accounted for 44 of the 75 largest services TNCs and dominate a wide range of international service sectors.

- Finally, with regard to the composition of services trade and FDI in services, services trade for the countries listed in Table III is quite diversified with the largest items being financial services and "other private services" as well as transportation and travel, while FDI in services tends to be more concentrated in banking, insurance and certain distributive services.

Thus, the picture which Sauvant paints is one where, in spite of the basically domestic orientation of the services sector, services are undergoing a dynamic process of internationalization through foreign direct investment and, to a lesser extent, through trade, while the two instruments are often closely linked with each other both generally and in individual service sectors [Sauvant, 1987: 24-35].

Trade in telecommunication services is but one of the service sectors which balance-of-payments and other data should reflect and -- along with data processing, information services and some aspects of computer software -- constitutes what more broadly would be regarded as trade in telecommunications and data services. Useful information can be presented for the United States as derived from a 1986 study of trade in services conducted by the Office of Technology Assessment. Internationally traded telecommunications services, comprising "payments to U.S. carriers by American customers on outgoing calls as well as access payments by foreign carriers on incoming calls", totalled $2.3 billion in 1983 out of $103.2 billion in total U.S. telecommunications revenues and represents only a very small portion of total U.S. services trade. However, in balance-of-payments terms, these telecommunications services would actually turn up as a negative sum since $1.7 billion of that figure was passed on in access payments to foreign carriers while foreign carriers remitted $0.9 billion to U.S. carriers for access on incoming calls [U.S. Office of Technology Assessment, 1986: 91-94]. Telecommunications services then represent only a small component of total U.S. services exports and actually turn up as a net negative item in the balance of payments, despite the fact that revenues from international services as part of total U.S. telecommunications industry revenues have been growing roughly twice as rapidly as domestic service revenues. Moreover, it should be remembered that international service revenues relate only to basic voice and data and a more accurate picture of internationally traded telecommunications and data services would include as well value added network service which are embedded as a portion of foreign revenues of "information services" (total: $2.9 billion in 1983) as well as leased-line revenues which likewise are embedded as a portion of foreign revenues in data processing (total: $2.6 billion in 1983) [U.S. Office of Technology Assessment, 1986: 72-73 and 61-63]. Finally, any comprehensive accounting would also take into account foreign direct investment in telecommunications services but this is likely at this point in time to be minimal given the fact that most countries maintain strict control over provision of basic telecommunications service, although FDI in value-added services is opening up in some countries. What should be crystal clear from the U.S. experience, however, is that internationally-traded telecommunications and data services are relatively small in revenue terms but that this measure is not really a very accurate gauge of the overall importance of this services sector.

BIBLIOGRAPHY

18 U.S. C.A. Sec. 2511 (3) repealed by Foreign Intelligence Surveillance Act of 1978, Pub. L. 95-511, 92 Stat. 1797 (1978), replaced by Exec. Order no. 12,333, 46 Fed. Reg. 59941 (Sec 2.5) Dec. 8, 1981.

Aho, Michael and Jonathan D. Aronson (1985). *Trade Talks: America Better Listen.* (New York: Council on Foreign Relations).

American Banker (1986). Sept. 8, 1986.

American Institute of Aeronautics and Astronautics, Inc., Dec. 1986.

Analysis and Forecasting Group (GAP) (1988). Open Network Provision (ONP) in the Community. Brussels.

Aronson, Jonathan D. and Peter F. Cowhey (1988). *When Countries Talk: International Trade in Telecommunication Services.* Cambridge, Ma: Ballinger, for the American Enterprise Institute, Washington DC.

Aronson, Jonathan D. (1984). Computer, Data Processing, and Communication Services, in Robert M. Stern (ed.), *Trade and Investment in Service Industries: U.S.-Canadian Bilateral and Multilateral Perspectives.* Toronto: University of Toronto Press, for the Ontario Economic Council.

Aronson, Jonathan D. and Peter F. Cowhey (1984). *Trade in Services: A Case of Open Markets*, Washington DC. American Enterprise Institute for Public Policy Research.

Ascher, Bernard and Obie G. Whichard (1987). Improving Services Trade Data, in O. Giarini (ed.), *The Emerging Services Economy.* Oxford: Pergamon Press, 155-81.

Atlantic Council (1987). *The Uruguay Round of Multilateral Trade Negotiations under GATT: Policy Proposals on Trade in Services.* Report of the Atlantic Council's Advisory Trade Panel, The Atlantic Council of the United States, Washington DC, November 1987.

Balasubramanyam, V.N. (1973). *International Transfer of Technology to India.* New York: Praeger.

Baldwin, Robert E. (1985). "Negotiating About Trade and Investment in Services - Comment", In: Robert M. Stern (ed), *Trade and Investment in Services: Canada/U.S. Perspectives.* Toronto, 195-199.

Ballance, R., and S. Sinclair (1983). *Collapse and Survival: Industry Strategies in a Changing World.* London: Allen and Unwin.

Balle, A.P. (1982). Het gebruik van glasvezelkabel in lokale telecommunicatie netten, 's Gravenhage: Staatsuitgeverij.

Bar, Francios and Michael Borrus (1987). From Public Access to Private Connections: Network Policy and National Advantage. Paper presented at the Fifteenth Telecommunications Policy Research Conference, Airlie House, VA, Sept. 27-30, 1987.

Bardach, E. and R.A. Kagan (1982). *Going by the Book: the Problem of Regulatory Unreasonableness, Philadelphia*: Temple University Press.

Basche, James R. (1986). *Elminating Barriers to International Trade and Investment in Services.* New York: Conference Board, Report #200.

Bauer, J.M. and M. Latzer (1987). Impact and Policy-Challenge of Telecommunications Liberalisation for a Small and Open Economy: A Case Study of Austria. World Telecommunications Forum, Part 4 (Geneva, 22-24 October 1987).

Bauer, J.M. (1987). De-regulierung als industrie politisches Instrument, Wien: Institut fur Volkswirtschaftstheorie und politik Wirtschaftsuniversitat.

Baumol, William J. and John C. Panzar and Robert D. Willig (1982). Contestable Markets and the Theory of Industry Structure, San Diego.

Baumol, William J., Robert D. Willig (1981). Fixed Costs, Sunk Costs, Entry Barriers, and Sustainability of Monopoly. *Quarterly Journal of Economics.* Vol. 96, 405-431.

Becker, J. (1986). New Information Technologies (NITs) and Culture: the European Response, The Hague: EC/Fast: COM 8 Conference.

Bergstern, C.F., T. Horst and T.H. Moran (1978). *American Multinationals and American Interests*. The Brookings Institution, Washington DC.

Bernstein, Robert (1988). Point-of-Sale Technology Reaches a Crossroad, *Canadian Datasystems*, (February 1988), p. 48.

Bhagwati, J.N. (1984). Splintering and Disembodiment of Services and Developing Countries. *World Economy*, No. 7 (June, 1984), 133-44.

Bhagwati, J.N. (1987a). International Trade in Services And Its Relevance for Economic Development, in O. Giarini (ed.), *The Emerging Service Economy*. Oxford: Pergamon Press, 3-34.

Bhagwati, J.N. (1987b). Trade in Services and the Multilateral Trade Negotiations. *World Bank Economic Review*, 1 (September, 1987), 549-569.

Bleek, Joel A. & Lowell L. Bryan. (1988). The Changing World of Banking,: The Globalization of Financial Markets. *The McKinsey Quarterly*, (Winter 1988), pp. 17-38.

BNA, Inc. (1985). UNCTAD Meeting on Technology Transfer Fails to Reach Agreement of Code of Conduct. Daily Report for Executives, June 7, 1985, DER No. 10, L-8.

Branscomb, Anne W. (ed.) (1985). *Towards A Law Of Global Communications Networks*. New York: Longmans.

Brazil - Ministry of Communications (1986). Telecommunications in Brazil.

Brenton, M.E. (1987). The Role of Standardisation in Telecommunications. *Trends of Change in Telecommunications Policy*. Paris: OECD/Committee for Information, Computer and Communications Policy.

Bressand, Albert (1988). Computer Reservation Systems: Networks Shaping Markets, in A. Bressand and K. Nicolaidis eds. *SWF Services World Economy Series* (second Volume), Ballinger.

Breyer, S. (1982). *Regulation and its Reform*. Cambridge, Mass.: Harvard University Press.

Brock, G.W. (1981). *The Telecommunications Industry: The Dynamics of Market Structure*. Cambridge, Mass.: Harvard University Press.

334

Brock, W.E. (1982). A Simple Plan For Negotiation Of Trade In Services. *World Economy*, No. 5 September, 1982, 229-40.

Brock, Gerald (1981). *The Telecommunications Industry*. Cambridge: Harvard University Press.

Bruce, R.R. and J.P. Cunard (1987). WATTC-88 and the Future of the ITU: Realism about the Limits of Regulation. Washington: Debevoise & Plimpton.

Bruce, Robert R. (1987). Definition of Services: Line Drawing, Industry Structure and Institutional Arrangements, in OECD, *Trends of Change in Telecommunications Policy*. Paris, 67-98.

Bruce, Robert; Jeffrey P. Cunard and Mark D. Director (1985). *From Telecommunications to Electronic Services*. London: Butterworths for International Institute of Communications.

Bruce, Robert R., Jeffrey P. Cunard, and Mark D. Director (1987). The *Telecom Mosiac*. Borough Green, United Kingdom: Butterworths for the International Institute of Communications, London.

Buchanan, James M., Robert D. Tollison, Gordon Tullock (eds.) (1980). *Toward a Theory of the Rentseeking Society*. College Station.

Burnett, J.T. (1986). Information, Banking Law and Extraterritoriality. *Transnational Data and Communications Report*, January 1986, 17-18.

Burns, W.G. (1988). Technology, Politics and the Customer in the Global Telecommunications Marketplace, (6 June 1988), Speech at University of Vermont.

Burton, R.P. and R.D. Malmrose (1987). Impact of Privacy Laws on Religious Bodies. *Transnational Data and Communications Report*, June 1987, 5-9.

Business Week (1988). Enterprise Networking: Key to Your Company's Future. Special Supplement, April 11, 1988.

Butler, R.E.(1988a). Search for a New International Telecom Framework, *Transnational Data and Communications Report*. March, 1988, 17-21.

Butler, R.E. (1988b). Interconnection and Trade: Priorities for WATTC-88 and for the International Community, Keynote Remarks at the ThinkNet Commission, Paris 13-14 June 1988.

Canada Consulting Group Inc. *The Traded Nature of Canadian Financial Services* (date not known).

Canada, Senate of, Second Session, Thirty-third Parliament, 1986-87, Proceedings of the Standing Senate Committee on Foreign Affairs (a) Issue No. 8, Tuesday, 17 November 1987; (b) Issue No. 11, Tuesday, 15 December 1985.

CEC/ESCO (1985). Complementarity of Satellite and Terrestrial Systems. European Satellite Consulting Organization.

Cleghorn, John (1987). Managing an International Institution in an Industry in Transition, *Business Quarterly*, Vol. 52, No.1 (Summer 1987), pp. 96-101.

Coalition of Service Industries, The (1988). A Multilateral Agreement on Trade in Services, Washington D.C., April 21, 1988.

Codding, George A., Jr. and Anthony M. Rutkowski (1982). *The International Telecommunication Union in a Changing World*. Dedham, Mass.: Artech House.

Commissie Steenbergen (1985). Signalen van straks: Een nieuwe richting voor de PTT's Gravenhage: Staatsuitgeverij.

Commission of the European Communities (1987). Green Paper on the Development of the Common Market for Telecommunications Services and Equipment, COM(87)290; Summary Report. Brussels.

Commission of the European Communities (1987). Towards a Dynamic Economy - Green Paper on the Development of the Common Market for Telecommunications Services and Equipment, COM 290. Brussels.

Commission of the European Communities (1988). Towards a Competitive Community-wide Telecommunications Market in 1992, COM 48.

Corbet, Hugh (1977). Prospects for Negotiations on Barriers to International Trade in Services. *Pacific Community*, April 1977, 454-470.

Corden, Warner Max (1974). *Trade Policy and Economic Welfare*. Oxford: Clarendon Press.

Corden, W.M. (1974) The Theory of International Trade, In Dunning J.H. (ed) *Economic Analysis and the Multinational Enterprise*. London: Allen and Unwin.

Corrigan, Gerald E. (1987). Financial Market Structure: A Longer View, Federal Reserve Bank Speech (January 1987).

Crawford, Morris H. (1988). EC '1992: The Making of a Common Market in Telecommunications, Program on Information Resources Policy, Center for Information Policy Research, Harvard University, Cambridge, MA.

Cuadra and Elsevier. *Directory of On-Line Data Bases*, v. 7, no. 3.

Curcen, N. and M. Gensollen (1987). Determining Demand for new Telecommunications Services. *Trends of Change in Telecommunications Policy*. Paris, OECD/Committee for Information, Computer and Communications Policy.

Dang Nguyen, G. (1986). *A European Telecommunications Policy: Which Instruments for Which Prospects?* Brussels/Florence: European Policy Unit, European University Institute.

Davidow, Joel (1985). Antitrust and Transfer of Technology Rules: Recent Developments. *The CTC Reporter* (United Nations), No. 19, Spring 1985.

de Sola Pool, I. (1983). *Technologies of Freedom - On Free Speech in an Electronic Age*. Cambridge/Massachussetts - London/England: The Belknap Press of Harvard University Press.

Diebold, William, Jr. and Helena Stalson (1983). Negotiating Issues in International Service Transactions, in William R. Cline, ed., *Trade Policy in the 1980s*. Washington, DC: Institute for International Economics.

Digital Eequipment Corporation (1987). Green Paper of the Commission of the European Communities on Telecommunications: Statement of Interest. Brussels.

Dizard, Wilson P. (1984). U.S. Competitiveness in International Information Trade, *The Information Society*, No. 2 (1984), 179-216.

Dizard, Wilson P. and Lesley D. Turner (1987). Telecommunications and the U.S.-Canada Free Trade Talks. Paper published by the International Communications Project of the Center for Strategic and International Studies, Washington, DC (mimeo).

Donges, Juergen B. (1986). Whither International Trade Policies? Worries about Continuing Protectionism. Kiel Institute of World Economics, Discussion Paper, No. 125, October 1986.

Dosi, G. (1981). Technological Paradigms and Technological Trajectories - A Suggested Interpretation of the Determinants and Directions of Technical Change. Sussex: European Research Centre, Horck IAP/2.

Drake, William J. (1988) WATTC-88: Restructuring the International Telecommunications Regulations. ThinkNet Commission, PROMETHEE, Paris 13-14 June 1988.

Dunn, Donald A. and Octavio Sampaio (1988). Pricing Interchange Access, Center for Economic Policy Research, Stanford University (mimeo).

Economist, The (1985). The Importance of being Nice, Retaliatory, Forgiving and Clear, November 9, 1985, 93.

Economist, The (1985). The World on the Linc. Nov. 23, 1985.

Ergas, Henry (1984). Monopoly and Competition in the Provision of Telecommunications Services, and International Aspects of Telecommunications Regulation, in *Changing Market Structures in Telecommunications*. Amsterdam: North-Holland, 3-16 and 17-29.

Ergas, Henry (1987). Regulation, Monopoly and Competition in the Telecommunications Infrastructure, in OECD, *Trends of Change in Telecommunications Policy*. Paris, 1987, 45-66.

European Commission/FAST II (1988). Sous-Programme: Communications - Synthese des Resultats. Bruxelles, Janvier.

338

European Commission/GNS (1987). A Possible Structure for a Services Agreement (Discussion Paper). Submitted to GATT Group of Negotiations on Services (GNS), Brussels.

European Community (1988). European Community - United States Second Plenary Meeting on Telecommunications. Airlie House, Virginia 3-4 March.

European Studies (1986). For Whom the Bells Tolls: Responses to Accelerating Change in International Telecommunications. Brussels, European Studies/AGB.

Eurostrategies (1988). European Integration and Telecommunications - International Consultative Forum on the Telecommunications Green Paper of the Commission of the European Communities - Briefing Memorandum. Brussels, Eurostrategies, February 1988.

Everard, James A. (1988). Trade & Investment in Services: OECD Agreements and the GATT, Institute for Research on Public Policy, 1988.

Eward, Ronald (1985). *The Deregulation of International Telecommunications*. Dedham, Mass.: Artech House.

Feketekuty, Geza (1980). Statement on Transborder Data Flows and Trade in Services, before the Subcommittee on Government Information and Individual Rights, Committee on Government Operations, U.S. House of Representatives, April 21, 1980.

Feketekuty, Geza (1981a). Statement on Transborder Data Flows and Trade in Services, before the Subcommittee on Government Information and Individual Rights, Committee on Government Operations, U.S. House of Representatives, March 31, 1981.

Feketekuty, Geza (1981b). Statement on Trade in Telecommunications Equipment and Services, before the Subcommittee on Telecommunications, Consumer Protection, and Finance, Committee on Energy and Commerce, U.S. House of Representatives, April 29, 1981.

Feketekuty, Geza (1982). Statement on Effect of Deregulation of Telecommunications on Trade in Services, before the Committee on Commerce, Science and Transportation, U.S. Senate, June 14, 1982.

339

Feketekuty, Geza (1985). Negotiating Strategies for Liberalizing Trade and Investment in Services, in: Robert M. Stern (ed.), *Trade and Investment in Services: Canada/U.S. Perspectives*. Toronto 1985, 203-214.

Feketekuty, Geza (1987). Trade Policy Objectives in Telecommunications. Paper published by the International Telecommunication Union in connection with the Legal Symposium of Telecom 87, a conference organized by the International Telecommunication Union in Geneva, Switzerland in October, 1987.

Feketekuty, Geza (1988a). Telecommunications and Trade: Implications for GATT and ITU, *Transnational Data and Communications Report*, XI May, 1988, 16-22.

Feketekuty, Geza (1988b). *International Trade in Services: An Overview and Blueprint for Trade Negotiations*. Cambridge: Ballinger.

Feketekuty, Geza and Jonathan D. Aronson (1984a). Meeting the Challenges of the World Information Economy. *The World Economy* 7, 63-86.

Feketekuty, Geza and Jonathan D. Aronson (1984b). Restrictions on Trade in Communications and Information Services. *The Information Society*, No. 2 (1984), 217-48.

Feketekuty, Geza and Kathryn Hauser (1985b). Information Technology and Trade in Services. *Economic Impact*. Washington DC: United States Information Agency.

Fforde, J.S. (1957). *International Trade in Managerial Skills*. Oxford, Blackwell.

Financial Times (1987). Plan for Freer Trade in Services, December 18, 1987.

FIDE (1984), Europe and the Media - Reports Volume I. The Hague: FIDE.

Forester, Tom (ed.), (1985). *The Information Technology Revolution*. Cambridge MA: MIT Press.

Freeman, C. (1986). The Challenge of New Technologies, Paris, OECD - 25th Anniversay Symposium, October 1986.

Fun, M.A. (1983). A survey of recent results in the analysis of production conditions in telecommunications, in L. Courville, A. de Fontenay, R Dobell (ed.), *Economic Analysis of Telecommunications - Theory and Applications*. Amsterdam/New York/Oxford: North-Holland/Elsevier Science Publishers B.V.

GATT (General Agfeement on Tariffs and Trade). Preliminary Negotiations on Services, (1984-86), National Studies on Services, 17 in Total Submitted Between January 1984 and November 1986.

GATT (1986a). Ministerial Declaration of the Uruguay Round, MIN.DEC., 20 September 1986.

GATT (1986b). Launching of Uruguay Round, *GATT Newsletter*, October, 1986, 1-6.

GATT (1987b). Group of Negotiations on Services. *GATT Newsletter*, January-February, 1987, 1-6.

GATT (1987b). The Uruguay Round and Trade in Services, Background Paper presented to the North South Trade Roundtable, Third Session, Geneva, 6-7 November 1987.

GATT, GNS (Group of Negotiations on Services) (1987a). Communications from Brazil, MTN.GNS/W/3, 11 March 1987.

GATT, GNS (1987b). Communication from the European Communities, MTN.GNS/W/29, 10 December 1987.

GATT, GNS (1987c). Communication from Switzerland, MTN.GNS/W/30.

GATT (1988a). Communication from the United States, MTN.GNS/W/40, 16 May 1988.

GATT, GNS (1988b). Communication from Japan, MTN.GNS/W/40, 19 May 1988.

Gazette, The Montreal (1988). Saboteur's Deadly 'Virus' Threatens Computers. Jan 8, 1988, A-12.

Giarini, Orio (1987). *The Emerging Service Economy*. Oxford: Pergamon Press.

Gibbs, Murray and Mina Mashayekhi (1988). Services: Cooperation for Development. *Journal of World Trade*, 22, April, 1988, 81-108.

Gibbs, Murray (1985). Continuing the International Debate on Services. *Journal of World Trade Law*, No. 19, May-June, 1985, 199-218.

Gibbs, Murray and Mina Mashayekhi (1988). Services: Cooperation for Development, forthcoming in A. Bressand and K. Nicolaidis eds. SWF Services World Economy Series (second volume), Ballinger. Services World Forum, 1988.

Giersch, Herbert (1985). Perspectives in the World Economy, *Weltwirtschaftliches Archiv*, Vol. 121, 409-426.

Gilhooly, Dennis (1988b). Unlocking the Network: Can Open Network Provision Create Real Competition in Services? *Communications Week International*, July 1988.

Gilhooly, Dennis (1988a). Commercial Common Carriers: Too Little, Too Late?, paper presented at the IIC Telecommunications Forum, held in Brussels, Belgium, July 14-15, 1988.

Goldstein, Judith L. and Stephen D Krasner (1984). Unfair Trade Practices: The Case for a Differential Response, *American Economic Review*, Vol. 74, 283-287.

Goncharoff, K. (1984). Bulletin Boards go Electronic. *New York Times*, Nov. 18, 1984, Sunday, Late Ed., Sec. 11 Long Island, p. 1, c. 2.

Gray, H. Peter, Services and Comparative Advantage Theory, in: Herbert Giersch (ed.), *Services in World Economic Growth*. Tubingen, forthcoming.

Green, S. (1985). Neo Nazis go High-Tech. UPI, 03/09/85, via NEXIS.

Greenaway and Milner (1986). *The Economics of Intra-Industry Trade*. Oxford: Basil Blackwell.

Grey, Rodney De C. (1985). Negotiating About Trade and Investment in Services, in R.M. Stern (ed.), *Trade and Investment in Services: Canada/U.S. Perspective*. Toronto: Ontario Economic Council, 181-193.

Grey, Rodney De C. (1986). The Elements of a General Agreement on Information Transfer/Trade (GAIT). Montreal: Atwater Institute, 1986.

Griffiths, Brian (1975). *Invisible Barriers to Invisible Trade*. London: Macmillan for the TPRC.

Grossman, Gene M. and Carl Shapiro (1985). Normative Issues Raised by International Trade in Technology Services, in R.M. Stern (ed.), *Trade and Investment in Services: Canada/U.S. Perspectives*. Toronto: Ontario Economic Council, 83-113.

Group of Negotiations on Services (1987a). Communication from Switzerland, MTN.GNS/W/30, Geneva 1987.

Grubel, Herbert G. (1987). All Traded Services are Embodied in Materials or People. *World Economy*, No. 10, September, 1987, 319-330.

Grubel, Herbert (1966). The Anatomy of Classical and Modern Infant Industry Arguments. *Weltwirtschaftliches Archiv*, Vol. 97, 325-342.

Guisard Ferraz, J.L. (1987). The Infrastructural Role of the Telecommunications Sector and Its Impact into the Economical Development. World Telecommunications Forum, Part 4 (Geneva, 22-24 October 1987).

Hague Convention on the Pacific Settlement of International Conflicts on 18 October 1907.

Hamelink, C.J. (1984). *Transnational Data Flows in the Information Age*. Sweden: Chartwell-Bratt.

Helleiner, G.K. (1981). *Intra-Firm Trade and the Developing Countries*. Macmillan.

Herzstein, Robert E. (1985). Applying Traditional Trade Principles to the International Flow of Information, in Anne W. Branscomb (ed.), *Towards a Law of Global Communications Networks*. New York: Longmans, pp. 313-30.

Hesse, Helmut (1988). Unbedingte order gedingte Meistbegunstingung als gestaltendes Prinzip einer Welthandelsordnung? *Jahrbuch fur Sozialwissenschaft*, Vol, 39, 235-244.

Hieronymi, O. (1987). *The Domestic and External Impact of National Domestic Policies: The Example of the Electronics Industry.* Carouge/Geneva: Battelle - Centre for Applied Economics, December.

Hill, T.P. (1977). On Goods and Services. *The Review of Income and Wealth,* Vol. 23, 315-338.

Hill, K.G. Anthony (1987). The Uruguay Round and Trade in Services (mimeo). 2 November 1987.

Hills, J. (1984). *Information Technology and Industrial Policy.* Beckenhand/Kent: Croom Helm.

Hindley, Brian (1988a). Service Sector Protection: Considerations for Developing Countries. *The World Bank Economic Review,* Vol. 2, 205-224.

Hindley, Brian (1988b). Problems and Prospects of Creating Integrated World Markets in Transportation and other Market Services, in: Herbert Giersch (ed.), *Services in World Economic Growth.* Tubingen, forthcoming.

Hindley, Brian and A. Smith (1984). Comparative Advantage and Trade in Services. *World Economy,* No. 7, December, 1984, 369-89.

Huber, P.W. (1987). The Geodesic Network - Report on Competition in the Telephone Industry. Washington: U.S. Government Printing Office.

Hudson, H.E. and L.C. York (1987). Telecommunications Investment in Developing Countries and the Generation of Foreign Exchange: The Impact of Electronic Funds Transfer. World Telecommunication Forum, Part 4 (Geneva, 22-24 October 1987).

Hudson, Manley O. (1944). *International Tribunals Past and Future.* Millwood, NY: Craus.

Huffbauer, G. and Chilas, G.J. (1974). Specialization by Industrial Countries: Extent and Consequences, in. Gierssh, H. (ed), *The International Division of Labour: Problems and Perspectives.* Tubingen, J.C.B. Molir.

Hughes H., and G.S. Dorrance (1986). Economic Policies and Foreign Investment with Particular Reference to Developing Countries of East Asia. Paper prepared for the Commonwealth Secretariat.

IBDD Supplement no. 4, 35.

IBDD Supplement no. 26,231 ff.

IBDD Supplement no. 29, 14-16.

Indian Institute of Foreign Trade (1987). *National Seminar on the Indian Service Economy in the 21st Century and International Trade in Services: Proceedings. 7 November 1987.*

International Chamber of Commerce (1988) Policy Statement, Worldwide Information Technology Without Barriers, Position Paper No. 10 (February 1988).

International Chamber of Commerce (1984). Information flows - Analysis of Issues for Business. Document No. 373/23, Rev. 3, December.

International Telecommunication Union. Administrative Council. (1987a). Resolution No. 966 - World Administrative Telegraph and Telephone Conference, June 25, 1987.

International Telecommunication Union. Administrative Council. (1987b). Circular Letter No. 188 - ITU Relations with GATT, July 28, 1987.

International Telecommunication Union. Preparatory Committee for WATTC-88 (1987). Report of the Meeting held from 27 April to 1 May 1987, Geneva.

International Telegraph Convention of Paris, May 17, 1965, 9 Recueil des Traites de la France 254.

INTUG, Usercomm 3 - Proceedings, (March 25-27 1987), London.

Jackson, John H. (1969). *World Trade and the Law of the GATT*. Charlottesville, VA: The Michie Company.

Jackson, John H. (1984). The Changing International Law Framework for Exports: The General Agreement on Tariffs and Trade. *The Georgia Journal of International and Comparative Law*, Vol. 14, 505-520.

Jackson, John H. (1987). The Constitutional Structure for International Cooperation in Trade in Services and the Uruguay Round for GATT. Unpublished paper, December, 1987.

Jackson, John H. and William J. Davey (1986). *Legal Problems of International Economic Relations*. Cases, Materials and Text., Second edition, St. Paul.

Jackson, John H. (1980). The Birth of the GATT-MTN System: A Constitutional Appraisal. *Law and Policy in International Business*, 12.

Japan Ministry of Post & Telecommunications(1988). International Economical Problems in Telecommunications. Tokyo, MPT, 1988.

Jaramillo, Felipe (1988). Balance of Interests Underlying Services Negotiations. *Transnational Data and Communications Report*, 11 August/September, 1988, 18-20.

Jarvin, Sigvard (1986). Arbitrating International Disputes. *Les Nouvelles* 15. MTN.GNG/NG 12/W/12.

Joskow, P.L. and Noll, R.C. (1981). Regulation in Theory and Practice, in Fromm, G. (ed.): *Studies in Public Regulation*. Cambridge/Massachusetts and London/England: The MIT Press.

Jussawalla, Meheroo (1987). The Information Revolution and its Impact on the World Economy. Paper prepared for the international seminar, Toward an International Service and Information Economy: A New Challenge for the Third World, sponsored by the Friedrich Ebert Foundation, (mimeo).

Jussawalla, Meheroo and Chee-Wah Cheah (1987). *The Calculus of International Communications*. Littleton, Colorado: Libraries Unlimited.

Katzen, M. (1982). *Multi-Media Communications*. London: Frances Pinter.

Keen, Peter. *Competing In Time*. Cambridge: Ballinger Publishing, 1986.

Kirkland, Richard I. Jr. (1987). The Bright Future of Service Exports. *Fortune*, June 8, 1987, 32-38.

Klodt, Henning (1988b). Industrial Policy and Repressed Structural Change in West Germany. Kiel Institute of World Economics, Working Paper No. 322.

Klodt, Henning (1988a). The Experience with Liberalization of Trade and Foreign Direct Investment in Services. Kiel Institute of World Economics, Working Paper No. 308, January 1988.

Komatsusaki, Seisuke (1988). A Summary of Questionnaire Survey on Deregulation/Regulation Situations in Telecommunications Services Area in 33 Countries. an unpublished paper prepared by a research group at the Research Institute of Telecom Policies and Economics, Tokyo, Japan.

Kosuge, Toshio (1987). International Telecommunications Issues - International VAN Services. Annual Report of Telecommunication Advancement Association, No. 3 July 1987.

Kosuge, Toshio (1988a). Liberalization of Telecommunications in NIC's Countries. Annual Report of Telecommunication Advancement Association, No. 4, 255-265, July 1988.

Kosuge, Toshio (1988b). Liberalization of International VAN. Tokyo, JIP-DEC.

Krommenacker, Raymond (1984). *World-Traded Services: The Challenge for the Eighties*. Dedham, Mass.: Artech.

Krommenacker, Raymond (1987). Uruguay Round Services Negotiations. *Transnational Data and Communications Report*, September 1987, 11-17.

Krueger, Anne O. (1974). The Political Economy of the Rent-Seeking Society". *The American Economic Review*, Vol. 64, 291-303.

Krugman, Paul R. (ed.) (1986). *Strategic Trade Policy and the New International Economics*. Cambridge, MA.

Labadi, A. and I. Sebestyen (1982). IIASA TPA-70 Gateway-Network Promotes International Flows of Scientific Information. *Transnational Data Report*, v. VD, no. 1, Jan/Feb 1982, 41-47.

Lanvin, Bruno (1986). *La societe d' information en suspens*.Paris: Futuribles.

Lanvin, Bruno (1986). Reseaux et competitivite, in Les services de communication du futur. *Bulletin de l'IDATE* No. 25, Montpellier, Novembre 1986.

Lanvin, Bruno (1987). International Trade in Services, Information Services and Development. UNCTAD Discussion Paper No. 23, Geneva.

Lanvin, Bruno (1987). Information Technology and Competitiveness in the Service Industry. Bulletin l'IRES No. 119, Universite Catholique de Louvain, Octobre 1987.

Lanvin, Bruno (1988). Information, commerce, international des services et developpement, in *L'Europe face a la nouvelle economie de service*, O. Giarini et J.R. Roulet ed., PUF, Paris, 1988.

Lanvin, Bruno (1988). Les service avances, infrastructure du developpement. *Mondes en Developpement*, No. 60, Janvier-Mars 1988.

Lanvin, Bruno (1988). Quels services pour quel developpement?, *Politica Internazionale*, IPALMO-Milan, Fevrier 1988.

Lanvin, Bruno (1988). Services Intermediaires et Developppment. *Revue d'Economie Industrielle*, No. 43, 1er Trimestre 1988, Paris.

Lanvin, Bruno (1988). Information, Services and Development: Some Conceptual and Analytical Issues, in Bressand and Nicolaidis 1988.

Lanvin, Bruno and Francisco Prieto (1986). Les services, cle du developpement economique? *Revue Tiers-Monde*, Paris, No. 105, Janiver-Mars 1986.

Lasden, M. (1985). Of Bytes and Bulletin Boards. *New York Times*, Nov. 18, 1984, sec. 6, p. 34, col. 1.

Lawrence, Robert Z. (1984). *Can America Compete?* Washington, D.C.

Leeson,K. (1987). Diversification of Demand for Telecommunications Services. *Trends of Change in Telecommunications Policy*. Paris: OECD/Committee for Information, Computer and Communications Policy.

Leone, R.K. and J.E. Jackson (1981). The Political Economy of Federal Regulatory Activity: The Case of Water Polution Controls, in Fromm, G.

348

(ed.), *Studies in Public Regulation.* Cambridge/Massachussetts and London/England: The MIT Press.

Levy, S. (1984). *Hackers.* Garden City, New York: Anchor Press/Doubleday.

Lewis, Barbara, (ed.) (1987). Technology in Banking. *The International Journal of Bank Marketing.*

Little, Arthur D. (1986). *Decision Resources Telecommunications in Brazil,* Cambridge, MA.

Malinverni, G. (1974). *Le reglement des differends dans les organisations internationales economiques.* Sijthoff, Leyde and IUHEI, Geneva.

Malmgren, Harald B. (1987). Negotiating International Rules for Services. *World Economy,* Vol. 8 No. 1, March1985.

Mansell, R., I. Miles, K. Morgan and G. Thomas (1988). Telecommunications Networking Strategies - The Evolution of Supplier/User Relations (background paper), England: Centre for Information and Communication Technologies, Science Policy Research Unit, March 1988.

McMahon, T. (1987). *Loving Little Egypt.* New York: Viking enguin.

Melody, W.H. (1986a). Telecommunication - Policy Directions for the Technology and Information Services. London: Economic and Social Research Council.

Melody, W.H. (1986b). Some Aspects and Public Policy of International Markets. *Global Networks and European Communities.* **Tilburg/The Netherlands: IVA/ISS (FAST Congress/COM-8).**

Melody, W.H. (1987). Telecommunication Implications for the Structure of Development, World Telecommunication Forum, Part 4, Geneva, 22-24 October 1987.

Mertens, J.F. (1986). The Development of Telecommunications: A Strategic Analysis. *Global Networks and European Communities.* Tilburg/The Netherlands: IVA/ISS (FAST Congress/COM)8.

Monssen, W. (1988). Airline Industry Takes Data Protection Seriously. *Transnational Data and Communications Report*, January 1988, 17.

Moran, T.H. and Pearson, C.S. (1988). Tread Carefully in the Field of TRIP Measures. *The World Economy*, Vol. 11, March 1988.

McCulloch, Rachel (1987). International Competition in Services. Working Paper No. 2235, National Bureau of Economic Research, May 1987.

Murdock, G. (1985). Intervening in Industry and Culture: Contradictions of Communications Policy. Florence: European University Institute Summer Conference.

Narjes, K.H. (1988). Telecom Policy Reform and International Trade, *Transnational Data and Communications Report (TDR)*, Volume XI Number 1.

Nayyar, Deepak (1987). The Uruguay Round and Trade in Services: Some General Policy Issues (mimeo). October 1987.

Nayyar, Deepak (1986). International Trade in Services: Implications for Developing Countries. Export-Import Bank of India. Commencement Day Lecture, Bombay, 1986.

New York Times (1986). Texts of the Statements Adopted by Leaders of 7 Industrial Democracies. May 6, 1986, A-12.

Nicolai, M.A. (1988). New Investments in the Financing of Trade. Royal Bank Speech, June 21, 1988.

Noam, Eli M. (1987). The Public Telecommunications Network: A Concept in Transition. *Journal of Communication*, Vol. 37, No. 1, Winter 1987.

Nussbaumer, Jacques (1983). Some Implications of Becoming a Services Economy, in J. Rada and Russell Pipe (eds.), *Communication Regulation and International Business*. Amsterdam: North-Holland, 23-37.

Nussbaumer, Jacques (1987a). *The Services Economy: Lever to Growth*. Boston: Kluwer Academic.

Nussbaumer, Jacques (1987b). *Services in the Global Market*. Boston: Kluwer Academic.

O'Brian, Peter (1988). International Structural Change in the Automotive Industry: A North South Perspective, Working Paper. No. 17. International Labour Office, Geneva, 1988.

OECD (1979). *The Usage of International Data Networks in Europe*. Study prepared by Logica Limited, London for the Information, Computer, Communications Policy Committee, Paris.

OECD (1980). *Policy Implications of Data Network Developments in the OECD Area*. Papers presented at a working session of the Information, Computer, Communications Policy Committee, Paris.

OECD (1983a). Transborder Data Flows in International Enterprises, (DSTI/ICCP/82.23). A report issued by the Information, Computer, Communications Policy Subcommittee of the Industry, Science and Technology Committee.

OECD (1983b). *Telecommunications: Pressures and Policies for Change*. Paris: OECD.

OECD (1986). Note by the Committee on Information, Computer and Communications Policy to the Trade Committee on Trade in Telecommunications Services. ICCP (86) 23, December 5, 1986.

OECD (1987a). *Trends of Change in Telecommunications Policy*.

OECD (1987b). Elements of a Conceptual Framework for Trade in Services. Note by the Secretariat, Paris.

OECD (1987c). Trade in Information, Computer and Communications Services: An Examination of the Relevance of the Conceptual Framework for Trade in Services. Note by the Secretariat, DSTI/ICCP, 86-21.

OECD (1988a). Trade in Telecommunication Network-Based Services. orking Party on Telecommunications and Information Services Policy, Directorate for Science Technology and Industry. Paris: OECD, June 1, 1988, 4.

OECD (1988). Telecommunication Network-Based Services: Implications for Telecommunication Policy (ICCP/87.5). A paper prepared by the

Secretariat for the Committee on Information, Computer and Communications Policy.

Ontario Premier's Council (1987). Competing in the Global Economy, Vol. 11, 1987.

Ostry, Sylvia (1987). Interdependence: Vulnerability and Opportunity, the Per Jacobsson Lecture, Washington DC, September 27, 1987.

Pacific Research Group (1987). Strategies for Japan's Communications Equipment Industry 1987, Japan/Tokyo: Pacific Research Group - A Division of Interworld Ltd.

Piernchiak, R.T. (1985). White Supremacists See Computers as Revolutionary Key. AP 03/03/85 via NEXIS.

Pipe, G. Russell (1987a). Towards New Telecommunications Regulatory/Regimes. *Trade Facilitation*, 1, 81-84.

Pipe, G. Russell (1987b). The Ultimate Bypass. *Datamation*, August 1, 1987.

Pipe, G. Russell (1988). Telecommunications Trade Rules: Implications for Services Providers, Manufacturers, Users and the ITU (summary of the proceedings). Congress for the Telecommunications Services Trade Project, Brussels.

Plank, Rosine (1987). An Unofficial Description of How a GATT Panel Works and Does Not. 4 *Journal of International Arbitration* 62.

Pogorel, G. (1986). Reseaux d'information et de communication et structures des firms. *The Bell Journal of Economics and Management Science*, Vol. 5, No.2.

PTC Quarterly (1985). SITA: A Worldwide Telecommunications Service for Airlines. December, 1985.

Rada, Juan (1984). Trade and Effects of Information Technology, in J. Rada and R. Pipe (eds.), *Communications Regulation and International Business*. Amsterdam: North-Holland.

Rada, Juan F. (1987). Information Technology and Services, in Orio Giarini (ed.) *The Emerging Service Economy*. Oxford: Pergamon Press for the Services World Forum, Geneva.

Randhawa, P.S. (1987). Punta del Este and After: Negotiations on Trade in Services and the Uruguay Round. *Journal of World Trade Law*, Vol. 21, 1987, pp. 163-171.

Regan, Edward J. (1988a). Telecommunications Policy Liberalization and User Needs. Presented at Interface '88 - The 16th Annual Conference for Communications and Information Networks, Chicago, Illinois, March 1988.

Regan, Edward J. (1988b). Telecommunications Policy Liberalization and Electronic Banking Services. Presented at Deregulation in the 1990's - Strategic and Regulatory Stakes for Telecommunications and the Information Economy, sponsored by PROMETHEE, Paris, 7-8 March 1988.

Reid, Ann Hutcheson (1985). Trade in Telecommunication Services: The Current Institutional Framework and the Potential for Change. Paper prepared for the Committee for Information, Computer and Communication Policy, Organization for Economic Cooperation and Development. Paris, Sept. 9, 1985, 16-25.

Reid, A. Hutcheson (1987). The Integrated Services Digital Network: A Presentation of Related Policy Issues, in OECD, *Trends of Change in Telecommunications Policy*. Paris, 99-114.

Rengaradjailou, R. (1987). Les Telecommunications au Bresil. Ambassade de France au Bresil.

Richardson, John B. (1986). International Trade Aspects of Telecommunication Services. *Common Market Law Review* 23: 385-399, Dordrecht/The Netherlands: Martinus Nijhoff Publishers.

Richardson, John B. (1987a). A Sub-Sectoral Approach to Services Trade Theory, in O. Giarini (ed.), *The Emerging Service Economy*. Oxford: Pergamon Press, 59-83.

Richardson, John B. (1987b). Services Negotiations: The Central Issues. *Transnational Data and Communications Report*, May, 1987, 13-16.

Richardson, John B. (1988). The Characteristics of a Successful Agreement on Trade in Services. Andean Pact Seminar on Services and Development, Lima.

Riddle, Dorothy I. (1986). *Services-Led Growth: The Role of the Service Sector in World Development.* New York: Praeger.

Riddle, Dorothy I. (1987). The Role of the Service Sector in Economic Development: Similarities and Differences by Development Category, in O. Giarini (ed.), *The Emerging Service Economy.* Oxford: Pergamon Press, 83-104.

Rivkin, Jack (1987). Trade and Finance: Toward a Global Market. Shearson, Lehman, June 1987.

Robinson, Peter (1985). Telecommunications, Trade and TDF. *Telecommunications Policy*, December, 1985, 310-318.

Robinson, Peter (1987a). An International Policy Framework for Trade in Services and Data Services: The Current Debate in International Organizations. Paper prepared for an International Seminar, Toward an International Service and Information Economy: A New Challenge for the Third World, sponsored by the Friedrich Ebert Foundation.

Robinson, Peter (1987b). From TDF to International Data Services. *Telecommunications Policy*, December, 1987, 369-76.

Roseman, Daniel (1988). Towards a GATT Code on Trade in Telecommunication Equipment. *The World Economy*, Vol. 11, 135-149.

Rubin, Michael Rogers (1986). US Information Economy Matures. *Transnational Data and Communications Report.* June 1986.

Rutkowski, Anthony M. (1986). Regulations for Integrated Services Networks: WATTC-88. *Intermedia*, No. 14, May, 1986, 10-19.

Sampson, Gary P. and Richard H. Snape (1985). Identifying the Issues in Trade in Services. *The World Economy*, Vol. 8, June, 1985, 171-82.

Samuelson, Paul A. (1939). The Gains from International Trade. *Canadian Journal of Economics and Political Science*, 195-205.

Sanders, Peter (1979). A Twenty Years' Review of the Convention on the Recognition and Enforcement of Foreign Arbitral Awards. *International Lawyer*, 13, 269-287.

Sapir, Andre (1982). Trade in Services: Policy Issues for the 1980s. *Columbia Journal of World Business*, Fall, 1982, 77-83.

Sapir, Andre (1985). North-South Issues in Trade in Services. *The World Economy*, Vol. 8, 1985, 27-42.

Sapir, Andre (1986). Trade in Services and International Telecommunications. Paper prepared for the CEPS/NBER Conference on Europe-United States Trade Relations, Brussels, June 12-14, 1986.

Sauvant, Karl P. (1983). Transborder Data Flows and the Developing Countries. *International Organization*. 37,2, Spring 1983.

Sauvant, Karl P. (1986a). *Trade and Foreign Direct Investment in Data Services*. Boulder: Westview Press.

Sauvant, Karl P. (1986b). Services TDF and the Code. *The CTC Reporter*. (United Nations) No. 22, Autumn 1986.

Sauvant, Karl P. (1986c). *International Tranactions in Services: The Politics of Transborder Data Flows*. The Atwater Series on The World Information Economy, No. 1. Boulder: The Westview Press for the Atwater Institute.

Sauvant, Karl P. (1987). Trade in Data Services: The International Context. *Telecommunications Policy*, No. 10 December 1987, 282-98.

Sauvant, Karl P. and Zbigniew Zimny (1987). Foreign Direct Investment in Services: The Neglected Dimension in International Service Negotiations. *World Competition*, October 31, 1987, 27-55.

Scherer, F.M. (1980). *Industrial Market Structure and Economic Performance*, 2nd. Edition. Chicago: Rand McNally.

Science, (1988). The Scourge of Computer Viruses. April 8, 1988, 133-134.

Schina, Despina (1987). *State Aids under the EEC Treaty, Articles 92 to 94*. Oxford.

Schott, Jeffrey J. (1988). United States-Canada Free Trade: An Evaluation of the Agreement. *Policy Analyses in International Economics, 24,,* Washington D.C.: Intitute for International Economics.

Schulte-Hillen BDU (1988). Expertenunterstutzung in Bereich des Handels mit Informationsdiensten als Beitrag fur die GATT-Dienstleistungstrunde. Koln: Technische Unternehmensberatung.

Screen Digest (1987). Background - Approach of the European Satellite Age, 225-232.

Shelp, Ronald K. (1981). *Beyond Industrialization: Ascendancy of the Global Service Economy.* New York: Praeger.

Shelp, Ronald K. (1987). Trade in Services. *Foreign Policy*, No. 65, Winter, 1987, 64-84.

Siniscalco, Domenico. Defining and Measuring Output and Productivity in the Service Sector. in Herbert Giersch (ed.), *Services in World Economic Growth.* Tubingen, forthcoming.

Snape, Richard H. (1988). Is Non-Discrimination Really Dead? *The World Economy*, Vol. 11, 1-17.

Snow, Marcellus.S. (1986). *Marketplace for Telecommunications Regulation and Deregulation in Industrialized Democracies.* New York: Longman.

Snow, Marcellus S. (1986). *Telecommunications, Regulation & Deregulation in Industrialized Democracies.* Amsterdam: North Holland.

Snow, Marcellus S. and Meheroo Jussawalla (1986). *Telecommunication Economics and International Regulatory Policy: An Annotated Bibliography.* New York: Greenwood Press.

Spencer, Barbara J. and James A. Brander (1983). International R&D Rivalry and Industrial Strategy. *The Review of Economic Studies*, Vol. 50, 707-722.

Spero, Joan E. (1982). Information and Telecommunications is a Trade Issue. *Intermedia*, No. 10, March, 1982, 9-11.

Spero, Joan E. (1985). *International Trade and the Information Revolution.* Cambridge: Harvard University Center for Information Policy Research.

Spero, Joan E. (1985). The Information Revolution and Financial Services: A New North-South Issue. Presented at the TIDE 2000 Conference on Telecommunication, Information and Inter-dependent Economies, Tokyo, 13 November 1985.

Stahl, H.J. and A. Burmeister (1987). Benefits of Telecommunications for Transportation Systems in Developing Countries, World Telecommunication Forum, Part 4, Geneva, 22-24 October 1987.

Stepp, L.S. (1987). Pope Uses Space Technology to Preach an Age-Old Message; Prayers Reach Worldwide Audience Estimated at 1 Billion. *Washington Post,* June 7, 1987, Sunday, Final Edition, A-28.

Stern, Robert M. and Bernard M. Hochman (1987). Issues and Data Needs for GATT Negotiations on Services. *The World Economy,* Vol. 10, March, 1987, 39-60.

Stevers, E. (1985). Computer Technology: A Political Tool? Amsterdam/Florence E.U.I. - Summer Conference.

Stigler, George J. (1971). The Theory of Economic Regulation, *The Bell Journal of Economics,* Vol. 2, 3-21.

Stigler, George J. (1981). Comment in G. Fromm (ed.), *Studies in Public Regulation.* Cambridge/Massachussetts and London/England: The MIT Press.

Stopford, J.M. and L. Turner (1985). *Britain and the Multinationals.* John Wiley and Sons.

Supreme Court (1976). Supreme Court in NAACP v. FPC 425 US, 662, 669.

Taylor, A.D. (1983). Problems and Issues in Modelling Telecoms Demand in Courville, L., A. de Fontenay and R. Dobell (ed.), *Economic Analysis of Telecommunications-Theory and Applications.* Amsterdam/New York/Oxford: North-Holland/Elsevier Science Publishers B.V.

Taylor, R. (1988). Analysis of Telecommunications Evolution in the Community for the Period October 1987-March 1988, Brussels: European Research Associates.

Taylor, W. and H. Williams (1987). Regulatory Change and Organisational Responses: Unintended Consequences in Telecommunications Policy-Making. Newcastle/Amsterdam: ECPR-Congress.

Temin, Peter and Louis Galambos (1987). *The Fall of the Bell System*. New York: Cambridge University Press.

Tomlinson, J.W.C. (1970). *The Joint-Venture Process in International Business: India and Pakistan*. Cambridge, Mass, MTI Press.

Transnational Data and Communications Report (1987). Free Speech in Space: Satellite Images for News Media. August 1987, 9.

Transnational Data and Communications Report (1987). September 1987, 2.

Tweedale, D. (1988). Businessmen Complain About Sanctions Against Panama. UPI, April 15, 1988 BC Cycle via NEXIS.

UNCTAD, (1985). Services and the Development Process. TD/B/1008 Rev.1, New York.

UNCTAD (1986). Collusive Tendering. TD/B/RBP/12/Rev. 2, Geneva.

UNCTAD (1986). *Services and the Development Process: Further Studies*. TD/B/1100, New York.

UNCTAD (1987). Final Act of UNCTAD VII, Geneva, 3 August 1987.

UNCTAD (1987). Studies on Restrictive Business Practices Related to the Provisions of the Set of Principles and Rules: Tied Purchasing Practices. UNCTAD, TD/B/RBP/18/Rev. 1, Geneva, 11 November 1987.

UNCTAD (1988). Services. TD/B/1162, Geneva, March 1988.

UNCTAD (1988). *Trade and Development Report*. Geneva: UNCTAD. Part II.

358

UNCTC (1980). Transnational Corporations and World Development, Third Survey. New York.

UNCTC (1982). Transnational Corporations and Transborder Data Flows: A Technical Paper. New York, 1982.

UNCTC (1983). Transborder Data Flows and Brazil. United Nations Sales No. E.83.II.A.3, New York.

UNCTC (1986). *The United Nations Code of Conduct on Transnational Corporations.* UNCTC Current Studies, Series A, no. 4, United Nations Sales no. E.86.II.A.15.

UNCTC (1987). Transnational Corporations in the Service Sector, Including Transborder Data Flow: Report to the Secretary General. E/C.10/1987/11, New York.

UNCTC (1988). *Transnational Corporations in World Development: Trends and Prospects.* New York: United Nations, Part IV.

United Nations Chronicle, August 1986, via NEXIS.

United States Business Advisory Committee (1985). SPAC Recommendations for the U.S. Trade Representative.

United States Business Advisory Committee (1986). SPAC Report to the U.S. Trade Representatives.

United States Congress, Office of Technology Assessment (1986). *Trade in Services: Exports and Foreign Revenues - Special Report.* Washington: GPO.

United States Congress, Office of Technology Assessment of the U.S. Congress (1987). International Competition in Services: Banking, Building, Software, Know-How. Washington D.C., Congress of the United States Technology Assessment.

United States Federal Communication Commission (FCC) (1987). Notice of Inquiry and Proposed Rulemaking in the Matter of: Regulatory Policies and International Telecommunications. Washington D.C., CC Docket No. 86-494/FCC 86-563-36961, January.

United States Trade Representative, Office of the (1987a). Update on U.S.-Japan Trade Issues. Washington.

United States Trade Representative, Office of the (1987b). U.S. Tables Uruguay Round Proposal on Services Framework Agreement. Washington.

United States v. Bank of Nova Scotia, 69 F. 2d 1184 (11th cir. 1982), 740F. 2d 817 (11th cir. 1984), 84-2 U.S. Tax Cas. (CCH) P9802.

USA Today (1988). New Law May Make Swiss Bank Accounts a Lot Less Secret. June 24, 1988, 8B.

Utton, M. (1988). The Likely Impact of Deregulation on Industrial Structures and Competition in the Community, England: Economist Advisory Group Ltd.

Van Tulder, R. (1987). The Squeezed Position of the Small European Countries in the International Telecommunications Struggle. Amsterdam: ECPR Congress.

Vanguard/U.K. Department of Trade and Industry (1987). The Economic Effects of Value-Added and Data Services. London: Department of Trade and Industry - U.K.

Vienna Convention on Diplomatic Relations, April 18, 1961, Arts. XXVII, XXIX 23 U.S.T. 3227, 3239, 3240, 500 U.N.T.S. 95, 108, 110.

Wall Street Journal (1986). Dow Jones News Document, 860404-400. April 4, 1986, 10.

Walters, I. (1985) Barriers to Trade in Banking and Financial Services. Thames Essay, No. 41, Trade Policy Research Centre, London, 1985.

Wellenius, B. (1987). The Changing World of Telecommunications: Policy Options in Developing Countries. World Telecommunication Forum, Part 4, Geneva, 22-24 October 1987.

Wildman, Steven S. and Stephen E. Siwek (1988). *International Trade in Film and Television Programs*. Cambridge: Ballinger.

360

Wilson, J.Q. (1980). The Origin of Regulation in J.Q. Wilson (ed.), *The Politics of Regulation*. New York: Basic Book, Inc. Publishers.

Winham, Gilbert R. (1986). *International Trade and the Tokyo Round Negotiation*. Princeton: Princeton University Press.

Woodrow, R. Brian (1988). Internationally-Traded Telecommunications Services: Concept and Scope, Domestic Context, and International Environment: A Report to the Canadian Department of Communications, Ottawa, DOC, 1988.

Woodrow, R. Brian (1988). Canada-U.S. Telecom Accord: Status Quo or Signpost? *Transnational Data and Communications Report*, March, 1988, 17-21.

Xinhua General Overseas News Service, via NEXIS, June 13, 1986.

Zorkoczy, P. (1982). Information Technology. Bath: The Pitman Press.

INDEX

Access to data, 7, 11, 165
   and conflicts of interest, 301-302
   and economic development, 296-297
   and litigation, 294-296, 303
   and political sanctions, 296
   and remote-sensing satellites, 293-294
   by media, 292-293
   importance to users, 288-291
   in databanks, 291
   types of, 291-297
   via leased lines, 292
   See also Vulnerability of data
Appropriate regulation, 10, 52-53
   and international trade, 157-159, 192
   meaning of, 157
Arbitration, 205-206, 208-212, 214
   definition of, 219
Atwater Institute, 12

Balance of payments, 47, 195
   and data services, 77-81
   and services, 76-77
   in the GATT, 75-77, 80, 320
   See also Developing countries
Bank for International Settlements, 109
Banking services. *See* Financial services
Bhagwati, Jagdish, 47, 79, 131, 194-195
Butler, Richard E., 27-28

COCOM, 218

Comparative advantage
   and infant industries, 183
   of developing countries, 58
   theory of, 32-33, 69
Competition in telecommunications, 11, 191, 230-231, 236-237
   and technological change, 257ff
   and trade liberalization, 191-192
   changing rationale, 270-273
   domestic regulation, 273-274
   history and background, 257-260
   in basic services, 267-268, 270
   in network management, 268-269
   international, 274-278
   in value-added services, 269-270
   nature of, 266-270
"Constitutional" analysis, 15-17, 41
Consultation, 204-205, 214

Data, access to. *See* Access to data
Data services, 4, 11
   and corporate strategy, 149-150
   dispute settlement, 212-217
   functions of, 5-6
   trade in, 15, 17-23, 32-36, 148-153
Declaration on Trade in Services. *See* Uruguay Round
Declaration on Transborder Data Flows. *See* OECD

Deregulation. *See* Telecommunication regulation

Developing countries,
  and information technologies, 110-111
  and market access in TNS, 242
  and trade liberalization, 4, 44-45, 60
  balance of payments, 74-81
  concerns of, 4, 38, 43-45, 52, 59-68, 150-151
  software exports, 111, 152
  telecommunication services in, 227-228
  See also Comparative advantage; G-10; Infant-industry considerations; Labor Movement; National objectives; Preferential treatment;Restrictive Business Practices; Technical assistance

Dispute settlement, 10, 50, 200, 203-217
  between private economic agents, 207-211
  between States, 203-207
  interaction between the two spheres, 211-212
  See also Data services

Electronic Data Interchange (EDI), 112-113, 125

Establishment. *See* Right of Establishment

FDI. *See* Foreign direct investment

Feketekuty, Geza, 25, 65-66, 86

Financial services, 5, 6, 56-57
  and market presence, 146-147
  cash management systems, 196-107

foreign exchange, 106-107
payment systems, 107
retail services, 108-109
swaps: currency and interest rate, 109-110
trade in, 105-110

Foreign direct investment, 9, 10, 37, 62, 79-81, 85, 132-135, 325-329
  impact on trade, 139-141, 187

Framework for trade in services, 3, 4, 6, 7, 10, 33, 39, 44, 47-50, 83-84, 97, 188-189, 309
  and institutional procedures, 200, 214, 216-217
  impacts on telecommunication services, 124

Frazee, Rowland C.,
  "Frazee Initiative", 118

Free Trade Agreement,
  Canada-U.S., 53-55, 87, 115-116, 122, 124, 138, 250
  U.S.-Israel, 122, 250

GATT, 8, 9, 16, 24-25, 28, 51, 53, 55-56, 60, 62, 71, 74-75, 86-87, 102, 118, 176-177, 184-188, 193
  and relationship with ITU, 126-127, 179
  dispute settlement, 206-207, 213-216, 320-321
  history of, 181-182
  Part IV, 74, 82, 84, 164

General Agreement on Tariffs and Trade. *See* GATT

Gibbs, J. Murray, 83-84

Green Paper, 66-67, 87, 169-170, 226-227

Group of Negotiations on Services. *See* Uruguay Round

G-10 (Group of Ten Developing Countries), 55-56, 61

Havana Charter. *See* GATT, history of,
Hill, K. G. Anthony, 63-64, 69

ICAO, 8, 70
IMF, 77, 94
Infant-industry considerations, 7, 67-68, 74, 183
Information services. *See* Data services
Information technologies,
   and economic development, 112-113, 115
   and trade in services, 119
   impact on agriculture, 103
   impact on developing countries, 110-112
   impact on education, 103-104
   impact on financial services, 105-106
   impact on health, 104
   impact on transportation, 104
   opportunities for service industries, 113
   world sales of, 102
   See also Developing countries
Institutional procedures,
   difficulties in telecommunication and data services, 198-200
   enforcement, 200, 218
   rule development, 200, 217
   surveillance. *See* Monitoring
   traditional difficulties, 197-198
   See also Dispute settlement
Integrated Services Digital Network. *See* ISDN
Intellectual property rights, 54
INTELSAT, 18, 66, 177-178

International Civil Aviation Organization. *See* ICAO
International Coordinating Committee on Strategic Trade with Communist Countries (COCOM). *See* COCOM
International Monetary Fund. *See* IMF
International Telecommunication Union. *See* ITU
International Trade Organisation (ITO). *See* GATT, history of
ISDN, 27, 117, 224, 229-230
ITU, 8, 18, 20, 26-28, 34, 64-65, 70, 86, 117-118, 174-176
   Plenipotentiary Conference, 127
   relationship with GATT, 126-127
   See also WATTC-88

Jackson, John H., 206, 240

Krommenacker, Raymond, 31

Labor movement, 9, 51, 55, 60-61, 138, 187
   See also Temporary presence
Liberalization of trade in services, 3, 44-45, 70, 73-74, 143, 309
   and national objectives, 9
   as a means to an end, 93
   aspects of, 186-189
   in data services, 190-194, 235-237
   in telecommunications, 192-193, 235-236
   of financial services, 147
   See also Developing countries
Liberalization clubs, 185-186
   European Community, 185

EFTA (European Free Trade Association), 185
Malmgren, Harald, 29, 59
Market access, 7, 11, 22, 84, 187. *See also* Market access in TNS; National treatment
Market access in TNS, 162
  airline model, 252-253,255
  and trade-offs, 251-253
  definition, 243
  history and background, 245
  past precedents, 249-251
  right of interconnection, 245, 247-249
  right of non-establishment, 245-246
  See also Developing countries; Free Trade Agreement; Right of Establishment; Right of Presence
Market-Oriented Sector-Selective (MOSS) Talks, 250-251
Mashayekhi, Mina, 83-84
McCulloch, Rachel, 57-58
MFN. *See* Most-Favored-Nation Principle
Monitoring, 201-203
Monopolies, 270-273. *See also* PTTs
Most-Favored-Nation (MFN) Principle, 9-10, 53, 62, 69, 94, 167, 181
  and trade conflicts, 185
  applicability to trade in data services, 189-193
  applicability to trade in services, 186-189
  arguments against, 184-185, 194
  conditional, 167, 185
  history of, 184
  in GATT, 181, 315

in international trade, 181-186
multilateralism vs reciprocal bilateralism, 185
non-discrimination, 193
objectives of, 184
unconditional, 184-185, 188-189, 193-194

National objectives, 43-70
  Brazil, 61-63
  Canada, 53-55
  Developing countries, 55-64
  European Community, 50-53
  for telecommunication and data services, 64-68
  India, 60-61, 67-68
  Switzerland, 53
  United States, 45-50, 53-55
National treatment, 49, 58, 69, 145, 151
  and market access, 240
  and market access in telecommunication services, 242-243
  and market access in trade in services, 241-242
  and Right of Presence, 136-137
  in GATT, 316-317, 240
Nayyar, Deepak, 58, 60-61
Non-discrimination, 49, 94, 146-147
Non-reciprocity. *See* Preferential treatment
Nussbaumer, Jacques, 30-31

OECD, 8, 22, 24, 27, 33-35, 62, 65, 109, 118, 239
  Declaration on Transborder Data Flows, 22, 24, 311-313
Organisation for Economic Cooperation and Development. *See* OECD
Ostry, Sylvia, 66-67

Performance requirements, 54, 136, 141-144, 153
Post, Telegraph and Telephone Administrations. *See* PTTs
Preferential treatment, 74
  in services, 82-84
  in the GATT, 81-82, 321-324
  of developing countries, 74, 81-87
Presence,
  franchises, 133
  joint ventures, 133
  licensing agreements, 133
  management contracts, 133
  See also Right of Presence
Protectionism, rationale for, 182-184
PTTs, 15, 19-21, 36, 115, 117, 121, 189-191

RBPs. *See* Restrictive business practices
Reciprocity, 69, 94
  and Right of Presence, 137-138
Regulation. *See* Telecommunication regulation; Appropriate regulation
Reid, Ann Hutcheson, 34-35
Re-regulation. *See* Telecommunication regulation, deregulation
Restrictive business practices, 74, 87-91
  and developing countries, 88-89
  in services, 88-89
  U.S. industry view, 90-91
Ricardo, David, 32, 182
Richardson, John, 63, 70
Right of Establishment, 10, 37, 69
  and foreign direct investment, 132

conceptual issues, 132-136
in context of services, 103, 120, 143-147
in context of trade in goods, 138-143
Right of Presence, 10, 37, 69, 131-132
  and national treatment, 136-137
  and reciprocity, 137-138
  in context of services, 143-147
  in context of trade in goods, 138-143
  subsidiary rights, 135-136

Sampson, Gary P., 30, 79, 138
Sauvant, Karl P., 134-136, 148, 326-328
Selectivity, right to, 84-85
Services,
  appropriate negotiating fora, 178-180
  classification, 30-32, 143, 186
  definition of trade in, 33-36, 68-69, 166
  history of debate on, 241
  in world economy, 3, 12, 41, 43, 148, 325-329
  in world trade, 3-5, 102, 325-329
  tradeability, 4, 6, 11, 17, 31, 166
  trade in, 3, 4, 28-32, 36-40, 43-44, 241
  See also Data services; Developing countries, concerns of; Liberalization; Telecommunication services; Uruguay Round
SITA, 5, 19, 125, 289
Smith, Adam, 28
Snape, Richard H., 30, 79, 138

Société internationale de télé communications aéronautiques. *See* SITA
Society for Worldwide Interbank Financial Telecommunications. *See* SWIFT
Spero, Joan, 56-57
Standards. *See* Telecommunications
Subsidies, 49
SWIFT, 5, 19, 107, 125, 288

Technical Assistance, 74, 91-93
  and data services, 92-93
  and services, 91-92
  to developing countries, 91-93
Technology transfer, 59-60
Telecommunication and data services. See Data services
Telecommunication network-based services (TNS), 20-21.
  See also Market access in TNS
Telecommunication-policy perspective, 17, 23, 25-28, 32, 35, 86-87, 127, 283-284
Telecommunication regulation, 9, 231-235, 278-285
  and data services trade, 165-167
  and technological change, 162-165
  Brazil, 173-174
  classification, 158
  concept of, 155
  corporate strategy, 160-162
  deregulation, 122, 172, 190
  effects on trade in data services, 156-157
  European Community, 167-170
  in relation to trade rules, 281-285
  Japan, 172-173

sources of ineffectiveness, 155
United States, 170-171
Telecommunications,
  costs, 116
  infrastructure, 11, 22
  national differences in competition, 279-280
  network management, 229-230
  objectives of telecommunication negotiations, 283-284
  objectives of trade negotiations, 282-283
  policies, 114-116, 226
  standards, 117, 280-281
  users, 229-230
  vulnerability of facilities, 117-118
  See also Competition in telecommunications
Telecommunication services,
  classification, 191, 261-266
  corporate perspective, 114-119
  market, 230-231
  providers of, 163, 228-229, 234
  tradeability, 121-127
  See also Competition in telecommunications; Developing countries
Telecommunication technologies,
  impacts on world economy, 160, 225-228
  new developments, 159-160, 223-225
Temporary presence, 37, 51, 54-55.
  See also Labor movement
Tiwari, N. D., 67
TNS. *See* Telecommunication network-based services
Trade agreements covering telecommunication services,
  GATT-administered, 127
  impacts, 124

objectives, 123
Trade liberalization. *See* Liberalization
Trade-policy perspective, 17, 23-26, 28, 32, 123, 126-127, 282-283
Transborder data flows (TDF), 9, 33, 85, 148-149, 151
and Brazil, 61-63
See also OECD
Transparency, 48, 69-70, 94, 200-203, 236, 309

UNCTAD, 8, 59, 87, 98, 131
UNCTC, 8, 10, 24, 61, 63, 148, 151
United Nations Centre on Transnational Corporations. *See* UNCTC
United Nations Conference on Trade and Development. *See* UNCTAD
Uruguay Round, 47, 72-73
Declaration on Services, 3, 9, 61, 72-73, 158-159, 181, 309-310
Negotiations on services, 9, 10, 16, 24-25, 50, 68-70, 83, 125-126, 137, 176-180, 188, 309-310
Usage conditions for leased lines, 164

User-group networks. *See* SITA; SWIFT
Users' access, 84-86, 162
Users' perspective, 11, 101-120

Value-added network services. *See* VANs
VANs, 230-231, 254-255
Vulnerability of data,
and sovereignty, identity and dependence, 300-301
to 'hacking', 298
to judicial proceedings, 299-300
to natural disasters, 298
to negligence, 300
to political sanctions, 299
to terrorism, 298

Walters, Ingo, 147
WATTC-88, 8, 26-27, 64, 174-176, 231
WIPO, 179
World Administrative Telegraph and Telephone Conference. *See* WATTC-88
World Bank, 24, 115
World Intellectual Property Organisation. *See* WIPO